Gypsy-travellers in nineteenth-century society

Gypsy-travellers in nineteenth-century society

DAVID MAYALL

Lecturer in History, De La Salle College,
University of Manchester

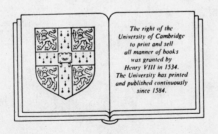

The right of the
University of Cambridge
to print and sell
all manner of books
was granted by
Henry VIII in 1534.
The University has printed
and published continuously
since 1584.

CAMBRIDGE UNIVERSITY PRESS

Cambridge
New York New Rochelle Melbourne Sydney

Published by the Press Syndicate of the University of Cambridge
The Pitt Building, Trumpington Street, Cambridge CB2 1RP
32 East 57th Street, New York, NY 10022, USA
10 Stamford Road, Oakleigh, Melbourne 3166, Australia

First published 1988

Printed in Great Britain at the University Press, Cambridge

British Library cataloguing in publication data
Mayall, David
Gypsy-travellers in nineteenth-century
society.
1. Gypsies–Great Britain–History
–19th century
I. Title
941'.00491497   DX211

Library of Congress cataloguing in publication data
Mayall, David.
Gypsy-travellers in nineteenth-century society.
Revision of the author's thesis (doctoral).
Bibliography.
Includes index.
1. Gypsies–Great Britain–History–20th century.
I. Title.   II. Title: Gypsy-travellers in 19th century
society.
DX211.M39 1987   941'.00491497   87–6634

ISBN 0 521 32397 5

Contents

Illustrations

Preface and acknowledgements

It has often been a matter of puzzlement and not little amusement to others as to how I became attracted to Gypsies as a subject for research. My first explanation, not altogether seriously offered, is that I was embarking on a voyage to rediscover my origins. This stems from a story I was told in childhood by my mother that I was the son of a Gypsy confined in the same hospital ward, the name tags being somehow confused. Following any naughty behaviour I was threatened with being sent away with the next group of peg-sellers to visit the house. From an early age I was led to believe that the Gypsies were a different people, a group apart to be feared and scorned. Yet the real attraction lay not in a search for a separate and distant race but rather with a group which seemed to stand in firm opposition to major features of nineteenth-century society, notably permanency of settlement and wage-labour employments. This itinerant group functioned within a sedentary-based society and yet apparently resisted attempts by various agencies at their religious, moral and economic reform, whether taking the form of voluntary and philanthropic endeavours or by means of coercive and legislative pressure.

From such beginnings developed a full-time study which led first to a doctoral thesis and then on to this revised form. Along my own often peripatetic path many people have helped considerably with obscure references, advice and criticism. Special mention and gratitude is due to Colin Holmes for his initial supervision and subsequent encouragement and interest. I am also grateful to Mary Mallon for her thorough reading of the manuscript, and to Helen Corr and Hosein Piranfar for their most useful comments on parts of the text. Further thanks to the following who each contributed much of value: Tony Delves, John Field, Elaine Fishwick, Van Gore, Nigel Goose, Richard Russell, David Smith, Tony Sutcliffe, and finally to Beryl Moore, Sheila Ashden and Beverley Eaton for their secretarial assistance. I would also like to acknowledge the help provided by the many librarians and archivists who managed to identify much relevant material. Particular mention is due to the staffs of the Sydney Jones Library (University of Liverpool), the Brotherton Library (University of Leeds), the Inter-Library

Loan Department (University of Sheffield) and the archivists at the Dorset and Surrey Record Offices. I also thank the Twenty-Seven Foundation for the award of a grant towards the cost of revising and preparing my original study for publication.

I am grateful to the Bodleian Library for permission to reproduce photographs and illustrations.

1

~~~~~~

Introduction

Gypsy-travellers occupy a unique position in sedentary-based societies by virtue of their physical and ideological distance from the main features and trends of the host structures. They stand apart from the majority of the population both culturally and economically, with their resistance to incorporation into the wage-labour market and persistent reliance on the family as the key economic unit serving to isolate them as a distinctive fringe group in any society which stresses permanency and settlement. It would, though, be an exaggeration to suggest that Gypsy-travellers occupied a central and prominent position in relation to the major issues emerging through the dramatic years of nineteenth-century industrialisation. Nevertheless they did drift in and out of the margins of the debate, touching along the way such areas as economic change and the role of itinerancy in the developing economy, and the changing aspects of leisure and culture. Responses from settled society brought into sharp relief the nature of policing and controlling a marginal, minority group, highlighting the expanding role of the state and the processes of policy-making. The function of evangelism and the reclamation of heathens to spiritual and secular responsibility and respectability needs to be seen in this context.

In order to make sense of the emergent industrial society and its consequent evils religious bodies adopted a stridently evangelical tone. In searching for evidence of amorality, irreligion and idleness many of the new missionaries decided to look no further than the camps of the Gypsies. In the laissez-faire age of the early nineteenth century responsibility for the supervision of the Gypsy-travellers was left predominantly in the hands of these evangelical and voluntary bodies, though this should not be taken to imply that the state did not play a supportive role. Increasingly this voluntary system came to be replaced by more extensive state initiatives, at local and national level, in which the endeavours of George Smith of Coalville formed an important milestone. In carrying on the grand British tradition of philanthropy he continued and extended the work of evangelical Christianity into more secular forms, taking his crusade not only to the subjects of his concern but also to the public at large and to Parliament. But the question of

1

responses is not merely one of conflict between travelling and settled cultures. The particular case of the Gypsy-traveller is further complicated by the imposition of the concept of race on the travelling structure, constructing hierarchies according to racial characteristics. The three major themes which emerge are, therefore, the role of travellers as a mobile labour force and the pressure for change from modernising influences; the position of a group marginal to the socialising instruments of an industrialising society; and, finally, the identification of a minority by reference to culture and race, explanations which could be both complementary and contradictory.

Each of these various areas forms the basis of major historical enquiries and controversies, addressing important conceptual problems concerning the nature of the state and the methods of maintaining conformity and consensus in a society undergoing fundamental transformation. Rather than concentrating the scope of this study I decided in favour of a more expansive approach in the hope of highlighting the links and overlaps between each theme. Evangelism blended with philanthropy, both travelling alongside state policy-making. The policing of travellers involved a complex system of formal and informal arrangements, which in turn raised questions of public versus private duty. The arguments used by the defenders of the repressive policies directed against the travellers combined notions of criminality and race with heathenism, economic rationality and the imposition of minimum standards of health and education. Moral and religious reasoning were thus balanced by an economic and political rationale, both appealing to instinctive common sense as the foundation for support. A survey of the whole period shows that the motivation for these responses, their articulation and expression, stemmed from and borrowed different arguments as justification. But such a study also reveals that the purpose of each response, the desired long-term goal, was remarkably similar: to bring an end to the economic, social, political, religious, cultural and ideological embarrassment caused by a particular group of people.

Choosing to look at this section of the travelling community over a period of dramatic and fundamental change created a number of difficulties. Chief of these was the problem of retaining a clear sight of the very different worlds in which the Gypsies found themselves from the beginning of the period under survey until the end, especially in the face of strong elements of continuity among the group itself. Gypsy-travellers were by no means unaffected by the major changes taking place in society and the economy, yet their main features of self-employment and the adoption of travelling as a way of life remained the stable bases of their existence. In this sense it is possible to see the retention of basic characteristics from pre-industrial times through to the period of advanced industrialisation. Other groups and classes experienced profound changes in relation to work, leisure and political life but although the life-style of the Gypsy-traveller was affected it did not radically alter.

Always prepared to adopt and adapt, the Gypsies managed to hold on to their basic identity. It is the negotiation with the developments taking place in wider society and the economy that forms the central strand running throughout this work.

In the early decades of the century the travellers performed significant roles in the imperfect supply and demand conditions of the time, contributing goods and services to the economic and social life of the village. When the emphasis within the domestic economy shifted from the rural to the urban sector this role was exposed as an anachronistic and unwanted vestige of a past stage in economic development. Always morally and ideologically unacceptable to the dominant culture of sedentary society the travellers, by the latter decades of the nineteenth century, had also lost much of their former importance and relevance in the socio-economic sphere. At this moment the marginality of travellers to the structures of a sedentary-based, industrialising state became increasingly apparent and the problem of the accommodation of the travelling population then became a matter of much concern. Travellers were seen to stand apart from the cultural and ideological pressures towards conformity with a settled way of life and so with regular employments and deference to strict time-discipline, both features becoming more evident as the century progressed. Their way of life was seen as unnecessary, causing more problems of a practical and ideological nature than their existence was likely to solve. The state had come to play a growing part in controlling the industrial workforce, in the factory and the home, and this group existing on the margins of society was not to be exempted from attention.

This is to express the problem in terms of the specific context of the relationship between travellers and the structures and mechanisms of a developing, capitalist state. Although it is necessary to take account of the particular political and economic nature of the dominant society, it is also important that the frame of reference and analysis should not be too narrow. Antipathy to travellers was not restricted to a particular epoch or political system, but was rooted in a long-standing conflict between the travelling and sedentary ways of life. The expression of this conflict in the nineteenth century came most vociferously from the supporters of the emergent bourgeois ideology, which denigrated the traveller and the itinerant way of life for standing opposed to the forces of civilisation and advance. At times this appeared in the guise of concerned religious agencies and individuals who combined notions of industriousness and thrift with those of moral rescue and the evangelistic desire to save certain groups in society from themselves. On other occasions the clamour for control was more directly associated with officialdom and authority, with police and local government officers shouting together for suppression. Behind all the cries was the sometimes active but more usually tacit approval of sedentary citizens.

Individuals were often able to establish favourable associations with the Gypsies, chiefly by means of a useful and acceptable economic and social relationship, but society as a corporate body voiced unanimous opposition. The cautious acceptance of the early part of the century was increasingly replaced by unqualified intolerance. Impressions borrowed from numerous sources enabled the various agencies to embroider their arguments with racial categories which established a hierarchy among travellers containing Romanies, didakais or half-bloods, and *gorgios* or *gaujos* (non-Gypsies).

From the twin elements of nomadism and racial separateness developed a host of stereotypes about travellers which in turn profoundly affected responses. In general, all classes were united in their antipathy but, unlike the case of other minority groups, whether racially or culturally defined, popular persecution of travellers was not rooted in fears of real or perceived threats to jobs or status but rather in contempt for alleged parasites made such by the travelling ways of life and/or hereditary factors. Although much of the animosity was directed specifically at itinerancy itself this was frequently embellished by differentiating the habits and ways of travelling people according to racial characteristics.

Perhaps the most significant contribution to the association of a group of travellers with a Romany race came with the formation of the Gypsy Lore Society. In 1877 a letter appeared in the journal *Notes and Queries* requesting that interested persons set about collecting Gypsy songs and ballads as it was feared that Gypsy camps were rapidly disappearing from the commons and lanes and with them was vanishing a unique culture. The feeling grew among folk lorists that they had a duty to capture and preserve the history of the Gypsies before it was lost altogether. A reply to this letter suggested that a club or correspondence society be formed for this specific purpose. From these initial promptings and under the initiative and leadership of David MacRitchie of Edinburgh, the Gypsy Lore Society was founded in 1888.[1]

The declared objective of the society was to investigate the Gypsy question 'in as thorough and many-sided manner as possible'.[2] Membership was to be world-wide and the hope was to save Gypsy lore from exinction in every corner of the globe. The members' findings were to be published quarterly in the *Journal of the Gypsy Lore Society*. In practice the 'thorough' investigation of the Gypsy problem meant research into the language, history, ethnology and folk lore of the Gypsy race. The members of the Society saw the problem in terms of questions concerning origins and their intention was to identify the 'true' Gypsies and locate them as a race apart. The emphasis was firmly and almost exclusively on kinship and cultural patterns and not on social change or politics. The Society appeared at the time of the debate surrounding the registration and regulation of van- and tent-dwellers by means of the Moveable Dwellings Bill, yet the contributors to the Journal turned their backs on current issues and continued their searches for a dying language and genealogical lines. Controversial topics were noticeable only by their absence. The lorists were concerned about a decaying language and culture but not about a threatened and persecuted people. By avoiding such problems as registration, enforced settlement and harassment they distanced themselves from the present-day reality of Gypsy existence and looked only for the myth and mystery of Gypsies in the past.

However, by 1892 the Journal had ceased to exist and the Society entered a period of decline lasting fifteen years. Renewed concern about the Gypsy question in the opening years of the twentieth century perhaps contributed to the Society's revival in 1907. During this period the Gypsy was under threat of persecution and harassment almost as great as anything experienced in the past. In England there were attempts at control by means of the Moveable Dwellings and Children's Bills and active persecution by local authorities. It was even rumoured that representatives were to be sent to a proposed European conference, to be held at Berne in the summer of 1908, to discuss methods of ending for good the Gypsy 'disgrace'. Support for the proposal was mixed: some praised this attempt to rid civilised society of the 'dregs of humanity',[3] while others, less in evidence, condemned it as a genocidal conspiracy by the statesmen of Europe 'to wipe out the last traces of the Romany from the Western Continent'.[4] The atmosphere and mood forced the revitalised Gypsy Lore Society to acknowledge that the Gypsy did not live in a social and political vacuum, immersed in strange taboos and ancient rites. Articles were at last published in the Journal relating to political matters. However, concern about social and political issues did not last and the social-anthropological and folk-lore content remained dominant. The discovery of new dialects excited more interest among the Society's academicians, philologists and ethnologists than did new instances of repression and persecution. The war again caused the Society to enter a second period of decline which was not to be reversed until 1922.

The contemporary importance of the various issues surrounding a nomadic population, and especially this issue of race and racial stereotyping, is made readily apparent by even a cursory look through recent newspapers or by glancing at the television. Relations between a travelling and a settled society still show the same degree of conflict and antagonism seen in the nineteenth century. Often the same arguments, based on myths, inaccuracies and generalisations, are repeated time and again. Newspaper reports illustrate the persistence of persecution and local authority harassment; television programmes can still take the title 'They Steal Children, Don't They?'; and active members of anti-Gypsy organisations shout about the 'filth and pestilence' surrounding a group who 'are not humans', offering petrol bombs as their solution.[5] Likewise, the notion of the 'true' Gypsy is still called forth with the same degree of conviction as at the end of the nineteenth century. The superstitious aura engulfing the Romany lingers on with, for example, the disastrous fire at the Alexandra Palace in London in the summer of 1980 being blamed by some on a 100-year-old Gypsy curse uttered when they were turned off their camp site so the Palace could be built.[6] Many people today would also tell a similar story to that of Gaius Carley who, writing of his childhood in Sussex in the 1890s, recalls laughing at a Gypsy woman who had a hole in her stocking. In retaliation the woman put a curse on the incautious writer: 'She put the wind up me properly. I have been careful who I have laughed at since.'[7] The similarities between the arguments and stereotypes used, and the hostility and persecution shown in the 1880s and 1980s, are striking in their closeness and consistency. Antipathy to the travelling population remains virulent and virtually unanimous. There is no more a workable solution being offered now than there was 100 years ago concerning the question of how successfully to accommodate this marginal group.

The three themes mentioned in the opening paragraphs form the organising strands that run throughout the various parts of this study. The first section comprises the empirical base by means of its discussion of the Gypsy population in England and Wales, locating it geographically, socially and economically, and illustrating by examples the texture of everyday travelling life. This is followed by an assessment of the fundamental issue of ascriptions, perceptions, images and stereotyping. Essentially, there were three main definitions of a Gypsy which though different were not necessarily mutually exclusive. These covered a romantic race, a degenerate race and a group of outcast travellers. Responses were conditioned and informed by stereotypes evolving from each of these. The term 'Gypsy' could thus be applied to a racial elite to be found at the top of the pyramidal ordering said to exist among travellers. It could also apply, in a generic sense, to a much larger group of travellers sharing a way of life and having occupations in common, though identifiable from the artisan or vagrant traveller by cultural differences, a tendency to live and camp in groups and their adoption of a variety of self-employments. This incorporates regional and temporal variations in the ascriptions given to the travellers, as well as combining under one heading the many terms used to differentiate between the group according to such criteria as occupation, appearance, name, language and race. By this definition, which is the one adopted throughout the book, all gipsies, Gypsies, Egyptians, pretended Egipcions, fortune-tellers, tent-dwellers, van-dwellers, didakais and tinklers are grouped together.

The remainder of the work is concerned with responses to this varied travelling community from sections of the host, sedentary society. Historically the response of any society to the presence of Gypsies has been at best qualified tolerance and, at worst, open hostility and persecution, with the arguments used to justify this depending on irrationality, superstition and blind fear as much as on balanced and logical reasoning. The persecutors found their excuses in differences, alleged and real, in the areas of culture, race, religion and criminality. Each of these was said to reveal the Gypsies not only as separate and distinct but also, and importantly, as harmful to the interests of the community and the nation state. In contrast to the new ways of civilised, industrial society their culture was seen as backward and primitive. To add to this, their racial characteristics were thought to incline them towards dishonesty and deceit, heathenism, immorality and a profound disinclination to any form of honest and productive toil. In reaction to the presence of such a group who could be criticised, feared and scorned on any number of accounts, religious and philanthropic individuals and agencies led the way in the early nineteenth century in an organised endeavour to reform and settle the travelling population. They were assisted in their efforts by the generally persecutory activities of the police and magistrates, themselves responsible for the control and surveillance of the marginal and deviant sections of society. Following this came attempts by philanthropists and local authorities to secure effective legislation to curb the Gypsy 'menace'. Formal and informal agents of the dominant culture worked together, though not always harmoniously, in an attempt to find an effective solution to the itinerant 'problem'.

By looking in this way at responses to travellers and travelling it is hoped that the position of itinerants in society, and the relationship between this group and the settled population, will be clarified. Clearly this could not be achieved by looking at the nature of travelling life alone. It is also necessary to show how and why the travellers were defined and perceived by various organisations and agencies, from evangelist missions and the legislature to local authority reports and literature.

Any attempt at reconstructing the nomadic way of life in the nineteenth century, and how it was seen and understood by the travellers themselves, must inevitably be flawed and incomplete as they left behind very little in the form of written records. Theirs was primarily an oral culture which it is now unfortunately too late to tap by detailed social-anthropological survey. But to say they left little is not to suggest that autobiographical material by travellers is non-existent. Extensive research into working class autobiographies of this period has revealed a number of useful items relating to travellers and itinerancy.[8] Autobiographies written by travellers take a variety of forms, partly a reflection of the different backgrounds of the authors and of the extent of their association with the travellers' culture. Works written by navvies, vagrants and tramping artisans contain much of merit and interest but only in exceptional circumstances did the authors abandon their links with sedentary society. It was usually the case that their contact with an itinerant life-style was temporary and short-term. Life histories by those able to claim a stronger attachment to the travelling culture, by ancestry or long-term rejection of settled habits, were fewer in number and again vary greatly in their value. Perhaps the best known is *The Book of Boswell: Autobiography of a Gypsy* (1970), a transcript of a tape-recording made by Silvester Gordon Boswell and containing a most useful account of his life on the roads. Of less value is the disappointing and misleading work by Samuel Loveridge, entitled *No. 747. Being the Autobiography of a Gipsy* [1891]. Although allegedly written by Loveridge the narrative was put into 'an acceptable literary and publishable form' by 'F. W. Carew', the pseudonym of A. E. C. Way. While he includes some comment on travelling the author spent only five years on the road (when aged nine to fourteen), and much of the remainder of the text describes his life in service. For a later period the various volumes of reminiscences of Dominic Reeve[9] provide a welcome challenge to the romantic illusions found in Petulengro's *A Romany Life* (1935), Manfri Wood's *In the Life of a Romany Gypsy* (1973), and the didactic evangelism of Cornelius and Rodney Smith.[10]

On the whole, then, information on the travellers has to come from outside observers, some of whom had a great deal of contact with the people while others had little or none and wrote more from hearsay and speculation than fact. Of considerable value in locating the large number of printed items relating to Gypsies and travelling is a volume entitled *A Gypsy Bibliography*, compiled by George Black and published in Edinburgh in 1914 (a provisional issue appeared five years earlier). Black lists references to works relating to European and British Gypsies providing a full, if not entirely accurate, checklist of several hundred items. This has recently been brought up to date in a supplementary volume by Dennis Binns. Further guides to printed works can also be found in the catalogues of the Scott Macfie Gypsy Collection at the University of Liverpool and the Romany Collection at the University of Leeds.[11]

The quality and value of the many items available in printed form have proved to be highly uneven. To impose a rather simplified model on the various works, they can be said to favour one of the definitions outlined earlier. Although the mixing of stereotypes by some writers and the ambiguous and contradictory nature of some works could make the classification awkward, it was nevertheless generally the case that one tendency dominated their writings. This enables us to identify whether the author was describing a separate race, romantic or degenerate, or a larger cultural grouping of travellers.

The writers who claimed to have identified a separate race of Romany Gypsies were to be found mainly in the romantic school of fictional writers or else associated with the Gypsy Lore Society, though their influences clearly would have extended further than these narrow confines suggest. Writings of people such as George Borrow and the mainstays of the Gypsy Lore movement, notably Henry Crofton, Charles Leland and Francis Hindes

Groome, were very much a part of a general trend in Victorian thought that emphasised race and origins. Having found variation among travellers and identified foreign origins, theories of genetics were then used, often crudely and deterministically, to explain the characteristics of the group. In such a way a framework was formed within which responses were conditioned. Also in accordance with contemporary concerns, more was written about language and etymology than about the people themselves.

Yet despite these important reservations, these writers and the large number of contributors who published articles in the *Journal of the Gypsy Lore Society* offer perhaps the most substantial and essential of all the many and various sources, not least because of their bulk. If read with a care to criticism, an eye for omissions and a realisation of the attempt to impose false limitations on the group selected for study, then much of value can be extracted. A major drawback of this source is the tendency to fall into a comfortable acceptance of the opinions expressed and to become complacently convinced of the importance of ceremony and ritual in the everyday lives of the travellers. Such a failure is most clearly in evidence in the recent work of Elwood Trigg.[12]

Standing alongside these essentially racial works were those by authors who, though they may have subscribed to a belief in the existence of the Romany Gypsy, were not concerned with locating a separate race but instead sought to advertise the conditions of life of a large travelling group urgently demanding the attention of reformers. John Hoyland and James Crabb were among the first to publish works with this emphasis, and their importance was not missed by later writers who frequently drew from them for evidence.[13]

The 1880s were perhaps the heyday of the Gypsy as a subject, with articles published in a wide array of newspapers and journals. Much of the responsibility for the attention given to the Gypsy 'problem' must rest with the philanthropist George Smith of Coalville. Having turned to the issue of the reform of the children of travellers, he published widely and profusely on the subject. Many criticisms can be levelled at his first book dealing with this matter, *Gipsy Life: ʋeing an Account of our Gipsies and their Children, with Suggestions for their Improvement*, published in 1880. It is badly written and poorly argued, relying on exaggeration to draw lurid pictures and on anecdote combining freely with hearsay and factual information. Although the more serious of these problems were rectified in later books his distorted arguments remained convincing to an audience wanting to be convinced.[14] This presentation of wild speculation and unsupported assertions in the form of factual 'truths' can be seen in works as varied as W. and J. Simson's *A History of the Gipsies* (1865) and miscellaneous government publications.

Serious research into travellers and itinerancy has been steadily increasing in recent years, originating from various disciplines and revealing many approaches and perspectives.[15] At no time since the late nineteenth century has the question of the travelling population received such attention. It is hoped that the flaws and weaknesses of earlier works are not repeated, here and elsewhere.

PART 1

Nomadism

2

Itinerancy as a way of life

Travelling was an essential part of nineteenth-century economic and social life, with the various itinerant groups performing important functions both before the development of an efficient communications and trade network and also after, though in a modified form. John Swinstead, writing in the 1890s, identified seven classes of traveller which covered the uncommercial tramps, unemployed artisans, showmen, Gypsies, horse-dealers, hawkers and cheap-jacks.[1] This short list, for it can scarcely be termed a classification, touches only the surface of the vast, mobile labour force. John Sampson also attempted a categorisation, linking a particular type of traveller with the distinctive style of language, or cant, used by the group:

Up and down the devious dusky streaks between city and village, and village and city, go the tattered tribes of *dromengeros*, wild birds of passage, differing widely among themselves in note and plumage, but united in their common enmity to the plump city-bred pigeon – the Saddlers with their picturesque rhyming cant, the Hawker and Driz Fencer with their back slang, the Mush Faker with his *nedhers kena thari*; the Potter or Mugger with his mask cant, the Crocus Pitcher with his peculiar lingo, the Shalla-bloke, Tramp or Mumper with their ephemeral flying cant, and the Irish tinkers . . . chief among these are the Gypsies, the aristocrats of the road.[2]

An earlier attempt to make sense of the variety of groups who to some degree adopted an itinerant or outdoor style of life was provided by Henry Mayhew. He constructed a travelling spectrum of rural nomads which placed the respectable tramping artisan at one end and the unrespectable tramps and beggars at the other, with a mediate grouping of 'pedlars, showmen, harvest-men, and all that large class who live by either selling, showing, or doing something through the country'.[3] He then went on to identify the urban and suburban nomads who followed outdoor occupations in and around the large towns, such as beggars, prostitutes, street-sellers, street-performers, water-men and cabmen. But this attempt to distinguish between rural and urban nomadism, and between different kinds of rural nomads, is somewhat misleading. The variations and gradations between the rural nomads are not always as apparent as Mayhew suggested and may simply have represented different stages of life of the individual or of the diverse living patterns and means of earning a livelihood which correspond with the changing seasons of the year.[4]

There was a similar fluidity between the rural and urban nomads. Many of the former took to itinerant and marginal employments in the urban areas during the winter months, in the same way that many of the urban nomads travelled the countryside at certain times of the year, notably during the hop- and fruit-picking seasons. A more important criticism, though, concerns the use of the term 'nomads', commonly associated with ideas of tribalism and communalism. As stated, Mayhew's main criterion for identifying the various types of nomads, rural and urban, was that of occupation. Essentially, he placed on the same nomadic spectrum all whose employment necessitated an outdoor existence for some period of time. Such a classification is clearly too sweeping. Similarly, Swinstead's categorisation is made too broad by the adoption of travelling generally as his criterion. While these writers admittedly identify an interesting tendency towards mobility within Victorian society, they also conceal as much as they reveal by indiscriminately grouping together a miscellaneous assortment lacking any identity as a group.

In order to understand and appreciate the complexity and nature of the itinerant population, it is necessary to narrow the scope and make an important preliminary distinction that separates a sub-group of travellers from this larger group of mobile labour. This can be achieved initially by differentiating between those who travelled in order to obtain employment but otherwise adopted and conformed to a sedentary way of life, and those who, with their families, took to travelling *as a way of life in itself*, at least for a sizeable part of the year. In the first group can be placed the tramping artisans, navvies and agricultural labourers. In the latter can be grouped the showmen, hawkers, horse-dealers, Gypsies, travelling potters and the like.[5] The differences between the two groups included minor points of style as well as more fundamental distinctions. For example, Gypsies tended to travel as a family group, camping on waste or common land, by the roadside and in barns. On the other hand, the tramping artisan usually wandered alone, leading a solitary life and staying in lodgings, club houses and inns. Perhaps more significant was the nature of their various employments. The artisan was a wage-earner, dependent on selling his limited and specialised labour skills to others, and for whom tramping was a customary response to regional trade depressions.[6] In contrast, the Gypsies and travellers were self-employed and independent, following a wide variety of itinerant callings and trades, whose earning power was based largely on their own efforts and wits. The only time when they did not conform to this pattern of independency was during the season when agricultural labour was in high demand, with the opportunity for short-term employment and a regular and guaranteed income over a fixed period persuading them to enter the harvest fields, fruit-growing farms and hop fields. Even during the winter period, when travelling was usually curtailed, this self-styled and self-imposed economic independency distinguished them from their town neighbours. For these months they generally continued their trades as hawkers, pedlars, costermongers and street-sellers.

This sub-group of travellers comprises the subject of this study. The question of ascription and perceptions will be dealt with in a later chapter, but for present purposes it is sufficient to term this group Gypsies or Gypsy-travellers. They possessed a certain unity owing to their itinerant life-style and their independent, self-disciplined means of earning a livelihood. It is these considerations that assist in distinguishing between the many groups and occupations listed by Swinstead, Sampson and Mayhew, permitting a narrowing of the focus on to a nomadic, family group within the broader, travelling mass while not losing sight of either the breadth or even the blurrings of the boundaries. The common elements which bind together this sub-group and permit them to be seen by outsiders as separate and distinctive remain, in terms of responses, decisive. This, though, is not to imply uniformity or homogeneity within this smaller class of itinerants. The members of this sub-group differed from each other in terms of occupation, race, wealth, the extent of their migrancy, the types of dwellings used and even the reasons for adopting such a life-style.

The diversity of the migrant population, of that part of the labour force described by Raphael Samuel as comprising a vast 'reserve army of labour', would suggest that the reasons for its existence were many and various. In relation to the non-nomadic mobile labour force isolated earlier, itinerancy was a direct result of the individual's need to sell his labour. There is no such obvious correlation in respect of the nomadic sub-group, and there is no clear answer to the question whether the type of occupation pursued was a product of an itinerant life-style, or vice versa. The historical antecedents would be largely untraceable and the evolved interrelationships and traditions would render meaningless any simple explanation. Even so, four factors have been offered, at various times and with different degrees of emphasis, to explain the existence of a nomadic population.

The first, which was commonly held in the latter part of the nineteenth century, suggested that travellers, and especially Gypsies, were afflicted with an uncontrollable 'wanderlust'. It was in their blood, a part of their nature, and it was as natural for them to move as it was for the majority of the population to remain in one place. Itinerancy was believed to be a product of genetic determinants and, by extension of the logic, was present in some races and not others. Those Gypsies who adopted a sedentary way of life were either conveniently disregarded or else were said to be of 'impure blood'. More reasonably, itinerancy was said to result from socialisation to a travelling way of life. Clearly, being raised as a nomad and being accustomed to the rigours of travelling from an early age would undoubtedly have increased the likelihood of inter-generational itinerancy. Occupations demanding mobility naturally followed from this. Thirdly, employment criteria were thought to be uppermost: nomadism and mobility were economically essential in order to secure a regular income. Finally, it was suggested that itinerancy was the means of escape adopted by the 'refuse' and 'outcasts' of sedentary society, whether fleeing from industrial employments and the constraints of civilised society or merely from the hand of the law. These various arguments isolate heredity, cultural continuity, economic practicality and ideological rejection as the chief determinants, each contributing in some measure to the adoption and retention of a travelling life-style.

Moving on from the many reasons for adopting an itinerant life-style, it is also possible to identify a number of differences in the actual practice of travelling. Again, it is useful to return to the work done by Raphael Samuel in this area. He divides the travelling population into four categories according to degrees of itinerancy. To begin with he distinguishes the habitual wanderers, who moved from place to place with no regular settlement, from those who kept regular winter quarters in the towns. Apart from these were a further group who travelled only during the summer season but who otherwise remained in one location, and, finally, there were others who made frequent visits to the country but never moved far from their home base. John Hoyland found evidence of this range among the London Gypsies in the early nineteenth century, with some remaining in London all the year except for their occasional attendance at nearby fairs. Others sought to widen the market for their goods and services by travelling 20 or 30 miles from the metropolis into the neighbouring counties, where farm work could also usually be obtained. A final group preferred to use London only as their winter base, travelling the remaining months throughout the Southern and Midland Counties.[7]

It is important to make this identification between the different types of migrancy, and the decision of when and how far to travel would have been subject to a number of considerations, not the least of which was a personal assessment of employment opportunities and hawking capacity. The adoption and reliance upon a variety of itinerant callings meant that the means of earning a living required the ability to pursue different trades when the occasion demanded, and also the freedom to travel in response to demand. That is, the extent of itinerancy was guided by the degree of success, in money or kind, achieved in the various towns and districts.

The range and duration of the Gypsy-travellers' wanderings were neither carefully planned nor chaotically irregular. Circuits were followed and certain districts were regularly visited, with the exact route and length of stay in any area dependent on the nature of the relationship between the Gypsies and the local community as expressed in terms of the success of the hawking ventures, the response of the police, local authority officials and local residents, the condition of the camping ground, and the desire for change.[8] Personal considerations thus mixed with free choice, need and persuasion to provide the key considerations.

Samuel's model provides a convenient framework for the initial classification of travellers and itinerancy, but it needs to be further refined. In order to focus attention more sharply on the nomadic sub-group it is necessary to suggest a relationship between the extent of migrancy, the type of abode and the nature and location of the site of the dwelling-place. The categories used by Samuel correctly cut across factors such as occupation, race and age, yet variables of abode and site need to be added to his emphasis on the spread and range of migrancy. If migrancy was long in the amount of time spent on the road and wide in terms of the area travelled, then each stop tended to be relatively short and the sites for the camps temporary. Any area of waste ground, forest or common land, private land (often without the owner's consent) or a suitable roadside verge served as a short-stay site for these travellers. The types of abodes varied from vans and tents to barns, sheds and the open air. The lone traveller, with few possessions, tended to dominate the latter categories while the nomadic families seemed to favour the more protective vans and tents.

When migrancy was short and narrow, if not for all seasons then at least usually for the winter months, more permanent sites, or settlements, were erected. Secluded locations in forests or on land leased for long periods were the most preferred alternatives, providing some security of tenure and relative freedom from harassment. The sites varied in size and in the number of occupants from one family to several, and also in the degree of permanency, from two or three months to half a century or more. Such settlements, the larger of which came to be described as 'van towns', were to be found at various times in the period under review in and around London, in Epping Forest, near Woodford, at Battersea, Wandsworth, Hackney Marshes, the Notting Hill Potteries and elsewhere.[9] Similar camps could also be seen at Boughton Green in Northamptonshire ('the fluctuating capital of gipsydom in the Midlands'), in Altrincham, on the South Shore at Blackpool, in Birmingham, in the New Forest and on the Malvern Hills, on the outskirts of Manchester and in the mean streets of Leeds, in the quarries of Headington and by the Welsh lakes, on the Bohemian Estate at Eastwood, and in Norwich, Lowestoft, Southend, Gorleston and Buxton Heath.[10]

To argue for the existence of permanent sites is not to imply that all the inhabitants were necessarily a permanent feature also. Simply, it should be taken to mean that given the large numbers of Gypsies who used the sites, and given the diversity of the extent and duration of their travelling, these locations were the central bases of the comings and goings of a large and varied group. This would have been most noticeable in the summer, but even during these months many of the sites were in continual use, containing a nucleus of fixed residents. Indeed, some of the vans at the 'headquarters' of the van population near Wormwood Scrubs, Battersea, were no longer moveable, having lost their wheels.[11]

These large and regular sites provoked a great deal of concern and interest precisely because of the number of travellers congregated en masse and the semi-permanency of the dwellings. On any day the numbers on site could have been supplemented by philanthropists, journalists, philologists, lorists, sanitary officers, missionaries, police and local government officials. Whether by sympathisers or critics the Gypsies were hounded from all sides, suffering interrogation about their lore and language, subjected to the evangelistic endeavours of the missionaries or persecuted by the various agencies of the state.

Not all who curtailed their travelling during the winter, or who otherwise fell into the short and narrow migrancy range, lived in these settlements or even on sites in vans and tents. The tendency in the winter months was for the travellers to migrate inwards towards the centres of large populations and then find accommodation according to preference, availability and resources:

those who have houses empty the furniture out of their vans into the houses, and live the regular ordinary life of the working-man, but with more general experience.

Some remain in their vans by preference, and take up a place at the Agricultural Hall, Islington, the Drill Hall, Portsmouth, and similar places, for which they pay a larger rent than is supposed.

But others can neither do this nor even purchase the privilege of staying in an inn yard sheltered by the adjoining houses, and these . . . have to keep moving on . . . with their squalid vans or smoky tents.[12]

Winter lodging in houses and flats was not merely the preserve of the wealthier travellers. Vernon Morwood, writing in the mid-1880s, noted the tendency of Gypsies to rent accommodation 'in the most wretched houses in the low localities of our large towns'.[13] Many other authors also commented on this habit, often in an attempt to refute the claims by the 'wanderlust' theorists that the Gypsies could not be settled.[14]

This habit of temporarily terminating itinerancy in favour of settled abodes was apparent throughout the nineteenth century and no large town seems to have escaped this seasonal influx. But it was to London that a great many were attracted. Both John Hoyland and James Crabb noted the mass migration from the Midland Counties to London which took place during the winter.[15] The general impression formed by Morwood for the latter decades of the century was no less applicable to London a quarter of a century earlier:

some of the gypsies during the winter months take up their tents and live in houses. But when they do so, they make the place of their abode in the lowest parts of the metropolis. They leave the country and suburban districts of London . . . and make their dwelling in some low court in Kent-street, Shoreditch, and Golden-lane, St. Luke's; where two and three families of them will huddle together in one small room, with no chairs, tables, or beds.[16]

This picture of travellers living in non-moveable dwellings for the winter months could also be seen, though in better circumstances than those described above, at Kirk Yetholm in Scotland. For much of the century, the Gypsy occupants of Tinklers Row retained the travelling traditions of summer migrancy and winter settlements. However, the balance swung increasingly in favour of reduced travelling and permanency, a tendency that dated from around the latter third of the century, in Scotland as elsewhere in Britain. At first it seemed that only a few individuals were taking up permanent residences for the whole year, though still relying on itinerant callings as their source of income, but from the late nineteenth century the existence of large numbers of house-dwelling Gypsies came to be noticed by a variety of writers.[17] By this time the slow drift had turned into a more expansive slide into sedentarisation, and, eventually, colonies of Gypsies were identified:

The gipsy element is found in many if not most villages in the south of England. I know one large scattered village where it appears predominant – as dirty and disorderly-looking a place as can be imagined, the ground round every cottage resembling a gipsy camp, but worse owing to its great litter of old rags and rubbish strewn about. But the people, like all gipsies, are not so poor as they look, and most of the cottagers keep a trap and pony with which they scour the country for many miles around in quest of bones, rags and bottles, and anything else they can buy for a few pence, also anything they can pick up for nothing.[18]

This trend towards sedentarisation, in the nature of dwellings if not always in employment, should not be overstated. Although affecting an indeterminate though not insignificant proportion of the travelling community, there were still great numbers who modified their way of life rather than accept this important step towards permanent settlement. These changes in the duration and range of migrancy, and of the type of dwellings used by the travellers and their location, should not obscure a significant continuity. The range of migrancy discussed earlier, in terms of its duration and area covered, was apparent at the beginning of the period under review just as it was at the end. Some travellers had always travelled long distances and for long periods, while others followed a more restricted itinerant lifestyle. Following on from this, there were regular and permanent sites throughout the century. As early as the eighteenth century settlements of Gypsies could be found close to the new urban communities in the East and West Midlands, notably that of Tinkerborough outside Stafford.[19]

To argue that the wide migrancy spectrum was always present should not be taken to mean that the emphasis did not alter. Indeed, certain trends are apparent. By the latter decades of the nineteenth century the majority of travellers were grouped at the end of the scale that travelled shorter distances for fewer months, with the inevitable result that larger and more permanent sites grew up on the edges of the towns and cities. With the increased geographical concentration of the population there was no longer the same economic need to travel in small groups over wide areas.

This voluntary adaptation to change coexisted with other external factors which threatened and encroached upon the travelling way of life. The most notable of these were the attempts by missionaries and philanthropic humanitarians to force settlement on the travellers; persecution and harassment by law officers and state officials; the challenge posed by technological developments and industrial advance to traditional crafts and employments; finally, the enclosure movement and building and development schemes which took away many of the regular and customary camping grounds. The first three of these factors will be discussed in later chapters.

The enclosure movement gathered momentum throughout the century, taking away increasingly large areas of common land. The impact on the nomadic population was felt early on with accounts of Gypsies complaining of the difficulties occasioned by enclosure dating from the opening decades of the century.[20] Much land was enclosed under Private Acts between 1834 and 1849, under the Commons Act of 1876 and by an Act of 1851 passed for the disafforesting and enclosure of Hainault Forest. Epping Forest, the other great resort of the Gypsies, also suffered a series of enclosures throughout the first part of the nineteenth century. Furthermore, a considerable quantity of land had been partitioned by agreement and also under the sanction of the Statute of Merton. In the two years from 1871 to 1873 the area of commons had been reduced from 8,000,000 to 2,633,000 acres.[21] The effect of this on the Gypsies was dramatic:

Their old haunts are no longer their homes. The wide-stretching table-land around their present temporary retreat, once their own, as if by right of purchase, is now cultivated and enclosed; ploughed fields are interspersed among the smooth, turfy, breezy downs, and utility has replaced the picturesque. The gipsy tent rises no more from the green sward . . . so it is in the woodlands. Trees are felled, and houses built, and the wanderers . . . seek their leafy abodes in vain.[22]

Similarly, the roadside verge was no longer a convenient or practical alternative in quite the same way as it had been in years past. The wide 'slang' by the roadside of mid-century England, where the horses could pasture free of charge, were now guarded and reduced, and the pressure to move on from the rural police and local authority officials was consistent and tiring in its effect. A Gypsy named Lovell stated unhesitatingly that these developments had 'finished the old style gypsy'.[23]

The situation for the Gypsies was scarcely any better in the towns. For example, in London the regular haunts of the Gypsies at Crystal Palace, the 'Potteries' district of Latimer Road, and elsewhere, were subject to housing and building programmes.[24] By the 1880s Notting Dale, Willesden, Wormwood Scrubs and Kensal Green were all closed to the travellers. Reclamation of waste land, building projects and railway extensions were, for the Gypsy-travellers, the urban equivalents of rural enclosures.

The effects of these combined developments were various. Enclosure and the rural police tended to force the Gypsies off the country roads and into the towns. Here they congregated in large encampments, located generally on land rented either from sedentary landlords though also occasionally from the more wealthy Gypsies, or else in rented accommodation in low tenements of the slum areas. Homes were found in the damp cellars and garrets of the towns and cities.[25] The drift towards permanent settlement was taking place in town and country alike, affecting the Gypsies of Yetholm, London, Dorset, Kent and all the counties between.

With a way of life under such serious threat those not willing to accept settlement or engage in a running battle with the authorities looked further abroad for their solution. The wide open spaces of America proved to be more attractive as the century progressed, to the extent that it came to be described as the 'true Canaan' of all travellers.[26]

The selection of which path to take depended to a great extent on individual preference, which in turn must have rested on the perceived and real threat experienced by the travellers from the various assaults on their camping-grounds and employments from both impersonal forces and the particular whims of the different local authorities and policing agencies.

NUMBERS AND DISTRIBUTION OF THE TRAVELLING POPULATION

Having identified the subject of this study, its unity and diversity, and the long-term trends bearing on the travelling community, it remains now, before detailing the geographical location of the travellers, to consider the size of this group. Contemporary assessments were frequently based on impressions and distortions and were intended to have shock value rather than any element of numerical accuracy. At one extreme, James Simson estimated the number of Gypsies in the British Isles to be 250,000, 'and possibly double that number'.[27] This wild assertion was not the product of any systematic enquiry but rather stemmed from his belief that a child born of a couple with any Gypsy ancestry, however remote, was still a Gypsy. Numbers could thus increase only in a startling ratio. By way of contrast, there were other commentators, notably the lorists, who believed that the 'true' Gypsy, or Romany, had almost entirely died out by the late nineteenth century. The numbers of Gypsies had diminished almost to nothing, and the lorists were hurriedly collecting data on the culture and superstitions of the few who remained before they too were extinguished beneath the heavy feet of a rapidly advancing civilisation. However, the lorists conceded that numbers of *other* travellers were probably increasing. These were not the Romanies, who by the late nineteenth century had supposedly lost many of their distinguishing characteristics, but were instead the half-breeds, the allegedly dirty and disreputable offshoots of pure Romany stock. In between these two extremes came George Smith of Coalville, who estimated the Gypsy population to be from 15–20,000, and taken with other travellers of whatever description, the size of the itinerant population was calculated to be around 30,000.[28] Smith's method was far from scientific, relying on generalisations about nomads elsewhere from his limited experience of them around London and the Midlands. His conclusions were based on the assumption that each family consisted of six members and that the ratio of 1,000 Gypsies for every 1,750,000 of the inhabitants of London would be true for the rest of the country also. Other estimates varied from between 1,500 and 36,000.[29]

Closely bound in with these various assessments were the issues of definition and, following on from this, of responses. The lorists attempted to establish fundamental differences, rooted in race, between the various types of travellers and so tried to preserve a romantic image of the 'true' Gypsy, who was in a decline. The perceived growth in numbers of other travellers was of the half-breeds with diluted blood. A crude use of eugenic theory enabled the lorists to distance themselves from these travellers and to side with those who called for the persecution or reform of this group. Smith, on the other hand, did not trouble himself with such distinctions, and acted as the effective spokesman for local authority officials and other concerned parties in advertising the existence of a large group of nomads living in depravity on the fringes of civilisation, yet parasitical upon it.

The claims that the size of this group was increasing can be attributed to a number of causes. It is possible that the writers were simply adopting scare-mongering tactics and by providing statistical proof that the numbers of travellers had increased they hoped to provoke some immediate action. The tendency to exaggerate the impression that the number of idle, unclean, uneducated, parasitical itinerants was on the increase gave some justification to the persecution carried out by local authorities in their attempts to rid themselves of what was considered an unwanted menace. The existence of these travellers proved to be an open and visible sore. They were said to contribute nothing to the economy of the nation, while at the same time living in open defiance of all educational and sanitary laws. They could not, so the argument continued, be left to die a natural death: their numbers had grown so large that their demise had to be assisted.

Such claims may not have been deliberately misleading and it is probable that the number of van- and tent-dwellers appeared to have increased rather than decreased by the end of the century. It has been noted already that as the century progressed the extent and duration of the circuits travelled gradually diminished in scope and shortened in time. The general tendency was to remain close to, or within, major towns in semi-permanent encampments. The number of such sites grew and more Gypsies used them more often, with the consequence that larger groups of travellers were seen.

Alongside this development, more people were looking for the Gypsies. Whether the motives were philanthropic, official, charitable or hostile, the result was that more Gypsies were found and new sites discovered. For some it became a matter of urgency to break down the itinerants into clearly defined component categories. Their concern was with locating the pure-stock Romany who had become submerged beneath the rising tide of travellers lacking true Gypsy ancestry. To others, such attempts at categorisation were secondary to the more evident and pressing problem posed by the existence of a van and tent population, irrespective of its varied racial origins.

Although it is now possible to assess critically the bias of contemporary commentators, it remains a matter of considerable difficulty, if not impossibility, to give accurate figures for the size of the nomadic population. The number of travellers on the road would have varied with such factors as the season of the year, the inclemency of the weather and the vagaries of the different trades. Even though any attempt at enumeration has to be qualified by such considerations as these, the census reports provide the best if faulty indicator. The findings of the enumerators are tabulated and illustrated in Table 1 and Diagrams 1 and 2.

The 1841 census was taken on the 7th of June and that of 1851 much earlier on the 31st of March, but from then on the data on travellers were collected

Table 1 *Persons found dwelling in barns, sheds, tents, caravans and the open air (England and Wales), 1841-1911*

Year	Barns, sheds, tents, caravans and the open air			Barns and sheds			Tents, caravans and the open air		
	Total	Male	Female	Total	Male	Female	Total	Male	Female
1841	20,348								
1851	15,764			8,105			7,659		
1861	11,444	7,410	4,034	4,314	3,372	942	7,130	4,038	3,092
1871	10,383	6,246	4,137	2,358	1,921	437	8,025	4,325	3,700
1881	10,924	6,615	4,309	2,355	1,947	408	8,569	4,668	3,901
1891	15,983	9,469	6,514	3,149	2,548	601	12,834	6,921	5,913
1901	14,219	8,175	6,044	1,645	1,317	328	12,574	6,858	5,716
1911	30,642	19,948	10,694						

Source: Census of England and Wales, Reports and Appendices (1861–1911).

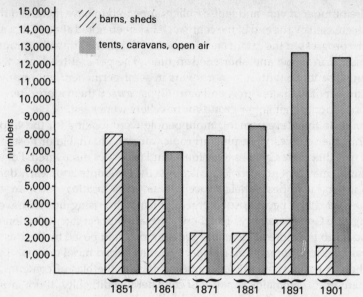

Diagram 1 Number of persons found dwelling in barns and sheds, and in tents, caravans and the open air (England and Wales), 1851–1901.
Note: the returns for 1841 and 1911 did not distinguish between the two types.
Source: Census of England and Wales, Reports and Appendices (1861–1911).

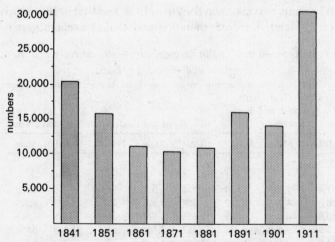

Diagram 2 Total number of persons found dwelling in barns, sheds, tents, caravans and the open air (England and Wales), 1841–1911.
Source: Census of England and Wales, Reports and Appendices (1861–1911).

sometime during the first week of April. Though perhaps a little early for some, this was about the time that summer migrancy began. This seasonal fluctuation did not pass unnoticed by the enumerators: 'in winter they shrink into dwellings, and in summer they swarm again in the fields, which have irresistible charms for the vagabond race, as well as for their near relatives the hop-pickers and haymakers. Mixed among them are found some of the victims as well as some of the outcasts of society.'[30] The nature of the directive issued to the enumerators, to quantify the number of persons sleeping not in dwelling-houses but in barns, sheds, caravans, tents and the open air, illustrates an intention to separate productive workers (such as canal boat-men and tramping artisans) from groups considered non-productive and with no specified occupation. Having identified the group to be counted, a further distinction was then made between those dwelling in barns and sheds, and those dwelling in tents, caravans and the open air. The reports for 1891 and 1901 further subdivided these groups according to gender, which showed most clearly the disproportion between males and females in the category of barn- and shed-dwellers. In 1891 there were 2,548 males and 601 females, and 1,317 males and only 327 females in 1901. This imbalance was by no means so apparent in the case of dwellers in tents, caravans and the open air, where the corresponding figures were 6,921 and 5,913 for 1891, and 6,858 and 5,716 for 1901.[31]

Barn- and shed-dwellers were, then, predominantly male, probably travel-ling alone. In contrast, the tent, caravan and open air population were more likely to be families, travelling as a group. The lone tramp and itinerant agricultural labourer were more likely to appear in the former category, with the nomadic groups that form the subject of this study in the latter. But the distinction is by no means clear-cut. At least until around mid-century, when caravans first appeared in significant numbers, nomadic families frequently took to lodging in barns and the out-houses of farms, some only erecting a tent when a stay in a barn was not possible.[32] This practice seems to have diminished by the second half of the century, though, as shown by the census taken in Surrey in 1913, this was not entirely the case.[33] However, in broad terms, the distinction remains valid.

Perhaps a more important obstacle in the way of accurate enumeration than the selection of suitable categories was the practical problem of ensuring that all travellers were included. Some would have accidentally avoided the enumerators by being on the move when the count was being taken or else by being hidden in some secluded location. Others regarded the census officials, as they did all figures of authority, with a mixture of suspicion, fear and contempt. Contact with such persons was often deliberately avoided as it invariably meant that trouble and inconvenience followed close behind:

At the time that the census officers were taking the census, gipsies and van-dwellers were either hiding in some out-of-the-way corner or back yard, or were on the road moving out of one district into another . . . purposely, to evade the census officers, because they imagined that the census officers were on their track for breaking the laws of the land.[34]

Even when given the census papers they either removed to another part of the country before they could be collected, or else returned inaccurate forms,

for, without education, without that general knowledge which will enable them to understand the work in hand, and probably, in many instances, not certain of their age and other particulars, they have, very likely, aided by prejudices, thrown obstacles in the way, and given no very clear account.[35]

Furthermore, the timing of the census would have excluded travellers still in their winter lodgings and Gypsy horse-dealers, basket-makers, tinkers and the like, who may have been listed separately under their several occupational headings. To balance against these omissions the figures are likely to have included tramps and showpeople.

The census officials were well aware of these inadequacies and inconsistencies, and the report for 1871 noted that the figures for vagrants, Gypsies, criminals, prostitutes, and the like, were so imperfectly returned that no benefit could accrue from the publication of their statements. It was thought that only the police could provide accurate statistical information. Both the 1881 and 1891 reports admitted that the numbers given must necessarily be an underestimate, for 'the detection and enumeration of this nomad population is manifestly one in which chance must have a great share'.[36] Despite these problems the census returns provide the best numerical guide available.

It can be seen from Table 1 and Diagram 2 that the travelling population as a whole experienced a steady decline down to 1871, and then began an upward climb climaxing in a massive growth between 1901 and 1911. No explanation is offered for this 115% increase. The answer is not to be found in a later dating for the enumeration for the count was taken on the 3rd of April, following the customary pattern. Natural population growth could account for some of the increase, though perhaps it was due simply to improved methods of enumeration rather than to various and diverse factors which at best could account only for a small proportion of the growth. The graph showing the composite elements of this total picture, Diagram 1, reveals that though starting from a position of approximate equality in 1851, the disproportion between those dwelling in barns and sheds, and those in tents, caravans and the open air, widened steadily during the period until, by 1901, the latter group outnumbered the former by a ratio larger than 7:1.

Finally, the reports from the latter part of the century are useful in illustrating the geographical distribution of the travellers. For the reasons given earlier, the following diagrams (3 and 4) have been constructed to show

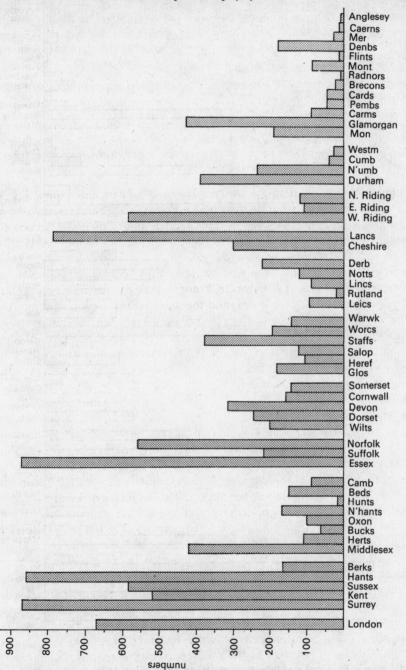

Diagram 3 Regional and county populations of dwellers in tents, caravans and the open air (England and Wales), 1891.
Source: Census of England and Wales, Area, Houses and Population, 1891, Vol. 2, Table 8 (1893), p. xxxv.

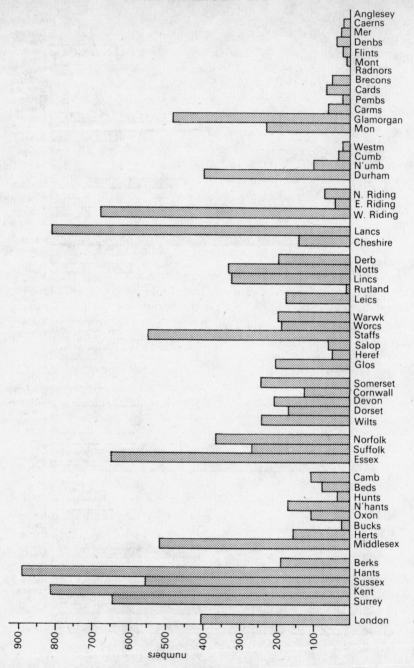

Diagram 4 Regional and county populations of dwellers in tents, caravans and the open air (England and Wales), 1901.

Source: Census of England and Wales, Summary Tables and Index, 1901, Table 23 (1903), p. 137.

the regional and county distribution of dwellers in tents, caravans and the open air only.

Both diagrams illustrate the concentration of travellers in the six counties around London, and in the neighbourhood of other industrial centres in the Midlands and the North West. Yet it is also clear that almost every county in England and Wales had some travellers within their boundaries, to a greater or lesser extent. Not surprisingly, their numbers are highest in the larger counties with the most dense populations. The pattern for 1891 and 1901 shows similar peaks and troughs, reaffirming the impression derived from various sources for the period as a whole. It should be remembered that although the absolute numbers were relatively high in some cases, their proportion of the population of a particular county and of the country remained very small.

GYPSIES OF THE NEW FOREST

The New Forest in Hampshire had been a regular stopping place for Gypsies throughout the nineteenth century. The number of travellers, as they were known locally, who camped within the Forest was subject to a series of fluctuations. Every travelling range was represented, from those who migrated only short distances from the Forest boundary to those who travelled throughout the Southern and Midland Counties, returning to the Forest with the arrival of winter.[37] To take a high average, the numbers camped at any one time would have been approximately 60 families, consisting of perhaps 400 persons. In August and September, when travelling was at its peak during the harvesting and hopping seasons, this number was greatly reduced with probably only half a dozen families remaining.[38]

Even though considerable numbers of Gypsies lived at different places in the Forest, there were still areas where it would have been impossible to find a Gypsy tent. Shelter, dryness, running water and proximity to a suitable market for their wares were the main considerations. The most popular areas which conformed to these requirements were, in the north, at Godshill Wood, Whinyates, Crock Hill and Copythorne; in the east at Ipley, Pennerley, Lady Cross and Norley Wood; at Poulner Pits, Picket Post, Burley and Thorny Hill in the west; at Bransgore, Shirley Holmes, Pennington and Setley in the south; and centrally at Rufus's Stone, Bartley, Buskett's Lawn and New Park.[39] Earlier in the century the Stanley family encamped at Marl-pit Oak and Gally Hill and just outside the Forest boundary camps were located around Bournemouth and at Blackhill.[40]

The problem of definition arises again when attempting to identify the inhabitants of the Forest. Various authors stressed the need to distinguish between the Gypsies, cheap-jacks, strolling outcasts, itinerant beggars, charcoal-burners, and van- and tent-dwellers. The case of the charcoal-burners was made easy because of their distinctive mud and grass abodes and the nature of their work, but any attempt to differentiate between the remainder is far more complicated. One popular solution was to separate them according to their surnames, and to this can be added the further criteria of the ability to speak the Romany language and whether the home was a tent or a van. Some commentators used these factors to argue in favour of racial variation among the travellers. Those who bore the surnames of Stanley, Lee, Eyre, Cooper and Burton were said to be the 'real' Gypsies of pure descent, estimated to comprise perhaps one quarter of the nomadic population of the Forest by the late nineteenth century.[41] Yet this distinction was not even agreed to by the travellers themselves. Although the Stanleys and the Lees were the most frequent visitors to the district in the early decades of the century, the Stanleys certainly did not consider they originated from the same racial ancestry as the Lees, thinking of themselves as the 'better sort of travellers'.[42] Not only the Lees but the remainder of the Forest-dwellers also were summarily dismissed as half-breeds, a mixture of tramp and Gypsy. Included in this much larger group were the families Lakey, Sherred, Doe, Sherrard, Sherwin, Sherwood, Wells, Blake, Green, Wareham, Barnes, and many others.[43]

The gradual disappearance of the Romany language allegedly provided further evidence of this dilution of the 'true' Gypsy blood. In the last decade of the nineteenth century it was reported that the New Forest Gypsies still understood and used, 'more or less', Romany, although in a very incomplete form. In general, Romany words were interspersed with ordinary English, and in using this hybrid form of language they differed from the old Gypsy families who were said to speak exclusively in the Romany tongue.[44]

The final distinction used was between the tent-dwellers of the Forest, who were supposed to be the descendants of the old tribes, and their van-dwelling brethren, or 'Romany of the towns'. The van-dwellers, to Henry Gibbins, were emphatically not residents of the Forest, but were merely a group who passed through on periodic visits. They were mostly cheap-jacks, or hawkers of various wares, at which they drove a profitable trade as evidenced by their expensive vans and horses. Although Gibbins' main intention was to draw a contrast between the respectable 'true' Gypsies living in the tents and the 'unruly' van-dwellers, he was reluctantly forced to concede that at least some of the latter kept their homes clean, their horses well-groomed, and their children well cared for. Griffith agreed that the 'true' Gypsy was rapidly disappearing from the Forest, and that three-quarters of the inhabitants were 'mumpers' or half-castes, but differed from Gibbins over the finer points of definition. He distinguished between the van-dwellers and those who had, at best, a pony and cart and, at worst, no more than a canvas sheet for a cover, but ascribed the differences not to whether the people were town or country

1 A portrait of a group of New Forest Gypsies towards the end of the nineteenth century.

Romanies, or to whether they were Romanies or half-castes, but instead to the more obvious variable of wealth.

The employment spectrum of the Forest population was considerable in its scope and variety, and the cycle of occupations pursued was adaptable to changing market demands and seasonal fluctuations. The travellers made baskets from withies, mats of heather, brooms, beehives, clothes-pegs and meat skewers; they repaired pots, kettles and umbrellas, sharpened knives, mended and bottomed chairs, collected rags and bones and swept chimneys. The women sold fortunes, flowers, love-charms, 'medicines' for diseases, rabbit skins and an assortment of other wares. In the summer many families travelled to Surrey and Kent to help in haymaking, fruit-picking, harvesting and hopping.[45] The list of occupations given to Alice Gillington as late as 1911 by a Forest-dweller illustrated both the range and continuity of their employments.[46]

The adaptability to the changing seasons was not only a response to changes in demand but also to the availability of the raw materials for the manufacture of the goods. In summer the men concentrated on making beehives of grass or straw and basket work, while the women gathered seasonal flowers for sale in the towns. In the winter the men switched to making clothes-pegs and meat skewers and the women made up artificial flowers from the pith of rushes and moss. It was the common practice for the men to remain at home and manufacture the articles, while the women and children toured the towns and villages hawking the items. If the householder could not be persuaded to buy any of the wares then the female Gypsy would either offer to tell fortunes or simply play on the sympathies of the listener by telling tales of sick husbands and dead children.[47]

In consequence of this dependence on the female, the movements of the family were conditional largely on the success, or failure, of these hawking and begging ventures. Griffith was surprised they managed to survive at all under such hand-to-mouth conditions and concluded it could only be done by 'very hard and ill paid work'.[48] Gibbins, on the other hand, had no such sympathy with a life he saw based on decadence, filth and idleness, the only cure for which was compulsory house-dwelling.[49] Although writing about the same group of people for almost the same period, these two writers were capable of seeing very different things. Where one saw differences in race the other saw discrepancies of wealth, and if one talked of hard work the other recognised only idleness. But it is not merely a matter of whether the Gypsies were either idle or hard-working as their pattern of employments were subject to seasonal variation, which had an important bearing on the nature and extent of their money-earning capacity.

The summer months provided the opportunity for some relief from the hardships and shortages of winter, and many of the Forest-dwellers travelled to the harvest fields, hopping grounds and strawberry fields of Surrey and Kent. Employment was plentiful, regular and temporary. Compared with the normal winter income relatively high wages were earned in a short period of time, and this was used to restock their hawking baskets, renew their wardrobes and carry out repairs to their vehicles and homes. Any that was left was spent in relaxed enjoyment at the fair held at Downton, near Salisbury, early in October and which served as a convenient social meeting place for the Gypsies on their return from hopping. For others it was neither necessary nor desirable to travel so far afield as some of the local Gypsies owned their own strawberry fields, employing Gypsy children as pickers.[50] Gibbins again had his own personal assessment of this picking employment cycle:

Gipsies, like convicts, are noted for their love of picking, and sometimes, unfortunately (for them), make five seasons in the year instead of four; . . . first in the spring he did a bit of pocket-picking at the race meetings, secondly in summer he did a bit of flower and fruit picking, thirdly in autumn he did a bit of hop-picking, fourthly in winter he did a bit of wood-picking, and fifthly (the rest of the year) he did a bit of oakum-picking.[51]

Although a similar cynicism and guarded reserve remained as part of the response to the Gypsies there were also other testimonies which preferred to praise rather than condemn this group, offering as evidence their civility, politeness, amenability to kindness and, to the incredulity of many critics, their general sobriety.[52] Moreover, some local farmers testified that Gypsies acted not as depredators of property but rather as protectors, safeguarding against poachers and sheep-stealers.[53] Contrary opinions thus served to stand many of the customary stereotypes on their heads. Relations with the local community were even so well advanced as to lead to amorous alliances being formed between the Gypsy lads and village girls and domestic servants. Finally, they were not known to have committed crimes of robbery or violence, and an elderly local magistrate told Gibbins that during the fifty years he had served on the Bench the most serious crimes of the Gypsies had been stealing small trifles such as a fowl or a rabbit, or some park railings for firewood.[54]

By the first decade of the twentieth century the number of tent- and van-dwellers in the Forest had greatly decreased and the Stanleys and Lees, formerly so prominent, had gone from the area. Some of the success for drawing the Forest inhabitants away from what was seen as a harsh and mean existence was claimed by the missionaries and reformers.[55] Perhaps more potent factors which drove them away or into houses nearby were the effects of enclosure and economic pressures. The neighbouring towns and villages no longer served as an adequate market for their wares and it became increasingly difficult to earn enough money to provide a daily sustenance. Moreover, about half of the original Forest had been taken over as private property, and during the summer months holiday-makers disturbed the former calm. Finally, Forest laws only permitted the travellers to remain for forty-eight hours in one place for fear that they could claim squatter rights. The net result was that the Gypsies either moved away altogether, settled in the Forest cabins, or formed small, sedentary colonies in the nearby towns and villages.[56]

Thorny Hill became one such settlement. Eric Winstedt estimated the number of Gypsies who settled there as around 700, though contemporary newspaper accounts placed the figure much nearer to 100.[57] They lived in thatched cottages rather than tents and vans, and marriages with the villagers were not uncommon. Family associations remained strong, though, and it was not considered unusual for three generations to live together as one household. Despite becoming house-dwellers they retained certain of their former habits and summer travelling remained an important and essential custom. Even when not travelling, the women, at least, were still dependent on hawking for providing for the family. On Tuesdays, Thursdays and Saturdays they were taken first to Christchurch and then on to Bournemouth in order to sell flowers. The men were chiefly occupied in strawberry-growing, brickmaking and farming.[58] Impersonal forces had thus acted to constrain the Gypsies' traditional way of life and persuade them to take up a sedentary existence, which was to lead to their total absorption into the local community.

'METROPOLITAN GYPSYRIES'

London and the surrounding districts remained the undisputed heart of the travelling population throughout the period under review. Even when pushed from the central areas the Gypsies continued to base their varied comings and goings from the fringes of the city into the surrounding counties. Thus it was in and around the metropolis that sizeable numbers of itinerants travelled, and their camps were to be found almost everywhere. When the season arrived for the commencement of travelling large numbers could be seen radiating from this centre, only for the direction to be reversed with the end of hop-picking and the onset of wintry weather. London proved to be a convenient and large market for hawking and street-trading, and a place where relative anonymity took precedence over conspicuousness. Vagrants, beggars and tramps were a common sight, and camps of people living in tents, in the open or under the arches of the London bridges were a regular feature of the landscape and environment. In London, then, was to be found the largest number of Gypsy-travellers situated in a geographically limited area. As has been seen before, the numbers would fluctuate with the seasons, and the types of travellers who camped here varied considerably in the nature and extent of their itinerancy and the permanency of their dwellings.

In the main the Gypsies camped, during the summer, on the edges of the metropolis in the forests, on the waste ground and on the commons. The winter months saw many of them migrate further inwards to seek alternative sites and lodgings in the mean streets of the city. Camp sites varied from the idyllic surroundings of the woodland and forest to the slum regions of the Notting Hill Potteries. They settled on waste land of every description, from yards belonging to public houses to pieces of common land over which no authority claimed any rights. The result was that they could be found in almost all areas of London. A London city missionary, writing in 1858, supported this picture of the widespread dispersal of the Gypsy encampments:

the circuit of my district has necessarily been large, taking in Woodford, Loughton, Barkingside, Wanstead, Barking, Forest-gate, Stratford, Barking-road, Bow-common, Hackney Wick, Holloway, Blackheath, Greenwich, Plumstead-common, Streatham, Norwood, Wandsworth, Wimbledon, Putney and Barnes-common, Hammersmith, Chiswick, Kensington, Potteries, Paddington, Battersea, Shoreditch, and Borough.

All these are regular stations, where I generally meet with gypsies. In addition to these places I visit the hop-gardens in Kent and Surrey during the hop-picking season; also the fairs in the neighbourhood of London, with Epsom races, in quest of gypsies.[59]

Before the widespread advance of the enclosure movement Norwood was perhaps the principal rendezvous of the London Gypsies.[60] This afforested area was, at the start of the century, wildly rural, largely uncultivated and thinly populated. Although the 1808 enclosures deprived the Gypsy-travellers of many of their traditional sites, they did not remove entirely from the district but instead migrated into neighbouring Dulwich, adding to the colony already there.[61] Their former site in Norwood came to be known, after their departure, as Gipsy Hill. In 1876 they signalled their intention to remain in the area when one of their number purchased a field in Lordship Lane, Dulwich, specifically for the purpose of accommodating his travelling relatives and friends, much to the annoyance of the inhabitants in the nearby mansions and 'residences of high character'.[62] Other suitable locations were found about the woods and lanes at Anerley and Penge, and in the Epping and Hainault Forests to the north-east of the city.

The romanticism of the picture of the wild Gypsy, living *al fresco* in tents and shelters, applied in general only to the first part of the century, and later only to a small section of the Gypsies. As the century progressed this image rapidly became part of the romantic myth that surrounded the Romany people. The reality of the situation in the metropolis, which was becoming increasingly apparent, was far less appetising. The Gypsies pitched their tents and halted their vans in areas of transition, on brickfields and on waste ground, on sites of intended buildings and where buildings had been pulled down. They encamped in the midst of ruins, chaos and filth, and many of their camps were in such depressed areas that they were said to be satisfied to put up their tents 'where a Londoner would only accommodate his pig or his dog'.[63]

The degeneration of the commons from pleasant green lands to industrial waste sites was a marked and clear phase that accompanied the development of the metropolis as a major industrial centre. In 1871, for instance, Wandsworth Common, a popular resting place for the Gypsies from the beginning of the century, was more of a nuisance than a place of recreation and enjoyment:

Its surface was bare, muddy and sloppy after a little rain, undrained, and almost devoid of trees or seats. It was covered with huge gravel-pits, many of them full of stagnant water, which, in addition to being very offensive, constituted a positive source of danger owing to their great depth and want of protection.[64]

Twenty years later their vans were camped on the waste land near the railway arches in Wandsworth and Battersea. The conditions had not improved, with

2 A Gypsy camp near Latimer Road in the Notting Hill district of London showing the philanthropist George Smith of Coalville handing out sweets to the ragged Gypsy children.

thick mud and garbage everywhere. For the dubious privilege of remaining there the Gypsies were paying between 2s. and 2s. 6d. a week in rent. By 1896 there were said to be five such colonies in these two parishes.[65]

A vivid picture has been provided of a typical encampment which was found in Donovan's Yard in Battersea, near to the South-Western railway line. Here could be seen rows of 'living waggons' surrounded by palings, walls and arches, outside of which sat the women and children engaged in needlework, gossiping or the family wash. The inside of a van was described as 'a pocket edition of home as known to many thousands of house-dwellers – the vast public of the one-roomed tenement'.[66] A fireplace, table and bed was all that could be accommodated within the confined space. Some owners had sold their horses on arrival to save the cost of keeping them over winter, and would buy replacements when the time again came to travel. But the site also contained 'moveable' dwellings that had been made more or less permanent fixtures by having their shafts, wheels and axles removed. The Gypsy inhabitants of Lamb Lane lived in equally appalling conditions. They had drawn up their caravans and pitched their tents in the spaces between the rows of houses tenanted by labourers in the foundries and the gas and water works. The yards were no more than areas for the deposit of garbage and yet they provided camping places for the Gypsy-travellers.[67]

However, these conditions favourably contrast with those which existed in Kensington, around the Notting Hill Potteries. Even the sites on the Thames mud-flats and Plumstead Marshes were described as salubrious compared with those at Notting Hill.[68] Whether from historical or geographical causes, tramps and travellers who entered London from the north and west had long used the district as a temporary halting place. Some stayed a night, some a week, maybe even months and years, but in general the travellers moved on, often to St Giles's or Whitechapel, only to return again on their later travels. Each time, though, some would have remained and Charles Booth commented that Gypsy blood was in evidence among the children in the schools, and was even 'noticeable in the streets'.[69]

The area only became known as the Potteries from the 1830s onwards, about which time it also attracted a large colony of pig-breeders. By 1849 the residents were living at a density of 130 to the acre, and the number of pigs was upwards of 3,000.[70] Many of the residents lived in converted railway carriages and vans. During the years 1846–8 the living conditions had deteriorated rapidly, with vast quantities of semi-liquid pig manure and other organic matter lingering in the cavities dug up by the potters and brick-makers. These conditions contributed to the alarming statistic that the average age of death was just eleven years and three months compared to thirty-seven years for London as a whole.[71] Following the cholera epidemic of 1848–9 'the conditions of filth, disease and insanitation in which its inhabitants were found to be living and dying gave the area a notoriety perhaps unsurpassed by any other district in London'.[72] It was not until the 1870s that conditions began to improve with the introduction of better systems of drainage, prosecution of pig-owners and the decline of pig-breeding as a regular business.

Yet despite the squalid environment, the Gypsies flocked to the area in large numbers, and those living in or near Latimer Road were estimated to comprise from forty to fifty families by 1862.[73] It was about this time that missionary work in the area was thought to have led to some transformation in the Gypsy way of life. Many were said to have given up the traditional Gypsy 'vices' of drinking, swearing and fortune-telling. Others had allegedly abandoned the Romany language and gone through Christian marriage services. A mission tent was erected in 1869, though the endeavours of the missionary worker were to be cut short by an outbreak of scarlet fever and the insistence of the local authority that the camp be broken up. As a result many took to living in 'melancholy looking cottages',[74] in sheds and out-houses, or in tenements 'so closely packed together that little sun or air can penetrate'.[75] Some, however, managed to evade the authorities and continued to live in dilapidated vans at the back of rows of houses and in 'narrow courts and

3 The inside of a Gypsy van at Notting Hill. The images of overcrowding, broken furniture and neglected children were calculated to excite sympathy and support for George Smith's proposals for a Moveable Dwellings Bill.

dingy lanes'.[76] Once settled in more permanent dwellings it was inevitable that travelling began to decline.

Other colonies of Gypsies, or van towns, similar to that described above, could be seen at Smethwick, between the railway arches at Clapham Junction, at Woodford, Wandsworth, Plaistow Marshes, and many other places besides.[77] Of these, the camp on the borders of Wanstead Flats, in Cobbold Road, was a 'picture of order, cleanliness and industry'.[78] It comes as no surprise to learn that the occupants of this site were not ordinary Gypsies living in unhospitable surroundings and unpalatable conditions but were instead a colony of evangelists. Although then living in five vans they did aspire to greater respectability and were in the process of building two 'neat little houses'. These Gypsies were held as a shining example for others to emulate as well as proving conclusively that such people could be civilised, educated and converted, thereby providing encouragement to missionaries and philanthropists.[79]

This type of encampment remained exceptional, the majority being of the Notting Hill variety. They flourished mainly during the winter months, experiencing a steady outflow with the arrival of spring, but it was increasingly the case that a core stayed on the sites throughout the summer months. The main sites, at Notting Hill, Wandsworth and Battersea, all retained a small nucleus.[80] With the return of bad weather over the winter months this core was added to:

As soon as the cold weather sets in the members of the various gipsy tribes whose headquarters are London and its suburbs, may be seen with their brown babies and their houses on wheels, the gay green and yellow paint with which their panels are bedecked, dulled and blistered by the sun of a long summer, leisurely making their way to the winter settlements. These are not far. There are two or three at Camberwell, and one at a place called Pollard's Gardens, near the Waterloo Road. Peckham boasts several; they may be found at Homerton in the back slums of Lambeth, and among the potteries between Notting Hill and Shepherd's Bush. Lock's Fields, Walworth, is a favourite spot with the fraternity.[81]

The return of the Gypsies to these places was regular and expected, and the areas of waste ground were often reserved and kept vacant for winter hiring. Other major sites in mid-century were at Kensal Green and Wimbledon Common, with around seventy Gypsies camped on the latter at Christmas 1831.[82] Others left their tents and vans for lodgings in houses. In general, these were at Bull's Court, Kingsland Road, Coopers' Gardens, Tottenham Court Road, Banbridge Street, Bolton Street, Church Street, Church Lane, Battle Bridge, Tunbridge Street, Tothill Fields and White Street.[83] Occasionally a Gypsy family would enter one of the houses in Deptford which was managed under the Octavia Hill scheme. They brought with them almost no furniture, and 'the walls would remain as bare as they found them, while old and young sat upon upturned boxes about the small grate, as contentedly as if it were a camp fire'.[84]

Clearly, just as the nature of the camp sites differed from place to place, over time and between individual families, so too did the type of their homes. At the beginning of the century the Norwood Gypsies lived, if possible, in the barns and out-houses of the local farmers, but a more usual home for most travellers was the tent or covered cart. These tents took on many shapes and sizes, varying from simple canvas or blanket tents, otherwise known as 'kraals', to large, dome-shaped constructions. The kraals on Mitcham Common in November 1879 were uncharitably though not incorrectly described as 'some kind of stitched-together rags thrown over sticks'.[85] A fuller

4 A typical Gypsy encampment sited in the wooded areas around London in mid-century.

description of a typical Gypsy tent in the same region at the same time is given below:

The tents are oblong and simple. Rods are stuck in the ground, and bent over to form a sort of waggon-shaped roof, tied together by strings, and covered with coarse brown cloths pinned or skewered together, and pegged to the ground. A narrow trench is cut around to prevent rain-water from flowing into the tent . . . Sitting cross-legged is the order of the day, there being neither chairs nor stools; and as tables are as scarce as chairs, the meals are spread on the ground, perhaps with a cloth for a little approach to tidiness, pots, pans, platters, and trenchers are pretty abundant; knives and horn spoons are used, but seldom a fork. A kind of brazier forms the fireplace, with a crook and a kettle for cooking. A pail and a water-cask, a box or two for cloths, and blankets to serve as bedding and bed-clothes, nearly fill up the list of goods and chattels.[86]

The Gypsies on Finchley Common about 1818 constructed more solid dwellings. Tent-shaped wattle huts were made from the boughs of trees and shrubs, covered with turf, and erected over a shallow hole in the earth.[87] However, despite the ease with which they could be constructed and their undoubted resilience to the climate, these huts do not appear to have been a common feature.

It was not until around mid-century that Gypsies took to living in vans,

5 A Gypsy camp on Mitcham Common.

which again varied from the small, crowded and squalid vans to the larger and more fancifully decorated type normally associated with the Romany. Other outdoor dwellings included various huts and wooden buildings, and under the numerous railway arches.[88] Finally, many Gypsies also lived in houses, and not only during the winter. Both John Hollingshead and Charles Booth felt it necessary to distinguish between the Gypsy inhabitants and their neighbours, said to be the lowest class of vegetable vendors.[89] The criterion for distinguishing between the groups is not made clear in either case.

Most of these colonies broke up with the onset of spring, and the months of April and May witnessed the beginning of the exodus of Gypsies from their winter camps. Some travelled far into Norfolk and the Midlands, others contented themselves by working in the market gardens of the London suburbs until July, when they crossed to Woolwich for fruiting, and then on to Sussex and Kent for the harvesting and hopping seasons.[90] Seasonal employment of this kind was an essential ingredient of summer migration. The nearby fairs, seaside resorts and race-meetings were also a major attraction, and Epsom during Derby week was overrun by Gypsies who either told fortunes, traded horses or set up coconut establishments. At the fairs they were the proprietors of 'Puff and Darts', 'Spin 'em Rounds', and other games.[91] Sometimes they even created their own fairs and built primitive swings and roundabouts on plots of waste land, with the motive power being provided by 'ragged boys running round and pushing bars radiating from the centre pole'.[92]

The summer season was also a particularly profitable time of the year for the Gypsy fortune-tellers. The parks of Richmond, Greenwich, Windsor, and the other resorts of the summer visitors from the towns, were much frequented by colourful Gypsy women with bright headscarves and droopy earrings.

For the same reason many Gypsies encamped about Blackheath, Woolwich-heath, Lordship Lane, near Deptford, and Plum Street, near Woolwich. But perhaps the most popular of all for the fortune-tellers was the once famous summer resort of Beulah Spa Gardens, Norwood. Indeed the reputation of the Norwood palmists was such that a small book entitled *The Norwood Gypsy Fortune Teller* was said to have been in great demand among young women of all classes.[93]

Apart from these primarily seasonal incursions into the self-employment cycle of the Gypsies, the usual occupations of the travellers were also practised. The Gypsies who camped for the summer in the woods about Anerley and Penge carried on their trades of making clothes-pegs and butchers' skewers, offering their services as tinkers and knife grinders, horse-dealing and fortune-telling.[94] Hawking and tinkering thus remained as the mainstay of Gypsy employments. Yet their occupations were even more diverse than this picture allows. Hoyland's list of Gypsy lodgers in London at the beginning of the century shows that a great many trades were followed, including those of chair-bottoming, basket-making, rat-catching, wire-work-ing, grinding, fiddling, selling fruit, fish and earthenware, and mending bellows. Although three were found to be employed on a regular basis, as a canal worker, lamplighter and journeyman saddler, the majority still relied on their own ability to maintain an existence and were dependent on selling their wares or skills directly rather than being employed as hired wage-labourers. This variety of occupations and the dependence on self-employ-ment was a feature retained throughout the century.

Thomas Herne, living in Gipsy Square in the Notting Hill Potteries, had a sign board on his cabin advertising his trade as a brush and cane chair-bottomer in the 1860s. Although aged about ninety years he still walked the streets touting for business.[95] Similarly, the Christian Gypsies on Wanstead Flats in the 1880s were employed primarily in chair-mending.[96] These street menders were a common sight about London, carrying from house to house their bundles of canes and rushes and performing the necessary repairs on the doorsteps or in the gardens.[97] They did not have the regular wages of those who worked for the dealers, but profits would generally compensate for this. The usual charge was from 8d. to 1s. per chair, according to the quality of the cane, the size of the seat and the estimated wealth of the customer. The cost of the raw materials, the split and dressed cane, varied from 2s. 6d. to 4s. per pound weight, which covered from six to eight chairs.[98] The work was precarious, though, and the profits were rarely sufficient to maintain a minimum standard of living on their own and needed to be supplemented by other work.

Another similar type of trade often adopted was that of umbrella-mending. The 'mush fakers', as they were commonly known, called from house to house and when their services were required they sat in full view of the other inhabitants of the street so as to attract further possible custom. Having repaired the umbrella the mush faker would ask if the owner had any others which were beyond repair. In return for these the repairer would reduce his charge and with just two or three broken and torn umbrellas he could make one 'tolerably stout and serviceable gingham'.[99] If he was unable to obtain old umbrellas by this method he would buy up a quantity of broken ones from Petticoat Lane.

It was likely, therefore, that the male would be, variously, a basket-maker, chair- and sieve-mender, tinker, horse-dealer, peg- and skewer-maker. At times he would stay at home manufacturing small items for sale, and at others he would leave the camp to go tinkering old kettles and saucepans, grinding knives and scissors or selling oranges.[100] The women usually left the camp to go out hawking and in south London were said to sell to the rich and poor alike.[101] The major change that took place during the century was that the items hawked were no longer primarily of their own manufacture. Even so it is still possible to find examples of Gypsies selling home-made clothes-pegs well into the twentieth century.[102] The other major home craft was that of 'chinning the cost', or making butchers' skewers, sold directly to the butcher at around 1s. per stone.[103]

But these were dying trades and by the end of the century the items hawked were of greater variety and were generally bought from a wholesaler. These wares included small wool mats, vases, cheap ornaments, brooms, brushes, clothes-props and pegs, fern roots, cottons, laces, and other odds and ends. A supplier of these wares gave his impression of these people to John Thompson:

some travelling hawkers make heaps of money, but they never look much above the gutter. I once knew one, Old Mo, they called him; I used to serve him with his wares, brushes, baskets, mats and tin things; for these are the sorts of goods I send all over the country to that class of people. Cash first, you know, with them. I would not trust the best of them, not even Mo, though he used to carry £9000 about with him tied up in a sack in his van. He is now settled at Hastings; he has bought property.[104]

This informant believed that most of these hawkers made considerable sums of money as their trade expenses were only nominal and their profits usually large. He offered 'proof' of this by telling a story of one such hawker who owned houses yet lived in his van and carried on his itinerant trade in the suburbs. However, for most the likelihood of property-owning was remote for, in his opinion, any profits were squandered on drink and gambling.

It is apparent, then, that all adults, male and female, played crucial roles in the domestic economy. The importance of the children also should not be underestimated. While the young girls travelled round with their mothers, the boys either assisted their fathers in the manufacture of various items at home or else went out hawking on their own. The grown-up lads of Lamb

Lane used to buy flowers in Covent Garden and then went round the suburbs selling them to house-dwellers, particularly on Saturdays. They arrived at Covent Garden at 4 a.m., spent 4s. to 6s. on flowers, and then sold them the same day, bringing in a profit of around 3s.[105]

This variety in the types of occupations pursued by the nomadic population was used by some writers in an attempt to confirm distinctions between the London travellers based on race. From such a foundation differences were found in physical characteristics, the extent of cleanliness of persons and variations in cultural patterns. The Gypsies were at the top of the scale, representing cleanliness, honesty and respectability, in the fashion of the 'true' Romany. This group then identified others below them, and in a descending order of filth and degradation were to be found the *chorodies, koramengre* and *hindity-mengre*. The dark Gypsies lived in clean and tidy tents and vans, spoke the Romany language and followed honest and respectable trades in woodworking and traditional rural crafts. The *chorodies*, a term meaning low, mean and contemptible, were said to have coarse, vulgar but fair (Saxon) complexions. Their racial descent was from English rogues and outcasts, and in the main they spoke English, though with some cant expressions and bastard Romany intruding into the conversation at times. They lived in the 'vilest' tents and broken and filthy caravans, with the men chiefly engaged in tinkering, basket-making and stealing, while the women hawked and told fortunes. Although they were described as 'ferocious, depraved and repulsive', they nevertheless stood above the *kora-mengre*, or 'fellows who cry out'. In every respect this group was one further step removed in the direction of dirt and depravity, even though they were said to come from the same ancestry as the *chorodies*. Their distinguishing feature was their occupation as itinerant sellers, travelling around with vans loaded with an array of rush-chairs, mats, rugs, mops, brooms, brushes, pots, pans and other household utensils. At the bottom of the scale came the *hindity-mengre*, or 'filthy people'. These were of vagrant Irish descent and were tinkers by trade, though they were also apparently experts at making from brass buttons the showy rings passed off by their womenfolk as gold.[106]

This interpretation attempted to isolate distinct racial categories and then argue backwards that from this could be identified differences in regard to employment, physical features, wealth, abodes and by extension to such other variables as the extent of travelling and the affixing of various stereotypes. While it should not be denied that the travellers would have indeed shown variations in the categories mentioned it would be wrong and misleading to suggest these stemmed from a racial foundation. *If* the Romany Gypsy existed and could be identified, both questionable assumptions which are challenged in chapter 4, it would still not necessarily follow, as has been suggested here, that he would be clean, dark, able to speak the Romany language and pursuing woodworking or rural trades. Moreover, while accepting that important differences did exist between travellers, they were also bound by certain unifying elements which to the majority of the settled population were of more significance than any fine points of distinction among them. They were united by a common life-style which revolved around nomadism and self-employment, and by a shared day-to-day existence and the experience of marginality *vis-à-vis* settled society.

These two studies of the way of life of the New Forest and London Gypsies are intended to provide some insight into the pattern and structure of itinerancy, illustrating how the Gypsy-travellers lived and worked. They also provide some introduction to the question of the nature of itinerant employments, the problematic issue of definition and the way in which this tied in with a complex web of racial, cultural and occupational categorisation. These two case studies provide the specific examples. It remains now to broaden the analysis.

3

From fortune-telling to scissor-grinding

It is no surprise that the conditions under which the travellers lived varied from camp to camp and family to family: 'Society on wheels, like every other sphere, has its patricians, and plebeians, its upright and religious, its idle and undeserving.'[1] Yet, for the most part, the nature of their existence remained similar, especially in relation to the types and range of occupations pursued. Some writers considered the travellers' employments from a negative aspect, alleging they did not perform 'real' work but rather occupied themselves with as little toil as was compatible with survival. They were thought to be idle, parasitical and beggarly, with no belief in the value of work.[2] Such a view was, and is, based on perceptions of the relationship between a settled/host society and a marginal social group who were thought to be parasites. But such relations are not entirely one-sided and can even take on necessary and mutually beneficial aspects to such an extent that the emotive and value-laden descriptions of host and parasite demand a more considered appraisal.

Although the Gypsies did not depend on selling their labour for a wage, like the majority of the sedentary population, they did rely on the settled members of society to purchase the variety of goods and services which they presented for sale. For this reason the goods offered, and the areas travelled, were closely linked to the changes and developments taking place in the wider society. The general move from the country to the town was a feature of both the sedentary and travelling populations – the Gypsies had to move with their market. This tendency was most apparent towards the end of the century, yet had always been of seasonal occurrence. Summer travelling in rural districts was replaced during the winter months by the need to reside in or near to the centres of a large and concentrated population.

On the one side, then, was dependence, but what of the other? Summarily, the family-based economic unit, a distinguishing feature of the Gypsy-travellers, undertook employments which the sedentary workforce were unable or unwilling to adopt. In the early decades of the century the Gypsies toured the largely inaccessible rural areas (as they had in centuries previously) offering their goods, services and labour to a population not otherwise served. Travellers appeared in remote areas as purveyors of news, sellers of cheap goods, repairers of general household items, as seasonal labourers and as itinerant entertainers contributing their musical talents to village feasts and festivities. While each of these features became threatened as the century progressed, with other agencies intruding to ensure their regular and permanent provision, the travellers did not simply die out. They adapted to the changed industrial environment by taking up new crafts, altering the old ones and offering a wider variety of goods for sale in the more densely populated areas.

For purposes of analysis Judith Okely placed the spectrum of Gypsy employments under four headings: the sale of goods not made by the travellers (horses, fruit, vegetables, pots, pans, needles, pins, jewellery); the offer of services such as tinkering, knife- and scissor-grinding, umbrella-repairing, chair-bottoming and entertaining; seasonal labour (agricultural work, fruit- and hop-picking); the provision of goods and services largely the monopoly of the Gypsies (pegs, baskets, beehives, fortune-telling), incorporating traditional rural crafts and long-established skills.[3] Such a classification provides a convenient model with which to assess the various occupations whilst perhaps suffering from a too rigid distinction between the groups. It is not always clear in which category a particular employment should be placed: fairground entertaining could be described as both a seasonal (summer) employment and a service. Similarly, some of the pegs and baskets were made by the Gypsies in the time-honoured fashion while others were bought directly from a wholesaler. Finally, the link between hawking and fortune-telling was such that the offer of goods and the provision of this particular service went firmly hand-in-hand. A further refinement to the model can be made by adding divisions between the various types of employments according to gender. Whereas the men were engaged at various times in occupations that fell under each of these headings, it was not usual for women to be employed in the service or craft trades. In general, craft items were manufactured by the men while it was the responsibility of the women to hawk the items from door to door.

PEDDLING GOODS AND FORTUNES

The sale of goods was the thread that ran through the whole of the Gypsy employment spectrum. The only time when hawking was not carried on full-time was during the season of summer agricultural work, and even then it would have been practised in between moving from farm to farm. The ability of the women to sell their miscellaneous stock of useful, cheap and regularly used items was crucial to the family economy. An old Gypsy recognised the importance of the role played by the female members of the group when he told a city missionary in 1859, 'I should not like my daughter to marry a gypsy man, but I know if my sons marry gypsy women, there is sure to be a living for them, for they will scrat [*sic*] a bread from somewhere, though it would puzzle a lawyer to tell how they got it at times.'[4] Flora Thompson has perhaps provided a clue to this puzzle:

When a door was opened to them, if the housewife appeared to be under forty, they would ask in a wheedling voice, 'Is your mother at home, my dear?'. Then, when the position was explained, they would exclaim in astonished tones, 'You don't mean to tell me you be the mother? Look at that, now, I shouldn't have taken you to be a day over twenty'.

No matter how often repeated, this compliment was swallowed whole, and made a favourable opening for a long conversation, in the course of which the wily 'Egyptian' not only learned the full history of the woman's own family, but also a good deal about those of her neighbours, which was duly noted for future use. Then would come a request for a 'handful of little 'taters, or an onion or two for the pot', and, if these were given, as they usually were, 'My pretty lady' would be asked for an old shift of her own or an old shirt of her husband's, or anything that the children might have left off, and, poverty-stricken though the hamlet was, a few worn-out garments would be secured to swell the size of the bundle which, afterwards, would be sold to the rag merchant.

Sometimes the gipsies would offer to tell fortunes . . .

. . . The gipsies paid in entertainment for what they received. Their calls made a welcome break in the day.[5]

Many writers condemned this persistence as thinly disguised begging, and claimed that people preferred to give the Gypsies goods or money simply to get them to move on.[6] Whether seen as welcome entertainment or unwanted cadging, these doorstep visits were at the heart of the Gypsies' economy.

The items offered for sale changed with the seasons, depending on the availability of raw materials for the manufacture of craft goods and the vagaries of seasonal demand for different wares. The variety of goods is impressive both for its range and adaptability. Artificial flowers were made and sold throughout the winter and real flowers when in bloom. In the winter of 1898, about Christmas time, an old Gypsy was seen close to Primrose Hill, London, selling holly, mistletoe and herbs.[7] One group established a minor reputation selling cart grease (claimed to be pure fat but in fact made up of potatoes, yellow turnips and grease) and in London the Gypsies formed a part of the very large street army of mobile traders.[8] Fruit, vegetables and flowers were sold alongside gravel, wood and coal.[9]

The Somerset Gypsies, in mid-century, hawked home-made brushes and brooms, pots, pans, tinware and other small items.[10] Travellers in Sussex some years earlier were found to be selling wooden spoons, trenchers, bowls, shoe horns, drinking cups made of horn, tin pots and pans, crockery, dusters, hardware, jugs, brooches, watch keys and the inevitable brooms and brushes.[11] Staffordshire was travelled by Gypsies earning a living by making and repairing small iron and tin wares and by the manufacture and sale of coarse earthenware and birch brooms.[12] Others bought up at low cost the cast and faulty articles from the various earthenware manufactories at Tunstall, Burslem, Hanley, Stoke and Longton, to repair and resell at profit. In short, anything was sold that did not require a large initial capital outlay, which was small and light and which people with limited resources were prepared to buy because of the items' practical usefulness and cheapness. However, while hawking provided a subsistence it could not be said to offer hope of riches. At best the hawkers secured sufficient income to maintain a day-to-day existence. Poverty and hardship could easily result from a series of slammed doors and the constant threat of hunger served as the chief reason for these door saleswomen's reluctance to leave a household without selling something, however small, whether a pin, a pot or a fortune.

The importance of the hawker, pedlar and street-seller in the rural and urban environment should not be underestimated. They filled a gap created by an irregular demand and supply situation, whether caused by temporal or financial factors. Consider, by way of illustration, Alexander Somerville's account of the Gypsies' role in the Border regions:

We lived inconveniently distant from shops and towns; and they supplied us with many things, such as spoons, crockery, tin-ware, and sieves, and repaired so many things at prices exceedingly moderate, that my impression of their usefulness was, that we should have had to do without some articles of use, or pay very dear for them elsewhere, if the tinklers had not come round periodically to supply us.[13]

Later in the century a speaker in the House of Commons claimed that the 'tyrannical monopoly' of the single village shop was held in check by the competition provided by the itinerant hawkers.[14] In the towns the provision of cheap goods was centred chiefly in the poorer districts, and the travelling hawker was distinguished from the sedentary tradesman by the character and means of his customer: 'the pedlar or hawker is the purveyor in general to the poor . . . the class of travelling tradesmen are important, not only as forming a large portion of the poor themselves, but as being the persons through whom the working people obtain a considerable part of their provisions and raiment.'[15]

Even so, the homes of the wealthier classes were not entirely free of the Gypsy hawker, although it would seem that fortunes were sold easier than the cheap wares. It was said that the servant maids of London willingly paid their sixpences and shillings to the Gypsy women in order to hear about their matrimonial prospects before the rest of the household had risen for the morning.[16]

The belief that Gypsy women possessed magical powers which enabled them to see the future was common among the superstitious of all classes. This impression was further enhanced if the Gypsy, dressed for the part by wearing colourful headscarves and droopy earrings, was old, ugly and with

6 A Gypsy knife-grinder.

the appearance of a 'wild-eyed hag'.[17] To be told your fortune by a ragged
hawker would by no means have sounded so convincing and the game had to
be played with equal conviction by both parties. Superstitious beliefs among
the general population were fed by the Gypsies' marginality to conventional
society, by the mystery and myths surrounding their present existence, and
by a romantic image of their origins and past lives. Even today fortune-telling
is still carried on by the numerous 'Gypsy Lees' at fairs and holiday resorts
with little noticeable diminution of its popularity.

Just as the media now exploit this particular susceptibility by the publication of daily horoscopes, so did the Gypsies in times past. Some claimed to
believe in their own ability to foretell events, though this perhaps stemmed
from a desire to perpetuate the image and convince the interviewer of their
magical powers. Others recognised that it was a supreme opportunity to
obtain financial reward by pandering to the weaknesses of the superstitious
and curious. John Clare, the well-known poet, recorded in his memoirs how
in their private moments the fortune-tellers made fun of their alleged powers,
inventing the stories they were to tell the following day and generally scoffing
at the foolishness of those who came to listen to them.[18] Not surprisingly,
only good was foretold, with tales of tall, dark strangers, wealth and travel

7 The aged, haggard Gypsy reading the palm of the young, innocent country girl in charming rural surroundings.

being repeated time and again. The dream of better things to come in the material world was the secular reply to the religious promise of an improved unwordly state.

Although fortunes were sold throughout the year as an adjunct to hawking, it was a trade also subject to some seasonal variation. Come the summer, with its succession of fairs and race-meetings and with the parks, gardens and resorts filled with holiday-makers, the Gypsies sought to mine this potential gold field. They maintained a regular presence in the Beulah Spa

8 Broom-selling and chair-mending were important elements of the Gypsy employ-ment spectrum, involving traditional craft skills and the use of freely available raw materials.

Gardens and several notorious fortune-tellers had long frequented the Rosherville and Springhead Gardens near to Gravesend, and one, Avis Lee, had been there for twenty-six years. Her particular experience offers a glimpse into the changing nature of leisure provision during the nineteenth century. At first she paid no rent and took 5s. or 6s. a day, but by the middle

1860s she considered herself fortunate to earn that amount in a week, for though she may have taken up to £4 in that time she now had to pay £30 for the season's rent, a victim of the inflationary commercialism progressively intruding into the realm of non-work life and activities.[19]

Fortune-telling was an activity which required the complicity and willing participation of members of settled society and which was partly a product of the imposition on the Gypsies of an expected mode of behaviour derived from a persistent and forceful image of the mystical, Romany culture. It seems likely that the voluntary part played by the customers of the fortune-tellers, together with a commonsense view of the harmlessness of the activity, resulted in the ambiguous attitude displayed by the magistrates. Fortune-telling had been declared illegal in 1864 and some magistrates felt it necessary to use this as an excuse to increase the tempo of persecution against the Gypsies.[20] Others, though, were not so willing to give their backing to this particular form of legal pressure on itinerancy. For example, Mr Harrison, at Ashton-under-Lyne, dismissed all fortune-telling cases that came before him with the remark that 'it served silly people right if they lost their money'.[21]

Less subject to prosecution but equally open to misinterpretation was the trade of horse-dealing. The many fairs held throughout the country served as the locations for the horse trade, among the best known being Appleby, Turton and Boughton Green.[22] For some outsiders this trade was deserving of criticism, suspicion and mistrust, and the Gypsies were often accused either of having stolen the animals or of sprucing-up old and worn horses. At Cobham Fair, for example, 'five-pound screws' were allegedly transformed into elegant horses by a process of clipping, singeing and beautifying.[23] It may not have been until the rain had washed the dye from the skin that the purchaser would discover his mistake.

The unreservedly antagonistic George Smith of Coalville claimed that the horse trade served merely as a further pretext for the practice of Gypsy deceit and cunning. He reported a conversation overheard at Boughton Green Fair:

I heard some gipsies chuckling over the 'gingered' and 'screwed' horses and ponies they had sold during the fair, and arranging which of their party should hunt the customer out the next day, to buy back for a five-pound note their palmed-off 'broken-winded' and 'roaring old screws' which they had sold for seventeen pound or twenty pound during the fair . . . Many of the horse-dealing gypsies are dressed nowadays as farmers, and by these means they more readily palm off their 'screws'.[24]

One can only express surprise – and doubt – that Smith again chanced to be in the correct place at the correct time to hear such a concise condemnation of this deceit. That the Gypsies occasionally bought back stock that had recently been sold is evidenced in the following extract from a notebook kept by

Sylvester Boswell, but which indicates sound business sense rather than calculated and deliberate fraud:

	£	s.
Bought of garned		
a poney Cost	7	10
and sold to Mr. Smith of		
Felexsolm for	9	0
sold the black mare that		
Cost	3	15
to Ealey for	5	10
bought the same poney		
again at	5	10
and sold again to Mr.		
Simons at Barnett Fare for	9	0[25]

Moreover, horse-dealing was a regular business which depended on a joint reputation of expert knowledge and trustworthiness which inspired the confidence of farmers and other buyers.[26]

Indeed, such trading between travellers and members of settled society suggests a relationship of trust and respect rather than intolerance and abuse, based on an acknowledgement of the Gypsies' traditional expertise. Accusations of cheating – though undoubtedly applicable in certain situations – have to be seen chiefly as the product of the desire to paint the Gypsies in the blackest possible colours. To have admitted that horse-dealing was honest, profitable and useful to both seller and purchaser would have been to chip away at the myth of the unproductive parasite that generally engulfed these travellers.

THE SALE OF SERVICES

Apart from the sale of goods the Gypsies also secured an income by offering for sale their various services. The trades of chair-bottoming and umbrella-mending have been noted earlier, and appear to have been especially popular with the travellers living in or near cities. Also engaged in servicing the social and practical needs of small communities were the travelling entertainers, knife- and scissor-grinders, rat-catchers, and the repairers of tin ware, copper kettles and agricultural implements. Many travellers even preferred to describe themselves as tinkers, stressing the long tradition of this occupation among their ancestors.[27] Others became renowned for their particular skills with, for example, the Lockes and Smiths of Oxfordshire being regarded as extremely able iron-workers.[28]

To obtain work involved much walking, long hours and small earnings. Chairs were bottomed at prices ranging from 1s. and scissors ground and reset at from 2d. to 2s. 6d., with the price adjusted according to the circumstances of the owner.[29] Only in rare cases could sufficient money be accumulated to insure against illness and old age, and contemporary sources often referred to Gypsies in their eightieth and ninetieth years who continued to tramp the streets for trade.

Clearly not everyone employed in these service trades could be regarded as true travellers, a further example of the crossover between the settled and travelling communities and the coincidence of occupational interests pursued by members of the opposing cultures. Many street-traders were only itinerant in the sense of travelling the streets for custom, otherwise following a sedentary way of life. Their work took them from district to district and town to town but their cultural life was rooted in the ways of the settled community. Others were travellers in both economic and cultural terms and service trades were merely one point on a varied employment spectrum. However, the distinctions were often blurred and it has been noted earlier that Gypsy-travellers and their families also adopted a sedentary existence for many months each winter. Yet despite the different cultural and ethnic origins of the street-traders they were generally welcomed into the working class communities on their regular visits. Children and adults alike were attracted by the colour and vitality of the entertainer, sympathetic to the pathos of the elderly organ-grinder, intrigued by the work processes of the tinker and grinder, and keen in their anticipation of a variation in diet offered by the many food hawkers.

In the early part of the nineteenth century village feasts, fairs, wakes and weddings formed a central feature of rural social life. A key element of each was the presence of the Gypsy entertainers:

> At every village feast and fair
> The Gipsies' music would be there.[30]

And not just their music for they were also in attendance as bear-leaders, acrobats, dancers, harp-players and carol-singers.[31] Moreover, they entertained not only at fairs and annual feasts but also at private parties, in ale-houses where they played dance music for the 'young people of the working class', in streets and from door to door.[32] The Buckland family, who lived in the Headington Quarries near Oxford in the 1840s, provided shows at Whitsun and in November and the local morris-dancing team included a Gypsy named Samson Smith, who was also the leading fiddler. Such integration in the leisure activities of the local community ensured that the Gypsies became an acceptable semi-permanent fixture and it was not uncommon for marriages to take place between the travellers and the locals.[33] Such activities were treated by the rural working class as an important element of their traditional pastimes and for this reason the Gypsy entertainers could find not only temporary acceptance in the rural community but also a genuine welcome for the part they played in the pattern of country life.

Yet these leisure activities were not without their critics. James Crabb voiced a generally held puritanical disgust with the manners of the 'lower orders' and grieved over the mixing of Gypsy musicians with the most degraded sections of society who frequented pubs and drinking parlours. The adult entertainers excited the 'unholy dance' with their violins and tambourines and, worse still, they were said to introduce their chidren to this environment as soon as they were able to perform on any instrument. The inevitable consequence, in Crabb's opinion, was that the children would soon become drunken brawlers and wife-beaters.[34]

Although this form of rural entertainment declined with the gradual demise of such traditional leisure patterns Gypsies were still engaged as fiddlers at village feasts, wakes and weddings well into the 1880s.[35] Even in the twentieth century the Gypsy fiddler was able to drive a thriving trade, as evidenced by the experiences of Tommy Boswell who earned his living in the villages of the Berkshire Downs and other groups of Gypsies in Wales.[36] Indeed, the local and sometimes national repute of one or a group of entertainers was a feature throughout the period. At the beginning of the century James Allan was a well-known and popular figure around Northumberland and it was largely through his efforts that the bagpipes were recognised as a Gypsy instrument in the Scottish Lowlands, the Border regions and the north of England.[37] Sammy Draper was similarly famous around the inns of Hertfordshire in the 1860s and 1870s, accompanied by his daughter,[38] and the families of Gray and Shaw were likewise noted for their tours of East Anglia, Oxfordshire and neighbouring counties with dancing booths and violinists.[39] But probably the most noted of all the Gypsy entertainers was a band calling themselves the 'Epping Forest Gypsies'.

This group began touring the country giving balls and opening their camp to visitors early in the 1860s. They started to break up in 1874 and fell to pieces altogether in 1878 when the various members dispersed to Ireland, America, Norfolk, Blackpool, Birkenhead and Liverpool. George 'Lazzy' Smith (not to be confused with George Smith the crusading reformer) claimed to have originated the idea of charging admission to their sites, tents and dances. He recognised and exploited the general public interest generated by their presence, especially when accompanied by an appearance of the tribe's 'King and Queen'.[40] It was said that civil war, international conflict, national politics and local stories of murder all took second place behind smoking cigars with male Gypsies and drinking tea with the females.[41]

Not surprisingly there was a vociferous section of the public who did not fall under the Gypsies' spell. Tents were reported to be 'wretched-looking' and 'utterly bare of comforts', and the presence of a light-skinned child in the camp prompted journalists to revive mythical images of child-stealing, moonlit magical incantations and unholy rites.[42] Town officials and clergymen repeated the customary charges of theft and prostitution and sought to discourage the public from visiting the camps.[43] Yet their appeal was largely unheard and despite, or perhaps because of, these rumours and allegations the Gypsy balls remained crowded. It is unlikely the Gypsies themselves could have dreamt up a more effective publicity campaign advertising their differences with the local population.

In 1866 the group were camped on the moor at Newcastle, on their way to Edinburgh, where they spent some time in the summer and winter of 1867 and the spring of 1868. From there they travelled through Manchester and on to Kidderminster, arriving in the summer of 1869. By this time the local press had come to modify their approach and now praised this clean and tidy group of travellers who presented a startling contrast with the Gypsy camps usually found in the Midlands. Their tents had now become roomy, clean and amply decorated with fabrics and furnishings which gave an Eastern air. The Gypsies themselves were no longer separate and disdainful but were well-dressed, communicative and easy-going, apparently content to continue unassumedly with their other trades of horse-dealing and fortune-telling. During the next few years the band also visited Swansea, Newport, Bath, Bristol and Taunton. By March 1871 they were to be found in Binsey Lane, Oxford, where it was claimed that nearly everyone in the city who could spare the time had been to the encampment.[44] Although exaggerated, this impression serves to confirm their widespread popularity and appeal. The Gypsies left for Banbury at the beginning of April and later moved on to Leamington and Cheltenham. Subsequent reports were given of their visits to Wales, Holywell, Liverpool, Hull and Manchester.[45]

These itinerant entertainers with their well-ordered camps and evident appeal were atypical of the general lot of the nineteenth-century Gypsy. They were primarily entertainers, or showmen entrepreneurs, and in order to maintain public interest, friendship and curiosity they had to exploit to the full the romantic myth of the mystical Easterner. Even after the disbandment of the group 'Lazzy' Smith did not entirely disappear from the public eye. At the Liverpool exhibition of 1891 he reappeared with a reconstruction of a spacious oriental-looking Gypsy tent which again fed the public's desire for romanticism and mysticism among these people.

CRAFT SKILLS

It was not usual for the money obtained from entertaining to be sufficient to sustain a family, and an existence was maintained only by combining this with other occupations. Diversification of skills and interests, together with rapid adaptability, were the necessary keys to survival. Nowhere were these qualities better shown than in the craft ability to transform natural and plentiful raw materials into novel, attractive or useful, saleable items.

The Gypsies were renowned for their dexterity in manufacturing a wide variety of small items, such as rings, nails, knives, seals, needles, horn spoons and sometimes articles made from tin, brass and copper. They also worked extensively with the materials found in plenty around their sites, especially wood and grass. Brooms were made of heather, whips of plaited rushes, and doormats of dry grass stems tightly bound and woven together with strips of fresh bark or bramble.[46] Gorse was cut to make walking sticks and umbrella handles, beehives were created from straw and artificial flowers were moulded from turnips.[47] Basket-making was also common and comprised a chief occupation among the Gypsies of Bethnal Green, using materials gathered from the Essex Marshes and neighbouring farmland. Although by the 1880s the travellers were able to buy cheap, ready-made baskets imported from France some nevertheless preferred to continue the craft tradition.[48] The demand for baskets of all descriptions meant that the Gypsies had to turn their skills to the manufacture of receptacles for fruit, coal, wood, lobsters, beer and a range of other commodities. By this flexibility borne out of necessity they managed to retain some control of this limited but steady market.

Heather and birch brooms had remained as the staple manufacture of the Gypsies of Ashdown Forest in Sussex for a period of around 200 years. The method of production had changed little in that time:

As a rule the heather is cut in winter, and kept until it is seasoned. Then it is tied together and trimmed, according to its destination. An admixture of birch is valued as giving it 'a better head'. The binding is done on a 'binding horse', which presses the heather or birch together. In this position it is tied with withes or 'splints', peeled off hazel rods. Some brooms are made with 'bats' or handles, others without. They vary in size and to some extent in quality.[49]

Housebrooms sold at between 2s. and 2s. 6d. a dozen, while stable brooms fetched twice that price, and brewers' brooms even more. This occupation was combined with selling bracken, underwood, peat and turf to farmers until they became the innocent victims of a lawsuit which restricted the gathering of these items for personal use only.[50]

Perhaps the two most traditional of all Gypsy crafts were those of skewer-making and clothes-peg-making.[51] About 1905, W. Raymond visited a family of Gypsy peg-makers in Somerset, in the neighbourhood of the Quantock Hills. In order to make the pegs the Gypsy needed a ready supply of willow, which was taken from the roadside, and a supply of tin, obtained from shops and rubbish tips. The only tools required were a pair of pincers, hammer, stake, knife and nails. The Gypsy would sit in front of the stake, about two inches in diameter and a foot high, and the stages that follow are best described by Raymond himself:

'That's to cut off the clothes-pegs on,' said he. He sat down on a bag . . . drew a sheath knife, took a willow wand already peeled, and measured the length by means of a piece of hazel cut half through at the right distance and split down to the cut. Then he hammered the knife through the willow, using the stake as a block. He chucked the little five inch piece upon a heap of hundreds of others which he had cut off during the day.[52]

The wood was then dried before being finished by nailing around it a ring of biscuit tin, which was to prevent the split from going too far down. Occasionally, the manufacture was carried out by all the family, with each member specialising in one operation and so providing a fine example of the family division of labour. Around the turn of the century a day's work at this would bring in, at most, the grand total of 3s.

Skewer-cutting was a common employment among the poorer Gypsies and, like peg-making, a great amount of labour would result only in modest returns. Although 2,000 skewers could be cut in one day, this was likely to take from seven in the morning until late at night, for which they would receive about 1s. for every 14 pounds' weight.[53] One Gypsy analysed the work involved: 'It takes a deal o' work to earn a penny at skewer-making. A dozen cuts to a skewer, and a dozen skewers for a penny, that's a hundred and forty-four cuts a penny.'[54] Such industry was based in traditional rural craftsmanship and involved imagination, skill and long hours of labour. While not wishing to go to the opposite extreme of romanticising this craft aspect, the nature of this labour should serve to counter the more customary cries concerning the Gypsies' alleged propensity for idleness and avoidance of 'real' or 'honest' toil. What these terms betray is not the attitude of the Gypsies to work but rather that of the commentators. Confrontation with a group holding on to an independent and self-styled pattern and structure of work, existing within a society increasingly keen to establish the virtues of time-discipline and wage-labour, caused the commentators to react with vitriolic abuse. The travellers' insistence on remaining apart from the new economic relationship also served to isolate them from the related aspects of modern life *vis-à-vis* leisure, education, religious training and pressures to conformity with the new organisation of society. The Gypsies' economy was unquestionably based on real toil for the alternative was starvation and hardship. It was not whether they did or did not work that formed the grounds for the attack but rather the *nature* of that work, more readily identifiable with pre-industrial than industrial formations.

SEASONAL EMPLOYMENTS

The months from March to November formed the height of the travelling season. Fairs and race-meetings formed a major feature of the itinerant's calendar. They gave some structure to the timing and route of itinerancy, vesting it with purpose and direction. Such occasions served the economic function of providing a convenient location for large numbers of people to engage in the serious business of horse-dealing and the less serious pleasures of games and amusements.[55] Also, they acted as a social forum drawing travellers from around the country and becoming the meeting place for families and friends.[56]

The following evidence given before the 1839 Commission on the Constabulary Force described how the travelling calendar could be largely, or even wholly, determined by attendance at fairs and race-meetings:

Boughton Green Fair, near Northampton, in June every year, thousands of people assemble there; the police from London come to it. Then there is Lincoln, April fair; Boston, May fair; Newmarket in May, then to Birmingham or Sheffield fairs; then to Coventry, to Newport Pagnall (Bucks.), then back to Boughton, and there is a place called 'Stow Green Fair'. Then Peterboro' summer fair, then Fairlop Forest, 10 miles from London, there I have seen the most gypsies, hundreds at a time. Then to Liverpool spring meetings, and then follow the races in all the midland and northern counties, ending up with Doncaster. Then comes on the winter fairs – Nottingham goose fair, Leicester cheese fair, Ottley Statties, Knaresbrough, York; then come down to Sheffield fair, 28th November, then end up until Wrexham fair begins the year on the 6th of March.[57]

While not suggesting that the route plotted above was carried out by many, it nevertheless indicates the extent to which fairs and meets were a central feature of the travellers' life. Moreover, this route touched only the surface of the number of fairs that were held each year. Horse fairs took place at Ashrigg Hill, Topcliffe, Appleby, Brigg, Boroughbridge, Thwaite, Brampton Hill, Middleham Moor and Lee Gap, to name just some of the more important. Brough Hill was considered to be the largest horse fair in the Midland and Northern Counties, held during the last week in September and attracting Gypsies from Scotland, Ireland, the Isle of Man, and from many of the English counties. Around London the best known were at Wandsworth, Greenwich, Deptford, Blackheath and Clapham, and Wanstead Flats was known as the 'Gypsy Fair' owing to the great number of Gypsies who made it their first gathering of the travelling season.[58] Further out of London, in the Epping Forest, Fairlop fair was held on the first Friday of July and was described by George Smith (Gypsy) as 'a little gold mine to the members of our tribe'.[59]

Such occasions were not always greeted favourably by the authorities. Although a good deal of legitimate business was transacted at the meetings there was also much that was not so firmly on the correct side of the law. Fairs and race-meetings attracted well-meaning trippers whose intention was to enjoy a day out, and whose hard-earned wages lay loose in their pockets, the prey of robbers, thieves, pick-pockets and confidence tricksters. Added to this was the menace caused by the many encampments situated by the roadside, on waste ground and even on the race course itself. The Rev. J. Wilson of Folkingham registered his discontent with the Constabulary Force

Commissioners, complaining that the fairs brought into the district the 'refuse and scum of society', offending the respectable citizens who were unable to obtain any protection, support or assistance from the police.[60] Similarly in Surrey where two streets of a town were annually taken over for the Gypsy fair. The main business, conducted in the middle of the highways, was horse-dealing, although many side-shows and amusements contributed to the festivities. Yet those in authority decided that the fair was a physical and moral nuisance and needed to be modified or repressed.[61] In this criticism can be seen the seeds of concern growing among the middle classes and town notables with unregulated and unsupervised street and leisure activities. Rational recreation and supervised clubs, associations and games were proposed as alternatives.

Moreover, not only was the activity of the street fairs the subject of disapproval, but the Gypsies themselves were also occasionally singled out for especial victimisation. In 1838 the Mayor of Oxford issued an order for the exclusion of Gypsies from St Giles's Fair.[62] This brought a poetic reply from the Gypsies, entitled 'The Gypsies' Humble Petition and Remonstrance Addressed to the Worshipful Mayor of Oxford':

> O Mr. Mayor, O Mr. Mayor!
> What have we gipsies done or said
> That you should drive us from the Fair
> And rob us of our 'custom'd bread?
>
> O had you seen, good Mr. Mayor,
> Our wond'ring, weeping, wailing band,
> And marked our looks of deep despair
> When first we heard your stern command;
>
> Could you have witness'd, Mr. Mayor,
> How, young and old, and weak and strong,
> Excluded, branded, cold and bare,
> We sat astounded all day long;
>
> Your heart had ach'd good Mr. Mayor,
> And felt that gipsies too were men;
> Then deign our losses to repair,
> Nor drive us thus to try the pen.
>
> Alas! 'tis true, good Mr. Mayor,
> Our friend Sir Walter Scott, is dead;
> But heav'n that hears the Gipsies' pray'r,
> May raise another in his stead.

Dread not the name, good Mr. Mayor,
No more the witch's pow'r we claim;
But still we are the Muse's care,
And Oxford Poets guard our game.

What place then so unfit, good Mayor
A war against our tribe to raise,
As that which lately fill'd the air
With Gipsy-lore and Gipsies' praise?

You welcome Lions to the Fair,
Tigers and monkeys, Punch and Fool:
Then suffer us, another year
To hold there our Gymnastic school.

Meanwhile farewell, good Mr. Mayor,
Your frowns, dismiss, resume your smiles;
We'll leave off cheating, take to prayer,
And claim thy patronage, St. Giles![63]

Apart from the fairs, seasonal work was provided by the changing demands of the farming calendar which for a period of a few months required large numbers of temporary, migrant workers to be employed. Interestingly, though, it was a popular belief among some nineteenth-century commentators that agriculture was an industry to which the Gypsy had the greatest antipathy, an impression fed by the idea that the Gypsy had a natural and instinctive aversion to anything that approached hard labour and physical toil.[64] Often, however, the aversion was not of Gypsies to agriculture but of farmers to employing Gypsies. Crabb noticed the hostility to Gypsies was so great that they were never employed by some farmers if any others could be hired instead. In 1830, at one hop plantation, Gypsies were barred from some grounds while common beggars and well-known thieves were taken on in preference.[65] This was not a parochial arrangement to benefit the local poor but rather a positive act of discrimination. Nor apparently, if he found work, should the Gypsy expect fair treatment. An old shepherd pointed out that the unstable and restless Gypsy 'must not look for the same treatment as the big-framed, white-skinned man who is as strong, enduring, and unchangeable as a draught horse or ox, and constant as the sun itself'.[66] In some places they were paid less wages than other workers, perhaps amounting to from 2s. to 4s. a week less per man, and were called upon to do things that the other workers would not do.[67] Once again, though, the antipathy of some has to be balanced against the friendliness of others. A lady in Hampshire always employed Gypsies to watch her hop grounds, finding them to be trusty watchmen and good servants. Another farm in Hampshire was worked entirely by a group of Gypsies.[68] It would seem, then, that for every farm which was barred to them there would be another which would be welcoming.

Agricultural employments were to be found chiefly in the Southern and Eastern Counties, where it was possible to follow the stages of the agricultural cycle through the months by crossing from farm to farm and county to county in pursuit of the ripening crops.[69] From April to June work could be found in the market gardens of the London suburbs and in haymaking, followed by turnip-hoeing, pea-picking (or 'peas-hacking'), wheat-fagging, strawberry-picking and assisting with the corn harvest. In September the round of employments was completed by fruit- and vegetable-picking and hopping, principally in the counties of Kent, Sussex, Surrey, Hampshire, Herefordshire and Worcestershire.[70]

Pea-picking was carried on chiefly in the market gardens of Essex, Lincoln, Suffolk and Kent, and to a lesser degree in Norfolk, Worcester and Yorkshire. Dr Farrar estimated that between a quarter and a third of the persons employed in this occupation were van-dwelling Gypsies.[71] They were said to be especially favoured as they provided their own accommodation; and, because they were accustomed to temporary abodes and an outdoor life, they were thought to have a standard of living and level of health far above that of the ordinary seasonal labourer.[72] Women and girls were often employed in preference to males, their nimble fingers being considered particularly advantageous.[73] Payment was at a flat rate of 8d. a day. Although the season may have lasted for up to eight weeks the duration of the harvest on any one farm was short, perhaps a few days. On at least one occasion the pickers stayed in a single village throughout the summer, but this was made possible only by their turning to other work, notably vegetable harvesting.[74] It was the common practice for the Gypsies to move on.

Following the harvesting months of July and August the Gypsies arrived at the fruit and hop farms in early September. Fruit-picking was again largely reserved for females, working a sixteen-hour day. This sexual division of labour was not apparent in the hop fields, a seasonal employment for men, women and children of the poor classes from near and far.[75] Those counties with a high acreage under crop were the most dependent on the mass importation of 'foreign' labour and it was estimated that 80% of those employed in mid and east Kent were strangers.[76] In general, the hoppers were drawn from the Irish poor, the families from the slum areas of London, the unemployed, and 'nearly all the gipsies in England'.[77] Dr Farrar obtained information on the numbers of 'foreign' and Gypsy pickers in 1906, and the information is given in Table 2. In compiling the returns the clerks of the various rural district councils did not make clear the basis for distinguishing Gypsy pickers from other migrant labourers. It would seem reasonable to

Table 2 *Number of 'foreign' and Gypsy hop-pickers in the seven main hopping regions, 1906*

Region	'Foreign' pickers	Gypsy pickers	Total
Kent	74,748	5,614	80,362
Sussex	2,550	276	2,826
Southampton (Hants.)	1,599	810	2,409
Surrey	200	10 (?)*	210(?)
Herefordshire	12,900	0	12,900
Worcestershire	113,359	555	13,914
Shropshire	118	0	118
Total	205,474	7,265 (?)	212,739 (?)

* *Two or three families.*
Source: *Dr Farrar's Rpt to the L.G.B.., pp. 8–10.*

assume the problem of defining what is meant by a Gypsy, whether a Romany or merely a traveller, would have again intruded in the compilation of the statistics. It may be that Herefordshire and Shropshire sent in 'nil' returns because the clerk in charge did not see any group who conformed to his interpretation of what the term describes. Other counties appear to have taken the ownership of outdoor accommodation as the major criterion in identifying the Gypsy from the rest, this factor assisting in the elevation of the Gypsy-travellers above their fellow-pickers in the eyes of interested observers.[78] The Gypsies' way of life was only seen in a favourable light when it could be directly compared with that of a large group of urban poor cramped into temporary and overcrowded huts and troubled with the consequent complications of disease and sanitation. They were generally welcomed by the farmer for in providing their own accommodation they presented him with one less difficulty to negotiate, and the rigours of an outdoor existence were faced with a stoicism unlikely to be present in groups less accustomed to such trials.

PRESSURES CHALLENGING ITINERANT EMPLOYMENTS

Gypsy occupations were of a general and varied kind that mixed the legal with the illegal, the skilled with the unskilled.[79] They remained, for the most part, independent of the system of wage-labour and their reliance on self-help and an ability to turn their hand to almost anything was a fine example of Victorian attitudes to private enterprise. Earnings were usually small and the work temporary, insecure and subject to regular seasonal fluctuations. They travelled during the summer, finding employment as casual agricultural labourers, entertainers and the like, and remained in one place for most of the winter months. During this time they took up a number of trades and occupations, including as gas-stokers, tinkers, street-sellers and hawkers.[80] The mainstay of their occupational calendar, the hawking of different items by the female Gypsy, was also subject to seasonal and geographic variation. Items were sold according to what was available in a particular region: pots in and around the Midlands and the North, flowers in the South, and baskets about London. Beehives were sold in the summer and cutlery, nuts and oranges in the winter. The trade in umbrella-mending would, similarly, have been more profitable in the wet months.

The occupational structure remained dominated by the family as the essential work unit. Each member, from the youngest to the oldest, contributed in some way to the family income while still keeping largely independent of the hired-labour system. Although different families sometimes combined to work together it appears more usual for each to have been economically independent. Work itself was a continuous activity and there was no rigid division between work and leisure which, by the late nineteenth century, was an increasingly apparent feature of the industrial economy. The working day began early and finished late, affecting the old and young indiscriminately. An aged Gypsy lady, said to have been 115 years old, was working in a harvest field only a few weeks before her death.[81]

A major factor in the ability of travellers to maintain an existence was precisely the diversity and multiplicity of their employments, with the variety of work in which they engaged altering with the passage of time. The change in the nature and emphasis of employments, and in the goods and services offered for sale, were forced on them by the developing state of the environment in which they lived and altering market conditions. It has already been noted that the contribution made by travellers in filling the gap in the rural supply and demand economy was far from insignificant. Yet with the growth of the railways, improvements in systems of transport and communications, and with the diffusion of the conveniences of the city into the countryside, this gap was being adequately filled without the assistance of the travellers. Permanent retailers were distributing similar items to those hawked by the Gypsies at a lower cost.

The nature of the items hawked also suffered from the pressure of competition from industrially manufactured goods. The process which had begun by the time John Hoyland was writing about the Gypsies in the early years of the century had advanced immeasurably by the latter part. Increasingly the articles sold were not of their own manufacture but were machine-made, and industrially produced tin ware and other goods were now thought to yield greater profits for less physical effort. Baskets were bought in rather than home-made and, as Charles Godfrey Leland noticed, within days of the end of the hopping season the Gypsies went, 'almost *en masse'*, to buy baskets in Houndsditch.[82] It was suggested that hawking had become an excuse for begging and fortune-telling as people were no longer prepared to buy items at the door that could be found more cheaply elsewhere.[83] Gypsy Lovell summarised the development thus:

we make an honest living out of selling clothes-pegs . . . Business? No, it's not what it was. Machine-made pegs are undercutting us. They turn them out by boxes holding sixty dozen apiece . . . [But] they're no good compared with those cut by hand! They split after they've been used a time or two. Ours last for months.[84]

Perhaps as a result of this the Gypsy-travellers now often sold directly to shops and retailers in bulk rather than in small quantities from house to house.

The service trades of tinkering, repairing and entertaining were also being threatened. Cheap, new manufactured items were readily available, and the days of the itinerant entertainer became numbered with the development of a formal time-discipline that clearly segregated work from leisure and signalled the march forward of Rational Recreation.[85] Wakes, feasts and large wedding festivities were rapidly disappearing from the countryside calendar, and again the trend had begun early: 'England is no longer "Merry England", our merry games, our merry meetings, our wakes, fairs and festivals have given way to Bible societies, mechanics' institutes, and saving banks.'[86] Seasonal employment in harvest fields and hop farms was also increasingly less in demand. The use of agricultural machinery, the mechanisation of harvest work and the employment of farm labourers on a more permanent basis all combined to reduce the need for temporary, seasonal hiring.[87] A similar movement was taking place in the hop fields. The acreage under hop was reduced by over a third between 1878 and 1907. Improved cultivation had increased the yield, hops were by then able to be kept in cold storage, and less were being used in the manufacture of beer.[88]

The list of pressures, trends and developments acting to challenge the structure and form of the Gypsies' economy is therefore as impressive as it was irreversible. Essentially the travellers' resistance to industrial capitalism's dominant economic formations revealed the group as sharply anachronistic, a position that was to become progressively more acute as time passed. By the latter decades of the century there was apparently no further economic rationale for their existence. They were no longer needed to serve the demands of the remote rural areas, goods were replaced rather than serviced, social life was undergoing a dramatic transformation and crafts skills lost out in the competition with mass, factory production. All these factors pointed to the conclusion that the Gypsies would inevitably be forced to accept the logic of industrialism and take up sedentary-based employments. The Gypsy-travellers were urged to face up to the reality of events and accept that their way of life and methods of earning a living were no longer of relevance in the modern world.

This, though, was to reckon without two important factors. First, the trends and changes described were necessarily uneven in their impact. They took place at different times, at a different pace and with varying strengths in the various regions of the country. There are a good many first-hand accounts of rural life in the 1920s and 1930s painting a picture of life unchanged in many of its essentials from a much earlier period, with scissor-grinders, umbrella-repairers and chair-bottomers still a regular feature of the itinerant country scene.[89] A niche therefore still remained for the travellers many years after objective criteria would have denied them such a place. This persistence of traditional patterns is just one side of the story. The other is the refusal of the Gypsies to accept calmly the economic logic of the pressures on their way of life. They recognised the need for changes and sought to adapt where necessary, moving from village to town and abandoning old trades in favour of new activities more suited to the times. Although this demanded some modifications and shifts in emphasis in their nomadism and self-employment these two features nevertheless remained as the chief characteristics distinguishing them from the settled population. A less resilient culture and less adaptable economy would have crumbled under the impact of these forces, yet the result was not collapse and incorporation but rather consolidation and adaptation.

PART 2

Images

4

Romany or traveller – definitions and stereotypes

The impressions and stereotypes formed about nineteenth-century British Gypsies revolved around two contrasting perspectives which represented them either as an itinerant group or as a Romany race. By considering how the Gypsies were defined by the legislature, philanthropists and others, it will be possible to see how the often contradictory stereotypes evolved and how responses were conditioned by mistaken and misguided assumptions. Some commentators viewed Gypsies as just one, indistinct and unremarkable part of a large and ill-defined vagrant population, discussed briefly in the opening chapter. Others viewed them as a distinct and separate race whose culture and heritage should be preserved and respected, whether in the imagination or through practical efforts in the collection of folk-lore material. Another group borrowed the same arguments to identify the Gypsies as a race apart, but then proceeded to attack them on the grounds that their race possessed hereditary characteristics not romantic and desirable but rather harmful and destructive to the individual and society. Essentially, my concern is with the application and use of theories of race, blood purity and genetic determinism to define the features and characteristics of a minority group. It needs to be asked whether recourse to concepts of racial distinction was valid in regard to Gypsy-travellers in the nineteenth century, and what were the intentions and consequences of such interpretations.

FICTION AND THE GYPSY LORISTS

The use of romantic notions of a separate, mysterious race of Gypsies was a device frequently adopted in poetry and fiction of all descriptions, from the 'highbrow' works of Sir Walter Scott, George Borrow, Charles Dickens and D. H. Lawrence to the anonymous 'penny dreadfuls' and railway literature.[1] Whether the Gypsy was an incidental acquaintance or the main character, foreign origin was the basis around which images were drawn of a romantic people, living an idle, natural, *al fresco* life, camped in secluded woods and forests. Physically they were dark, supple, agile and handsome, possessing a temperament that was wild, fierce and defiant. The beauty and grace of the bewitching Gypsy maiden attracted many admirers in a variety of stories. The use of the male stereotype of the lithe and handsome Gypsy was adopted less frequently, though perhaps most familiarly in D. H. Lawrence's *The Virgin and the Gypsy*. Romance and adventure among an exotic people formed the main themes.

George Borrow is perhaps the best known of all writers whose books contain Gypsy characters and their way of life as the central element. The Gypsies of his semi-autobiographical novels certainly fit the picture described above of a foreign people with their own language and laws, determined to maintain their separateness from non-Gypsies. Yet although he had some contact with the subjects of his writings, the reader is in fact told very little about the people. Borrow's tendency to generalise, to appropriate Gypsy words from other authors (including mistakes) without acknowledgement and to romanticise and exaggerate the mysterious and picturesque meant that the resultant picture was far removed from a factual study of Gypsy life.[2] Even so, Borrow's novels contributed greatly to the appearance of Gypsies in a range of romantic literature and provided an important stimulus to the growth of gypsiology which appeared at the time. Indeed, many writers, whether novelists or journalists, referred frequently to Borrow for inspiration, and his romanticism filtered through to the pictures they were to present:

Formal, hedge-clipped, much-inclosed, well-farmed law-respecting, vagrant-hunting England has few sights left so racy in their savour of wood smoke and open air, so delightful in their grouping of form and blending of colour, so helpful to the green landscape, so suggesting of escape from the mill-horse round of daily life and labour as the wayside camp of the gipsy horde.[3]

Such romanticism pre-dated Borrow and would long outlive memories of his work, yet his particular influence should not be forgotten.[4] He stood as the figurehead for the romantic elevation of the Gypsy to the status of chief protagonist with the forces of progress and advance, resisting the crushing organisation of society and the routine and restraints of civil life.[5] They stood for freedom against the tyranny of law, for nature before civilisation and for simplicity before complexity. This instinct for liberty was held as the symbol for the aspirations of all who challenged the repressive forces of modernisation.[6]

These writers did not go unchallenged though, and their emphasis on imagination rather than fact or experience was often criticised. George Smith of Coalville, the crusading philanthropist, said they looked at Gypsy life through 'tinted or prismatic spectacles', dismissing them all as 'daisy-bank sentimental backwood gipsy writers'.[7] Many other commentators warned against being misled by the representations of the stage or books.[8] But just as these criticisms were mounting the romantic movement resurged and gained in strength with the emergence of the numerous Gypsy lorists. They took this romantic picture, mixed it with the developing sciences of anthropology, genealogy, ethnology and philology, and emerged with a full-blown racial theory that had the notion of blood purity as the unifying theme.

Perhaps the most noted writers who adopted this vision of a small Gypsy elite of 'pure' blood were the many contributors to the *Journal of the Gypsy Lore Society*. They sought to identify the 'true' Gypsy and show him to stand above the common traveller, morally, socially and educationally. He was to be presented as the real aristocrat of the road. Their task was made more urgent by the belief that this purity was being eroded, and with it was disappearing the lore and culture of these distinct people. Scientific enquiries permitted the lorists to isolate to their own satisfaction a Romany race of pure pedigree and to make assertions about the high moral character and cultural distinctiveness of this people. The notion of blood purity assisted the isolation of the Romany Gypsy from other half-blood travellers, variously termed *posrats*, didakais and mumpers, and from non-Gypsies, otherwise called *gaujos* or *gorgios*.

The lorists attempted to construct a picture of the past and present respectability of the Romany Gypsy to set in contrast with the alternative presentation of travellers' camps, situated on waste ground, with a loosely constructed canvas tent for shelter, skeletonised horses feeding nearby, utensils and rubbish scattered about, a woman cooking, a man lazing, and swarms of ragged and unwashed children competing with each other to be the first to beg from the stranger or passer-by.[9] Such a situation had nothing to commend it to the old Gypsies who could remember better days, nor to the gypsiologists who found such a state contrary to reasonable conceptions of social order. To link the Romany Gypsy with a class of travellers living in poverty on the verge of society was opposed to the romanticised image they wished to paint of a persecuted race that had remained noble and culturally distinct amidst great adversity. Some of the 'pure' race still lived in the late nineteenth century, though in rapidly decreasing numbers:

Gipsies! Why, there aren't no gipsies now . . . All the old families are broken up – over in 'Mericay, or gone in houses, or stopping round the nasty poverty towns. My father wouldn't ha' stopped by Wolverhampton, not if you'd gone on your bended knees to him and offered him a pound a day to do it. He'd have runn'd miles if you'd just have shown him the places where some of these new-fashioned travellers has their tents.[10]

In short, a sub-group of Romany Gypsies of 'pure' blood, with a culture and characteristics distinct from all others, had been distanced from the larger group of travellers. Accusations of poverty, filth, depravity, immorality and a multitude of other vices then being levelled at the travelling population were denied by the lorists only in relation to the Romany. They agreed the mass of travellers, of diluted or no Romany blood, were of the type described by

9 The original caption for this illustration was 'A farmer's pig that does not like a gypsy tent'. A popular criticism of the Gypsies was that they lived in the most insanitary conditions and were content with an existence that would not have been tolerated even by animals. Note the conflict here with the cleanliness taboos (*mokadi*) said to be associated with the 'true Romany'.

George Smith of Coalville, local authority officials and other critics.[11] This group were simply a low breed of itinerants only loosely connected, if at all, to the Romany. Just as purity of blood was used to explain positive, worthy features and the distinctive culture of the Romany, so its dilution could be used to explain the weakening of these features and the appearance of negative characteristics.

The essential paradox of the lorists' approach was that their enquiries began only when they considered the Gypsies' distinctiveness was being eroded, having long been in the stages of a steady and progressive decay. The isolation and purity of the race were thought to be disappearing with the abandonment of traditional habits and customs, and the degeneration of the Romany language.[12] Their work became a desperate attempt to salvage some vestige of separateness for a group they saw as becoming virtually indistinguishable from the rest of the travelling population. Their arguments about the present, however, were firmly embedded in a vision of a mythical and romantic past which they intended to confirm rather than question. The very need to publish books and articles which argued emphatically and unswervingly for a distinct and separate race of people was recognition that this identity was itself of the past. Moreover, their researches provided much evidence indicating the opposite of their premises and conclusions, illustrating the invalidity of their approach and interpretation in the contemporary context.

There emerged from the writings of the romanticists, lorists and their disciples several key features interrelated and united by concepts of racial descent and the maintenance of purity of blood. The 'true' Gypsy was identified as distinct and separate both from other travellers and from the settled population. Chief among these features was the question of origin, an issue which dominated the early numbers of the *Journal of the Gypsy Lore Society*. There was no agreement over the original location of the Gypsies, or the timing of their first migrancy. Some favoured Egypt as the homeland, suggesting the Gypsies were forced to become an itinerant tribe as punishment for making the nails hammered through the hands of the crucified Jesus. Other writers looked instead to India and the impetus given to travelling by the fearsome rampaging of Timur Beg in the late fifteenth century. The Indian theory was especially popular by the late nineteenth century, relying heavily on the philological links between the Romany and Indian languages. There was, however, little disagreement among the lorists that the travellers were able to trace their ancestry to a foreign land.

The next stage in the argument was to indicate how the group had managed to retain an ancestral purity, a linking chain with their foreign origins, by marrying only within the tribe, hence resulting in a select group with 'pure' surnames and the survival of a distinct language. By maintaining this selective in-breeding their fundamental characteristics were said to remain undiluted. Any attempt to break with this tradition could result in the offender being cast out and denied any further contact with his family.

Having thus laid the foundation for the racial distinctiveness and separateness of the group, the structure began to take a fuller shape. Layers were now added regarding the Gypsies' particular physiognomy, dress, behaviour, attitudes, culture and polity. The completed picture could take on many different hues according to the position of the observer: neutral, white and glowing, black and undesirable. Moreover, features considered attractive to some could also be wholly repugnant to others. The Gypsies' alleged independence was seen both as a natural virtue and as evidence of an undesirable rejection of the conventions of the dominant society.

Perhaps the most popular of the stereotypes surrounding the Gypsy concerns physical appearance. Complexion was said to be swarthy, hair curly and black, eyes dark with a pearly lustre.[13] The mode and style of dress was frequently portrayed as showy and colourful, with headscarves, trinkets and droopy earrings in abundance.[14] As a tribe they were thought to be fiercely proud and independent, even the most poor refusing any contact with charitable agencies and state institutions such as the workhouse and poor relief. They were free-living and free-loving, with a sexual appetite matched only by their wanderlust, itself a product of the possession of black blood, or *kalo ratt*.[15] The wild nomadic spirit was transmitted by birth and could not be controlled or denied: 'There is in the gypsy a power stronger than all others, a power that severs old ties, and that is their unsubjugated wandering instinct. We come across it in the gypsy in a more intensified and at the same time possibly more primitive form than in any other wandering people.'[16] Confinement within four walls was thought to be anathema to the tribe[17] and many evangelists believed it an impossible task to persuade the Gypsy to settle and so go against natural impulses.

Statements regarding polity formed a further component of the stereotyped image of the Romany traveller. Few commentators were able to write about the Gypsies without stressing their marginality to the dominant social and political institutions. They were said to be uninvolved in the politics and structures of the wider, host society and were instead ruled by internal organisations dependent on dark, mysterious meetings and which called to mind the secretive rituals and practices of freemasonry.[18] The meetings, or councils, were likened to a judicial court which demanded the attendance of all the tribes in the locality. They adjudicated disputes and passed judgement on those who offended tribal laws, perhaps resulting in the expulsion of the offender from the Gypsy brotherhood. Decision-making on less serious matters was left to the patriarch of a particular group who was most commonly referred to, with his wife, as the King and Queen. Novelists, journalists and other commentators paid especial attention to this feature. Tales of Kings, Queens, Princes and Princesses appealed to the popular imagination with visions of riches and grandeur. Considerable publicity was given to the Gypsy colony at Kirk Yetholm where a dispute over succession provided excellent copy for the reporters, with stories of 'a sort of civil war' taking place before the title was rightfully claimed.[19]

The overall representation of the 'pure' and 'true' Romany was completed with alleged evidence concerning their adherence to a series of taboos, rites, ceremonies and beliefs. All cultural factors were taken into consideration and covered, among others, death and marriage, taboos concerning women and superstitious portents which determined when they could travel. Closely associated with the notion that Gypsy life was guided by omens and ritual was the romantic relationship they were said to have with nature. They were seen as a primitive people living a natural life untroubled by the cares of civilisation, able to preserve intact their magical beliefs and practices.

Marriage was said to consist of the ceremony of jumping or crossing broomsticks,[20] and other rather more elaborate customs.[21] Similar rituals surrounded divorce, in certain instances requiring a display of nudity and the sacrifice of a horse.[22] Traditions associated with death included the burning of the property of the deceased, the relinquishing of some habit of the dead person by the remaining members of the family,[23] the pouring of ale over the grave and the burying of some keepsake with the corpse.[24] These practices were still carried out even if they resulted in the surviving members of the family being reduced to poverty.[25] Most commentators ignored the practical reasons for such practices – fear of infection, prevention of quarrelling over inheritance, the impracticality of a nomadic group accumulating material possessions[26] – and instead favoured superstition and mysticism. The burning or burying of goods was thought to avoid the taboo of the corpse and the ghost of the dead man was said to be placated by providing, in an ethereal form, the items needed in the spiritual world.[27]

Also central to many nineteenth-century gypsiologists was the belief in the widespread existence and practice of *mokadi* regulations.[28] These fell into two categories. The first covered taboos associated with female sexuality and were based on the idea of contamination by women. The second category covered 'uncleanness' regulations governing diet, the use of eating utensils and the washing of clothes. Anything associated with femininity, whether food preparation, clothing, long hair or menstruation, were all included in the codes of behaviour. These determined what women could touch, where they could sit and what they could do. If a menstruating woman crossed a stream then the water was immediately contaminated and the family would have to move camp. Childbirth was singled out for exceptional treatment with the woman being physically ostracised from the family and the main body of the camp. Uncleanness taboos were based on the principle of contamination, especially in relation to eating habits, and anything touched by a *mokadi* person had to be destroyed. This included food handled by a menstruating female, a food dish touched by an animal, and even food dishes washed in a bowl usually reserved for clothes. The list of regulations is endless and, when accompanied by the range of other codes of conduct determining behaviour compiled by the lorists, it becomes easy to assume that ritual and ceremony dominated the lives of the Gypsies. They seemed unable to eat, sleep, travel, wash, drink or give birth without first consulting some omen or belief.

Contemporary evidence collected by the gypsiologists, and subsequently reinforced by Judith Okely's much later studies, would suggest that travellers indeed hold and practise distinct cultural forms.[29] The problems arise not in whether these customs were followed by most or some nineteenth-century travellers but rather in the attempt to attach to these practices a racial analysis in which non-adherence advertised exclusion from the inner 'elite' of racial 'pures'.

What we have, then, is a conglomeration of images, each contributing to the overall picture of how the 'true' Romany should look and behave. Building from a base of racial separateness the various commentators constructed a not entirely unsympathetic vision of the proud Romany: a tousle-haired, black-eyed, brightly-dressed people of Oriental and travelling ancestry, living outdoors throughout the year. They were ruled through their own political structures and organisations, indulging in traditions and ceremonies alien to the native culture of the host society. This was the ideal type, an image made familiar by, among other devices, popular literature. The issue of race was central, with these characteristics derived from and reinforced by racial attributes in a link of inevitability securing birth with behaviour, attitudes, language and appearance.[30]

RACE: THE BASE FOR HIERARCHY AND ANTIPATHETIC STEREOTYPES

Having created the desired image the next stage was to explain the relationship with other travellers. By distinguishing them as a race apart, defined by hereditary and cultural characteristics, the Romany was distanced not only from the indigenous settled population but also from non-Gypsy nomads. A clear hierarchy was constructed with the respectable Romany at the top of the scale, the aristocrat of the road. Working downwards, through declining morals and heightened degeneracy, came the tramps and vagrants at the bottom. The half-bloods were located somewhere in the middle. To confuse the 'true' Gypsy with these *posrats* of diluted blood was presented as a grave error that led to much injustice being directed towards the clean-living Romany. The latter, declining in numbers as the century progressed, were superior in manners, morals and occupations to their degenerate and impoverished 'mumply-brothers'.[31] These half-breeds were said to have inherited all the vices of the Romany and the *gaujo* but none of their virtues.[32] Elements of each of the factors used to identify the Romany were perhaps to be found in the half-blood, though to a degree related directly to the extent which the 'pure' blood had been intermixed and diluted. Although other factors could intrude into this hierarchy, including conditions of existence, van- or tent-dwelling and employments, these followed rather than preceded the essential and primary determinant of race.

A variety of terms identified the scale of this hierarchy. The 'true' Gypsies were the Romanies or Romanichels, while the half-bloods were the *poshrats, pushcats*, didakais, mumplies, mumpers, *posh and posh*, or *posh-kalo*. Tramps were variously called hedge-crawlers, hedger-mumpers, can-men and dossers.[33] Some occupational categories remained closely linked to racial variation, such as *chorodie* (English rogues, tinkers and travellers), *kora-mengre*

(English hawkers) and *hindity-mengre* (Irish tinkers). The terms tinker, tinkler, mugger and potter more usually cut across racial divisions.[34]

The arguments permitting the creation of a travellers' hierarchy based on race, with the elevation of the 'pure-blood' Romany as the central feature, were adopted overtly and tacitly by most people. This model was used to argue for regional differences between travellers, with the persistence of language and customs evidencing racial purity. It also served to romanticise the Romany and place him in a position of unassailable virtue.[35]

Any attack on this vision was deflected by the lorists by recourse to the stand-by notions of racial impurity. Evidence of Gypsies denying their basic and instinctive wanderlust by either settling in winter lodgings or abandoning travelling altogether was explained by mixed blood: it was the 'mumpers' who sneaked from the tent to the relative warmth of bricks and mortar while the true Romany warmed his black blood by the camp fire.[36] The image of the noble savage unable to control his instinctive nomadism thus remained secure. Any dilution in appearance, behaviour or customs was attributed to the same cause.

Gypsies themselves and local authority officers borrowed this notion of a distinct race with distinguishable characteristics, the one to deflect criticism and the other to justify persecution of the mass of travellers. Part of the Gypsy-travellers' defence against accusations of dishonesty and immorality was that they, always the 'true' Romanies, were not blameworthy and that responsibility rested with the half-blood degenerates who also followed a nomadic way of life. In the late 1890s a writer on Gypsies visited a camp of van-dwellers, one of whom strongly condemned his English tinker and 'cadger' neighbours: 'They are undoubtedly scourges to all game preservers in our district, snare hares and rabbits and pick up pheasants' and partridges' eggs wherever they have an opportunity . . . Unlike the English van people also, the gypsies do no wilful damage and are scrupulously correct in paying for the grazing of their horses.'[37] Likewise, Sylvester Boswell rued the disappearance of the 'pure' and worthy Gypsies, retaining only a contempt for the 'modern half-gorgified gypsies'.[38] Complaints against travellers thus stemmed not from the actions of the Gypsies but from those of the nailers, potters, tramps and wandering cadgers.[39]

Even George Smith of Coalville believed that the objects of his concern were not travellers who possessed Gypsy blood but rather those who followed Gypsy habits. The old-fashioned Gypsies were dead, forced off the roads by the Enclosure Acts and persecution, to be replaced by a 'new race' who had taken to travelling primarily to escape rates and taxes.[40] While there was a general consensus that the old-style Gypsy had disappeared, few agreed with Smith that the 'new race' were persons recently arrived from sedentary society. Instead they were a mongrel people, descended from the Gypsies but with much diluted blood: 'Already the old black blood has been crossed and re-crossed; the pure gypsy is as scarce as a black swan; the old customs have been perverted; the old language has been nearly lost; the traditions are forgotten.'[41] New theories of racial purity were thus used to locate a minority of 'true' Gypsies, and to afford them some honour and praise for their racial integrity. The identification of this elite group had the further effect of isolating a larger group of racial 'impures' whose characteristics, behaviour and manners received no praise from any quarter. An excuse could be found for travelling if it was genetically determined and instinctive, the preserve of a small group. No justification existed for travellers maintaining an itinerant life-style without this claim to predetermined impulses.

For the moment I will leave intact this racial base and its superstructure of stereotype as it was also the case that other commentators built from the same foundation of racial separateness to compose a rather different and this time unsympathetic image. Having outlined this second racial construct I will return to consider both structures and their foundation more critically.

Perhaps the most overtly antagonistic and antipathetic of all the images presented of a race of Romanies was that likening the people to animals: 'The Gypsies are nearer to the animals than any race known to us in Europe'.[42] This statement appeared in an article entitled 'In Praise of the Gypsies'! The intention, then, was to place the Gypsies on the lowest possible level of human existence.[43] They were said to eat more like beasts than men, subsisting on animals that had died of disease and the discarded refuse of settled society.[44] They were described as drinking more like swine than human beings and, to continue the metaphor, possessed the animal traits of cunning, deceit and aggression. These vitriolic denunciations were then extended and amplified by further accusations of treachery, idleness, parasitism, heathenism and vice.[45] Scarcely any aspect of their character, way of life or emotions went unnoticed or uncriticised. However, probably the most potent of the antipathetic stereotypes was that associating the Gypsy race with various crimes.

It was a common reaction for the settled population to look on travellers with suspicion. The moment they appeared in a district was the time the crime rate was usually reported to have risen. If anything went missing, whether livestock, bracken or children, the travellers became the obvious suspects. They were the ideal scapegoat as they were suspected by everyone and supported by none. Whether the rate of crime did increase, and whether the travellers were responsible in any case, is impossible to determine. They would not have been entirely free from blame, but it was also the case that local residents took this opportunity to increase illegal activities such as poaching. The 1839 Commission on the Constabulary Force gave official sanction to the popular association between itinerancy and criminality, reporting that the most prominent body of delinquents in rural districts were vagrants.[46] For a man placed in circumstances of suspicion to call himself a traveller was thought an admission that he was deserving of guilt; to call himself a Gypsy was confirmation.[47]

Gypsies, as part of the travelling community, thus came under an umbrella condemnation of inevitable criminality. Some even accorded them special status as a race of hereditary criminals and outlaws. The appearance of a family of Gypsies made clear the apportioning of blame for any mis-demeanour or mishap:

If a hedge was broken down – if a sheep was missing – if an inroad was made on the henroost, who but 'the gypsies' were the perpetrators of these outrages. The speckle-backed hen, the best breeder in the yard, layed no eggs, a gypsy-woman had been seen on the premises. The red cow gave but two pints of milk – no wonder – 'the gypsies' were encamped just below the meadow gate. Calumny did not stop here; John, the plough-man came late to his work (the idle rascal had been spending his wages at the ale-house), the fault was laid at the door of the black-eyed Aegyptian, the daughter of Tom the tinker.[48]

To be called a Gypsy was therefore to be attributed with the ability to do untold damage not only to property but also to established morality and social discipline. But perhaps the most common accusation was that the Gypsy 'race' possessed a particular propensity towards stealing. This was said to be due to hereditary factors and also to result from their way of life and occupations in that regular thefts were necessary in order to supplement their financial income and vary their diet.[49] Whatever the causes, the almost casual assumption that gypsyism was merely another name for a nomadic, thieving way of life can be frequently found: 'I saw a great many Gypsies and their tents, likewise, some very good horses, which no doubt they had stolen, for I believe there are not many, of that sort, that are not guilty of thieving or poaching or some bad crime.'[50] They were accused of stealing everything from sheep, horses and children to grass for their horses and bracken to make fires. In the much-quoted example of prosecution for horse-stealing, pro-vided by James Crabb, the Gypsy was singled out for especially harsh treatment and was given no hope of mercy by the judge.[51] This combination of Gypsy with thief was also taken one step further with the claim that everything to which the Gypsies turned their hands was associated in some way with dishonest practice and criminality.

Their traditional skill with horses and prominence at horse sales meant that they could be accused of both stealing and 'doctoring' the animals.[52] Attendance at fairs also permitted other criminal activities, and the Hampshire Gypsies were said to have organised leagues of young men into hierarchically structured groups of thieves.[53] Other occupations, 'sometimes real – more frequently pretended', were seen as cloaks for less honest pursuits and mere sham for a variety of impostures.[54] They carried rushes and pretended to be chair-menders, 'though they have never mended a chair in all their lives', and the hawking of small articles from door to door was simply a pretence for carefully noting what could be pilfered later.[55] Hawking was also considered a pretext for begging, playing on the susceptibilities of the gullible, fortune-telling and 'ringing the changes'.[56] Likewise, the trade of rat-catching was merely a means of gaining admission to farms where the Gypsies could then kill the animals, achieved either by suffocation or poisoning.[57]

A crime believed to be the exclusive reserve of the Gypsy race was that of child-stealing:

When they saw the gipsies they drew back behind their mother and the baby carriage, for there was a tradition that once, years before, a child from a neighbouring village had been stolen by them. Even the cold ashes where a gipsy's fire had been sent little squiggles of fear down Laura's spine, for how could she know that they were not still lurking near with designs upon her own person? . . . She never really enjoyed the game the hamlet children played going home from school, when one of them went on before to hide, and the others followed slowly, hand in hand, singing:

> I hope we shan't meet any gipsies tonight!
> I hope we shan't meet any gipsies tonight!

And when the hiding-place was reached and the supposed gipsy sprung out and grabbed the nearest, she always shrieked, although she knew it was only a game.[58]

Similarly, there was an old Scottish rhyme traditionally sung to fretful children:

> Hush ye, hush ye, dinna fret yet
> The Black tinkler winna get ye.[59]

Having taken the child from its true parents it was claimed that the Gypsies then disguised their captives by blackening them artificially with a dye made from green walnut husks, galls and logwood.[60] Stolen children, when old enough, were later married into the Gypsy fraternity to ensure that the resulting mixed blood gave stamina to the race.[61] Elsewhere, the practice was linked to the tribal and historic superstitions of the race.[62]

The net effect of these various accusations was that the romantic notion of the Romany came to be challenged. Animal-like behaviour and instincts were set against a proud independence, criminal practices against strict internal rules and organisation. Each, however, shared the common assumption of the racial separateness of the group. It is to this foundation we must now return.

10 A 'classic' portrait of the Romany Gypsy: dark-haired, black-eyed, dark-complexioned and wearing a headscarf and large ornamental earrings. Evidence of fair-haired and blue-eyed children in the Gypsy camps led to accusations of child-stealing and dilution of the pure, black Gypsy blood.

THE ROMANY DECONSTRUCTED

The superstructure of image and stereotype appears comprehensive and all-embracing, whether in its neutral, positive or negative aspect. Yet the essential premises on which this was constructed can be found wanting in every area. We are asked to believe that the Gypsies arrived in this country sometime in the early sixteenth century, driven either from Egypt or India. Already the supposition is that racial purity was upheld during the period of their extensive travels through various countries. The lorists then attempted to argue that this purity remained intact from the sixteenth to the nineteenth

centuries by the tribe marrying internally and prohibiting entry from outsiders. Such a claim collapses under the weight of its grandiose presump-
tions. Thomas Acton, a noted and important writer on the subject of the
British Gypsies, suggested that from the time of their first appearance in this
country they would have been mixing 'culturally, linguistically and genetically with the local population'.[63] Available evidence would seem to back up
this claim.

From the eighteenth century records of marriages with *gorgios* have been
preserved, indicating that such relationships were neither rare nor exceptional.[64] Proof of intermarriage between travellers and non-travellers is even
more plentiful for the following century.[65] But perhaps the most damning
evidence was provided by the lorists themselves. Francis Groome offered
three Romany pedigrees showing various degrees of intermarriage with
gorgios and in one of these, of Abraham Wood, marriages with *gorgios*
outnumbered those with Gypsies. Groome himself recognised that, despite
his desire to prove the opposite, not only was the trend towards intermarriage more pronounced by the latter decades of the century but also that it
was extremely difficult to draw a clear line between Gypsies and
non-Gypsies.[66]

Other writers casually acknowledged that non-Gypsy blood was to be
found in ancestral chains.[67] Thomas Thompson, a prominent gypsiologist,
showed that the majority of Lawrence Boswell's descendants had, by the
fourth generation, married outside the tribe.[68] Similarly, the Reverend
George Hall's notes on the pedigree of the Heron family showed the same
pattern (see Table 3). The trend would appear to be clear, confirming the
findings of other genealogists. Yet Rivers himself said of the table: '[the]
method is far from accurate, for the pedigree shows that many people bearing
true Gypsy names are nevertheless of mixed blood . . . The figures must . . .
be taken as only rough approximations.'[69]

What Rivers has hinted at in this admission reveals on closer examination
to be a serious and fundamental flaw in methodology. Information on

Table 3 *Marriages of the Heron family with non-Gypsies and those of mixed stock*

		Generation			
	B	C	D	E	F
Number of families	2	7	23	28	29
Number of marriages	10	37	71	64	34
Marriages with:					
(a) non–gypsies	1	0	7	14	5
(b) mixed stock	0	4	5	18	12

Source: W.H. Rivers, 'Notes on the Heron Pedigree Collected by the Rev. G. Hall',
J.G.L.S., New Ser., Vol. 7, No. 2 (1913), p. 91.

pedigrees was collected chiefly from oral accounts by the Gypsies themselves. Even disregarding lapses of memory and incorrect recollections, there
was also the problem of the Gypsies being reluctant to admit marriages with
non-Gypsies or with those whom they considered degenerate half-bloods.[70]
A more serious criticism concerns the assumptions made by the genealogists
in their adoption of the lorists' maxim that surnames were a convenient and
accurate guide to racial purity.

The idea that Gypsies could be identified by names probably dates back to
the time of their appearance in this country, and was referred to by Hoyland
and Crabb in the early part of the nineteenth century. The Gypsy lorists took
this and transformed it into a means of identifying the extent of purity among
travelling families. Charles Godfrey Leland even went so far as to produce a
list of names of pure-blood and half-blood Gypsies, giving to each family
group particular physical characteristics and directions where they could be
found.[71] This method, and the guidelines provided by Leland, were adopted
by many subsequent writers.[72] More recently it has even been suggested that
the high incidence of traditional Gypsy names among canal boatmen indicated their Romany ancestry.[73] Rarely has this methodological position been
challenged despite many discrepancies and flaws.

The surnames Buckland, Stanley, Clayton and Holland were commonly
associated with pure Romany ancestry, yet a more detailed look at their
family histories suggests all was not as it appeared. Edwin Buckland had been
born a peasant at Charlbury in Oxfordshire. He lived in a house until twenty-
seven years of age when he married a traveller and took to a wandering way
of life. He was even noted for speaking Romany with great fluency.[74] One of
the Stanleys was able to claim respectable ancestry with his great-grandfather
being a principal officer in the army and his father taking to the roads only
when the family fell on hard times.[75] The families of Clayton and Holland can
also be traced to sedentary origins. From the original families of the Hollands
of Barlestone and the Claytons of Barwell, there were said to be by the 1880s
seven families of the former travelling the country and fifteen of the latter.
This represented a total of around 150 adults and children who had taken to
gypsying in the last fifteen years since George Smith was writing in the
mid-1880s.[76]

Such examples indicate the impossibility of assuming any clear correlation
between surname and racial origin. One explanation for the weakness of the
method can be found in the following statement issued by the Gypsy Lore
Society:

all members are warmly urged to look through such Parish Registers as they can obtain
access to. Every entry in which the descriptions 'Egyptian', 'Gypsy', 'vagrant',
'vagabond', 'wanderer', 'stranger', or their Latin equivalents, occur, should be noted
down . . . Entries containing obviously Gypsy names should also be copied, even
when there is no description.[77]

Such vague and all-encompassing instructions were bound to lead to conflict-ing interpretations. The debate over whether or not the name Kemp indicated a 'true' Gypsy highlighted the problems.[78] Eric Winstedt, keen to uphold the existence of the 'pure' Romany, disputed that Kemp were a pure-blood family, and to support this opinion he cited from the parish registers the entry of the burial of a Kemp, 'a travelling man', at Carlton, Suffolk, in 1726.[79] To Winstedt this proved conclusively that this man was not a Romany. Lady Grosvenor, equally in favour of the Romany myth, used precisely the same type of evidence to show that the Buckland family were of Romany ancestry.[80]

The use of surnames to identify a separate race of Romany Gypsies is thus highly flawed. It fails to distinguish between the different groups of travellers with any degree of certainty, uniting as 'pure' Gypsies all travelling families with 'pure' surnames and the 'vagabonds' and 'hawkers' of the parish registers. Such a methodology denies rather than assists the likelihood of identifying racial origins.

Similarly, the argument that language provided the key to the differences between the Gypsies and non-Gypsies does not withstand critical examina-tion. The commonly held assumption was that all Gypsies were able to speak Romany to some extent, with the greatest fluency coinciding with the purest blood.[81] However, not all speakers of Romany were necessarily Gypsies. All such a hypothesis proves is that those who could not speak Romany were not Gypsies. The definition is exclusive rather than inclusive. This still leaves the problem of the extent to which the language had to be known and the degree of fluency with which it had to be spoken for an individual to be termed a true Romany.

It seems probable that a Romany language did once exist, and that it was widely spoken by travellers of every description. An itinerant whom Charles Leland met near Bath in 1876 admitted his knowledge of Romany and asked rhetorically if there was ever an old traveller who did not.[82] However, by the latter stages of the nineteenth century, the language had become increasingly corrupted. According to Robert Scott Macfie of the Gypsy Lore Society, Romany was subordinate to the vernacular grammar of the country, adding that the Gypsy noun had lost its nine cases and the verb its moods, tenses and persons.[83] The 'vulgar tongue' of nineteenth-century Gypsies combined Romany words with English, and conformed to the English method in syntax and sentence structure. The deep or old Romany dialect was said to be known only to a very few aged Gypsies.[84]

The reason suggested for this progressive decay of a language was the greater degree of intermixing taking place with the indigenous population, both as travellers and settled folk. Despite this, or rather perhaps because of it, language became a central concern among the Gypsy lorists, keen to record and preserve before it disappeared altogether from living memory. A by-product was its emergence as a major feature in isolating the 'true' Romany from the half-blood. Knowledge of a language was presented as a product of pure-blood ancestry and not of culture, again illustrating how, in crudely following the pattern set by late nineteenth-century social and scientific investigators, the lorists came to make exaggerated claims concerning origin and race.

A survey of the literature of the period indicates a persistent desire to identify, categorise, describe and reform the people of dark continents and the Empire. The existence of domestic travellers with a tradition of racial separateness offered the opportunity for writers, evangelists, folk-lorists and others to look at home for alien groups and cultures.[85] Inspired by a fascination with the separateness of the travellers from settled society they carried a missionary torch to illuminate the backwardness of this people in the midst of civilised society. Scientific tools such as genealogy and philology were applied with vigour and despite the existence of contradictory evidence, the lorists discovered the race they had set out to find. Assertions about behaviour, physiognomy, social and political forms were made with scarcely even a cautious proviso that appearances could be deceptive or the realisation that cultural elements could exist without being based in the traditional practices of a distinct racial group. By setting-up a picture of the Romany as dark-haired and dark-eyed the lorists and others were creating a myth lacking real or general substance. The presence of fair-haired and blue-eyed children in the camps of, by their definition, Romany families was greeted with a degree of alarm.[86]

A similar response was occasioned when the same camps failed to bring forward people dressed in the colourful Romany clothes. The New Forest Gypsies, for example, favoured 'the unlovely and ragged garments of the common tramp'.[87] T. Taylor, writing in the *Illustrated London News*, ridiculed the theatricality of the popular conceptions about the brightness and gaudiness of Gypsy dress, concluding that their appearance was rather a cross between a debauched game-keeper and a Staffordshire pot-hawker.[88] Although he sympathised with the notion of the 'pure' Romany, Taylor at least recognised their appearance was little different from the rest of the population. Reports of Gypsies dressing in bright and colourful clothes seem more suited to the romantic and fictional stereotypes, contrasting the manner and style of the group with the greyness of the expanding cities and growing slums. In this sense, they provided a distraction from the realities of urbanisation. Visits to camps invariably spawned an opposite picture, emphasising raggedness, hardship and struggle.[89]

Slowly, then, the Romany stereotype begins to crumble. The lorists' arguments for a separate and noble race are found to rest on weak supports, thereby also damaging the range of antipathetic images and the notion of a

hierarchical ordering among the travellers. But the destruction of one construct begs the question with what is it replaced?

There can be no doubt that in the context of any sedentary-based society
travellers exist as an identifiably separate group, but to attempt to differentiate between them according to racial characteristics has been shown to rest
on insufficient and suspect foundations. Instead of searching for inner racial
elites it is of more value to acknowledge diverse ancestry and then to attempt
a definition which stresses the ethnic, cultural and occupational identity of
the group. When the foreign Gypsies arrived in the early fifteenth century
they would have met a number of nomadic families already travelling the
roads, following a tradition of itinerancy and pursuing particular occupations. Crucially, the indigenous travellers did not remain aloof from the new
arrivals. There are records of intermixing between the Egyptians and native
'loyterers', outcasts, highwaymen, smugglers, vagabonds, tinkers, pot-haw-
kers and umbrella-menders from 1612 on,[90] and by the nineteenth century
the group of Gypsy-travellers would have been able to trace their origins to
each of these groups and others besides.[91]

Controversy developed over the definition of particular categories of
traveller. As has been shown, this was to lead to the development of
hierarchies founded chiefly on origin though also informed by occupation.
Disagreements arose over whether tinkers, potters or muggers could correctly be termed Gypsies, with the lorists refusing them this title unless their
ancestry could be proved. In many instances, however, such occupational
categories were used interchangeably with Gypsy. More comprehensively, it
was common for gypsyism to be linked to any form of nomadism.[92] It was the
contrast and conflict between two opposing ways of life that formed the
kernel of the issue. Differences between travellers came second to fundamental similarities which marked them not from each other but from the ways and
customs of settled society. Arguments could be wrapped in racial clothing to
justify and excuse persecution, but this was merely concealment. The clash
was more fundamentally between two different ways of life increasingly
moving in opposite directions, the standards of one being flagrantly disregarded by the other.

NOMADIC STEREOTYPES AND THE CLASH WITH SETTLED SOCIETY

Travellers in general were considered to be separate from settled society and
in some way different from the sedentary inhabitants. Henry Mayhew
identified nomads as a separate race distinguished by their high cheek-bones
and protruding jaws, among whom there was a greater development of the
animal than of the moral or intellectual nature of man, and who possessed
certain characteristics:

The nomad . . . is distinguished from the civilised man by his repugnance to regular and continuous labour – by his want of providence in laying up a store for the future – by his inability to perceive consequences ever so slightly removed from immediate apprehension – by his passion for stupefying herbs and roots, and, when possible, for intoxicating fermented liquors – by his extraordinary powers of enduring privation – by his comparative insensibility to pain – by an immoderate love of gaming, frequently risking his own personal liberty upon a single cast – by his love of libidinous dances – by the pleasure he experiences in witnessing the suffering of sentient creatures – by his delight in warfare and all perilous sports – by his desire for vengeance – by the looseness of his notions as to property – by the absence of chastity among his women, and his disregard of female honour – and lastly, by his vague sense of religion.[93]

By implication, settled members of society possessed characteristics opposite to the above, such as thrift, materialism, industriousness and high morality. The travellers' inability to save money, respect property, work industriously and live morally clearly offended Mayhew's conception of social order and progress.

A further illustration of the long-held connection between sedentarisation and respectable behaviour, and between itinerancy and antisocial behaviour and attitudes, is provided by Luke Pike:

Before the Norman Conquest a man who had no lord was to be accounted a thief; in the reign of Elizabeth a man who had no lord and no master was to be accounted a vagabond . . . the houses of correction were filled with 'idle labourers that would not work for the wages taxed, rated and assessed by the justices of the peace', and 'strong tall persons, having no land, money or lawful occupation'.[94]

By the nineteenth century these attitudes were being repeated more and more frequently, and by persons of varying backgrounds and objectives. Criticisms made by the early trade union leaders about the demoralising effect on character engendered by itinerancy, thus making the traveller unfit for the settled industrial occupations, could have been made by any number of critics from any class.[95] Simply, travellers of whatever description were considered rogues and vagabonds of the worst type, whose way of life, habits and characteristics were not acceptable to members of a society structured chiefly around permanency of settlement. Yet the very same society which criticised itinerancy in such strong terms also demanded its existence by its reliance upon a measure of nomadism and labour mobility to compensate for seasonal and regional fluctuations in trades and employments. Toleration of a necessary evil rather than acceptance was, though, the justification for the perpetuation of this marginal group.

Into this context of general antipathy to nomadism wandered the Gypsies. From the moment they first appeared in great numbers, in the reign of Henry VIII, they were deemed vagabonds. They were viewed with such disfavour not so much because they practised palmistry, or even because they were suspected of various felonies, but rather because they 'went from shire to shire'. By the laws enacted in the reign of Philip and Mary they were able to avoid the various penalties directed against them only by leaving their 'naughty, idle and ungodly life and company, and be placed in the service of some honest and able inhabitant of the realm'.[96] The early legislation, notably of 1530 and 1554, singled out the 'Egipcions' for capital punishment or deportation. By the time of the Elizabethan Poor Law (1596) the frame of reference had been extended to include all persons 'pretending themselves to be Egipcyans or wandering in the Habite Forme or Attyre of counterfayte Egipcians'.[97] The category had become diluted and broadened, itself an acknowledgement that distinctions could no longer be made. Subsequent legislation continued this expansive approach with the Vagrancy Act of 1824 simplifying earlier provisions, removing any ambiguities and avoiding racial categorisation.[98]

When it came to hurling abuse and affixing stereotypes the differences between the vagrants and travellers were soon forgotten. They had a freedom resented by the householder and were seen as marginal to the normal forces of law and order. Those travellers who did not work, or were not seen to work, were thought of as idle mendicants; those who did were said to pursue sham and vagabond employments which evaded hard and real toil. In short, they were seen as unwelcome and unsavoury parasites. The nomadic way of life stood in defiance to that experienced and suffered by the sedentary population. It rejected materialism, conformity and subjugation to industrial discipline. Anything that suggested eccentricity and unconventionality was treated with an interest qualified by reserve and suspicion.[99]

By the latter decades of the nineteenth century these rather amorphous and ill-defined antipathetic sentiments were fuelled by mounting evidence concerning illiteracy, sanitation and morality and the possibility of infectious diseases being transmitted by travellers. The earlier, more moralistic emphasis on the need to extinguish itinerancy to prevent licentious and parasitic behaviour became superseded by an appeal to common sense. The expressed concern over the moral and physical dangers posed by the itinerants was apparent throughout the century, but the difference was that the emphasis had been modified. George Smith of Coalville was a prime influence in effecting this change. His numerous publications in newspapers, articles and books portrayed the travellers not only as idle, beggarly and parasitic but also as unclean, uneducated, unhealthy and amoral conveyors of infectious diseases. And if this was not sufficient, they were also highly prone to criminal acts.

Smith conformed with tradition in his isolation of itinerancy as the great evil to be cured, with failure to find a remedy likely to have disastrous consequences: 'By travelling in vans, carts, and tents they escape the school boards, sanitary officers, rent and rate collectors; and today they are – unthinkingly, no doubt – undermining all our social privileges, civil rights, and religious advantages, and will, if encouraged by us, bring decay to the roots.'[100] Smith did not condemn the Gypsies as a race, only the itinerant, Gypsy way of life. To support his argument that settlement was the only solution he presented examples of sedentary Gypsies who were industrious, clean and religious. They complained to him about their lack of education, and related stories of their former life on the road which concentrated on a series of crimes, fights and child-stealing. They all, without exception, commented how pleased they were to have given up wandering. In contrast, with a distinction too convenient to be treated without considerable scepticism, travellers were presented as the complete opposite of the respectable, settled families. Occasionally Christian van-dwellers may be found, living in clean, tidy vans in pleasant surroundings, but they were a rarity. The remainder came in for unreserved criticism.

The accuracy of these various allegations was of less importance in terms of responses than the fact of their constant repetition and cultural transmission from one generation to the next: 'I have heard so much about their being a predatory and dishonest race, that I am compelled to think that what anybody says must have some truth in it.'[101] This particular writer was forced to submit to popular consensus despite having had personal contact with the Gypsies, an experience that showed them to be an honest and 'serviceable class of persons'.

The strength of the stereotyped themes and images lay in their emphasis on generalisations borrowed and learned from others, which were constantly repeated in newspapers, literature, folk lore, common hearsay and nursery rhymes. Each time the separateness of the Gypsy from settled (civilised) society was stressed, either as a distinct racial group or as a debased and debasing nomadic outcast. Responses were based on persistent but mixed stereotypes, the one founded in a romanticism of a distinct people but which also became adapted in terms showing a marked antipathy to an 'alien' race and culture, and the other based in a long-standing hostility and mistrust directed at the whole nomadic population.

The overt racism contained in the association of malicious stereotypes with a separate alien race was perhaps the least common of these various nineteenth-century perspectives. However, this position came to the front most clearly when the country experienced periodic visits from foreign Gypsies, notably with the arrival of the Greek Gypsies in 1886 and later followed by the Hungarians, Serbians, Germans and the Calderari Gypsy coppersmiths from Hungary in 1911. [102] As obviously of foreign origin as they were of nomadic disposition, these Gypsies offered the lorists an opportunity again to romanticise about past origins, strange beliefs and customs. In contrast, almost every other section of the community responded with horrifying xenophobic crudity. Local authorities would not tolerate their existence, violent conflicts occurred frequently with the police, indigenous travellers gloated over their harassment, and the local townspeople stoned them and spat at them. Here antipathy to the Gypsy, the nomad and the foreigner was seen in the most extreme forms.

The most commonly held views, in relation to indigenous travellers, subscribed to the romantic elevation of the Romany and the actual denigration of all other non-Romany travellers. These positions did not, as might appear, stand in contradiction to each other, but rather interacted in a complementary and self-reinforcing manner. Lorists could borrow from both sides to argue that the subjects of their studies were always the 'true' Romany, while the dirty and degenerate criminals of other writings were necessarily the half-breeds or non-Gypsy travellers. Conversely, the travellers encountered by philanthropists such as George Smith and the local authority officials, many of whom were directly influenced by his work, were regarded only as half-breeds and never the 'true' Gypsies whom they exalted along with the lorists. Both groups thus held identical positions, and claimed to be studying different sections of the hierarchically organised travelling community. Apparently, on their visits to the Gypsy camps, their paths never crossed. Pro-Gypsy sentiments were, then, reserved for a small section of travellers, found and visited by the lorists, though seemingly not by anyone else. For all others the Romany remained an elusive figure, bathed in a fictional, romantic light. Antipathy to travellers was thus double-edged, composed of racial flights of fancy and alleged empiricist objectivity concerning their manner and conditions of life.

CONCLUSION: MARGINAL, MOBILE, MINORITY

The whole question of perceptions of Gypsies, and of responses to them, has to be viewed from within the much larger framework of attitudes and responses to itinerancy in general and to a separate, 'alien' race and culture. The motivation behind the concern over an itinerant population, no matter how varied, is not hard to understand. Travellers offended every sense of good order and morality. They existed on the fringes of society, and of the economic and political spheres, and this marginality to, or rejection of, a conventional, settled mode of life made them suspect and unwelcome. They were to be feared for the implicit threat their existence posed to a method of thinking that was increasingly to stress immobility and regularity, and to be resented for remaining apart from the pressures towards conformity, whether legal, institutional, cultural or the many, subtle pressures towards socialisation. Yet they were also envied for managing to retain some independence and individuality. On the whole, though, the balance of opinion was very heavily weighted against them.

Itinerancy, vagrancy, vagabondage and mendicity were terms used almost interchangeably. The problem was compounded by the belief that the numbers of the class were forever increasing, boosted at various times by, for example, those thrown on to the roads following the reduction in the size of the militia after the end of the Napoleonic Wars and also the influx of Irish poor as a result of the mid-century potato crop failure.[103] Reports of Chief Constables, to be found in the Public Record Office, testify to the expressed concern over vagrancy and its perceived increase.[104] The depth of concern over this problem is illustrated well by the large number of Bills put forward, and Acts passed, covering this issue throughout the nineteenth and early twentieth centuries.

Added to this was the antipathy that developed towards a group allegedly of foreign origin, who had managed to retain distinctive characteristics over the centuries. Myths thus emerged concerning freemasonry practices, strange rites and customs inimical to the British way of life. Peculiarly Gypsy traits compounded the impressions which formed around nomadism into an all-embracing hostility, shared by all members of settled society, irrespective of class. The settled labourer had no more sympathy for the Gypsies than the lord of the manor. Essential to this response was the belief that they were different from, and apart from, settled society, whether this was identifiable in terms of low moral, physical, religious and educational standing, or in peculiar dress, manners and customs. On the whole, they were not regarded as a threat, either economically, politically or in any sense other than to property or health. To accord them the status of a threat or challenge was thought to give them a measure of importance and respect they did not deserve.

The basis of the racial definition, namely of blood purity as determining ethnic identity and cultural habits, has been found to suffer from serious methodological flaws to the extent that it eventually crumbles under the pressure of overwhelming contradictory evidence. The assumption that the Gypsies were a separate race and were identifiable as such, has thus been challenged and it has been shown that the attempt to locate the 'real' Gypsy is doomed to fail if blood purity is sought as the crucial and decisive factor. But to deny the Gypsy-travellers racial unity and separateness is not to suggest that they did not form a relatively cohesive group distinguishable both from settled society and the large amorphous collection of travellers of every description. The key to this distinctiveness, though, is not to be found in any racial explanation but rather in cultural patterns which incorporate a particular life-style and employment habits which are essentially the product of itinerant descent.[105]

PART 3

Responses

5

Evangelism and the reforming mission

Responses to Gypsies have always exhibited a series of fluctuations and ambiguities. They could be welcomed as entertainers and vendors of small wares almost simultaneously with being greeted as 'gyppos' and treated with disdain, contempt and fear. They were both the appealing, romantic savage and the degenerate, villainous outcast. Condemnatory generalisations appeared frequently in newspapers, insults were shouted at them in the streets, and on at least one occasion the constant provocation of the Gypsies by local schoolchildren led to retaliation and eventually resulted in one fatal injury.[1] However, for most people contact with these travellers was minimal and short-term, and no sooner had the abuse been cried than it was forgotten. Only when the camps had become more permanent and settled did the local population rally in active and vocal opposition. But the Gypsy-travellers lingered on in some people's consciences, playing on popular fears and allowing the development of adverse stereotypes.

Local authorities and the legislature were forced into taking action in an attempt to curb what were considered the more unacceptable excesses which resulted from a travelling way of life. The harshness of these responses varied over time, from place to place and individual to individual, and will be considered fully in a later chapter. Suffice it to say here that the edicts and persecutions which were carried out before the nineteenth century sought to eradicate the Gypsies from this country by transportation, banishment and execution. Yet such extreme measures proved impracticable and were gradually abandoned. The hanging of a number of young Gypsies at Northampton in 1780 can be taken as the symbolic watermark that signalled the end of the excessively severe persecution of previous times.[2]

From this date it was realised that persecution alone would neither improve the Gypsies nor drive them out of the country. The best that could now be hoped for was their reformation, to be achieved by their being educated to the ways of settled society. Although persecution was to continue, often excessively harsh and grossly unjust, this iron-fisted method gradually eased its grasp to allow the emergence of other forces which set about the task of reclamation. A major part of this duty fell to the evangelist

97

missionaries: 'Law, rigid stern justice alone could do no good with them, and consequently handed them over to the minister of love and mercy.'[3] With a realisation of the failure of legislative measures and a belief that the number of Gypsies was increasing, evangelists of every description, whether concerned individuals or members of organised missionary agencies, took up the travellers' cause with varying degrees of enthusiasm and energy. Their aim was first to bring an end to the Gypsies' wanderings and then to correct the laxity of their morals. Notions of moral rescue combined with a desire to reclaim marginal groups from their independent existence and to prepare them, and especially their children, for industrial occupations which relied on values of dependence and submissiveness.

It is not my intention to discuss the reasons for the upsurge in evangelism which accompanied the early stages of the economic and social revolution of the late eighteenth and early nineteenth centuries. This is a task which I shall leave for others more qualified in the history of religion. My objective is more limited and is concerned primarily with identifying the nature of the evangelistic response to Gypsy-travellers by considering the aims of the missionaries and the justification provided for their actions. It is important, however, not to lose sight of the fact that this represents only the religious-based, voluntary attempt to reform and civilise the nomadic population. It is necessary to take into account other responses – whether philanthropic, humanitarian or legislative – in order to have a fuller picture of the reaction of settled society and how the balance between the components of the picture was constantly changing.

The first known public appeal calling for the Gypsies' reformation appeared in the *Public Advertiser* in 1778, yet this appears to have evoked no response.[4] The barriers of ignorance and hostility were so great that many potential reformers did not even turn to the task, believing it to be impossible. The Gypsy people were thought to be a race beyond recall.[5] Perhaps the most significant advance towards arousing serious interest in the Gypsy problem came with the English translation of Heinrich Grellmann's treatise on the subject, entitled *Dissertation on the Gipsies* (1787). Although the book was concerned primarily with Continental Gypsies it was the first real attempt to provide information on this class of travelling people, and to illustrate the urgent need for their social and religious reformation. Coming at the time when the Sunday-school movement was the physical embodiment of a general evangelistic zeal for reform and improvement directed at the poor and under-privileged children of the working classes, to be achieved through teaching virtuous religious principles and elementary reading and writing, the call to reform the Gypsies (and especially their children) aroused considerable interest among religious communities.[6]

By the opening decades of the new century this missionary fervour had gathered some momentum. For the time being, however, reformation was to remain a literary call rather than actual practice. The debate was next taken up in the pages of the *Christian Observer*.[7] Several correspondents contributed their thoughts and proposals at great length, and the letters were unanimous in their criticisms. The language used was uncompromising in its opposition to the travelling way of life and in its detestation of the people. One correspondent had even written a letter on the subject as early as 1801 which he had intended to send to the Society for Bettering the Condition, and Increasing the Comforts, of the Poor. He thought better of it, though, as 'any attempts to civilise a race of beings so degraded, and held in so much contempt, would be considered so very visionary, that I gave up the idea'.[8] The language used by these early reformers illustrated their harsh and uncompromising attitude, with constant reference to the Gypsies' savage life, wretched existence, spiritual misery and the way their degraded state offended the society upon which they were parasitic. The image of the Gypsy as a vagrant pest living a depraved life in the midst of a civilised and refined society was thus made very clear. To some, such as the correspondent above, there could be no solution as the magnitude of the problem rendered it insoluble. But there were others who were far more optimistic about the possibilities for change. They believed that true reform could come about only if the Gypsies were 'reclaimed from their vagrancy', or forced to settle, and were 'acquainted with the Saviour'. Missionaries were exhorted to go among them and do this work, financial assistance was offered, and a meeting was called to discuss the matter, though this never materialised. Other proposals put the onus of responsibility on to the parishes to which the Gypsies belonged with the demand that they provide homes for the travellers and persuade them of the benefits of settlement by the offer of employment for the adults and free schooling for the children.[9]

Already, the problems which confronted the missionaries were emerging. More people called for reform than were prepared to act, parishes were unwilling to take responsibility, and any inducements to settle, such as the provision of employment, suffered from local opposition. Finally, the mere fact of their travelling militated against prolonged contact with missionaries, and so with 'educating and elevating' influences. Despite these problems, though, the missionary ball had been set rolling, helped on its way by the next major series of correspondence calling for reform which appeared in the *Northampton Mercury* in 1814,[10] and by the interest taken by the Quakers, resulting in the publication of a book on the subject by John Hoyland in 1816.[11] Again, the emphasis of the correspondents to the *Northampton Mercury* was on 'calling the wanderers home', by providing them with an asylum of some description which would encourage their reformation and persuade them to abandon their 'accustomed vices'.[12] This theme was expanded on by 'Junius' who called for four to six villages to be built for them in different parts of the country. However, these were not to be purely Gypsy colonies, and the hand of paternalism was not far away. A house or a farm was to be attached to the village where a 'respectable person' was to be placed in order to carry out supervisory duties. Children were to be educated at sex-segregated schools and when old enough were to be apprenticed to a useful trade. Moreover, the scheme was not proposed as a voluntary remedy. Any Gypsy found wandering was to be placed in the nearest station, 'and should any either leave their residence, or refuse to accept of this asylum, I see no reason why the law should not be enforced upon them with the greatest severity'.[13]

Here, then, was a call to the legislature to introduce a Bill designed specifically to deal with the problem of 'troublesome mendicants' by forcing compulsory settlement. It was thought that such a plan would benefit both the Gypsies, by raising them out of wretchedness to comfort, and also the community, by making property more secure and less prone to plunder or parasitism. A characteristic of all these early demands was that they were argued with strong moralistic and religious fervour from a position of almost total ignorance about, and certainly a lack of any real contact with, the people whom they sought to reform. The proposals sought to destroy the travelling way of life, split up families by removing the children to schools and by apprenticing them to various trades, and by making their actions and activities subject to the control and supervision of an overseer. None of this was considered possible unless organised on the principle of absolute compulsion.

The missionary drive took a significant step forward in 1815, when a meeting was called by the Quakers to discuss the possibility of reforming the Gypsies. It was decided that a great deal more had to be known about the people, and the responsibility for this fell to John Hoyland, a member of the Society of Friends. A circular letter and questionnaire was drawn up and sent to the clergy and laity in most of the counties of England, and Hoyland himself supplemented the material obtained with details from personal visits to their camps in Northamptonshire, Hainault Forest and Norwood.[14] The results of his findings and the replies to his questionnaire were published as a book, which was to become one of the most important and influential written about the Gypsies in the nineteenth century. The circular mixed sympathy with the degraded and persecuted Gypsy with a desire to spread the word of Christ and to reclaim undesirable and parasitic elements so as to benefit society as a whole. To allow the Gypsies to continue their itinerant and marginal existence meant, according to Hoyland, they would remain only parasites and depredators. The primary objective was to transform them into 'useful citizens'.

It was acknowledged this would not be an easy task. Although possessing a certain amount of sympathy for these people, Hoyland condemned them for their lack of religion, their propensity to wander, their thieving habits and their tendency to idleness. The remedy was to enforce settlement, provide a rudimentary education and offer a sound religious training. The emphasis on retraining to the ways of settled society was to fall heaviest on the children, who were to be sent to charity schools when between the ages of six and fourteen years:

Their being placed among a much greater number of children, and those of settled, and in some degree of civilised habits, would greatly facilitate the training of Gypsies to salutary discipline and subordination, and the associations it provided for them out of school hours, being under the superintendence of a regular family, would, in an especial manner, be favourable to their domestication.[15]

On leaving the charity schools the boys were to be sent out as apprentices and the girls were to enter domestic service. Inducements, such as amounts of cash to assist in clothing and the buying of tools, were to be offered. Hoyland pleaded equally with the Gypsies and with the sedentary population to accept this solution. The Gypsies had to accept a drastically altered way of life and the break-up of the family, and the settled members of society had to abandon their antipathy to employing Gypsies. To achieve any kind of lasting change, force necessarily had to be applied on the Gypsies and persuasion on the rest.

There remain three further published sources from this early period that evidenced the depth of concern among Christians. The first was by Samuel Roberts, and although he was writing at the same time as Hoyland his attitude to the Gypsies was markedly dissimilar.[16] He rejected the common image of the Gypsies as lawless vagrants, and instead showed a greater respect for their way of life and family ties. However, Roberts' desire to remain unconvinced by the arguments of his contemporaries on this subject led him to adopt a similarly extreme, though contrasting position. He saw them as 'more sinned against than sinning', and any crimes they committed were ultimately the responsibility of a settled society which forced the Gypsies into illegal activities partly by a hostile attitude which automatically treated them as criminal outsiders and also by approving legislation which made it a crime to put up a tent, graze a horse and build a fire. But even though Roberts admired them for their liberty and independence, and for the plain and simple life they pursued, he recognised their condition demanded amelioration. No less eager for their reformation and conversion to Christianity, he differed from other missionaries in his refusal to accept that force and compulsion were necessary to achieve these ends, favouring instead reciprocal feelings of love, confidence and gratitude.[17] This method, though, won few supporters and Roberts' writings and ideas never achieved the prominence that later evangelists accorded to Hoyland.

The two remaining published sources illustrating that the call for reform was very much alive, and in fact spreading out to the Gypsy camps, appeared, first, with the publication of a pamphlet by a clergyman of the Church of England, describing his missionary adventures with the Gypsies at York in the early 1820s.[18] Secondly, a letter proposing an alternative remedy to the Gypsy problem appeared in the *Wesleyan Methodist Magazine* in 1828.[19]

The York pamphlet described how a clergyman chanced upon a Gypsy encampment and having engaged the group in conversation then distributed religious tracts to them to be read aloud by those among their number who could read. He later came across another camp and, having again distributed bibles and tracts, gave a sermon and held a prayer-meeting. The aim of the narrative was to show the Gypsies in a more favourable light, not devoid of religious and moral feelings as was commonly supposed, but in fact 'ready and desirous for improvement'.[20] In their present condition they were useless to both the government and the country, and were injurious to its morals, and yet they wanted their own reform and were ready and able to accept any helping hand offered. The final call for reform worthy of note came from 'Scoto-Montanus'. In his letter to the *Wesleyan Methodist Magazine* he proposed that two or three small huts should be erected for Gypsies in each parish of England and Wales. The adults could then be put to work in fields or found other suitable employment, and their children could be apprenticed to trades and honest occupations. It was estimated that within two generations the Gypsies would be absorbed into the mass of the population.[21]

Although other calls for reform appeared in these years, these examples show the way in which the evangelistic movement gathered strength and provoked interest and comment. It can be seen that, with the sole exception of Samuel Roberts, the attitudes were harsh and single-minded in their determination to destroy the Gypsy way of life, by force if necessary. During these years of mounting concern Roberts provided the lone evangelical voice that respected the travelling life-style of the Gypsies. The remainder sought only to circumscribe and eventually eradicate the Gypsy and his way of life, seeing the problem from an evangelical, humanitarian and strictly conservative viewpoint. The dominant attitude was that the Gypsies had no religion or understanding of religious principles and morality and so had to be taught them. They had to be pulled from the poverty and degradation that characterised their existence and made into useful members of society, respectful of civil associations and order. On the whole the evangelists adopted the image of the Gypsy as a depraved outcast, without hope or comfort, unable and unwilling to escape from his low position and uncomfortable surroundings. This image, though, was subject to subtle variations, with some stressing the romantic 'natural' aspect of the travelling life, while others saw mainly the parasitic element. All, however, were agreed on the need for reform, to be achieved through forced settlement and religious education. The real work had to be done with the children as, to a large extent, the adults were beyond redemption. Reform, both in spirit and in practice, was intended to be oppressive and destructive of Gypsy traditions and ties.

The opening decades of the nineteenth century thus saw a growing evangelical call for the reformation of the Gypsies together with increasing efforts to provide information on a people about whom little was known or written. Grellmann, Hoyland and Roberts, the first writers to comment on Gypsy habits and ways of life and to speculate on their origin and language, were soon followed by others who, in a period of change, wrote about Gypsy life primarily to promote their own thoughts about the need for moral reform and stable social organisation. However, the early writers were faced with an extremely difficult task as centuries-old antipathy and ignorance towards this people had first to be broken down. The evangelists' call, although appealing also to humanitarian and conservative instincts, was heard by only a few. To the vast majority the Gypsies were either beyond hope or simply not worthy of time and consideration. Even so, a few beginnings were made into effecting a practical amelioration and reformation in the Gypsies' condition. The grandiose proposals for Gypsy stations throughout the country came to nothing more than a few minor efforts in this direction, all of which proved to be unsuitable and ineffective. The less ambitious plans for reform through education were relatively more successful.

The first practical attempt to educate Gypsy children, allegedly successful, appears to have taken place in Cambridge in 1810. A correspondent to the *Christian Observer* managed to persuade a Gypsy who had settled in the district for the winter to send his son to a new school established in the area.[22] The first account mentioned by Hoyland of Gypsies receiving education came from Thomas Howard, a Calvinist preacher and proprietor of a glass and china shop in Fetter Lane, London. In the winter of 1811 he had assisted in establishing a Sunday-school at Clapham, intended principally for the children of brickmakers, 'and the most abject of the poor'.[23] A Gypsy family named Cooper was lodged opposite to the school for the winter and a thirteen-year-old girl named Trinity applied for admission. Although turned down because she was a Gypsy she persevered and eventually gained entrance for herself and her two brothers. Howard commented that the Gypsy children were very attentive, and soon 'acquired habits of subordination, became tractable and docile'.[24] Both he and the children were sorry when, with the arrival of spring, the Gypsies left the area for their usual travels. This experiment acted as an inspiration to others, and Thomas Jackson, of Brixton-Row, minister of Stockwell Parish, admitted several Gypsy children to the sabbath school run under the direction of his congregation.[25] A final instance of Gypsy children receiving education in this period was held up as a fine example of the Gypsies' desire for improvement and of self-help. For four winters Uriah Lovell paid 6d. a week for each of his three children to attend a school for the Irish kept by Partak Ivery. Ivery confirmed that he had had six Gypsy children at his school, who, when placed among other children, were 'reducible to order'.[26] Some positive if tentative moves had thus been made to socialise the Gypsy children through the education system but, as yet, these remained sporadic and scattered.

Besides these largely insignificant educational efforts there was also the occasional excursions by missionaries into Gypsy camps, but again these did nothing more than merely scratch the surface of the reform problem. It was not until the Home Missionary Society and James Crabb at Southampton took up the problem that a more serious and long-term approach to the issue was adopted.

THE HOME MISSIONARY SOCIETY AND THE SOUTHAMPTON COMMITTEE

Although clergymen of the establishment, dissenting ministers and missionaries had undertaken occasional visits to Gypsy camps, it was not until 1820 when the Home Missionary Society took up the cause that the problem was approached in a more organised and deliberate fashion that contrasted with the spontaneous efforts of the early years.[27] The Committee of the Home Missionary Society had their attention drawn to the Gypsy problem by a letter from a Quaker woman from Bath, who urged the Society to take some action to reform the Gypsy people.[28] They responded by sending one sympathiser to the cause, the Reverend Cobbin, and one other who confessed his belief that reform was not possible, the Reverend Hyatt, to tour Cambridgeshire, Northamptonshire, Bedfordshire and neighbouring counties, in order to ascertain the present state and conditions of Gypsies. Both men returned dedicated to a mission they hoped would rescue a large section of the population considered destitute of moral and religious advantages. The Society denied that persecutions and prosecutions could have any positive effect, and instead called for visits to camp sites when in the neighbourhood and schooling for the children.

Again, the solution was thought to lie with educating the children away from their parents to the ways of settled society and persuading them to become apprenticed to a trade. It was recognised that two major obstacles worked against this plan. First, the expense, and secondly, the unwillingness on the part of Gypsy parents to part with their children. The Committee urged Christians of all beliefs to come forward to support this plan, but no such coordinated effort came about. Hyatt confessed sadly that few people cared sufficiently about the state of the Gypsies to take remedial action.[29] However, the H.M.S. remained committed to the cause and the pages of their journal, the *Home Missionary Society Magazine*, are sprinkled with references to the reform work undertaken in Gypsy camps by the roadside, especially

Hargreaves' work with the tent-dwellers in Gipsy Lane, Morcombelake.[30] Yet the work of the Home Missionaries could necessarily have limited effect as the meetings with the Gypsies were brief and only took place annually when the Gypsies revisited the missionaries' own stations. To combat this a Sub-Committee was set up in the late 1820s for the purpose of devoting full attention to Gypsy mission work. The first positive sign of success was that three Gypsies had been persuaded to settle in a town, six children had been put into an infants' school and one had become apprenticed to a carpenter.[31] Again, though, practical achievements were small. In order to find evidence of a more prolonged and continuous effort at the reformation of the Gypsies it is necessary to turn to James Crabb and the work of the Southampton Committee.[32]

Crabb's biographer, John Rudall, presented him as a man wholly in the grip of religion. His faith was his life and his mission was to encourage others to acquire it. He worked first of all with the prostitutes, poor, children, sailors and fishermen around Southampton, Romsey, Kingsland and Itching Ferry, being drawn towards these groups by a real concern for their moral well-being. Symptomatic of their spiritual condition was the general physical degeneracy and squalor found among this group, which Crabb sought to remedy by committed missionary endeavours. But whether from despair and resignation or perhaps because he was made aware of a group of people crying out even more urgently for the word of God to be given them, Crabb turned his attention to the 'outcasts and aliens from society, dwelling as heathens in a Christian land', the Gypsies.[33] The single most important event that caused Crabb to divert his attention from the working class poor of Southampton to a group of heathen travellers was the injustice and cruel treatment meted out to a Gypsy offender at Winchester Assizes in 1827. When two men were convicted of horse-stealing, the non-Gypsy was offered the hope of mercy, but when the Gypsy pleaded for his life the judge replied: 'No; you can have no mercy in this world: I and my brother judges have come to the determination to execute horse-stealers, *especially Gipsies* [my emphasis] because of the increase of the crime.'[34] To begin with Crabb took into his home two Gypsy children, whom he placed in an infant school. Following the death of one of the children the other was taken back from Crabb's care, and this, together with the alleged contempt shown by the other Gypsies to the women for giving up their children, must have caused Crabb to despair about his prospects of doing good with these people. He somehow managed to regain the Gypsies' confidence and a further three children were entrusted to him and again placed in the infant school. The parents of the children settled in a house in Southampton, the rent of which was paid by Crabb and a few friends.[35] These initial steps encouraged him to extend his work and a provisional committee was nominated on 12 November 1827, 'to take into serious consideration, without loss of time, the peculiar habits, character, and condition of the forlorn Gipseys; and to adopt such measures as might be considered best calculated to promote their general improvement'.[36] A Sub-Committee was immediately formed to collect information about the Gypsies, and a questionnaire was drawn up and sent out.[37] Although 12,000 copies were distributed to clergymen and laity throughout the country the appeal did not attract very wide attention, and nor did it bring in a large number of replies. The Sub-Committee bemoaned the lack of response in its Second Report, November 1828, and commented that it reflected a 'grievous unconcern' for the Gypsies.[38] Even so, Crabb was able to extract enough information to compile a book on the subject, and to drive him and his Committee onwards with their missionary endeavours.

Judging by the replies reprinted by Crabb and Rudall it seemed that very little had been done previously to ameliorate the Gypsy condition. Yet Crabb had support for his proposals, with the suggestion that the nobility and 'other classes of the higher orders' would subscribe to so worthy a venture.[39] Although unprepared to initiate any active steps towards the reform of the Gypsies, these classes of society appeared willing and ready to offer their moral and financial backing to such a programme. Others were more cynical, believing that reform could be achieved only by the compulsory domestication of the children, by bringing this 'idle, worthless set of wanderers' under the cognisance of the civil magistrate, or by first getting the Government to 'fix' or settle them.[40]

Crabb attempted to avoid the forceful and compulsory element. Although he shared with many of his contemporaries an abhorrence of the travelling way of life and the evil habits and characteristics it engendered, he did not think that forced settlement was the solution. Not only did reform have to be gradual to achieve any lasting effect but it also had to be voluntary. To force a Gypsy to settle in a town against his will was likely to create more problems than it would solve. Part of the difficulty here resulted from the nomadic disposition of the Gypsies which meant that the various members of the family would have been born in a number of different places. To return individuals to their place of origin would lead to a break-up of the family, something which was understandably wholly unacceptable to the Gypsies and which would have been strongly resisted. Moreover, unless they really wanted to settle with the necessary commitment to the ideals of a civilised and settled society, instilled in them by sound religious training, Crabb thought their morals stood in great danger of being more severely corrupted, 'and they would be capable of more extensive injury to society, should they take to their wandering habits again'.[41] The Gypsies' travelling way of life made the establishment of an institution such as a school of limited use, and in any case Crabb turned his back on any suggestion of forced teaching. He also believed that a travelling missionary was not the solution, not for reasons of potential success or failure by this method but because he thought such a task was personally inconvenient, expensive and 'highly improper'. A travelling life-style was considered as detrimental to the morals and character of the missionary as to the Gypsy and was offensive to all senses of decency even if the intentions were worthy.

In rejecting compulsion Crabb was adopting a long-term strategy, but before considering the methods proposed and practised by him and the Southampton Committee, it is necessary to bear in mind a few essential points. First, his moralistic fervour, high religious principles and complete disdain for the travelling way of life undoubtedly had a marked effect on his actions. Next, his attitude to, and impression of, the people on whom he focussed his attentions were of great importance in shaping his responses. Crabb saw the Gypsy way of life as one of poverty, hardship and deprivation, often in the most appalling material conditions. He related a story of a visit to a camp near Southampton and described in detail the physical discomforts of an outdoor life and the suffering imposed on the children. The mother of one of the families was a fortune-teller and 'swindler' and the father 'a most depraved character' who robbed from fences and folk and squandered his ill-gotten money on alcohol and extravagances.[42] Restraint, self-control and discipline were concepts Crabb believed were unknown to this people. But just as he was convinced of the immorality and irreligiosity of the Gypsies and the depraved and degrading conditions of their existence, so he was equally confident that they could be reformed if given the right encouragement and guidance.

To achieve this end the Committee proposed a general plan which they hoped would be adopted throughout the country, of engaging agents to make daily visits to the Gypsy camps, for the purpose of talking to the Gypsies, reading to them, and providing instruction for both adults and children. The emphasis was to be on the rising generation, but older groups were not to be ignored. Agents were to be found from among the 'lower orders' – pensioned soldiers and others – who had available time, could be hired cheaply and were said to be accustomed to the simple habits of the Gypsies. If every camp was visited daily, with some uniform plan of instruction being observed, then reform would speedily take place.[43] Testimonials on a card of good conduct were to be given them when about to move, to serve as an introduction to other persons interested in their reform in the next area in which they camped. Also, small financial donations were offered to discourage them from pilfering and to assist in paying rents and becoming apprenticed when they had the 'wisdom' to settle.[44] This aim of teaching the 'inconveniences, hazards and impropriety of a wandering life' was to be achieved by imbuing them with a sense of honesty and morality and instructing them in the Christian religion.[45] When this was achieved settlement would soon follow. Although Crabb avoided compulsion he did want to persuade the Gypsy parents to hand over their children to some philanthropist for education, and subsequently for sedentary employment. The erosion of family ties was to be eased by allowing the parents free access at any time to their children, and actively encouraging them to see their offspring at their studies when in the neighbourhood. This, then, was the theory, but what of the practice?

A concerted effort on a nationwide basis was a rather naive and optimistic plan, and although Crabb's work undoubtedly acted as an inspiration to others the reforming mission remained restricted to a few localities. However, the work of the Southampton Committee with the Gypsies of Southampton and the New Forest went ahead with enthusiasm. Crabb himself frequently visited the encampments in Hampshire offering the tent-dwellers advice, sympathy, practical help and religious instruction. A free school was opened by him which the Gypsy children were invited to attend, and he erected a mission hut and employed a lay teacher and preacher, at his own expense, for the adult Gypsies and poor of the district.[46] But it was soon decided that more assistance was needed and in 1828 the Sub-Committee appointed a man 'of Christian character' already acquainted with the Gypsies, Mr Cope, to visit their camps and give them instruction.[47] William Stanley, a settled Christian Gypsy, was also considered for employment as a visitor to the camps 'when the funds are adequate to pay the salary'.[48] These were soon forthcoming. Despite the absence of any great positive evidence of widespread reform the progress made was sufficient to encourage Crabb to extend his operations, and missionary work spread into the neighbouring counties, reaching a peak in May 1831 when Stanley and Crabb travelled over to preach to the Gypsies encamped on Epsom race course.[49]

Although the news of the work of the Southampton Committee was spreading far and wide, amongst both the travellers themselves and other interested groups, the event that brought Crabb and his mission into the public eye was the annual festival held for the Gypsies in the grounds of his house. The first was held in December 1829. Besides the Gypsies, the meetings were numerously attended by the gentry of the neighbourhood, and by persons from London and various parts of the country, who had a keen interest in the proceedings.[50] The Gypsies, numbering on average about 150, camped in a field adjoining Crabb's house. The meetings opened with hymns, prayers, Scripture readings and addresses, when Crabb attempted to persuade them of the advantages of industry and the blessings of social life. After the preaching came a meal, and the Gypsies, 'on this one day of the year, obtained a taste of the comforts of civilised life, and had an opportunity of contrasting its blessings with the miseries of a houseless, homeless, wandering life'.[51] After the meal blankets, clothing and bibles were distributed.[52] The meetings continued up to 1847 when Crabb was forced to discontinue his activities because of ill-health and old age. A final meeting, the nineteenth, was held in the grounds attached to the mansion of William

Betts in December 1848. The work of the Southampton Committee was then transferred over to the men who managed the Farnham Institution, discussed later.

An assessment of the relative success or failure of the work of Crabb and the Southampton Committee must necessarily depend on the criteria adopted. The aim of missionary work was clearly to encourage the Gypsies to settle, adopt the ways of settled society and be absorbed into the sedentary population. This was to be achieved, primarily, by the conversion of the Gypsies to Christian beliefs and practices. This provides a clear example of the common interest between the evangelists and the upholders of the new morality of the emergent industrial society, well illustrated in the following:

It was a leading object in every arrangement to endeavour *gradually* to overcome their early, deep-rooted habits of restlessness, sloth, and inactivity, and the evils arising from *gratuitous* charity, by stimulating them to Industrious and provident habits, and inducing them to contribute small weekly deposits out of their earnings for their future maintenance and clothing; thus raising the tone of *self-exertion*, and giving suitable encouragement when their personal efforts entitled them to some testimony of approbation [original emphases].[53]

Testimony to the shared ideals and objectives between the evangelists and the new town bourgeoisie is provided by the large amount of cash raised by subscription by the Committee, estimated to have totalled more than £20,000 for the period from when Crabb came to Southampton to the end of his ministry.[54] The figure may have been inaccurate, or even exaggerated, but the implication remains the same. But the question still to be answered is the extent to which it was money well spent, or rather invested.

It is difficult to establish the truth behind the various claims for the success or failure of the mission work owing to the obvious bias of the sources. The pro-Gypsy lobby and evangelists clearly wished to illustrate the great advances being made as a result of their endeavours. Consider, for example, the following quotation from the *Home Missionary Magazine*:

[Crabb] . . . proved them to be as teachable, to be as capable of learning trades, of being good labourers, work people, and servants – as steady, honest, and deserving, as the poor of any other class in the kingdom; and he has shown that more extended means alone are wanting to remove the great moral stain from among us, of having a heathen population in a Christian land.[55]

Those retaining a fundamental antipathy to the Gypsies held on to a strong cynicism about the claims made. The reports of the Southampton Committee, and its Sub-Committee, were full of references to the number of children being educated at Crabb's school, to those apprenticed to various trades, and to the families who had ceased to make the lanes and commons their home in preference for a permanent home and employment in Southampton and the neighbourhood.[56] For example, in the first year of the mission, six children had been settled at infant school, and by the following year were said to have 'exchanged their restlessness of body and unfixedness of mind for habits of attention and self-control'.[57] By the middle of 1829, twenty adults and children were said to be under moral and religious instruction, six women were settled in Southampton and were seeking employment, four boys were apprenticed to various trades and a number of small children were at school.[58] After five years of almost continuous persuasion forty-six Gypsies had been tempted away from their vagrant habits in favour of a settled state of domestication.

However, although some had taken to various employments, ranging from shoemaking and making Gloucester boots to charring, washing and mangling, this picture of apparent success is somewhat misleading. Of these forty-six, only twenty remained in Southampton for any length of time, with the rest either returning to the travelling way of life, entering service, removing to another town, travelling in the summer, or dying.[59] Furthermore, it seems to be the case that many of the twenty were women and children, being tempted to settle through the death, imprisonment or transportation of their husbands. Travelling was possible, but hard, without an adult male to assist in the bread-winning. Also, the long-term achievements of education and settlement are suspect, with the suggestion that the Gypsies adopted different faces for different people and circumstances, and even the reformed and educated children almost all returned to their old wandering life.[60] Finally, it was even alleged that the settled Gypsy adults mostly turned out more criminal and unhappy than their travelling brethren.[61]

Crabb's claim that the Gypsies' minds had become more enlightened and their characters more religious as a result of the evangelistic preaching is also difficult to substantiate. Attendance at the annual meetings was certainly not through any religious conviction and it was highly improbable that many, if any, came away converted to the Christian faith. The attendance of the Gypsies would have been based far more on pragmatic self-interest. Friends and relatives could be met in a convivial atmosphere, free from the worry of harassment from the authorities, and the prospect of free food and clothing acted as an additional incentive. Where the mission work and annual meetings may have succeeded was in drawing the attention of outsiders to the need for reform, showing that it was both desirable and possible, and by advertising that the presence of Gypsies need not necessarily be synonymous with dirt, squalor, depredations and petty crime. It is also possible that the constant entreaties of the missionaries persuaded the Gypsies away from excessive thieving and a general change in their habits. It was said that some had developed into steady, respectable workmen who treasured the bible, and whose morals were greatly improved.[62] The settled Gypsies soon lost all vestiges of their travelling way of life and were so keen to reject and forget their past that they even declined to attend the annual meetings, their presence being intended by Crabb to act as an example to others.[63] In fact, at one of the meetings Mr Sturges Bourne stated that in his long experience as a magistrate he had never known a quarter session or assizes held in the county in which there was not a Gypsy among the prisoners, but since the labours of Crabb and his associates there had not been one of them up for trial.[64]

Again, though, these claims, and the assertion that Gypsies had reformed their manners and ways as reflected in their absence from the courts, have to be treated with some reservations. Consider the following:

The magistrates, county gentlemen, and farmers, in the neighbourhood of Mr. Crabbe's (sic) gipsy colony, complain bitterly of the effects of his benevolent scheme – affirming that it subjects them to the perpetual depredations of swarms of vagrants of all sorts, and that the good man himself is the dupe of nine-tenths of these persons, who allow him for a time to reckon them among his reformed gipsies.[65]

It seems that for every claim there is a counter-claim. Crabb's belief that news of his labours had spread among the Gypsies seems positive evidence of the good being done until it is realised, as commented by Stanley, that the Gypsies at the Epsom races were under serious misconceptions as to the actual nature of the missionary work.[66] The question of the success or failure of the mission therefore has to remain unsolved, a casualty of unreliable and misleading sources. Crabb and his Committee were intent on advertising their achievements, however small, while the cynics and critics not only challenged the extent of the alleged successes but also saw them as hollow victories, with the Gypsies again deceiving the missionary by guile and deception in order to gain some immediate benefit or advantage.

If the attempt to reform the Gypsies had, at best, a limited effect then perhaps the influence of Crabb and the Southampton Committee should be sought in another direction, through the inspiration it provided to other evangelists. Following the example of the Southampton Mission, and as a result of the direct entreaties of Crabb, similar missions were commenced in earnest by the Reverend John Baird in Kirk Yetholm, by the Reverend John West at Chettle in Dorsetshire and then at Farnham, and by the London City Mission.

THE MISSIONARY ENDEAVOUR GATHERS MOMENTUM: KIRK YETHOLM

Baird's mission for the reform of the Gypsy population was centred on those who lived, at least for a part of the year, at Kirk Yetholm in Roxburghshire. There is no satisfactory account of how or when they came to settle though one estimate stated they had been there for three centuries.[67] By the nineteenth century they had become firmly established, living on Tinklers

11 The Gypsy dwellings and encampment at Kirk Yetholm in Scotland, the scene of
the reforming mission of the Reverend John Baird.

Row in houses with long-term leases.[68] In 1818 they were said to number fifty
persons, increasing to one hundred and twenty-six by 1862.[69]

They used to be known either as the tinklers, or tinkers, of Yetholm owing
to the men going about the area mending pots and other utensils, or as the
'Horners', from their occupation of making and selling horn spoons called
'lutties'. By the 1830s they had come to be called the 'muggers' or 'potters',
derived from the habit of buying faulty articles from the potteries of Staffordshire, which they then hawked chiefly around Northumberland and the
Border counties.[70] They were also known to assist with the reaping, and to
collect and sell rags and bones, old iron and broken crystal, as well as making
heather baskets, pitchers, fishing-tackle and besoms, which were sold by the
women alongside needles, thread, trinkets and other smallwares.[71] The
variety and nature of employments was said to be progressive, starting off in
youth by selling besoms and baskets and saving money to buy an ass and
cart, from which earthenware and other items could be hawked. Following a
period of relative prosperity the Yetholm Gypsies then slipped back into
poverty and wretchedness with old age. In the first part of the century this
emphasis on itinerancy occupied around eight months of the year, with the
Gypsies returning to their homes for the hard winter months.[72]

Even before the evangelist reformers had got to them they were said to be
much intermixed with the natives of the country and other wanderers, and
had even established other colonies in Kelso, Jedburgh and Coldstream.[73] Yet

their conditions of existence and way of life still marked them off from the sedentary-orientated householder and when on their travels they were condemned for causing an inevitable nuisance to landowners and the police. Similarly, their sedentary existence, even though this was the desired objective of the reformers, was also much criticised. Their homes, for example, were said to be generally poor, sparsely furnished and inferior to those of the ordinary day labourers.[74] Although there were times, such as the Shrovetide football game, when the Gypsies mixed freely with the rest of the villagers, for the most part their different ways of life kept the two groups apart.[75] On at least one occasion following the game the latent hostility erupted when the locals turned against the 'muggers', causing them to barricade themselves inside their houses to avoid the likelihood of violent and physical assaults. Relations were at best strained and below a thin line of tolerance lay a generally felt antipathy to the inhabitants of Tinklers Row.[76]

They were resented for their alleged propensities to thieving, poaching and 'blackguardism', and, added to these, were said to be prone to excessive drunkenness, brawling, idleness and allegedly had the ability to undermine the morals and industry of the neighbourhood.[77] Some commentators found particular cause for complaint against the male Gypsies who were accused of performing only the lightest of work, never 'draining, or digging, or plough-ing', and by leaving the womenfolk to carry heavy armfuls of goods from door to door they constituted a 'positive affront to manliness'.[78] A major part of the responsibility for their poor character was attributed not to race or blood but to itinerancy:

Their wandering . . . exposes them to many peculiar temptations, idleness and rapine lead them frequently into scenes of mischief and wickedness, and necessarily leave them ignorant, uneducated and uncivilised. Withdraw them therefore from this mode of life . . . and you save them from innumerable evils, and probably render them valuable members of society.[79]

Any benefits accruing to the travellers from their temporary winter settlement were negated by their insistence on taking to the roads again throughout the summer. Baird intended to break this tradition.

He was appointed minister of the parish of Yetholm in the spring of 1829. Although clearly aware of the Gypsy presence and problem in Kirk Yetholm, the early years of his ministry were marked more by improving the physical appearance of the two towns (Kirk and Town Yetholm) than effecting any reform among the tinklers. Yet it was not long before his priorities turned, seeking to reclaim the Gypsies from their vagabond habits and, through the educating and civilising effect of Christianity, transforming them into 'useful' members of society.[80] Again we can see the justification for persecution and control deriving from a concept of 'social citizenship' which divided society not in terms of class but according to their productive economic potential.

Baird viewed the problem in a similar way to Crabb, borrowed the same explanations, offered the same solutions, and likewise found the financial backing to put his proposals into practice. Both men shared the popular antipathy to Gypsies and to itinerancy then current among evangelists and those classes of society most concerned with the ideological, spiritual and moral welfare of the population as a whole. These latter groups were prepared to offer financial assistance not merely from evangelistic motives but from a desire to curb the excesses of a society which they sought to make increasingly efficient by enforcing regularity and conformity with their own image of how it should develop.

Baird's motives and standpoint are clear, betraying a keenness to expose the romanticism that surrounded these people as being a plethora of lies and mythical fantasy. He was unable to find any redeeming features in the people or their way of life and described them as a set of worthless, unprofitable, deceitful and dishonest vagabonds who hated all work and pursued only those occupations which covered and excused their idleness. In his opinion, they preferred to want rather than work and steal rather than want, they lacked any religious knowledge or principle, and were poor, ragged and dirty.[81] Baird was disturbed that such a situation had been allowed to carry on unchecked, accusing the community and magistrates of timidity and indifference for not preventing the Gypsy-travellers from wandering freely about the countryside.[82]

From the beginning Baird was prepared to use coercion to enforce his vision. He sought prohibitions against camping, selling without a licence, selling goods not of the Gypsies' own manufacture and even their own goods except in public markets and such places. He expressed grave doubts that the problem could be effectively resolved without the legislature imposing restraints and prohibitions upon the Gypsies' wandering habits and offering them encouragements to settle. Baird shared the popular assertion that the present state of affairs was believed to rest with the Gypsies' way of life rather than with the people themselves. That is, a cultural not a racial argument:

All their peculiar vices . . . are obviously traceable to their wandering life. This engenders idleness, ignorance, poverty, a fierce lawless temper, and to what crimes and evils will not these lead? They have so many opportunities, when unobserved, of indulging their thievish propensities, that they are bold and unblushing in the practice. Unaccustomed to any kind of control or restraint, but that exerted over them by superior strength, their passions, when excited, are fierce and ungovernable, and on such occasions they are addicted to the use of awfully profane language.[83]

This, and their cunning and revengefulness, made them, according to Baird, feared, hated, shunned and persecuted. In short, they were little better than 'demi-savages'; they were, indeed, 'a lawless nomadic horde'.[84]

Essentially, Baird's remedy was to encourage the Gypsies to settle, with the bulk of the persuasion again being directed at the children as the habits of wandering were thought to be too deeply ingrained in the adults to effect any significant reformation. In a letter to Crabb, written in December 1830, Baird commented that on the whole the Gypsies expressed a desire for the education of their children and settled homes and jobs for themselves. The parents were said to be willing to leave their children at home during the summer while they travelled, and that they should be trained for some trade. For themselves, they admitted a willingness to remain in their settled abodes if they could be assured of constant employment.[85] Baird's plan was to prevent the children from travelling with their parents, to send them to school and 'otherwise to attend to their temporal comfort and religious improvement'.[86] While their parents were absent the children were to remain in their own homes if they had a suitable person to look after them, or else were to be boarded with other families in the village. It was hoped that by this method they would be unwilling or physically incapable of following the wandering life of their parents. Furthermore, through their children and the closeness of family ties and the offer of regular employment, it was hoped the parents may also be persuaded to settle.

Such a plan needed considerable funding in order to pay the school fees, a salary to the teacher, an apprentice fee for boys and lodging expenses. It was estimated that at least £100 a year was needed but not until 1838–9, when a Society was formed in Edinburgh under the patronage of the Scottish Church for the purpose of 'The Reformation of the Gipsies in Scotland', did such funds become available. Although the intention was to reform all the Gypsies in Scotland it was decided to try out the experiment first on those at Kirk Yetholm. The responsibility for the task fell entirely on Baird's shoulders, and the First Report of the Committee elected by the Society acknowledged that they were 'little else than collectors for him of the pecuniary contributions necessary for his assistance'.[87] This they continued to do for many years, but with a gradual falling off in subscriptions in the period from early 1850 up to the death of Baird in November 1851, perhaps due to the realisation that the expenditure was not being justified by the results. Even when this happened Mr Baillie, a Committee member, paid the greater part of the expenses from his own pocket until his death around 1859. This event proved to be the final blow to the Committee and it broke up immediately. After 1861, when the work was carried on by the minister who succeeded Baird, expenses were paid by friends to the cause who lived in the neighbourhood and by a grant of £100 from the Ferguson Fund.

Baird's work was made undoubtedly easier by the guarantee of a constant supply of funds, and also by the fact that the Gypsies already had their own permanent homes in Kirk Yetholm, but he still recognised that there were some stiff barriers which needed to be overcome. Firstly, there was the problem of the general antipathy felt towards the Gypsies. This made aid, sympathy and cooperation difficult to obtain from neighbours and other villagers. Townspeople were reluctant to employ Gypsies or to take in their children as lodgers when their parents were away travelling, and the village children expressed an unwillingness to sit by the Gypsies or otherwise associate with them at school. Secondly, Baird had to contend with the Gypsies themselves, whom he saw as greedy, unreasonable, dissatisfied, deceitful and jealous. Finally, when they could be persuaded to settle it was immediately apparent that in comparison with their fellow-workers they had few or no clothes, tools or furniture. Engaged in the same work as other villagers they were a long way, materially, behind their nearest point of reference. It was realised that dissatisfaction could result from this experience of inequality, prompting a return to the roads. Some financial assistance was therefore necessary to facilitate the transition but all the while taking care that no challenge was made to the guiding principle that rewards waited upon a life of industry, honesty and virtue.

By February 1839 Baird was approached by the first Gypsy family willing to leave their children in his care. One of the barriers had been surmounted but the next proved, at least initially, more difficult. No family in the district had been persuaded to take in the children on any terms, and Baird had no alternative but to house them himself. Within about ten days, though, offers reached him from villagers who had changed their minds, and after that initial stumble he had no further difficulties in accommodating the children left behind. By 1841 five Gypsy children had been taken on as apprentices or servants or were engaged elsewhere in the locality and forty were attending school. Of these, seven to ten had been boarded out at a cost to the Committee of 2s. 6d. a week and the rest remained in their own homes with someone hired to look after them.[88]

Baird then had to face the next obstacle, namely that the parochial school did not have the room or facilities for a large influx of Gypsy children, thus rendering useless the freedom of choice given to the parents as to which school they wanted to send their children. As a result, by October 1842 a new school house had been erected and was ready for use. Every Gypsy child who was capable of attending the school did so, with two exceptions, and Baird was urgently making preparations for them all to remain at home throughout the year. His success or failure in this venture was not noted. Over the years the number of Gypsy children at school fluctuated between about twenty-five and forty, and it was stated that by the end of March 1839, twenty-six of these remained in Kirk Yetholm while their parents went off on their travels.[89] The sabbath school, opened in 1844, was attended by similar numbers. The aim was to reinforce the work done in the day schools by ensuring the children were given constantly to understand that in return for all that was being done for them they were never to follow in the footsteps of their parents but were instead to be trained for some settled employment. The effectiveness of these efforts was greatly diminished when the numbers at both day and Sunday schools decreased, largely the result of the attempt by the Committee to enforce parental responsibility upon the Gypsy adults by demanding from them payment for fees, clothing and maintenance. Some responded to this by cutting back on their travels, returning home more often to see and care for their children, and by shortening their itinerant season to be at home in the autumn when they were able to assist in harvesting.

The second part of the Committee's plan, to persuade the adults to settle and adopt regular employments, met with even less encouraging results. The Report for 1842 noted that 'the success hitherto has been next to an entire failure'.[90] Some had tried to settle but soon returned to their wanderings because few were disposed to employ them. By 1846 some gains had been made with four families leaving their travels to become settled and regularly employed, yet if the men found themselves even temporarily out of work the temptation to return to travelling was very strong.

An awareness of this led Baird to restate his belief that reform could be achieved only if evangelism was accompanied by legislative coercion. He called for the magistrates of the various counties to combine and adopt every means in their power to control the movements of the tribe.[91] Their response was to prosecute all those who camped by the roadside and lit fires at night, and strictly to enforce the laws requiring hawkers to possess licences.[92] At first the Gypsies avoided such harassment by moving into lodging houses but soon found this to be prohibitively expensive over long periods. They then took to narrower circuits, returning to their homes each night. The effect was to crowd the district and its potential market, causing the younger and stronger to look for other work, chiefly labouring, and so leaving the travelling to the more elderly. Such actions and modifications to their life-style were the clear result of the pressure imposed by rigorous policing.

The Reverend Adam Davidson took over Baird's work in 1861 and by 1864 he was able to report that there were only six nomadic Gypsy families left in the village, and even their children were attending school. Moreover, they were not only settling but were intermarrying with the villagers and working in service or at day labour like any other inhabitant of the village, many taking to farm labouring.[93] In short, they were becoming less distinct as a minority group and were being absorbed gradually into village life. It would seem that over twenty years of practical mission work, providing education and inducements to settle, had had some effect. But whether the gradual turn away from an itinerant to a sedentary existence was due to their religious reformation or to the fact that itinerant occupations no longer provided the sort of income necessary to maintain an adequate level of subsistence and to the increased efforts of the magistracy to curb travelling, must remain open to question.[94] On balance Baird and Davidson can be said to have been met with not inconsiderable success, in contrast to Crabb's work at Southampton, although the semi-settled state of the Gypsies and the pressures on itinerancy from other directions would appear to have been more instrumental than evangelist missionary activities in effecting settlement.

A rather less successful scheme, but one which was similarly inspired by the work of James Crabb, was undertaken by yet another evangelist reformer, John West, in the region of Chettle in Dorset.[95]

West was so impressed with the objectives and activity of Crabb at Southampton that in 1842 he erected two cottages in his parish of Chettle (Dorset) in each of which he placed a Gypsy family.[96] An acre of ground was provided for each family for cultivation and the children were placed in the local school. The most immediate problem West had to meet was local opposition, with the townspeople objecting both to the introduction of a 'nuisance' to the neighbourhood,[97] and to the likelihood of the mixing of the Gypsy children with their own in the schools. This prompted West into thinking in terms of a school built exclusively for Gypsy children.

His first step towards making this a reality was to issue a pamphlet entitled *A Plea for Educating the Children of the Gypsies*, which he dedicated to the M.P., Lord Ashley, and to the local nobility, gentry and magistrates.[98] At the beginning, the proposed school was to provide for the education and maintenance of twenty-four orphan Gypsy children under six years of age, or boys and girls of the same age from the largest and most destitute Gypsy families. Also, benevolent persons were called upon to 'sponsor' Gypsy children at a cost of about £5 per year. Plans were submitted to the government along with an application for a grant, which was approved and £100 donated.[99] Lord Ashley consented to be the patron of the scheme and the list of subscribers included parliamentarians, clergy and nobility. By December 1844 West was able to write that the fund had reached almost £500, and with the donations from Lord Ashley and others this had increased to £1,200 within twelve months.[100] A site was obtained at Farnham and on 24 July 1845 the foundation stone of the Farnham Gipsy Asylum and Industrial School was laid by the elderly Gypsy evangelist from Southampton, William Stanley.

Work on the school was slow, however, and with the death of West in December 1845 it lost much of its momentum. By the middle of the following year the Farnham Committee, which was to take over the work of the Southampton Committee in 1847, called a meeting to discuss ways of ensuring its completion. Although the asylum was eventually opened on 5 October 1847, with six Gypsy children in attendance, it never really flourished. The Committee found it difficult to find and keep staff and at least three schoolmistresses ran the school during its eight-year life-span. The local residents were suspicious and it was never significantly supported by the Gypsies themselves. By 1854 only forty-six children had been admitted in seven years and of these only five remained. In 1855 the decision was taken to close the school and the money received was to be used as a salary for a new missionary.[101] The first Gypsy school thus came to an ignominious end and even the handful of children educated there mostly drifted back into the travelling way of life.

By the mid-1850s the first wave of Gypsy evangelism appears to have tailed off. Crabb had died and the Southampton Committee had passed over responsibility, the Baird mission was suffering financial and other difficulties, and the Farnham School had closed, through a mixture of opposition and apathy. Moreover, the achievements of these early years had been small. Some Gypsies had been settled, some educated and some converted, but no great change had been effected with any great numbers. Yet the missionary movement continued, undaunted by these failures. The London City Mission, Alder at Chobham, and various missions with the New Forest Gypsies and in the hop fields, took up the banner.

MISSIONS IN THE METROPOLIS

One of Crabb's final appeals before he died was to the London City Mission, requesting they take up the Gypsy cause. This they did, but not on the lines already drawn up by Crabb and others. They considered the absorption of Gypsies into sedentary society by a policy of coercion would result only in increasing the urban slum problem. Instead, they sought to convert and educate the Gypsies and eliminate such 'vices' as gambling, drinking, brawling and fiddling, by going among the people with a bible grasped firmly in their hands.[102] Their missionaries visited encampments in most areas of the city and social gatherings were arranged in nearby halls offering bible readings, free teas, and 'short discourses of a simple character'.[103] One such party, at Notting Hill, survived for at least twenty years and was attended by up to 200 Gypsies.[104] In contrast with the earlier missionary endeavours less emphasis was placed on settling the Gypsies and persuading them of the benefits of 'useful toil' and rather more on their moral and spiritual reformation, suggesting a purer evangelism than had previously appeared.

Direct attempts were also made to secure the education of Gypsy children in and around London, and they were known to be in attendance at a variety of day, evening and missionary schools in the district of Notting Hill and the Kensington potteries. Towards the end of the century the Ragged School Union joined in the work and Mr Dyer, Superintendent of the Union, and nine voluntary workers opened up a mission for the Battersea van-dwellers in a railway arch, known as the Gipsies Hall, which was apparently very well attended in the evenings and on Sundays.[105] A partition separated it from a blacksmith's forge and D. L. Woolmer has graphically described the scene:

Despite the fact that smoke from the bellows will creep through crevices and contend for the mastery with the whitewash, despite cracks in the wooden wall and peep-holes which young rascals have bored through the other, despite the lack of numerous conveniences generally regarded as essential to any educational establishment, the place attracts overflowing numbers.[106]

The reasons for its success were partly due to the magic lantern shows held at 6 p.m. on Sundays, such a novelty then being a great attraction, but more importantly success was achieved because this was the one place where the Gypsy-travellers were guaranteed a welcome devoid of patronising paternalism. The Union also held tea parties at the Shaftesbury Welcome, Doddington Grove, near to the largest encampment.[107] Again the meetings seemed popular with the Gypsies and around 200 were said to attend.[108]

There is some evidence to suggest that a few Gypsies were won over by the words of the missionaries and abandoned such past sins as fortune-telling, fiddling and drinking, in favour of wholehearted commitment to Christianity. Some even became evangelists themselves and a small colony were to be found on Wanstead flats in the early 1890s, though they preached not to fellow-travellers but to the settled population.[109] The same was true of perhaps the most famous Gypsy evangelist of them all, 'Gipsy' Rodney Smith, whose conversion led him to turn his back on his former way of life while also exploiting its appeal by retaining the title of 'Gipsy' to give himself notoriety and publicity.[110] The other achievements of such missionary work, which had begun around mid-century and continued throughout the period under review and after, were of a much more general and less obviously spectacular nature. More Gypsies were said to attend religious services in the locality of their camps, many were now said to have proper Christian weddings, and others joined the Rescue (Temperance) Society.[111]

To balance against this, scorn was levelled at the missionaries' attempts 'to wash away the Gypsies' sins with tea', for although they may have been forced to listen to sermons and bible-readings, this by no means indicated inward and spiritual acceptance.[112] Moreover, the attempts of a group of people, said to be 'conceited and unpleasant', to persuade the Gypsies to give up tents, beer, tobacco and music were likely to have little effect. Francis Groome commented thus on the Gypsies' response: 'It would be amusing if they [the missionaries] could hear all that is said as soon as their backs are turned.'[113] Once again the actual extent of their achievements must remain open to question.

NEW FOREST GOOD SAMARITAN CHARITY, STANLEY ALDER AT CHOBHAM AND HOPPING MISSIONS

The New Forest, in Hampshire, was another major centre where Gypsies were subjected to a concerted missionary drive. Begun by Crabb, the endeavours continued throughout the period. In the 1880s and 1890s a missionary and his wife spent a good deal of time among the tent-dwellers, teaching them cleanliness, providing food and clothing, and instructing the children in reading and religion.[114] The achievements were small and gradual, but some Gypsies were persuaded to marry in church and others were talked into settling in houses.[115] This evangelistic zeal even affected an aged Colonel who lived near to the Forest, who attempted to bribe Gypsy girls into having Christian marriages by offering a gold wedding ring to any about to marry in this way. He did not account for 'Gypsy cunning' though, and some girls succeeded in getting two or three rings each while still remaining unwed.[116] Nonconformist ministers also held gospel meetings near to the Forest, though these were said to attract villagers and stragglers rather than '*bona-fide* Gipsies'.

This ran alongside the most serious and prolonged effort to reform the Gypsies of the Forest by the New Forest Good Samaritan Charity, set up in 1888–9.[117] The Charity offered spiritual assistance, practical help and instruction as to the benefits of a settled life. The success of their attempts at religious conversion cannot easily be estimated, though by 1909 they had encouraged over forty couples to marry in the orthodox fashion. Their practical aid was of more direct value. In the first ten years the Charity had provided fifty families with parcels of warm clothing, supplied two families with ponies and four with hawkers' licences, and several with money to assist them on their journey to the hop fields.[118] Their greatest claims concerned the number of Gypsies they had persuaded to adopt a sedentary way of life. The 10th Annual Report of the Charity claimed to have decreased the number of Gypsies living in the Forest by more than three-quarters. Eighteen families had been placed in cottages and ninety children had been clothed and sent to school, eleven boys had joined the militia and four girls had gone into domestic service. The rent was paid for those in the cottages, and they were given a weekly supply of groceries, tea and tobacco.[119] Some, though, soon returned to their former way of life. Priscilla Sherred, aged ninety years, only remained within the confines of a house for a short time. She explained: 'I couldn't abide that 'ere roof over my 'ed. I couldn't bide it no hows. If I'd a stopt there another day I should a died.'[120] However, others did remain and 'good employments', that is, sedentary employments, were found for the boys and fathers, and they were soon paying their own rents and earning an honest living.

The intentions and methods are very clear. By friendly advice and practical assistance the Gypsies were gradually pulled away from their tent life and into a *gorgio* existence. This antipathy to travelling underpinned the missionaries' work and objectives, and was made explicit in the 10th Report when Gypsy life was equated with that of the nomadic, thievish tramp, and was a way of life that 'should be made impossible'.[121] By regular contact with sedentary friends the Gypsy children were shown the comforts of house-living in stark contrast with the harshness and discomfort of tent life. Yet the reasons for settlement cannot be solely, or even chiefly, ascribed to the moderate success of this tactic and the work of the Charity. There were a number of forces in operation which gradually persuaded the Gypsies to move out of the Forest, the most important of these being economic and legal.[122]

One further individual remains to be named for his work with the Gypsies. Stanley Alder, a Home Missionary, was one of the teachers at the Farm and Shaftesbury Schools at Bisley, having responsibility for missionary work with the large numbers of Gypsies who camped each year at Lucas Green and Folly, Chobham. Alder had for some time visited their tents and conversed with them on religious subjects, though the mission proper was not begun until August 1881, with the first report on the work covering the period 1881–2.[123]

Alder and his fellow-workers were not blind to the immensity of the task which they faced. In short, he viewed the Gypsies as heathen, ignorant and wretched, for they played pitch and toss on Sundays, their children were in a dirty and wretched condition, they used the 'basest' language, misery and vice were prevalent and 'pernicious habits and corrupt influence' were rampant. The objectives and methods of the mission followed the familiar pattern. The aim was to change their habits and way of life by conversion and settlement and the method was by holding meetings and offering financial assistance to compensate the pecuniary difficulties of setting up a permanent home and adopting sedentary customs and employments.[124] The mission was said to have had the moral and financial support of the local clergy, gentry and of all classes and creeds, and the local press consistently recommended the mission work to their readers.[125] But there was also a strong body of local opposition which resented the encouragement given in bringing unruly, disreputable and dishonest Gypsies to the area.[126] Antipathy was shown by the scarcity of employment and homes for those who had decided to settle: 'If he wants a house the name of a Gipsy, or a man from tents, shuts the door against him.'[127] In 1891–2 this opposition was taken to its logical and inevitable conclusion. That winter saw the influx to the encampments of some twelve to fourteen vans and tents, eight or so more than usual, composed allegedly of an unlawful group of travellers who broke up hedges and quarrelled and fought with the villagers. While legal steps were being taken to remove them, a gang of youths decided to take the matter into their own hands and went in and broke up the camp and herded the tent-dwellers from the neighbourhood. Alder's work with the Gypsies was thus brought to an abrupt end.

The mission did not cease without having first registered some small successes, and Alder provided a concise summary of his work in the Report for 1889–90:

Ten years ago, only 3 out of 18 families could read even a little; no one cared to go to teach them God's message of love; the encampments were indeed awful dens of vice and blasphemy; the nights were hideous with their quarrels; their habits degraded. Now we have four tents at the Folly, where ten years ago there were 14; and four at Lucas Green, where there were from four to eight 10 years ago. Those families we placed in cottages eight years since never want to go back to tents. Some of the children who went to school have begun life for themselves, but prefer the cottage life to tent. We have five families now in cottages in this parish, and the children going to schools.[128]

In all, Alder had persuaded eight families to take up residence in cottages, though the employments of the men still bore the signs of their past, itinerant lives. One was a chimney-sweep, another a beehive-maker, while many of the other families still relied on seasonal labour and left their homes in the summer to begin the circuit of pea-picking, hay and harvest work and hop-picking. A few Gypsies attended Night Schools for the Improvement of Young Men in West End, and others attended the Penny Readings held at the West End and the Farm School, Bisley. However, Alder was forced to admit that, on the whole, the spiritual results were less encouraging than moral reform.[129] In terms of numbers settled and converted the success was again decidedly on a small scale.

It is evident, then, that the efforts of Alder and his associates were just one further evangelical attempt to reform the Gypsies to both the spiritual and secular ways of the majority. When on their travels they were met by local clergy who ministered to their religious needs, while more concerted attempts were made in the camps and van-towns of a more permanent nature.[130] The Gypsies met with the evangelists at race-meetings, and their seasonal migration to the hop fields in September was matched by an exodus of evangelist missionaries to the same places.[131]

For some individuals and agencies, such as the Church of England Missionary Association, the Hop-Picking Mission Committee, the London Oratory and the Church Army Mission, the evangelical drive was directed at the spiritual needs of all the hoppers, with no special emphasis on the Gypsies.[132] Others, though, saw this guaranteed gathering of large numbers of Gypsies, tied to one place for at least a couple of weeks, as a supreme opportunity for attempting their reform. Crabb and his fellow-worker, Stanley, were perhaps the first to grasp at this chance, visiting the Gypsy hoppers at Farnham in the autumn of 1830, distributing tracts and moral and spiritual advice. A public meeting was often held after the day's labours when God's words were related to the tired and hungry pickers. The London City Mission also looked to the hop fields, and the Annual Report for 1859 of one of their workers stated that he had made 1,017 visits to the Gypsy hoppers at Farnham, Surrey, and Kent, to the races and fairs, and had distributed 1,088 tracts and 127 readings of the Scriptures.[133] However, it was the mission work of Samuel Chinn that is deserving of most attention.[134]

Chinn began his work in about 1861 with the Gypsies who flocked to the Hampshire hop districts. He shared the common evangelical view of the Gypsy as a filthy and degenerate outcast and set about his reformation not by regular services but by going amongst them while they worked, being careful to make sure he helped to fill their bins whilst he talked. Gradually others joined him in his work, among them John Farley of the London City Mission. With more people setting about the task the visits became more extensive and regular. Camp meetings were held and open air services took place on Sundays. In time, the idea of a permanent mission tent superseded the more informal one-to-one conversion process of the earlier days. Although some opposition was expressed at the idea of having a tent containing 500 or so 'wild and lawless' people being erected in the hopping district at Binstead, Chinn went ahead with the scheme. Free tea was offered after work to entice the Gypsies away from the public house and into the mission tent. This proved to be a very popular meeting place and so it was decided to erect another at Selbourne, which met with an equally favourable response from the Gypsies. This was followed by another at Worldham, and then at Bentley, the latter despite the fact that a farmer offered £50 for it not to go up, as he feared it would become a centre for quarrelling and fighting. Although it was believed that the roughest class of pickers frequented the tent at Bentley, the farmer's fears proved groundless. In 1880 a tent was erected at Holybourne, to be soon followed by one at Wyck, making six in total, employing a total of about twelve to fifteen missionaries, with an annual expenditure of around £300.

The majority opinion seemed to be that Chinn and his fellow-missionaries had achieved a remarkable change among the Gypsies in the twenty-six years of their work. They found unqualified praise in the *Nonconformist*, the *Christian*, and *Word and Work*, and several magistrates were prepared to give testimony to the good results achieved:

[The mission] . . . has had the best effects, not only from the religious point of view, but also from the social point of view . . . The improvement in the behaviour of the immigrant hop-pickers . . . is remarkable.[135]

When I first sat on the bench it was a matter of course that numbers of hop-pickers were brought before us for assaults, sometimes most serious ones, and for drunkenness. In the last three years we have scarcely had a hop-picker before the bench.[136]

Although no statistics were available to prove these claims the magistrates' clerk unhesitatingly reported that crime among hop-pickers had reduced by almost 70% in six or seven years. G. Duncan, an employer, confirmed this impression and in his statement is a suggestion of the reasons for its popularity:

I have pleasure in bearing my willing testimony as to their [the tent services] beneficial influence socially, morally, and religiously, from the fact that the people when they have done their work have a comfortably-seated and well-lighted [*sic*] tent to go to direct, and are provided with well-made, excellent tea without charge, where they can eat their bread and cheese and butter or bacon in comfortable social intercourse, and where there is provided for them some kind of entertainment when tea is over, either by the magic-lantern, addresses, and a great deal of singing, which the people greatly enjoy, and all with a decided moral and religious tendency.[137]

The effect of this was that the local villages were blessed with order and peace and not riotous drunkenness, but any long-term reform must be doubtful. The mission had solved the problem of a great influx of strangers and travellers to a region for a short period each year by providing a free form of entertainment close at hand for the pickers. It is extremely unlikely, however, that the teachings decrying the pickers' moral turpitude and proposing Christianity as the means of reform had any significant lasting effect.

In conclusion, the end of the eighteenth century and the beginning of the nineteenth saw a move away from the objective of expelling and executing Gypsies towards reforming and absorbing them, of welding them on to the sedentary-based social system as orderly residents. The disappearance, dissolution or disbandment of this minority group were the desired aims in both cases. To begin with there was much talk, missions were proposed and a small number of Gypsies were accepted into schools. Such action, though, was directed only at small numbers and was of little consequence. Crabb's mission at Southampton was the first attempt to deal with the problem in a methodical and organised manner, and with any great numbers. This was then followed by a number of other similar ventures. Even allowing for the exaggerations and optimism of the evangelists' own claims about their work, it would seem niggardly to deny them any success in reforming morals or in persuading the Gypsies both of the benefits of a religious life and a settled existence. However, it needs to be stressed that in each of these areas their achievements were at best extremely limited, reaching only small numbers of Gypsy-travellers and reforming and converting even less. Perhaps of more significance than any list giving numbers of Christian Gypsies is an awareness of the causes of the antipathy shown to the Gypsies and a realisation that the reforming mission was an attempt to deal with a problem that legislation had not solved. The failure of evangelism in turn rekindled the legislative and persecuting drive.

There is no simple explanation for the general antipathy shown towards the Gypsies by the evangelists. Ethnic, religious, cultural and class factors joined together in a curious admixture. Ethnic factors were linked with the view of the Gypsy as an outcast and alien race marked by its propensities to crime, violence and vice. Religious arguments were used as a plea to Christianise the heathens at home before turning to those in the remotest parts of the world. Finally, cultural and class factors were mostly tied to their travelling way of life. Not only was this evidence of idleness and an aversion to the principles of a settled society, but it meant also that the conditions of existence were of the worst kind. The emphasis given to each of these factors varied between individuals and with these differences came modifications in aims and methods. However, the theme throughout was to show the Gypsies the benefits of sedentarisation and the evils of nomadism.

Travelling was the chief cause of the problem. It resulted, according to some interpretations, from the nomadic instincts of the Gypsy tribe and was a cause of poverty, vice and degradation. By a process of re-education the nomadic instinct could be curbed and the evils resultant upon a travelling existence would be destroyed. The ultimate aim of all the reformers was, therefore, the settlement of the Gypsies. Naturally, the methods adopted were various, involving different degrees of voluntarism and coercion, responsibility and obligation. Some sought to keep the Gypsies in one place and then re-educate them, others thought that settlement would follow from good teaching. Baird summarised the different tactics adopted to come to terms with the problem.

[It is] . . . no longer the object to extirpate, but to ameliorate; no longer to irritate, but to soothe; no longer, by severe and persecuting enactments, to inflame the worst passions of their nature; but, by instruction, by encouragement, by inculcating the doctrines and precepts of Christianity, to enlighten their minds, to influence their affections, and to reform their lives – to lead them to see and acknowledge the evils of their present wandering life, and induce them to relinquish it.[138]

The humble and inadequate attempts of the pioneering, but unassisted, individuals were successful to only a very limited degree. The most significant factor that emerged from the later evangelical efforts was not that more Gypsies were persuaded to settle and become Christians but that the work was no longer unassisted. The various reforming missions sought for, and found, moral and financial support from other classes in society equally repelled by the travelling way of life, and the parasitism and chaos, freedom and anarchy which it was seen to symbolise: 'A population living on the toil of others is certainly a serious burden for a state; in accord with morality, then, political economy advises the trial of regenerating the gipsies.'[139] Viewed in moral, political and economic terms, their incorporation into settled society was the motive of the reform endeavour. History had shown that violence was unable to achieve this end, and so support was given to evangelism, with its system of 'enlightened and persevering charity'.[140]

The evangelists were motivated by an awareness of moral and spiritual degeneracy, combined with a desire to contribute to the structural solidity of the nation by reforming 'low' elements to 'high' ideals. They approached the Gypsies with the same self-righteous missionary zeal that was usually reserved for distant 'savages' and 'inferior' races. Their uncompromising attitude and approach was largely a product of their belief that the Gypsy was an uncivilised savage, made so by race and by the nomadic life-style, and just as these missionaries were spreading their doctrines abroad it was equally essential, in fact more so, that these savages at home should be reformed and absorbed into the domestic social fabric.[141]

Attempts to discuss the reasons for the failure of the reforming mission are faced with serious methodological and historiographical obstacles. Contemporary writers on this subject nearly always wrote from a position of sympathy with the evangelists' methods and objectives. The methodology of these writers, whether the evangelists themselves, their biographers or interested outsiders, was thus to seek out the successes, not failures, of the people and their missions. There was an understandable reluctance to admit that their work was of limited consequence. More recently, Elwood Trigg has written from a similar perspective.[142] He recognises that an assessment of the relative success or failure of the evangelists' work must depend on the criteria used, yet it must be questioned whether the new criteria adopted by Trigg reflect any real grasp of the nature of the problem, and of the solutions proposed and tried. Trigg claims some success was achieved by introducing Gypsies to Christianity and by encouraging them to observe Christian rites and ceremonies. However, he also admits that on the whole the reform mission was a failure in terms of making them adopt a settled way of life and moulding them into a Christian people in the Victorian image.[143] Trigg's attempt to salvage some vestige of success and cause for optimism from the missionary endeavours, and his reluctance to admit to their failures, betrays his sympathy with their objectives.

Thus, when attempting to assess the reasons for the failure to achieve any lasting or significant reforms, there is the immediate problem that many of the writers who are relied on for source material were unwilling to concede that there was a failure. Even so, certain causes are apparent, and can be seen to be a product of both the evangelists' methods and how the Gypsies interacted with, and responded to, these approaches. Regrettably, sources offer only little confirmatory evidence and so, however probable, the causes mentioned here have to remain more supposition than fact.

The evangelists' didactic and often patronising method of preaching was likely to have alienated rather than converted, and their attempts to offer practical assistance were inhibited by the fact that nomadism lessened the duration and impact of the missionary work. A further claim was that the racial characteristics of the Gypsies made reform extremely difficult, if not impossible. Gypsy traits of deceit, suspicion, drunkenness and tendency to violence were said to make missionary work a hazardous and fruitless enterprise.[144] Moreover, a gradual but distinct diminution in the amount of moral and financial support offered by other interested parties and the general antipathy of the sedentary population made finding homes and employment for the reformed Gypsies a serious problem.

Finally, the reasons for the ineffectiveness of the attempts at the mass conversion and settlement of the Gypsies have to be sought from among the Gypsies themselves. Once again the inadequacy of the sources acts as a severe obstacle in obtaining support for any comments dealing with the response of the Gypsies to various missionaries. Despite this, certain points are worthy of consideration. If the problem is looked at from the perspective of the Gypsies a possible pattern emerges. The missionaries, in attempting gently to persuade or otherwise force the Gypsies to settle and adopt sedentary employments, were thus seeking to alter completely the Gypsies' way of life, and this clear intention would not have been missed by even the most ignorant and illiterate among the travellers. It would have necessarily involved a change in cultural habits, attitude and responsibilities. Freedom of movement, choice of employment, and of when and how to work, would have been taken from them and replaced by disciplined and servile labour. Subservience to external authority and participation in the wage-labour system would have replaced a much-valued independence. To moderate the impact of this transition the evangelists offered gifts, money, homes and advice. Clearly, the response of the Gypsies would have varied greatly. Some would have rejected entirely these overtures, no matter how amicably they were presented. Others would have gladly accepted all that was offered, and would have given themselves over to their benefactors' paternalism with a quiet conformity. Still others would have shown all the outward signs of acceptance while in reality changing little from their previous ways. Gypsies were more than willing to declare their conversion to Christianity if this brought with it a flood of gifts and a grateful response.[145] Thus, whatever criteria are used, the reforming mission has to be seen as a failure. The causes for this can be found in the evangelists' methods, aims and in that the Gypsies themselves did not want to be reformed in a way that would so drastically alter their way of life. Evidence of reform was little more than a token gesture.

To attempt to judge the missions is largely a fruitless task. Of more interest than the achievements of the various endeavours is the common pattern that embraces them. What each of the evangelistic episodes show, almost without exception, is that their aims go far beyond the limited desire to reform a heathen people to Christian ways. The objective of civilising the Gypsies to the ways of settled, industrial society, was just as important as religious conversion. This is made clear from the arguments adopted by the missionaries, with the language used making as many references to industriousness, thrift and sobriety as to heathenism or religious reform.

It is important, then, to see the work of the evangelists in the context of the general antipathetic response of settled society to an itinerant minority. Although this voluntary response continued throughout the whole of the period under review, the main thrust of their efforts was concentrated in the first half of the century. The work of the missionaries declined as the century progressed, partly due to the ebbing evangelical tide in general and also a consequence of the growing willingness and ability of the expanding state and its local government wing to take greater responsibility for this particular social 'problem'. It was not entirely the case that voluntary efforts were replaced by state-directed initiatives, but rather that the balance was shifting, while still remaining within the overall framework of an antipathetic reaction composed of many complementary components.

6

George Smith of Coalville and the legislative attack

Despite the disappointments of the early evangelistic attempts at reformation, some men of Christian conscience still sought to reform the Gypsies by means of conversion. Schools and travelling van schemes continued to be proposed throughout the century and the Gypsies remained a central concern of evangelist agencies.[1] Yet the tendency was to move away from evangelists and evangelism, and the concern expressed about the Gypsy problem took on an increasingly scholastic, practical, humanitarian and conservative tone. The reforming mission continued to operate but it became pushed further into the background and by the latter decades of the century the plea for religious conversion now came largely from the numerous Gypsy lorists, from Francis Groome through to the Reverend George Hall. Whereas the earlier reformers had seen religious conversion as going hand-in-hand with settlement, whether as a precondition or result, this was not the case with the evangelistic lorists. For these, the assimilation of the Gypsy into the culture and ways of settled society was to be prevented at all costs, not in order to protect the sedentary population from the demoralising and degrading ways of the Gypsies (as would have been an earlier argument) but rather to protect the distinctiveness of the Gypsy and his culture. Conversion was to be achieved by clergymen visiting the camps, spreading the Christian doctrine, and by teaching the children at schools. For these writers conversion and education were to be treated as ends in themselves and not as a step towards the acceptance by Gypsies of the ways of settled society. The Gypsy Lore Society and the numerous Gypsy lorists remained throughout their history true to this anti-assimilationist stance.

The continuing call for settlement now came from people with no less strong religious beliefs, but who possessed a different approach to the problem from the earlier evangelists. The intention remained to regulate and control those who pursued a travelling way of life with the ultimate aim of ending it altogether, yet the proposals and methods saw a move away from evangelism to a more rational scholasticism. The arguments put forward were no longer based on the need to reform the 'savage' at home but were rather to do with raising the lot of the degraded traveller and reestablishing some kind of balance with the sedentary population by making the traveller equally subject to the laws and controls falling on the settled man. Although rarely stated in such terms, reform was thought to be a political, social and economic necessity, and was to be achieved not by religious persuasion but by legislative coercion. The growth of the bureaucratic state and the increased efficiency of local government administration was thought to facilitate the process of enforcing regulations and restrictions.

At first appearances it would seem that there was a conflict between the Gypsy lorists and the proponents of settlement, between the assimilationists and the anti-assimilationists. However, these two apparently conflicting groups were in fact very close in their approach and interpretation of the problem, and the key to explaining this again brings us back to the ever-present theme of definition.

The Gypsy lorists held firmly to the racial view of the extent of 'gypsy-ness' being largely dependent on the amount of pure blood that flowed through the travellers' veins. It was only the pure-blood Gypsies, the 'real' or Romany Gypsies, who should be prevented from assimilating with the sedentary population, and it was their culture that needed to be preserved and recorded. The antipathy of the lorists to half-bred Gypsies and other travellers was equal to the fervent diatribes made by others about this group of nomads, and they too called for an end to be made to this 'poor imitation' of the Gypsy way of life. These half-breeds, it was claimed, served only to give the 'real' Gypsies a bad name, and were guilty of all the charges laid at their feet. It was they who were the thieves, beggars, illiterates and degenerates, not the Romanies. Any attempt to regulate and restrict the wanderings and activities of this 'mumply-group' was met with sympathy by the lorists. Their recourse to such a definition thus permitted, and even supported and justified, the persecution of the great majority of travellers.

Meanwhile, the pro-settlement lobby frequently excused the 'real' Gypsy from the unacceptable excesses of his half-blood brothers. It was regularly repeated that the intention was not to prevent the 'true' Gypsies from following their natural way of life. Instead, concern was directed at the 'imposters' and 'degenerates' who took up, or married into, this nomadic life-style. In the Parliamentary debate over the Moveable Dwellings Bill, in August 1885, Mr Kenny expressed support for the Bill, '[it] being aimed, not so much at genuine gipsies, as at people who pretended to be gipsies – people who were a great annoyance to those amongst whom they lived, and people who lived, to a great extent, by spoil'.[2] Such 'pseudo-gipsies' were also discovered in Lamb Lane by George Smith and a reporter from the *Weekly Times*:

For the genuine Gipsy tribe, and their mysterious promptings to live apart from their fellows in the lanes and fields of the country, we have a sentimental pity; but with such as these Lamb-lane people, off-scourings of the lowest form of society, we have no manner of sympathy; and we hope that a gracious Act of Parliament may soon rid English social life of such a plague.[3]

Although George Smith did not concern himself greatly with subtleties of distinction, and on the whole ignored the isolation of a Romany elite by the scholars, anthropologists and philologists, he nevertheless occasionally made reference to the 'true' Romany, who was in a more elevated position than the majority of travellers. To have done this too often, though, would have undermined the moral force of his argument as it would have amounted to an acknowledgement of the existence of a commendable and worthwhile group of travellers. But Smith and his fellow-persecutors were confident in their actions and thoughts for they were not seen to be condemning or attacking the romanticised Romany, who could exist comfortably in their imaginations, but only the depraved and outcast traveller. No one claimed to want the assimilation of a Romany race, with its own ethnic and cultural traditions, but only those travellers whose itinerant way of life conflicted with the interests of settled society. The arguments presented gave backing to the suggestion that it was the culture of travelling, not of a race, that was to be ended. George Smith of Coalville channelled this sentiment into a forceful legislative drive, intended to secure the circumscription of the travellers and their nomadic life-style.

George Smith was born the son of a local brickmaker and Primitive Methodist preacher at Clayhills, in Staffordshire, on 16 February 1831.[4] His background was one of poverty and deprivation, and, like other children of his class, at nine years of age he went to work for thirteen hours daily in the local brickfields.[5] Yet, in a supreme example of self-help fed by strong religious beliefs, he pulled himself out of the slavery of child labour by attending night school and educating himself from books purchased out of the extra wages obtained by working some nights at the brick-kilns.[6] Before long, Smith was running his own brick and tile yard in Reapsmoor, Staffordshire, where he first put into practice his evolving plans for the moral and spiritual enlightenment of his employees.[7] He then moved to a larger works at Humberstone, near Leicester, and eventually to Coalville, where he was employed by the Whitwick Colliery Company between 1857 and 1872. He resigned from this job following a disagreement with the management, ostensibly over the amount of time he was devoting to bettering the lot of the workers rather than the company.[8] While he was now free to devote all his attentions to his own personal missionary adventures with the brickyard children, the canal-dwellers and eventually with the Gypsies, his unemployed status meant that he was without any income to provide for his wife and family or to subsidise his work. As a result his furniture was sold to raise money and it became necessary to move from comfortable surroundings to a house that 'leaked water from all directions'.[9] In a very short time he had reduced his family to a condition of poverty and squalor equal to that which he came to abhor when it applied to canal-dwellers and Gypsies. Domestic comforts had to take second place behind his philanthropic endeavours.

From his personal life is seen perhaps the clearest insight of a single-minded devotion to work that characterised his entire life: 'He lived and moved and had his being in his work',[10] all the while showing 'indomitable perseverance and self-denial'.[11] Yet while his single-mindedness enabled him to continue in the face of hunger, poverty, distress and opposition, it meant also that he took a narrow and blinkered view of the cause for which he was fighting, a failing common to philanthropists and evangelists of whatever ilk. His biographer, Edwin Hodder, said 'He saw visions and dreamed dreams; he mistook for realities the unsubstantial images of the brain. It became difficult for him sometimes to discriminate between facts and fancies; it led him into a great deal of unconscious exaggeration.'[12] Indeed, his writings confirm this judgement containing many instances of plagiarism and generalisation, and were, in the last instance, so obviously one-sided as to do more harm than good to his cause.[13] His complete lack of sympathy both with the objects of his concern and with others whose nature and interpretation did not fit in with his own, served only to antagonise many individuals and groups.[14] This blind devotion to a single cause is well illustrated by his work with the nomadic population.[15]

It was not until Smith had completed to his own satisfaction his reform of the canal-dwellers, culminating in the passing of the Canal Boats Act Amendment Bill in 1884, that he felt able to turn wholeheartedly to the cause of the Gypsies, though his work among them had begun some years previously. For thirteen years he had laboured for the brickyard children and then the canal-dwellers in a state of complete deprivation and poverty. Even allowing for the unfriendly bias of the commentator, who was to oppose Smith over the issue of the Moveable Dwellings Bill, the following assessment of Smith conjures up a pitiful picture:

More like a *pīrdo* he was when he first come out; never a pair o' decent shoes to his feet, and his clothes al'ways in rags. I give him a pound o' soap one day to wash hisself [*sic*] with, for the dirt on the man was a sight to make anybody ashamed; and more 'an once I've gi'n him a *pos-bar* to pay his railway home. His wife relowed [*sic*] him so much money, but he used to get drinking it them days; and then he'd come begging to us, saying as how he wanted money for to provide schools for the children.[16]

Presumably this was said of Smith prior to the mid-1880s, from when his condition improved markedly. In November 1884 he received a Treasury order for £300 in recognition of the work he had done for the canal-dwellers, and immediately he put this grant towards helping forward the cause of the

Gypsy children.[17] Also in that month the *Pall Mall Gazette* issued a notice and appeal for monies to set up a George Smith Fund, and very soon this brought in a sum of £800, which prompted Smith to write in his diary for 31 December 1884: 'We are better off than we have been for many, many years. Thank God!'[18] His material position improved even further in 1885 with a grant from the royal bounty fund, and the closing of the *Pall Mall Gazette* Fund at the sum of £1,480.[19] With this he bought a house at Crick, near Rugby, and even managed to form a George Smith of Coalville Society, whose members were to assist him in his endeavours.[20] Thus, when he took up the Gypsy cause Smith was able to go about his work with a vigour revitalised by a measure of financial security.

It will have been apparent from earlier references to Smith that his attitude towards the Gypsy people, and the problem they caused, was uncompromising in its opposition and condemnation. He possessed a hatred, antipathy and disgust towards them drawn from his early experiences while working in the brickyards. Smith admitted to having had a 'nervous dread of the black-eyed gipsies encamped beside the brickyard', and many times was 'half-frightened out of my senses by gipsies and tramps'.[21] They stole his clothing, food, drink and, most hurtful of all, the first book he ever possessed.[22] Visits to encampments in the Midlands, London and even Scotland only confirmed these damning impressions. Smith desperately wanted to expose the 'truth' about present-day Gypsy life and so redress the balance upset by the efforts of novelists and others to paint the Gypsies white. Their contrasting positions are well shown in the following:

To dress the satanic, demon-looking face of a Gipsy with the violet-powder of imagery only temporarily hides from view the repulsive aspect of his features . . . The dramatist has strutted the Gipsy across the stage in various characters in his endeavour to improve his condition. After the fine colours have been doffed, music finished, applause ceased, curtain dropped, and scene ended, he has been a black, swarthy, idle, thieving, lying, blackguard of a Gipsy still.[23]

Smith's distaste for the 'backwood romantic gipsy novelists' was surpassed only by his antipathy towards the Gypsy.[24] No one could have been more comprehensive in his criticisms, which covered everything from education and morals to diet and dress. Often Smith compared Gypsies with savages and animals, and accused them of shocking ignorance and illiteracy:

A few days since I wended my way to a large number of Gipsies located in tents, huts, and vans near Wandsworth Common, to behold the pitiable spectacle of some 60 half-naked, poor Gipsy chidren, and 30 Gipsy men and women, living in a state of indescribable ignorance, dirt, filth and misery, mostly squatting upon the ground, making their beds upon peg-shavings and straw, and divested of the last tinge of romantical nonsense, which is little better in this case – used as a deal of it is – than paper pasted upon the windows, to hide from public view the mass of human corruption which has been festering in our midst for centuries, breeding all kinds of sins and impurities.[25]

At one camp he allegedly found no more than four or five out of almost one hundred adults and children who could read a sentence or write a letter. He generalised from his personal observations to state that not 2% of the 30,000 poor Gypsy children in the country were able to read or write, and he quoted a number of Gypsies who bemoaned the lack of literacy amongst their number.[26] To Smith, their total lack of morals expressed itself in the way they lied, cheated and demoralised all with whom they had contact by their degrading and crafty habits.[27] They were only able to maintain themselves by pilfering and poaching, fortune-telling and selling the odd item such as clothes-lines and clothes-pegs, although they seldom used such things themselves as they rarely washed.[28] They lived huddled together 'like so many dogs', regardless of either 'sex, age or decency', and with little respect for marriage ceremonies.[29] Their diet was 'little better than garbage and refuse', their dress, if any, was ragged and dirty, with the result they were among the main conveyors of infectious diseases.[30] The absence of religious feelings and sentiments was added almost as an afterthought.

Smith believed the romantic Gypsy of poetry and fiction had long since disappeared from the roads, 'and neither the stage, romance, nor imagination will ever bring him to life again in this country'.[31] Instead of scenes of sunshine, freedom and romance Smith substituted squalor, wretchedness, poverty, dirt and idleness, and talked of a people who 'live like pigs and die like dogs'.[32] In his opinion the tents and camps contained even more filth and disease than the overcrowded cabins of the canal boats and to add to this already appalling state of affairs, Smith was horrified by the ease with which the Gypsies escaped inspection and regulation. By taking to a nomadic way of life he saw them as avoiding taxation, rents, the Inspector of Nuisances and the School Board officer. Their existence was not officially recognised except at the time of a census when, at the expense of the householder, a register was made. Their living conditions were marked by indecencies and dangers to health and no government representative troubled to look into the problem.[33] Some change in the manner of their life was therefore thought essential. Smith viewed them as a danger and disgrace not only to themselves but also to the nation as a whole. It is little wonder that he called on the sanitary inspectors and public health officials to remedy the Gypsy 'problem' for he likened the people to a disease, describing them as a 'plague spot' which urgently had to be removed.[34] As with leprosy and other infectious diseases they were an anachronism in a Christian and civilised society, able to contaminate any with whom they came into contact.[35] Their alleged ability to reduce others to their own level acted as a threat to the whole of society, and through their parasitism they were believed to be delaying the spread of civilisation, negating a belief in material progress:

It is my decided conviction that unless we are careful, and take the 'bull by the horns', and compel them to educate their children, and to put their habitations, tents, and vans under better sanitary arrangements, we shall be fostering seeds in these dregs of society that will one day put a stop to the work of civilisation, and bring to an end the advance in arts, science, laws, and commerce that have been making such rapid strides in the country of late years.[36]

In short, Smith saw them as living in defiance of social, moral, civil and natural law.[37] Viewed from every angle, whether moral, educational, religious, sanitary, economic or political, their reform seemed essential.

Despite the generality and inaccuracy of many of Smith's statements and claims, he succeeded in awakening the general public to the seriousness of the Gypsy problem. Hodder commented thus on the importance of the press in publicising Smith's endeavours: 'His career is the best illustration I have ever come upon of the splendid willingness of the press of any country to hammer the proposed remedies of genuine philanthropists into the head and heart of the public, and compel adequate legislation to render them permanently effective'.[38] Editorial comments appeared in many papers and dialogues were conducted in the correspondence columns of national and local newspapers, often providing general support and corroboratory evidence.[39] Sometimes Gypsies and lorists wrote to point out that Smith was looking at 'mumply-travellers' and tramps and not the 'real' Gypsy at all but even so they also tended to sympathise with the black picture painted by Smith, but excluded from it the 'real' Romany Gypsy. Smith did not rely entirely on the written word to convert the general public and legislators to his cause, making good use of a range of resources to force home the message. He spoke at Social Science Congress meetings in 1879 and 1882, at Manchester and Nottingham, and began a lecture tour in 1885, speaking at meetings of the Young Men's Christian Association, at Leeds, Hull and elsewhere. In 1887 he lectured to the Association of Public Sanitary Inspectors on 'The Insanitary State of Gipsy Homes', and again at various Y.M.C.A.s and literary societies.[40] Yet he recognised he had not only to convince public opinion but also to win over the legislators, local authorities and the Gypsies themselves. He set about each task with equal determination.

Smith advertised the extent and nature of the Gypsy problem by dedicating his books on the subject to the members of Parliament.[41] He petitioned the House and engaged in an extensive letter-writing campaign, which was also directed at the local authorities.[42] Again his persistence achieved results as he came to be regarded as the authority on Gypsies and van-towns and it was in deference to his knowledge, or perhaps self-advertising, that he was called to give evidence before the Royal Commission on the Housing of the Working Classes, 1884–5. After he had appeared before the Commission Smith wrote in his diary that he was satisfied he had convinced the Commissioners that the cause of the Gypsy children was a good one.[43]

In an attempt to persuade the Gypsies themselves of the benefits of education and moral reformation Smith made personal visits to their camps, feasts and fairs.[44] He took with him illustrated pamphlets, picture-cards and literature which were distributed to the old and young alike, and to sweeten the effect of the elevating and didactic sermons he also took oranges and confectionery for the children and tobacco for the adults.[45] The Gypsy response to this propaganda campaign gave great encouragement to Smith. His proposals were said to have their 'heartfelt sympathy', even to the extent that financial assistance was given to help him in his work.[46] He even quoted the Gypsies themselves to give a personal flavour to this alleged support: 'Lor, bless you, my good mon, I'm reight glad you big fokes are going to do sommat in the way o' givin our childer a bit o' eddication, for they've nowt as it is.'[47] During November 1890 Smith, according to his own testimony, visited several hundreds of Gypsy families in the Midlands, distributing copies of his proposals to them all. He reported that all but seven were behind his schemes, and he subsequently received many letters of support from them.[48] However, Smith's crowning glory, and the most often quoted example of Gypsy friendship and support, was when the Lee family sold to Smith, for a nominal sum, a small copper and brass box, dated 1197, a family heirloom, 'for his long efforts to improve our condition and educate our children'.[49] The presentation took place at a large gathering of Gypsies at Plaistow Marshes in November 1888.

Smith wanted to give the impression of widespread backing yet his proposals did not meet with total support, and he had first to tackle the same pessimism and cynicism which had also greeted the earlier reforming evangelists. Some challenged altogether the notion that reform was necessary, claiming that crime and disease were not common among the Gypsy people. An Irish Gypsy wrote to the *Standard* praising Smith's efforts to improve the condition of his fellow-travellers, but also arguing that the Gypsy was neither morally degraded nor criminally inclined, stating there was not one Gypsy registered in the crime statistics for every five hundred criminals who attended religious services.[50] Smith replied to this criticism by drawing on ample 'evidence' to expose these claims as errors and the writers as romantics. A further challenge came from those who thought that the Gypsies' habits and ways could never be changed as they were a part of their nature, a product of 'untameable blood'. The Gypsies' nomadism, disrespect of property and rights of ownership and contempt for legislation were considered irrefutable characteristics.[51] The response to this was to distinguish the 'genuine Romanies', whose wanderlust could be understood and accepted, from the rest of the nomadic population, who could not be similarly excused.

Yet, on the whole, it was not his ultimate aim of ending the evils and excesses of itinerancy that was criticised or rejected, but instead the opposition was to his proposed methods. Parliament, the public and the Gypsies themselves were by no means unanimous in their support over the need to resort to the legislative process to secure the enactment of a Bill containing clauses considered both harsh and impracticable. To appreciate why this was so it is necessary to take a closer look at the clauses and provisions of the various Moveable Dwellings Bills, 1885 to 1894.[52]

THE ATTEMPT AT DIRECT LEGISLATION, 1885–94

Essentially, Smith sought to apply the principles and provisions of the Canal Boats Acts, of 1877 and 1884, to all moveable dwellings. This was to be achieved by the registration of all such dwellings; the compulsory school attendance of the children of Gypsies and van-dwellers; the enforcement of regulations concerning their dwellings, governing the amount of cubic space required by each individual and the separation of the sleeping accommodation of males and females; the power to enter the dwellings to inspect for health, sanitary and moral irregularities; and encouragements to Gypsies to localise and settle. By bringing what he regarded as the 'lowest dregs of society' within the educational and sanitary laws, it was hoped they would be taught loyalty, honesty, industrious habits and faithfulness, converting them into useful members of society. Improving the moral and physical condition of the Gypsies would lead, ultimately, to their social absorption.

The registration of all moveable dwellings, including tents, shows, caravans, auctioneers' vans, carriages, wagons and the like, was considered essential if regulation was to be effective. Without this it was not thought possible to enforce proposals regarding sanitary arrangements and education. Registration was to be by a certificate, issued annually at a stated, nominal fee, though with heavy fines for non-compliance. This would bring the owners of vans under the watchful eye of the authorities at least once a year. Even Groome supported the idea of registration, not because he thought it essential on regulatory grounds, but because of the benefits it would bring to the Gypsies. It would enable them to find camping grounds on application to the local police station and reopen sites that had been closed to them under the Highway and Commons Acts.[53]

More general support for the principle of registration was motivated by a similar desire to Smith's for regulation and control. There was a feeling that legislation should be enacted and enforced to control the 'nuisance' of the Gypsies and to impose minimum sanitary and educational standards. The press gave support to the principle, and Smith claimed to have received letters in his favour from many Chief Constables (some of whom requested even greater powers), county magistrates, town councils, various school boards and from different religious denominations.[54] The Association of

Sanitary Inspectors even passed a resolution in favour of the Bill.[55] In Parliament the response given to the clause was not unanimous approval. When the Bill was considered in Committee in 1889, Mr Stephens, a member of the Liberty and Property Defence League and a spokesman for the United Kingdom Showmen's and Van Dwellers' Protection Association, expressed the belief that the clause was 'entirely unworkable and cruelly oppressive'.[56] The demand to register with a local county council was intended to suppress the mode of life followed by the travellers, and would, in effect, 'force these people from a healthy, harmless country life, into our overcrowded towns, where they are not at all wanted, and where . . . it will be impossible for them to earn their living'.[57] Registration would have to be the responsibility of some local authority official as the council itself was not always sitting, and this involved handing over power to a person not under the direct control of the representative authority, and 'far more under the influence of the residents and landlords of the neighbourhood'.[58] Mr Stephens' persistent blocks, on this ground and others, proved to be the most serious obstacle confronting Smith in his endeavour to get the Bill approved.

The proposals regarding sanitary regulations met with an equally equivocal response. The Local Government Board had power over every dwelling in England, on land and water, to make regulations regarding health and sanitary matters, but as Smith pointed out, they had no effective power over moveable dwellings.[59] Similarly, although local authorities possessed the power to enforce bye-laws respecting the sanitary conditions of moveable dwellings, Smith considered that the powers were not great enough, and in any case very few of the 1,576 sanitary authorities had taken any steps to extend their influence over the van-dwellers. The need for such regulations was visibly apparent for all to see. Smith dismissed as nonsense claims that van-dwellers were a healthy people and that their encampments were not hotbeds of infectious diseases. To him, it was inconceivable that the people could be healthy and free of disease given the conditions under which they existed, and he was able to quote a number of respectable sources that, in his view, proved this beyond reasonable doubt. For example, the Gypsy children camped on Danbury Common

are daily passing before us untaught, and suffering in health through exposure to cold and wet, versed in arts of deception and quite inaccessible to influence . . . I am sure that those who dwelt *under tents* [original emphasis] must have perished or laid the foundation of fatal disease during the late severe weather.[60]

Similar testimonies were received from other, equally 'reliable' sources.[61] Consequently, clauses were put in the Bill governing the fixing of the number, ages and sex of the persons who were allowed to dwell in such temporary abodes, 'having regard to the cubic spaces, ventilation, provision for the separation of the sexes, general healthiness and accommodation', and the promotion of cleanliness in such dwellings and the prevention of the spread of infectious diseases. The problem of how to regulate regarding cubic space and ventilation in a tent, which may be no more than canvas stretched over sticks, was just one of the ways in which this clause was thought to be unworkable.

The real point of contention, though, rested with the way in which these regulations were to be supervised and enforced. Provisions were made in the Bill for any officer of the county or sanitary authority to have the power to enter the moveable dwelling between 6 a.m. and 9 p.m., 'on his motion', or if with a magistrates' warrant at any time. Lord Wemyss, of the Liberty and Property Defence League, reacted strongly: 'What! is not this a gross violation of the rights of the subject? Every gipsy's van is his castle, and he should be at liberty to make a pig-sty of it if he likes.'[62] Smith answered his critics by pointing out that the powers of entry were more stringent in the Canal Boats Acts, 1877 and 1884, the Housing of the Working Classes Act, 1885, and the Public Health Act, 1875.[63] Even so, opposition caused him to modify the provisions and, by stages, powers of entry applied only to the hours between 9 a.m. and 6 p.m. He now said that he did not want the power to enter vans and tents at night, 'as officers have under other Acts', and that the powers were given to local authority officers and not the police: 'I want to keep the policemen clear of the vans.'[64] Yet these amendments and appeals were to no avail and this clause proved another stumbling block.

Finally, the later Bills, though not the original presented in 1884, made provisions for the education of the children of the van-dwellers. The Elementary Education Acts of 1870 and after had been ineffective in extending the principle of compulsory education to the children of travellers, and Smith's earlier attempts to evoke positive response from Parliament had met with disappointing results. Mr Mundella, Vice-President of the Committee of the Council on Education, said in reply to a Parliamentary question from Mr Burt:

It is exceedingly difficult to devise any effectual scheme for the education of the nomadic population . . ., and up to the present we have received no suggestion for dealing with the subject which appears to be practical. The matter, however, is 'under consideration', and we propose during the recess to confer with the Local Government Board respecting it.[65]

Smith endeavoured to supply the practical solution by suggesting a clause should be inserted in the Canal Boats Act Amendment Bill to cover Gypsy children. Mr Burt warned Smith not to be too hopeful and was proved to be justified in his pessimism when the clause was blocked on its second reading, 18 April 1883, by Mr Salt, M.P. for Stafford.[66] No education clause was inserted in Smith's first Moveable Dwellings bill, partly because he had been seeking its insertion elsewhere and partly because he feared the education clause would be the block on which the whole package would fall. This omission was rectified in all his subsequent Bills. Smith suggested that a book be issued to the children in which their names and attendance at school could be entered and which would be taken from place to place and endorsed by the schoolmaster, showing the School Board Officer that the child was attending. The small extra cost incurred by educating Gypsy children was to have been paid out of the poor rates. The children would thus be brought under the Education Code, by means of a 'free, easy, single national system'.[67] It was not thought that the education obtained in this way would be entirely adequate, 'but through the kindness of the schoolmaster . . . and the vigilance of the School Board visitor, a plain, practical, and sound education could be imparted to and obtained by these poor little gipsy children and road-side arabs'.[68] There was little doubt or disagreement that provision ought to be made for the Gypsy children, and Smith was not slow to recount from helpful Gypsies stories and claims about their own ignorance and illiteracy. There was, then, widespread approval for the principal of compulsory education, but the dispute was over how that education should be imparted and the regulations enforced.

Clearly, one of the problems in enforcing compulsory schooling on a nomadic population was that it offended notions of individual liberty. The only way of ensuring that the minimum number of attendances was reached was by forcing the Gypsies to settle in a particular district or by preventing the children from travelling with their parents until they had satisfied the School Board Inspector. There were even greater problems involved with the attendance of Gypsy children at state elementary schools. Chief among these were those to do with cost and with the widespread antipathy shown to the children, whose attendance, it was thought, would harm the children of settled parents. First, it was claimed that Gypsy children increased the numbers at state schools but lowered the average of those passing the examinations, resulting in a lower government grant.[69] The *Caravan*'s plea that the grant should not act as a barrier to the education of any class of children strikes a rather despairing note. Perhaps an even greater obstacle was expressed in the manifesto of the Liberty and Property Defence League: 'The attendance of travelling children . . . would do very serious harm to schools . . . and if any attempts were made to enforce it very vehement and insurmountable opposition on the part of school managers, school teachers . . . would certainly be exacted.'[70] Hodder expressed a similar view, and in so doing provided a good illustration of how Smith provided his opponents with more than enough ammunition to shoot down his proposals:

There are . . . caste distinctions and class distinctions which deserve great consideration and respect, and personally, we sympathise with the teachers who protested that it would be a great moral wrong to flood their schools and bring their scholars under the contaminating influence of gipsy children, who, according to George Smith's own persistent showing, were the very scum of the earth, brought up in the midst of the grossest indecencies and profanities.[71]

The nature and extent of the proposals gradually filtered down to the Gypsies, either by Smith visiting their camps, explaining and distributing copies of the Bill, or by word of mouth, which tended to lead to such misunderstandings and exaggerations as seen among the Gypsies at Ascot who were under the impression that Smith's measures would result in their children being taken from them.[72] A careful study of the works of Smith, and others, brings to light sufficient evidence to show that, despite claims to the contrary, many Gypsies were opposed to the Bill and to Smith's methods of reform, and this opposition often expressed itself in a most violent manner. At Birmingham Onion Fair a group of van-dwellers turned against Smith and chased him up and down the streets of the city. Eventually, he turned to confront them, and managed to cool their animosity only by providing them with money for tea and lodgings.[73] At the Northampton races and the Leicester, and Market Harborough fairs, he was given police protection against the threat of violence from the van-dwellers, but at one they got close enough to chalk a large cross on his back, presumably as a target.[74] Similarly, the Gypsies insulted and roughly treated him at the Nottingham and Peterborough fairs, and only a blunt knife ensured that he left a group of Worcestershire Gypsies with his beard, and neck, intact.[75] At Ascot races his life was again under threat, and cries of 'Burn him alive' were heard. When a woman offered to pour paraffin over him and set fire to it, it was feared this was not merely an idle threat.[76]

The opposition was not always so spontaneous and emotional. Lazzy Smith, a Gypsy, took it upon himself to visit the House of Commons in order to speak out against the Bill and correct the impression of the Gypsies given by Smith. He was alleged to have shouted at those present in the House: 'Yer Lordships this man Smith never knowed a rale Gypsy. Them folks as 'e knows is tinkers an' peg-makers – the' ain't Gypsies.'[77] Once again, the best form of defence was to shift the blame. Yet the real force of opposition came not from the outbursts of individuals but from the organised efforts of the Liberty and Property Defence League (L.P.D.L.), and the United Kingdom Showmen's and Van-Dwellers' Protection Association (U.K.S.V.D.P.A.), later the Showmen's Guild. The two organisations often worked in cooperation, and offered a coordinated opposition.

The L.P.D.L. challenged the claims of the 'patriarchally got-up Mr. George Smith' concerning the health and character of the Gypsies, offering him financial support if he could prove any of his 'wild' assertions.[78] In general terms they stood opposed to Smith's attempts to introduce legislation necessitating state intervention and help, which conflicted with their own belief in laissez-faire. More specifically, the provisions of the Bill permitted the inspection and regulation of people's homes without sanction of a magistrate's warrant, thereby infringing individual rights. Their method of organising opposition was to send out many printed summaries and objections to federated societies, M.P.s, the press and elsewhere, and by the assistance of nine members in the House of Commons nine notices of motion for rejection of the Bill were placed and maintained on paper throughout the session when the Bill was to be presented.[79] In 1890 an appeal was addressed to all owners and occupiers of travelling vans, carts, wagons or tents to combine against the Bill.[80]

Opposition was thus mobilised inside Parliament and outside, at a grass roots level. Meetings were held, often with the U.K.S.V.D.P.A., to organise the opposition and rally public opinion. The latter association won the backing of Mr Stephens, M.P. for Hornsey, Middlesex, and it was largely due to his Parliamentary blocks that the Bill never went through. The U.K.S.V.D.P.A. was not, though, a pressure group that acted on behalf of all van-dwellers, despite its title and the fact that its stated object, as laid down in the Rule Book, was to protect the rights of showmen and *van-dwellers in general* against any possible harmful legislation.[81] From the first it was more concerned that the public should not confuse the Gypsies with showmen, and that the showmen class of travellers alone should not be brought under the restrictions of the Bill. The Association's chaplain, Reverend Thomas Horne, was keen to make this clear:

Mr. Smith fails to make any distinction between say the living vans of George Sanger and the most miserable ramshackle carts ceiled over with hoops and canvas; between the true and legitimate showmen and his family, well cared for, and the veriest wretch of a miserable gypsy – one who is a pariah among pariahs of the road – vitiates his whole scheme and justifies up to the hilt the strong language of outraged parents. The proposed legislation is the same old story over again; the punishment of the just for the unjust; and in this the injury is all the more glaring because it is quite possible to separate the evil from the good. Mr. Smith seems to have no power of discriminating between the wretched drink-besotten gypsy and the showmen proper.[82]

Founded in 1889, the Association emerged for the specific purpose of opposing the Bill. The first meeting of importance in relation to this was held in the Agricultural Hall, Islington, in 1890 and the following months saw a massive campaign of pamphleteering and petitioning. Many more meetings were held and the next of note was again at the Agricultural Hall in January 1891. One of these was even attended by Smith himself, there to address the large number of travellers and showmen present, but he was not given the chance as the audience clambered over the benches in order to 'tear him limb from limb'.[83] Smith managed to escape from the hall by the back door, later to be congratulated 'on my hairbreadth escape from the jaws of death'.[84] In 1892 further meetings were held in London, Manchester, King's Lynn and Hull.

The Association appeared to be in a strong position. Its campaign was efficient and effective, membership peaked at about 1,000 in 1893, and its finances were said to be good.[85] Ironically, the success of its efforts in opposing the Bill was to contribute to its decline and from 1894 to 1899 membership fell off drastically. Its problems were compounded by the setting up of other trade associations for fairground people which ensured that competition for members was tough. There was a small revival in its fortunes around the turn of the century when it challenged Private Bills and local authority bye-laws which threatened to place restrictions on the holding of fairs, but it relied on the generosity of 'Lord' George Sanger and others in order to survive. The renewed agitation for a Moveable Dwellings Bill in 1908 acted as a spur to the Guild, and it again mobilised protest to the proposals. The application and effectiveness of its opposition can be judged only by looking at the long, tortuous and eventually unsuccessful passage of the Bill through Parliament.

The Moveable Dwellings Bill was presented to Parliament for the first time in July 1885. It was immediately opposed on the grounds that it was a 'tinkering attempt at legislation', and, as Gypsies would probably soon have the right to vote, it would be well advised not to press for such legislation that would harass them.[86] Despite these objections the Bill was read for a second time but was then withdrawn without debate the following day. It next appeared two years later when it was introduced by a temporary coalition of Conservatives, Liberal Unionists, Gladstonians and Irish Nationalists. After a second reading it was referred to a Select Committee, which accepted it with minor amendments. It was then blocked as being too costly and eventually it 'suffered Parliamentary shipwreck in the Irish storm that had raged so long'.[87] It was rejected again the following year as a 'drastic measure'.[88] Meanwhile, a miserable George Smith watched on despairingly. When objections were again raised in 1889, Smith, 'in the intensity of his anxiety', lost his self-control and shouted out from the Gallery of the House of Commons, but was silenced by the ushers before he had managed to utter barely a word.[89] Whether his impassioned plea had any effect on the outcome of the debate is doubtful, and yet the Bill went its furthest to date when it was referred to a Committee of the House. But once more the Bill collapsed before objections. It was reintroduced in each of the following years up to Smith's death in June 1895, except 1893. Meetings between Smith and his opponents led to a series of minor modifications being made but in essentials it remained unaltered, and blocks continued to be put on with monotonous regularity. The Bill died along with Smith, no closer to being passed than it had been ten years earlier.

Why, then, did the Bill fail? The body of support which Smith claimed to have behind his proposals makes such an outcome all the more surprising. His backing was said to include the main body of the House, the press and public opinion, the Select Committee who had had the Bill before them, the various Government Departments which would have been called on to assist in its implementation, and the Scottish Home Office and Education Department.[90] Such exaggerated claims served only to anger his opponents. While Smith may have been justified in claiming wide approval and support for his idea of reform, the specificity of his proposals and his recourse to legislation were by no means so widely accepted. Moreover, whereas much of his support was in the form of tacit acceptance of the principle of reform, the opposition to his particular methods and proposals was active and effective. It has already been shown that standing opposed to his campaign were various journals (notably *Truth* and *Caravan*), sections of the press, many of the travellers themselves, and, of particular importance in terms of blocking the Bill, were the activities of the Liberty and Property Defence League and the U.K.S.V.D.P.A.

In effect, by the beginning of the 1890s, the tide was turning increasingly against Smith and his proposals. Many interests were opposed to it, and in Hodder's words, 'there was neither enthusiasm nor interest on its side'.[91] Even public sentiment came to be swayed by the argument that the Bill would interfere with the free and joyous life of the Gypsy. The ambivalence of the stereotypes, which permitted the existence of the romantic Romany alongside the degenerate Gypsy, served to strengthen the confusion and doubt over which side to support. However, the more the tide turned against him, the harder Smith swam against it, and the louder he cried out pointing to the truth behind his presentation of the Gypsy. His pamphlet *Gypsy Children: Or, a Stroll in Gypsydom* was an attempt to revive public interest and support. Evidence of the Gypsies' amorality, filth, irreligiousness and ignorance was again presented. Consider, for example, his account of an interview he had with a Gypsy lad in Epping Forest:

I asked what his name was. He answered, 'I don't know; I have got so many names. Sometimes they call me Smith, sometimes Brown, and lots of other names.' 'Have you ever washed in your life?' – 'Not that I know of sir.' – 'Were you ever in a school?' – 'No.' – 'Did you ever hear of Jesus?' – 'I never heard of such a man; He does not live up in this Forest.' – 'Where does God live?' – 'I don't know. I never heard of him neither. There use to be a chap live in the Forest named like that, but he's gone away a long time. I think he went a hoppin' in Kent.'[92]

It does not matter whether or not such an interview took place. Smith desperately and vividly created a conglomerate picture drawing in many threads, but it was the struggle of a drowning man. In the final instance the opposition's arguments against the Bill were more convincing than his own in defence of it. In the main, they relied on the criticisms that the Bill threatened individual liberty, that it was unworkable and that it was unnecessary.

The defence of the rights and liberty of the individual stemmed from a variety of motives. Some may have been genuinely concerned about the harassment of a minority group, and so sought to defend their interests. The Gypsy lorists and the U.K.S.V.D.P.A. could perhaps be included in this context, though it could also be said that the latter's opposition to the Bill was based less on ethical considerations and more on a desire to protect their not inconsiderable profits and investments which would be adversely affected by excessive regulation.[93] In contrast, the Liberty and Property Defence League characterised the debate over the Bill as, in all essentials, an ideological battle between laissez-faire and state intervention. In the name of defending individual rights, the League and its offshoots stood firmly opposed to anything that hinted at state intervention or, as they saw it, interference. The cooperation that existed between the League and the U.K.S.V.D.P.A. served to justify the motives of the other. Moreover, their claims that the Bill would harass and persecute the Gypsy were not without foundation. Its aim was to bring the Gypsies under the watchful eye of the authorities, and the proposed regulations would have necessarily interfered with how and where they lived. In the long-term it was hoped that their way of life would be brought to an end: persecution extended to its logical conclusion.

Accusations that the Bill was impractical and unworkable were also justified. Any attempt to impose the specific regulations outlined by Smith was made extremely difficult, if not impossible, by a number of factors. First, the Gypsies' nomadism made it difficult to track them down and enforce the provisions with any effectiveness as they had only to move on when approached by visiting inspectors. Next, it was said the character of the Gypsy acted against reform and regulation, and his fear and distrust of officials and authority would prevent cooperation. Thirdly, it was thought the proposals were too costly, and the reply that the expense could be met out of the poor rates, the income from the registration fee and from a government subsidy was not thought sufficient. Finally, the practical enforcement of many of the measures, particularly those relating to the education of the Gypsy children, was made difficult by the antipathy of those necessarily involved in their implementation, such as the schoolteachers.

The final thread of the argument of the opposition stressed that the Bill was unnecessary since legislation elsewhere more than adequately covered the problem. Appendix 1 lists the major Acts, for England and Wales, that had some bearing on the Gypsies and the travelling, vagrant way of life.[94] Their variety and extent is readily apparent. While the pre-nineteenth-century Acts were harsher in their provisions, threatening banishment and execution, than anything enacted or in force in the 1800s, it would be wrong to think that this was evidence of weakness or relaxation on the part of the legislature. Rather, it was a more realistic attempt to come to terms with the problem. The laws had become more generalised and the Gypsies, or Egyptians as they were once referred to, were no longer singled out for special legislative treatment. Their racial isolation in the early Acts had given way to their inclusion in less specific Acts that dealt generally with the problem of itinerancy and vagrancy, and it is instructive to consider the more important of these.

The various Hawkers and Pedlars Acts between 1810 and 1888 provided that all such travellers needed a licence to carry on their employments, thus resulting in the registration of all such nomadic salesmen and saleswomen. The occupations were essentially the same, but with the legal distinction that the pedlar went about on foot, carrying his wares in a basket or a wheelbarrow, and the hawker carried his goods in a cart drawn by a horse. A pedlar's licence cost 5s. and a hawker's £2. Most travellers would have had a licence of one kind or the other as it acted as an effective safeguard against the Vagrant Act, though some were issued illegally by forgers.[95] The 1824 Vagrancy Act was perhaps the most pernicious piece of legislation in force against Gypsies and travellers in the nineteenth century. It has already been mentioned that it gave considerable discretionary powers to magistrates, who showed little reluctance in enforcing it, and by sweeping the countryside as 'a remorseless drag-net' no nomadic family was able to feel immune from its generalised provisions.[96] Even at the time of its enactment it was criticised for its severity and was said to have been framed in a spirit unknown to the constitution, endangering the ancient liberties of Englishmen.[97] Yet to others the Act was thought far too lenient, especially when it was considered who were the objects of the laws: 'this "unruly brood" . . . [who] may be compared to the overflowings of a stream left to stagnate – impoverishing the land, and distempering the air; or like those lazy peccant humours of the body, which, unless dispersed, or purged away, weaken and eventually destroy the whole constitution'.[98] The summary power entrusted to the magistrates was believed to allow for a cheaper and speedier redress of wrongs than 'could possibly obtain by the tedious and expensive mode of trial by jury'.[99] The Act was frequently called upon to deal with the Gypsies by these powers, and many were prosecuted under its provision. Moreover, the Act gave power to police constables to carry out an effective persecution of the Gypsies by forcing them, under threat of prosecution, to move on unless tented on private property and by permission of the owner.[100] The Gypsies were able to counter this, up to a point, by taking out a Hawkers' and Pedlars' licence and, by encamping on the border of two counties, they were able easily to move across from one county to the other when challenged by the county officers who had no jurisdiction beyond the boundaries of their own shires.[101]

By the various Commons and Enclosure Acts, notably of 1899, and also by the Local Government Act (1894), local authorities were empowered to make bye-laws regulating village greens and commons. This had the effect of further restricting the places where Gypsies could encamp, reinforcing the

1835 Highway Act which penalised Gypsies who encamped on any part of the highway. The result of these laws was to close commons and highways as camping places. Captain Fullarton James, in his evidence to the Departmental Committee on Vagrancy in 1906, even went so far as to say that the effect of the 1899 Act in particular was to abolish the Gypsies.[102]

Not only were their traditional sites being barred to them, but those they were still permitted to use were being watched a great deal more closely. This was achieved mainly by recourse to Section 9 of the Housing of the Working Classes Act, 1885, which extended the provisions of the 1875 Public Health Act to vans and tents. By this, moveable dwellings were brought firmly within the sanitary laws. Any such habitation which was in such a state as to be a nuisance, or so overcrowded as to be injurious to the health of the inmates, could lead to the prosecution of the occupier. Next, it allowed for bye-laws to be made for promoting cleanliness in, and the habitable condition of, such dwellings and for preventing nuisances and the spread of infectious disease in connection with them. Finally, it allowed any person so authorised by the sanitary authority, or by a Justice of the Peace, to enter these dwellings by day. Smith said this about the provisions made under this Act: 'I thank God for the ninth clause. I have worked hard and long for this.'[103]

The only aspect of Smith's Bill not dealt with adequately elsewhere was that regarding the education of the children. The Elementary Education Acts, 1870 to 1902, had proved ineffective in extending the principle of compulsory education to travelling children, and attempts by Smith to have education clauses inserted in other bills had proved unsuccessful.[104] It was not until the Children's Act of 1908 that the principle of compulsory education was enforced in relation to the children of nomadic families, and then only for the months October to March. The children were required to have 200 attendances at school in a year, under threat of a substantial penalty if they failed to do so. Although this represented only about half the attendances required of other children, it did necessitate that, for the winter months at least, the nomads had to remain in one place. The Act was welcomed for the provisions it had made for the education of the vagrant children, yet it created an unanticipated problem, which appeared especially acute in Scotland. Because of their poverty and the antipathy shown them by sections of the settled population, their enforced settlement in the winter months resulted in their being accommodated in the worst properties of the slum districts, exacerbating an already bad housing problem. This, and the difficulty of finding employments, meant that the School Boards were often unwilling to prosecute if the law was disobeyed, and the courts were unwilling to convict. On balance, the provisions made in the Act for compulsory education mostly tidied up the final loose end of Smith's proposals, and effectually marked the realisation of his short-term objectives.

Thus, the Gypsies were a long way removed from the free and uninhibited life ascribed to them in the romantic novels. In the nineteenth century the law treated them as vagrants, rogues, beggars and vagabonds, having moved on from the racial implications of the much earlier legislation against Egyptians. Provisions already existed for the registration of travellers, for regulating where they could camp legally and under what conditions, and for supervision of their health, sanitary arrangements and schooling. Apart from educational provisions, the remainder of these controls were in existence at the time when Smith was campaigning for his Bill. However, to say that the laws existed is not to say that they were applied either in the manner or spirit in which they were intended, or that their practical application was as effective as was anticipated. It therefore remains, in the following chapter, to look at their operation at a local level, and, more generally, at the response of the local authorities to the Gypsy problem. It is in this context that the endeavours of George Smith should be assessed.

Smith identified the group who were at the root of the problem, provided a definition of them and gave publicity to their distinctive features and relations with sedentary society. Earlier attempts to accommodate the travelling population had failed and it was generally agreed that the time had arrived for more positive steps to be taken to assimilate this 'unruly' element. By the 1870s and 1880s the position of travellers in relation to sedentary society had become increasingly unacceptable, offering apparently less in the way of an economic and social contribution. It has already been suggested how their former, traditional role in rural society had come to be replaced. While the Gypsies modified their way of life and occupations according to changes in wider society their position appeared as increasingly marginal, working on the fringes of an informal economy. Smith was the first person to confront the problem of a travelling population living in the midst of an industrial and settled society, and one which closely resembles that which exists today. His findings and suggestions about the need and nature of assimilation formed the basis of contemporary responses of those, notably local authorities, who were forced into taking action.

7

The Gypsy versus magistrates, police and local authorities

Confrontation between the Gypsies and authority was most marked at the local level. Legislative enactments give an overview without really casting a great deal of light on the relationship between the Gypsies and the officials of the various authorities of settled society. The response of magistrates, police and local government officials most clearly illuminates the clash beween the nomadic and settled ways of life. Scarcely any authority looked on the Gypsies with favour and the major differences in terms of responses were in the methods used to regulate the problem. These varied from persecution by stretching the word of the law to its limit, to the turning of a blind eye until the matter had solved itself by the Gypsies moving their camp to another area of their own accord.

Up to the 1870s, when local authorities were given greater powers to impose their own bye-laws regulating Gypsies and van-dwellers, the chief means of confronting the Gypsy and vagrant problem was by recourse to the police and the courts. Gypsies were classed alongside criminals and rogues and prosecutions were frequent. In the later decades of the century prosecution for various offences, even if loosely defined as vagrancy, gave way to a more general and all-encompassing persecution and harassment by the authorities. Prosecutions against individuals and families were accompanied also by a wider persecution of the Gypsies in their camps, matching the tendency of the Gypsies to live in larger groups on the edge of cities. The issue was now of concern to both urban and rural authorities. However, the desire seems to have been to disperse the problem and move it on, evidencing a general unwillingness to accept responsibility for the measures taken.

THE POLICING OF TRAVELLERS

As might be expected, records concerning the policing of Gypsies and vagrants in the early part of the nineteenth century are very scarce, though it is clear from those that do exist that the various policing agencies kept up the tradition of persecution. Placards appeared by the roadsides and notices were printed in newspapers which ordered the Gypsies' apprehension and committal to prison.[1] Of the few which have survived the notice issued in Sussex in 1799 would have been typical:

At the respective General Quarter Sessions of the Peace, holden at Chichester and Lewes, the 15th and 17th days of January 1799 [*sic*].

The Majestrates met and Assembled at the abovesaid Sessions, having taken into their consideration the great number of Gypsies and other Vagrants of different descriptions infesting this County; were pleased to order, that if any Gypsies or other Vagrants of whatever description, should be found therein after the 25th day of March next, they will be punished as the Law directs, of which all Constables and other Peace Officers, are particularly Ordered to take Notice and apprehend all such Gypsies and other Vagrants, and carry them before some of his Majesties Justices of the Peace for the said County for that purpose; and if any Constables, or other Peace Officers after this Notice shall neglect or refuse so to do, they will be immediately proceeded against and punished with the utmost vigour that may be by Law for such their neglect or refusal.

> By order of Court,
>
> Wm. Ellis,
> *Clerk of the Peace, for the County of Sussex.*
>
> Horsham, 22d Feb. 1798 [sic]²

Gypsies and other vagrants were thus deemed guilty of an offence even before they were accused of any crime. Their mere presence as travellers and vagrants was sufficient cause for prosecution. The Northumberland magistrates issued similar notices and orders, demanding that active steps be taken to rid the county of 'rogues, vagrants and other idle and disorderly persons'.[3] To achieve this, rewards were given to constables for the apprehension of such persons and penalties were threatened if it could be proved that they had been negligent in this duty. Such action was thought to be 'the most effectual step towards driving these detestable characters from society, who by their lying stories and distressed appearances, too successfully work upon the feelings of the charitable and humane, and too frequently devour the portion of the fatherless and the widow, and those who are really afflicted'.[4]

Concern over the question of vagrancy was heightened during the years following the end of the Napoleonic Wars when demobilised sections of the militia added greatly to the vagrant numbers. It was considered essential to come down harshly on all travellers in order to curb what were regarded as their mendicant, poaching and other offensive and parasitical habits. In 1817 the Norfolk magistrates made the position very clear when they passed the following resolution:

That the clerk of the peace do give public notice in the newspapers circulated within the county of Norfolk, that all persons pretending to be Gipsies, or wandering in the habit or form of Egyptians, are by law deemed to be rogues and vagabonds, and are punishable by imprisonment or whipping. And the Chief Constables in their respective hundreds, and the petty Constables in their respective parishes, are required to put the law in execution, by apprehending such gipsies, or pretended gipsies, and to carry them before some of his Majesty's justices of the peace acting in and for the said county, in order that they may be dealt with according to law.[5]

Throughout the whole of the period under review the felt, or perceived, increase in vagrant numbers led to such demands being frequently repeated by magistrates and Chief Constables alike. Reports of the latter from around the mid-nineteenth century provide ample testimony to the desire to suppress the growing problem of vagrancy.[6] Although it is difficult to characterise the response of magistrates as a body, it nevertheless seems to have been the case that judging from past and present experience of their statements and actions in relation to the travelling population, the Chief Constables were able to rely on their assistance in securing the prosecution or removal of the vagrant elements.[7] Hoyland noted that in some places Gypsies were sent to prison under the Vagrancy Act without even being charged for committing depredations on property.[8] Similarly Crabb related stories of Gypsies who were arrested and taken before the magistrates on suspicion of having committed thefts, but when they had proved their innocence, against all odds, they were then proceeded against for having allowed their animals to stray, for living under a hedge, or some other pretext.[9] It was also stated that Gypsy fortune-tellers were flogged and openly discriminated against in the law courts.

Perhaps the most famous case of all, which resulted in questions being asked in the House of Commons, was that of the seven Gypsies committed to twenty-one days' hard labour by the Reverend Uriah Tonkin, at Hale, Cornwall, in 1864. Tonkin justified this penalty in a letter to the Home Secretary, Sir George Grey, reprinted in the *Cornish Telegraph*.[10] Prior to their appearance before Tonkin, one of the party had been apprehended at Redruth on the charge of vagrancy, but was discharged after promising to leave the neighbourhood. The next day she was only three miles away, and two of the party were now cautioned by the police for sleeping under a wagon not belonging to them. They travelled about begging and telling fortunes, and eventually camped on the Trelissick Estate, where they were said to have done 'a great deal of injury' by breaking down trees and lighting fires. At this point they were apprehended and brought before the magistrate. From the moment of their arrival in the district they had been closely supervised by the police, under direction of the Superintendent of the Police, as many thefts had been committed in the area and, as usual, the Gypsies were the chief suspects. Tonkin then examined the party 'individually and collectively', and finding they had no visible means of support and were unable to give a satisfactory account of themselves, as required by the Vagrancy Act, he considered it his duty to commit them to a lengthy period of hard labour 'for the safety of the county'.[11] When this latter phrase was read out in the House members expressed their approval with a chorus of 'Hear! Hear!'.[12] It is worth adding at this point that the party consisted not of a group of marauding adults but of a man, his wife and their five children, aged from eight to twenty years.[13]

Reaction to the sentence in the local press was one of surprise and indignation. It was stated that the law as interpreted by Tonkin made it illegal to sleep beside a haystack or in a tent, and there was fear that it set a dangerous precedent: 'soon it will be thatch, and so we shall soon have the police down upon all rascals below the grade of the twenty-pound house-holder'.[14] Tonkin's law was said to 'smite the poor' and the newspaper quoted similar opinions from the *Examiner* and the *Observer*, which expressed amazement at the severity of the sentence and which saw no wrong in sleeping under canvas. Mr George Hunt, M.P. for Northants North, raised the matter in the House and requested the Home Secretary to enquire into the circumstances of committal and conviction, with a view to securing a remittal of the sentence.[15] However, Tonkin's reply must have satisfied the Home Secretary, and the sentence stood.

In terms of the actual and specific response of the local policing agencies to the problem caused by travellers and vagrants, the rural constables needed little encouragement from their supervisors to carry out effectively their duties of watching, moving and apprehending this section of the population. Although the rural constables were, in the early part of the century, 'untrained, indifferent, unpaid, unwilling',[16] there were perhaps two chief factors that would have acted as an incentive for them to carry out an effective persecution of the nomadic population. First, at least before the reorganisation of the Constabulary Force, the rural constable was partly motivated by a desire for the bonus or reward that was often paid for the apprehension and successful prosecution of vagrants, perhaps amounting to 10s.[17] The second factor stemmed from the place of the constable in the local community. The constables, or their deputies, were appointed locally and had to carry out their policing duties often simultaneously with their own full-time employment. It was likely that a certain amount of local crime was committed by persons known personally to them, perhaps as friends or customers. In the local context self-interest and personal responsibility conflicted with their public duty as enforcers of the law. In such a situation it was not surprising that the 1839 Commission on the Constabulary Force had to admit that the constables often did not want to get involved with the acts of apprehension and policing generally.

From time to time travellers wandered into this inefficient and contradictory arrangement. Not being of the community there was no protective bond of reciprocity of friendship, custom and goodwill. In all senses they provided a convenient scapegoat to be accused of many local crimes. It suited the magistrates who wanted a conviction and the local population who sought to divert blame and attention to seek the offender in the Gypsy camps, irrespective of the true location of guilt. Local feelings and connections were absent and the inhabitants of the camp had no protection from persecution and prosecution. At times the watchful and supervisory eye of the local constable was used as nothing more than a warning and threat, but more usually it was translated into an active and persistent persecution, with the Gypsies being hunted like 'beasts of prey . . . from township to township'.[18] Crabb was eager to point to the numerous examples of such harassment on the part of the police, who, when challenged about this, replied simply that they were obliged to do their 'duty'.[19] The Gypsies were frequently moved on, under threat of prosecution for contravening the various Vagrancy Acts and the Highways Act, by which they could be summonsed as rogues and vagabonds for simply encamping on the highway or living without any visible means of subsistence. It was said this constant harassment was especially applicable in relation to the Gypsies dwelling in the south of England, resulting in their migration northwards in great numbers, although it is not possible to substantiate either of these claims.[20]

Perhaps the most blatant example of persecution and harassment took place in the south at the end of the eighteenth and the beginning of the nineteenth centuries, when the Gypsy encampment at Norwood, near London, was raided by the police, resulting in the eventual committal to prison of the entire group. The first raid occurred in 1797, when ten police officers broke up the camp by tearing down all the tents and taking to prison thirty men, women and children, who were proceeded against under the vague and all-encompassing clauses of the Vagrancy Act.[21] Yet their removal from Norwood was only temporary. In 1802 three Norwood Gypsies were arrested on suspicion of the murder of a Dulwich hermit, and in October 1803 several Gypsies from the area were in attendance at the Surrey Quarter Sessions to answer the charge brought against them by the Society for the Suppression of Vice for 'bringing idle persons about them at Norwood, to have their fortunes told on a Sunday'.[22] Although the charge of fortune-telling was proved, the Gypsies expressed contrition for their past and, on the promise of not repeating the offence, were freed.

The common was enclosed in 1808, but even this did not succeed in removing the Gypsies from the neighbourhood, and they were to be found in the woods of Dulwich College in that year, and in 1809 encampments were again seen at Norwood.[23] Six years later a further effort was made to remove them from the area:

On Sunday the police officers attacked the Gipsey encampment at Norwood, from which they made a precipitate retreat; they, however, captured three coach loads, together with their queen and princes Thomas and John! The officers were attacked by a rallying party of about 40, in an attempt at a rescue, in which they failed. They were committed as vagrants.[24]

But even this, combined with the progressive encroachments on their sites brought about by enclosures, did not entirely rid Norwood of the Gypsies. Around 1830 building began in the area in an attempt to turn Norwood into a health resort, necessitating the removal of the Gypsies from their long-established haunts. After this, they were to be found in the woods about Penge and Anerley, and also encamped in a field in Lordship Lane, in Dulwich, which had been purchased by a Gypsy capitalist.[25]

Such examples as these serve to illustrate both the individual and localised nature of the responses to the Gypsy-travellers and also the considerable discretionary powers, often abused by their extreme application, at the disposal of the police and magistrates. This was to undergo some modification by the middle decades of the century. The reform of the Constabulary Force, recommended by the 1839 Commission, affected different areas at different times, yet the overall effect was the gradual replacement of a highly parochial and amateur arrangement by one systematically rationalised, professionally organised and imposing a non-discretionary code of punishment. Such a development was not made compulsory until 1856, when the County Constabulary Act was passed. Methods of surveillance, harassment and persecution became increasingly efficient, and there are many references to the constant pressures exerted by the police on the travellers, driving them from the rural roads into the towns.[26] On occasions, camps were raided and the people persecuted simply on suspicion they might have stolen something.[27] By the end of the nineteenth century the travellers could be prosecuted, or threatened with prosecution, for sleeping out, overcrowding, possessing no dustbin, or neglecting to provide a proper water supply for their habitations.[28] Any travellers who set up camp in the district of the Metropolitan Police were immediately cautioned, and this invariably had the desired effect of removing the Gypsies from the area. If the caution proved slow to evoke a response then a further incentive to move on was administered to the travellers by seizing, or threatening to seize, their horses. The expense entailed in recovering their animals acted as a great deterrent to the Gypsies remaining in the district.[29]

In Worcestershire, Hertfordshire, Middlesex and other parts of the Home Counties, similar steps were taken, though the 'hunting' of the Gypsies did not always remain bound by the confines of the law, and in at least one instance the travellers were prevented from entering a district by the police drawing themselves across the road in a line, presenting an impassable human barrier.[30] In the East Sussex division persecution was less overt but scarcely less threatening, with a close surveillance being maintained over the travellers. Diaries were kept by various police stations recording the site and location of the camp, whether it was situated on waste land or private property, the names and numbers of the persons on the site, their date of arrival and proposed date of departure, and any complaints issued against them.[31]

The cooperation of all members of settled society, acting in unison against the vagrant travellers, was a major factor contributing to the general system of policing and surveillance. This may have extended to the participation of 'lay' members in the duties of policing or simply acting as the complainants who made the newspapers, council officers and the police aware of the travellers' presence and demanded that some remedial action be taken. The nuisances said to be caused by the travellers were extensive, ranging from camping opposite dwelling houses to contaminating water, stealing, lighting fires and using abusive language.[32]

From at least the eighteenth century onwards, rural policing was supplemented by groups of local inhabitants banding together to carry out specific policing functions. This is evidenced by the proliferation of locally organised associations for the prosecution of felons, brought into existence as a response to the inadequacy of the formal system.[33] Mr William Allen, who was in the legal profession at Higham Ferrers, Northamptonshire, commented that associations such as these made the situation of the Gypsies increasingly deplorable, for by persecuting them it pushed them further from the civilising habits of settled society.[34] In relation to this study, one of the most interesting of these associations was formed at Southampton in January 1818 to prevent depredations by Gypsies and vagrants. It was felt by a meeting of 'gentlemen inhabitants' of Southampton that the depredations committed by Gypsies and other vagabonds had increased to such a degree that it was necessary to enforce with greater strictness the existing laws for the apprehension and prosecution of such offenders.[35] Specially appointed constables were the means by which this was to be achieved, and anyone found 'remiss and negligent' in this duty was to be punished severely. The ten parishes and towns in the Association also swore to inflict the severest penalties on all offenders and vagrants who were caught. Likewise, in 1907 the 130-year-old Beare Green Society for the Prosecution of Thieves endorsed a suggestion that they turn their attentions to the increasingly serious Gypsy question.[36]

Elsewhere, local residents decided to take direct action themselves to remove the problem. In 1799, near Bath, a violent affray took place between the Gypsies and a farmer assisted by his neighbours, resulting in the successful eviction of the nomads.[37] It was even thought by some that such violent assaults were entirely acceptable and would have the approval of the law agencies. In 1874 a vigilante group visited a Gypsy camp at Sale, near Manchester, pulled down the tents and attacked the Gypsies, inflicting serious injuries. That the attackers thought they had the tacit approval of the authorities was shown when one expressed great surprise for his subsequent apprehension and conviction at the Altrincham Petty Sessions for what was described as 'a most gross assault'.[38] Even though the Gypsies may have offended notions of order, it would seem that at least some magistrates did not give their backing to unprovoked assaults.

Such forcible methods of securing the Gypsies' removal were common. In 1895 a gang of freeholders of Long Horsley Moor, Northumberland, physically expelled the Gypsies camped there, and in this instance their actions were given legal sanction by the subsequent judicial decision which banned the Gypsies from ever again using the moor as a camping ground.[39] Similarly, an army of farmers resorted to violence to remove the Gypsies camped at Effingham in 1908.[40] It was more usual for the police to be in attendance, ready and willing to give assistance in preventing a disturbance. The police were not legally able to move the Gypsies and their tents and vans from the camp site so they would wait for the group and their belongings to be deposited on the highway and then proceed against them for causing an obstruction and other minor misdemeanours. The Gypsies who camped in various parts of North Hampshire in the early 1890s were forced away by such combined action. Unable to move as they had no transport each landowner provided two or three horses, forcibly removed the Gypsies and their possessions onto the highway, and left it to the constables to ensure that the road was not obstructed by demanding that the Gypsies move on.[41] Such an effective combination of local residents and police also occurred at Ipswich in the opening decade of the twentieth century, when a committee of the Freehold Land Society decided to take their own measures to remove the Gypsies from a plot of land in Henniker Road:

10 or 11 committee men – all stout men – armed themselves with umbrellas, and proceeded to the meadow in question, there surprising 9 horses quietly cropping the valuable grass. The men spread themselves out in a half-circle . . . and advanced on the horses with flapping umbrellas. Eventually 7 were driven onto the road, and impounded by 3 constables.[42]

The result was that four Gypsies appeared at the Ipswich Police Court, and were fined a total of £3 18s. for doing wilful damage to growing grass! Although the initiative for persecution had been taken by others the police and magistrates were only too willing to assist in its effective implementation.

A QUESTION OF SHORT-TERM RESPONSIBILITY

The comprehensiveness of the policing of travellers by the various members and agencies of settled society appears impressive. But although in general terms the response was one of antipathy and persecution this is qualified by the realisation that the interpretation and application of the law varied from region to region and Chief Constable to Chief Constable. Also, this lack of uniformity could result in serious disputes among different sections of settled society as to where lay the responsibility for dealing with the problem of the travellers. On at least one occasion this led to a serious questioning of the legality of the various police actions when, in 1909, the Chief Constable of Surrey, Captain Sant, refused to sanction tactics he considered to be *ultra vires*. At the core of this dispute was the position and role of the lords of the manors. By way of an introduction to the disagreements at Surrey, it is instructive to consider an earlier expression of the issues, at Wimbledon, around mid-century.

During the late 1850s and early 1860s the 5th Earl Spencer, Lord of the Manors of Putney and Wimbledon, was receiving many letters and petitions from local residents complaining of the Gypsy and vagrant nuisance on Wimbledon Common.[43] The Putney ratepayers even held a meeting on the subject in 1860, drawing up a memorial which highlighted the need to curb the 'problem'.[44] In 1861 Earl Spencer replied thus to one such complainant, a letter showing many signs of anger, frustration and impotence:

Sir,

I regret that the Gypsies on Putney and Wimbledon Manors should again be troublesome.

I assure you it is not the first time that this question has been brought before me.

It has given me great trouble and annoyance because whatever I do my powers are so limited that I cannot take effectual means to get rid of the nuisance.

The defect in my powers lies in the difficulty of conviction, and the facility that exists for the gypsies to escape wherefore the summons can be executed . . .

The position is an extremely harassing and difficult one for my common keeper . . .

I assure you it is my earnest wish to do all I can for the neighbourhood in this respect: & my orders are strict to lessen the nuisance as much as possible.

I am willing to adopt any effectual way of putting down the gypsies.

It is curious that at this very time last year I annoyed a lady friend of Lady Spencer's by refusing to comply with her request, which was just the contrary to yours, that the gypsies might be allowed to remain on the Common in order that their children might go to school.[45]

The problem thus continued unabated, with as many as 130 Gypsies camping in a corner on the Common,[46] until it was decided the only possible effective remedy would be enclosure.[47]

Earl Spencer's proposals to sell Putney Heath, which comprised about a third of the land, and to turn the rest into an enclosed and fenced park, met with much opposition.[48] Such a solution served to annoy the commoners even more than his inability to remove the Gypsies from the common land. Although there was a general desire to preserve order and prevent nuisances on the Common, a Committee was formed in opposition to these specific proposals. The issues concerned, about the nature and legality of enclosure, were such that a Select Committee was called into existence to consider the arguments. In relation to the specific problem of the Gypsies much contradictory evidence was presented. Generally most of the witnesses provided testimony to the Gypsy nuisance, though there then followed great differences in the assessments of the menace posed by the Gypsy presence and the steps needed to bring about a solution. These varied from enclosures to policing of the commons by keepers, paid by a small rate contributed willingly by the local residents.[49]

The Select Committee eventually reported that it was both unnecessary and undesirable for any part of the Common to be sold or enclosed and as a result the proposals were subsequently withdrawn. A clash of interests and responsibility, over the rights of the commoner and the duty of the Lord to curb a menace taking place on his land, thus resulted in inactivity and a continuation of the Gypsy 'problem'. Similar conflicts occurred elsewhere, with perhaps the most lengthy and fully-documented in Surrey in the early years of the twentieth century.[50]

By the late nineteenth and early twentieth centuries the county of Surrey had developed into a main centre for British Gypsies. Pushed out of London by the combined actions of the Metropolitan Police, land agents, sanitary authorities and building developments, the nearby open spaces of Surrey provided a suitable and convenient alternative.[51] Furthermore, in Surrey, the Gypsies had the possibility of employment at Ascot races and on the local fruit, vegetable and hop farms.[52] During the winter of 1896 their numbers were so great that it was estimated that 10,000 were encamped in the county.[53] Although this is undoubtedly a wild exaggeration, it does provide an indication of how seriously the problem was perceived. The numbers, as provided by the census enumerators for the county of Surrey, are shown in Table 4. The numbers under the jurisdiction of the Surrey Constabulary,

Table 4 *Number of dwellers in barns, sheds, tents, caravans and the open air in Surrey, 1891–1911*

	Barns and sheds			Tents, caravans, and open air			Barns, sheds, tents, caravans, and open air		
	Male	Female	Total	Male	Female	Total	Male	Female	Total
1891	304	64	368	465	409	874	769	473	1,242
1901	136	26	162	344	305	649	480	331	811
1911*							994	924	1,918

*Note that the census for 1911 did not distinguish between the groups.
Sources: Census of England and Wales, Reports, 1891, 1901, 1911.

rather than the Metropolitan Police, were necessarily less, amounting to around 1,200 in both 1906 and 1913.[54] Although the actual numbers were far less than the estimates, the problem was still regarded as serious and one which required an effective remedy.

Most of the urban and rural districts of Surrey were inhabited to a greater or lesser degree by the travellers, though they were most numerous around Chobham, on Gomshall Marsh between Dorking and Guildford, on Wood Common, Worplesdon, at Netley Heath, Farnham, Hurtwood, Shere and West Horsley, and on the North Downs.[55] Each time they appeared the Gypsies and their camps were described in the most unfavourable terms. The people were said to be beggarly and parasitic, while their camps were an ugly blot on the natural beauty of the Surrey landscape:

An old pair of stays, two battered and draggled [sic] straw hats, three old boots . . . plenty of horse dung . . . innumerable old rags half trampled into the mud, large sections of clothing in the way of old coats, old skirts, old trousers, and all these mingled with a mass of tin cans, broken bottles, and bits of bones, skin and offal, and so forth and so on: such is the inventory of the Gipsies' resting-place.[56]

There was no shortage of people demanding that immediate action be taken, the problem was over who was to act and how. Essentially, the county council responded by seeking to secure effective local and national legislation (to be discussed later), while the lords of the manors, major landowners and the Chief Constable, Captain Sant, carried out a long battle in an attempt to apportion the responsibility and burden for physically moving on the travellers.

In the main, the Gypsy-travellers camped on private land belonging to local and absentee landowners. The debate concerning responsibility hinged on whether the Gypsies' removal should be undertaken by the owners of the land on which the 'nuisance' was being caused, or whether the problem was of a general and public nature and so should rest with public servants, the police and local authorities. There was no disagreement amongst the opposing parties that some remedy needed to be found.

The landowners' campaign centred on the figures of Reginald Bray and Lord Onslow, and their position is summarised by Bray himself in a letter to the Chairman of the Surrey County Council: 'There is no legal or moral duty on the landowners to remedy the nuisance. It is the duty of the State or the County Authorities.'[57] Together Bray and Onslow sought to justify this claim, advertise it and secure its effective implementation. There was no shortage of letters and petitions received from local inhabitants which they could bring forward as evidence of the public nature of the problem, and the general demand from local residents of all classes for a remedy.[58] One such petition was concerned with the travellers camped in and around Hurtwood:

We, the undersigned inhabitants of Holmbury St. Mary and district, beg to draw your attention to the large number of tramps and vagrants now frequenting this neighbour-hood and living on the Hurtwood Common and adjoining waste lands, in carts or wigwams. The children frequent the high roads and beg or endeavour to obtain alms under the pretense [sic] of selling something, while the men and women frighten the summer visitors and prevent ladies going about without an escort, and the village children from gathering [nuts?]. The lawlessness practised by these vagrants, with regard to the non-education of their children and the filthiness and, if not criminality, of their mode of life, set a bad example to our villagers and their life amongst us has a degrading influence. We have to ask that the law may be put in action against them with a view to their dispersal from the extensive waste lands of the district, and thus any temptation to others to join their evil course of life, removed. In order to effect this it will be necessary to employ a considerable force of Police, as if only one or two warn them off, they remove only a little distance or refuse to move off at all. Some of these vagrants come with vehicles drawn by horses, which are allowed to wander loose about the village and commons, and cause much annoyance by disturbing the residents during the night.[59]

Bray had had personal experience of many of these complaints and reported that he had repeatedly sent his agents to drive away the Gypsies, but this had proved ineffective for they simply moved back into another area of Hurt-wood, which extended over 20,000 acres.[60] Correspondence received from other landowners testified to a similar impotence and it was realised that for any measures to be effective, there had to be a concerted and unified effort on the part of all those concerned with the problem, landowners, local authorities, police and local residents alike.[61]

Bray set about organising the landowners of the district by circulating letters and reports about the nuisance caused by travellers. On 19 February 1909 a meeting was held at the home of Lord Onslow, when it was decided to form an association of the lords of the manors and the owners and occupiers of lands, shootings and houses in the county, for preventing travellers encamping within the districts inhabited by the members. A further meeting, on 28 April, decided to appoint patrols to turn vagrants off the land of members of what was then called the Surrey Anti-Vagrants Association.[62] At the outset the Association covered only the districts of Guildford and Dorking, though it was hoped that in time it would extend throughout the county.[63] Concern was expressed in some quarters about this 'Surrey tyranny . . . this manorial persecution',[64] yet the Association defended itself by claiming it was not persecuting or harassing the Gypsies who lived decent lives and earned their livelihood honestly, but only the disreputable and undesirable vagrants and travellers.[65] Although the local press initially gave support to the Association, the members delayed taking advantage of public backing by acting against the travellers until the Lords' Committee on the Moveable Dwellings Bill had reported. If possible, they would have preferred action to be taken by any but themselves. After June the Association had faded away and nothing more was heard of it.[66]

Part of the reason for its demise has to be found in the general feeling among the landowners that they would prefer to delegate their powers to any authority willing to act in moving the Gypsies, stressing that the problem was one demanding a solution from public not private authorities: 'I have made up my mind that I will not again interfere to protect the property of the ratepayers, or to save them from annoyance. I am convinced that this is a duty which ought not to fall upon individual landowners but upon public authorities.'[67] Increasingly the landowners' campaign became directed towards pressurising the local authorities to secure effective legislation and the local constabulary to act positively in removing the travellers from the district. While the pressure on the local county council was intended to secure a permanent remedy, the debate over the allocation of responsibility to take immediate action against the travellers was clearly the most pressing concern of the landowners.

Their demand that the local police force were morally, if not legally, obliged to move the travellers rested on the claim that a public nuisance should be treated by a quick and effective response by public authorities. Such action was necessary to prevent local villagers from taking the lead from other places to arm themselves and aggressively confront the travellers. Furthermore, it was argued, the police in other counties were only too willing to accept responsibility, and it was only in Surrey that the Chief Constable refused to act.[68] It was even suggested that the Gypsy nuisance in Surrey was exacerbated by the unwillingness of the Chief Constable to take any effective action, with the Gypsies being attracted to a county adopting a policy of non-harassment of itinerants by police officers.[69]

The claim that Captain Sant was unprepared to take any action was not entirely the case. He was willing to take any necessary steps against the Gypsies, but only by process of the law. Not only would the police be acting *ultra vires* in forcibly removing travellers from private land but also Sant was not prepared to allow the police to act as the agents or common keepers for private individuals, an action that both he and the Home Office agreed would set an unwanted precedent: 'It would not be possible for me to accept on behalf of my men the authority you have sent me for them to become your agents . . . the Police, who are servants of the public, cannot become the agents of private individuals.'[70] The police always acted when the Gypsies committed offences, and were always present when they were moved on by the lords of the manor or their agents, in order to prevent any breach of the peace, but had they taken any active part in the evictions they were technically guilty of assault.[71] On one such occasion, Sant, an Inspector, a police sergeant and twelve constables were present for an afternoon when a single agent of the lord of the manor, with the help of one young man and a horse, removed about fifty Gypsy vans from Chobham Common. The police were forbidden to assist, simply watching over the eviction until the vans were on the highway when they were able to insist that the Gypsies moved on or risk prosecution for obstruction.[72] Sant complained that the presence of so many constables was necessitated by the scarcity of Lord's agents, thereby increasing the risk of a forceful refusal from the Gypsies to move. The Chief Constable considered this wasted his scarce resources by preventing constables from carrying out more necessary duties elsewhere; when constables were challenged over complaints of neglect of duty, the usual excuse was that they were 'engaged in shifting gypsies'.[73] Their lordships received no satisfaction from Sant's replies and explanations and so petitioned the Home Office for support. To their dismay the Home Secretary gave full support to Sant and tersely commented that either the landowners should combine to employ one or more common keepers to carry out the duty of removing the Gypsies, or that it should be undertaken by the rural district council.[74]

The matter did not end entirely to the dissatisfaction of the landowners for they managed to get the approval of the local authorities for the appointment of a special uniformed constable, subject to all the normal police regulations yet to be paid for by subscriptions from the landowners and local residents.[75] The constable lived in a property provided by the landowners and was to receive his orders solely from those who paid his wages. His duty was to prevent Gypsies from encamping if possible, or otherwise to remove them when found encamped.[76] It was thought that a uniformed member of the county police would do more good than any number of keepers and it was optimistically hoped that 'we may now be within measurable distance of getting rid of the trouble'.[77] Yet, by the end of August 1913, there were still around 1,200 travellers within the district of the Surrey Constabulary.[78]

The picture so far is thus somewhat confusing and contradictory. Although the various members of settled society sought the circumscription of the travellers and their way of life, there was no convincing response that would effectively bring this about. The landowners' actions proved impotent and were, in any case, tempered and qualified by a desire to pass on responsibility for any action. There was a general response from police and magistrates of harassment and persecution, though even this has to be qualified by occasional examples of justice, humanity and an unwillingness to act outside the legal limits. The response of the local population at times climaxed in active attempts to move the travellers on, though it more usually remained at the level of verbal intolerance, with them acting as informal policing agents by complaining of the Gypsies' presence to the various police authorities. By the latter decades of the nineteenth century a new agency entered into the debate when powers were given to local authorities to enforce their own bye-laws and successfully implement national legislation at the local level. Official harassment of tent- and van-dwellers then took on a new aspect.

TRAVELLERS AND LOCAL AUTHORITIES: LONG-TERM SOLUTIONS

Popular antipathy to the Gypsies was such that there was never a shortage of people willing to bring the question of their presence in a particular district to the attention of the local council. Local residents protested at having dirty Gypsies and their equally filthy encampments as neighbours, expressing fear for their property, children and health, complaining that they were continually pestered for water and other items, and that the travellers' presence devalued nearby properties. In most places where the Gypsies encamped the problems, real and imagined, posed by their presence would have been debated in the council chambers. On occasions it was decided the Gypsies should be allowed to stay in the area on condition they pay the same levies as the ordinary householder, and there are instances of local councils attempting to extract from the Gypsies payment of rates and rent for the hire of fields.[79] At other times nothing was achieved beyond a general condemnation of the people and their way of life, with vague suggestions that, nationally, legislation should be introduced to curb the menace, and that locally the Gypsies should be given a push to move on. The latter was to be achieved informally by making life uncomfortable for the Gypsy-travellers and making them aware that their presence was not welcomed. Local residents were persuaded not to supply them with water, they were threatened with rates payments and refused permission to bury their dead in daylight.[80] On the whole, the problem was considered by these councils to be only temporary, and rather than go through the lengthy and expensive process of removing the Gypsies, it was deemed more expedient to let the matter run its course.

When the Gypsies had voluntarily removed themselves from the district, it was then possible that the council would take steps to prevent a recurrence of the problem by passing bye-laws which restricted the use of common land and prohibited the drawing of vans on it. In 1912 such a scheme was submitted to the Board of Agriculture respecting Northleigh Common,[81] and in 1916 the Wincanton District Council expressed its anxiety to spend money on draining, levelling and improving Leigh Common, and to supplement this by making bye-laws 'for the preservation of order'.[82] The Gypsy and Folk Lore Club was alarmed at this attack on what they considered to be the fundamental right to encamp on common land, and issued an appeal for funds to oppose the decision:

There is a growing tendercy (*sic*) for local bodies to 'preserve order' at the expense of the ratepayer, and to the detriment of the picturesque travellers on our country roads; and it is earnestly hoped that all ratepayers who object to such a waste of money on 'draining, levelling and improving', and all who revere the old-time traditions of the Gypsies – the coalporteurs (*sic*) of the Folk Tales of the world, will help to keep Leigh Common and all other open spaces free from such expensive, quite unnecessary and perfectly useless interference.[83]

Judging from the number of subscribers to the fund, the council had a great deal more support for their interference than the Folk Lore Club did for their reverence.

Perhaps more common than these responses of acceptance or qualified tolerance of the Gypsy presence was that which evidenced intolerance, antipathy and opposition. This was especially the case in places where the Gypsies were regular and relatively long-term visitors. In such instances the council most commonly relied on a mixture of informal harassment of the type described above and resort to the legal process in order to carry out a policy of regulation and persecution. This was achieved either by issuing injunctions to prevent them from setting up camp, or by the police and local authority officials enforcing a rigorous and comprehensive set of national and local legislation. In this their decisions and actions provided an effective complement to those of the police, magistrates, landowners and local residents.

If it could be shown that the travellers' camps would be dangerous to the health of the neighbourhood, then, under the precedent set by the case of the Attorney-General *versus* Stone, in 1895, the local authorities had the power to obtain injunctions to prevent landowners from leasing land to Gypsies. The Attorney-General, at the request of the Heston and Isleworth Urban District Council, applied for an injunction to prevent James Stone from allowing Gypsies, and 'other like people', from remaining on his land in Heston, or from using his land so as to be a threat to the health of the house-dwellers in the district. In addition, an injunction was applied for which was intended to compel Stone to 'purify' the surface of the same land.[84] From January 1894 Stone had allowed the Gypsies to camp on his land on payment of a weekly rent for each van or tent and where the only facilities provided were two defective and unusable water-closets. In no time, claimed the plaintiffs, the land was made dirty and untidy and this, added to the noise made by them, was adjudged by the council to be injurious to the health and peace of the neighbourhood. The council received many complaints from the local residents about the encampment, and some local medical practitioners testified that the camp smelt offensively, and their verdict was that 'there was an accumulation of matter, no means of draining, and no water for flushing purposes . . . the land was generally unhealthy, and as a direct result there had been several cases of illness in the district'.[85] In his defence, Stone claimed that the land was cleaned from time to time, that few complaints had been made about the Gypsies, that refuse was washed away once or twice a week and so the land could not be filthy or dangerous to health, and, finally, that the Gypsies themselves were an orderly and respectable set of people. He called a great number of witnesses to testify in his support, and was so convinced of the strength of his case that he promised if the local sanitary inspector could show any of the Gypsies to be of dirty habits then the offender would be immediately turned off the land. However, the plaintiffs persisted and although they dropped the claim that a nuisance was created by noise from the camp, they continued to base their case around the allegation that the encampment was a public nuisance and injurious to the health of the neighbourhood. The decision went conclusively in favour of the plaintiffs. The judge dismissed the weight of evidence produced by Stone's witnesses as being

> of a class whose views on subjects concerning cleanliness and sanitation were likely to be of an abnormal character, and opposed to the views of the ordinary citizens, and whose evidence did not impress me favourably, and some of the defendant's witnesses . . . were such partisans, and so extreme in their evidence as to make it worthless to the Court.[86]

By way of contrast, the plaintiff's witnesses could not be accused of bias or partisanship, were said to have given their evidence well, and were witnesses who could be trusted.

The legal decision, therefore, was that the Gypsies had made the land insanitary, offensive and dangerous to health. It was not practicable to proceed against the Gypsies themselves for they would simply give up their place on the site to others but, as the state of affairs had been brought about by Stone allowing them to camp on his land, then the responsibility for sanitary and health matters was adjudged to be his. Summary proceedings before a justice were deemed to be an inadequate remedy, and the district council was said to have been well advised and justified in bringing the matter before the High Court. The legal precedent had thus been set. Now, not only the Gypsies were liable to prosecution for contravening health and sanitary regulations, but so too was the owner of the land on which they encamped.

The means for proceeding against the travellers were many and various, as indicated by a breviate of some of the statutes listed in Appendix 1. Perhaps the most important of all these for the local councils was the Housing of the Working Classes Act, 1885, which gave local authorities jurisdiction over moveable dwellings deemed overcrowded, nuisances or injurious to health. More than this, it empowered urban and rural district councils to make their own bye-laws, subject to confirmation by the Local Government Board if outside London, and by the Home Office for London, governing the cleanliness and habitable conditions of tents, vans and the like, and for preventing nuisances and the spread of infectious diseases in connection with them. The Local Government Board issued model bye-law for this purpose, in order to assist their implementation and guarantee some measure of uniformity. By 1887 it was said that only Battersea had had their bye-laws accepted, and only two proposals had been received, from West Ham and Pontypridd.[87] The stamp of approval was not awarded indiscriminately, though, and in 1897 both the London County Council and Enfield Council had their applications refused.[88] In fact, it was thought that the Local Government Board and Home

Office were too harsh in their refusal to sanction all that was put before them, and Lord Clifford of Chudleigh, speaking in the House of Lords in 1908, said that he did not think many had been approved since Battersea.[89] This common belief was entirely unfounded as by 1906 bye-laws on the Local Government Board model had been made by eighty-six urban authorities, fifty seven rural authorities and two Metropolitan borough councils.[90] The number had increased to two hundred and eleven by 1909, and included forty-three by town councils, ninety by urban district councils, seventy-five by rural district councils and three by Metropolitan borough councils.[91]

In practice these bye-laws enabled local councils, by means of their sanitary authorities, to serve notices on persons thought to be causing a nuisance, and which required them to abate that nuisance in a given time. If this was refused or ignored then the matter was referred to the justices, who could impose penalties if the habitations were considered overcrowded or unfit for humans. Critics of these provisions argued that the bye-laws were not enforced, or were ineffective, as the Gypsies simply moved on when threatened with legal action, and in any case had been passed by only 211 of a possible 1,839 authorities. In answer to these criticisms, while the bye-laws may have been unsuccessful in achieving prosecutions in the law courts the mere threat of this had in fact been effective in moving the Gypsies, thus achieving the original and prime intention. Also, bye-laws would have been made only by authorities who felt a need for them. For example, the bye-laws encompassed most of the areas visited seasonally by Gypsy workers in the hop fields and on the fruit and vegetable farms.[92] Finally, even in the cases where bye-laws were thought necessary, few councils would have had the foresight to regulate the problem before it had arrived, and often the Gypsies would have moved on just as the wheels had been set in motion to get bye-laws approved. Invariably the matter was then dropped until the time of the next visit from the van- and tent-dwellers. The case of the West Parley Parish Council illustrates well the lengthy process of seeking redress against the Gypsy problem by recourse to making new bye-laws.

The matter was first brought to the attention of the council in 1896 when it was decided the best solution was to ask respectfully the owner of the land on which the Gypsies were encamped to refuse them this privilege. It was not until eight years later that the council was required to take further action, when a Sub-Committee was appointed to enquire into the legal aspects and practices in the county respecting van- and tent-dwellers. Neighbouring councils were asked to provide information on how they dealt with the problem, and the matter was just gaining momentum when the Gypsies left the area and it was allowed to drop. The question of enforcing bye-laws reappeared sporadically in the following year, and by April 1905 the district council passed a motion adopting bye-laws regulating tent- and van-dwellers. Yet the problem of the Gypsies remained an item on the agenda of subsequent meetings, when concern was expressed about the cost of enforcement, the question being made more acute by the presence of a Gypsy encampment on West Moors. A Sub-Committee with executive powers had been set up specifically to keep a close watch over the Gypsies, and the sanitary authorities and the Inspector of Cruelty to Children were instructed to keep the site under close observation.[93]

In 1911–12 the matter was again discussed, and concern was expressed that the model bye-laws were not being more effectively enforced. Local ratepayers were so dismayed at this apparent inactivity that a deputation was sent to the council to state their point of view: 'they [the Gypsies] were dirty and insanitary; the children ran wild and did not attend school, but went round the village begging, the trees and gorse were taken wholesale from the common and surrounding covers, and altogether they were a nuisance to the neighbourhood'.[94] They demanded that the bye-laws be put in force, effectively ridding the area of the Gypsies. Again, approval was given to this demand and another Sub-Committee was appointed to watch over the matter, 'with such delegated powers as the Council may in its discretion define'.[95] In May 1912 they reported they had done everything in their power to remove the Gypsies, and felt that responsibility now rested with the owner and others interested in taking action in the affair. The owner, Lord Salisbury, reacted by considering the possibility of making over a small portion of the common to the Gypsies, on which they could encamp at will on payment of a small rent. Although his intention was to try to civilise the Gypsies into a more regular and settled mode of living the rural district council reacted immediately by informing him that for years they had been struggling to rid the area of the Gypsies.[96] In 1914 the question of their settlement was still in abeyance, and the rural district council was still wavering over the best means of enforcing the various bye-law provisions.

Here is an example of a rural district council violently opposed to the Gypsy presence and yet not extending its opposition to effect their removal by prosecuting the Gypsies themselves or the landowner. The matter was repeatedly allowed to drop when the Gypsies left the area, so that the process had to be started anew each time the travellers returned. A careful watch was maintained over the encampments, yet, inexplicably, the authorities appeared reluctant to prosecute and take full advantage of their powers.

Elsewhere, the failure to pass and implement effective bye-laws was the result not of the fractured attempts by the local councils but was rather due to the refusal of the Local Government Board and the Home Office to give their approval to the proposals. Likewise, the attempts by various councils to secure Private Bills met with the same obstacles. East Ham Council in 1903, and Acton Council in 1904, applied to Parliament in Private Bills for special powers to deal with the Gypsies but both were referred to the Police and Sanitary Committee of the district to which they applied and both were rejected on the grounds that the local authorities had not used their existing powers and there was insufficient evidence of the nuisance caused.[97] In 1907 both York and Hull applied for special powers, but again both were refused.[98] Middlesex County Council had attempted to get an extension to their powers for dealing with the tent- and van-dwellers from as early as 1893, but the Home Office had repeatedly rejected the council's proposals, with the latter, in their turn, rejecting the alternatives suggested by the Home Office.[99] But in 1906 they were successful in getting a Private Bill passed, the first of its kind. Clause 31 of the Middlesex County Council Bill inflicted a penalty on any tent-dweller, squatter, Gypsy or other person who used as a dwelling-place any tent, van or similar structure situated within 100 yards of any street or house so as to cause annoyance, injury or disturbance to the residents. Furthermore, it was provided that a similar penalty would be imposed on any landowner who allowed his land to be so occupied.[100] The Act is especially interesting in that it was the first time Parliament had given legislative recognition of the different types of traveller living in tents and vans, by exempting from the provisions of the Act owners of vans attending fairs. Naturally, the Showmen's Guild was delighted: 'For many years we had been trying to evolve a clause that would effectively abate the nuisance and anger to the public health of the squatter and gypsy settlement, and yet be free from harm to the business interests of the travelling showmen.'[101]

The success of the Middlesex Council was something of an exception as there is little doubt the Home Office and the Local Government Board were reluctant to approve in wholesale fashion any extension of the powers already available to the local authorities. Part of the reason for this has to be found in the different ways that these bodies treated applications from urban and rural district authorities. Bye-laws were approved only in areas which were urban in character and where the seriousness of the nuisance could be proven. The efforts of rural authorities to prove the latter were clearly made especially difficult by the apparent official attitude that the travellers were accommodated better in a rural than an urban environment. Although the Home Office and Local Government Board did not dispute that the Gypsies were insanitary, paid no taxes and were a general nuisance, it was not felt the solution to the problem was by 'exterminating' them by local or general legislation.[102] Applications by councils for an extension to the powers already given them under, for example, the Public Health Act and the Housing of the Working Classes Act were considered unnecessary, unreasonable and invalid. It was realistically understood this would result only in transferring the problem from one locality to another, and it was feared the problem may then again become urban.[103] The problem could be more effectively dealt with in the rural context by systematic action on the part of the police and local authorities effectively enforcing existing provisions.[104]

Undoubtedly the most concerted and persistent attempt to secure both local and national legislation to deal with the Gypsy 'nuisance' came from the Surrey County Council. It is this attempt that identifies best the various positions of local and national government, the practical problems caused by the presence of Gypsy-travellers at the immediately local level, and the felt need for more precise and uniform provisions to accommodate the problem.

It has been shown previously that the Gypsy problem in Surrey was equally serious as anywhere in the country, if, indeed, it was not the most serious. The local council were well aware of this from an early date, and between 1894 and 1896 a series of bye-laws were proposed by the council against all tent- and van-dwellers. However, the Home Secretary refused to confirm these, demanding that before approval was given the council must provide clear evidence of the peculiar nature of the problem in Surrey, proving the existence of nuisances other than those of sanitation.[105] This task occupied a not insignificant portion of the council's time and attention up to the outbreak of the First World War. Essentially the council had to show that numerically the problem was of a serious nature and also that a general nuisance was being caused.

Reference has already been made to the various census figures concerning the nomadic population of Surrey. Although the council took the census on a night between the Epsom and Ascot race-meetings, the numbers were still not as high as would have suited their purposes. Reassurances were even demanded from the Chief Constable of Surrey that the enumeration was accurate, doubt being expressed over the complete absence of travellers from certain parishes.[106] Yet even the apparent scarcity of travellers in absolute numbers could be turned to the council's advantage, as shown by Table 5, compiled from the census figures for 1911. By this the council attempted to prove the problem was most severe in Surrey owing to the density of the nomadic population. But even though they could claim to have the highest density nomadic population per acre of counties with a relatively large travelling community (greater than 750), it should not be forgotten that no amount of juggling the statistics could hide the fact that the figure was nevertheless extremely small.

The second aspect of the campaign, to prove that a general nuisance was caused by the travellers, met with a greater degree of success and many statements were collected from local residents eager to register their complaints about the Gypsies. The impetus for the collection of country-wide evidence was provided by the unanimous feeling registered at a conference held in Kingston-on-Thames, in December 1897, for the local county authorities and other interested persons. The conference resolved, without dissent, that fresh legislation was required to regulate the tent- and van-dwellers both locally and nationally. To back these demands the many local authorities were instructed to collect all information about the nuisance caused by the

Table 5 *Density of travellers in counties with a nomadic population greater than 750, 1911*

Order of total nomad population	County	Area in acres	No. of nomad population			% per Acre	Order of %
			Males	Fe-males	Total		
1	Lancashire	1,194,919	1,179	714	1,889	.16	5
2	Kent	975,966	1,156	645	1,801	.18	4
3	Yorkshire, W.	1,773,529	1,170	625	1,795	.10	9
4	Derbyshire	650,369	1,128	527	1,655	.25	2
5	Surrey	461,829	994	524	1,518	.33	1
6	Hampshire	958,947	801	586	1,387	.14	6
7	Essex	979,532	705	457	1,162	.12	8
8	Yorkshire, N.	1,362,285	784	277	1,061	.08	11
9	Lincolnshire, Lindsey	970,423	771	215	986	.10	10
10	Durham	649,244	633	247	880	.14	7
11	Monmouthshire	349,582	584	200	784	.22	3
Total for England and Wales		37,337,537	19,948	10,694	30,642	.08	

Source: Surrey Record Office, CC 28/249A.

travellers, which was then to be collated and forwarded to the Secretary of State.[107] Many testimonies were assiduously recorded highlighting the Gypsies' propensity towards dirt, destruction, thieving, begging, quarrelling and fighting.[108] There is no indication whether the Secretary of State was presented with the evidence or whether the matter was allowed by the council to rest dormant but, whatever the reasons, there followed a period of eight years when the council appeared silent and inactive over the question. It was not until May 1906, on receipt of further complaints about the Gypsy nuisance, that a Sub-Committee met to consider a possible remedy.[109]

The report of the Sub-Committee again stressed the insanitary and offensive conditions caused by the travelling way of life, and the difficulty of enforcing restrictions on a migratory population. Moreover, it was reported that property was frequently either damaged or stolen, the Gypsies' children remained uneducated, and the local residents were generally intimidated by their presence. The need 'for dealing definitely with the Nomad classes' was thus emphasised, to be achieved ideally by national legislation which would register and regulate tent- and van-dwellers. If the Government continued to prove unwilling to initiate or facilitiate such specific legislation then the Surrey Council were urged to promote a Private Bill for their own county. A new stage of the campaign had thus begun, with Surrey Council taking the lead in urging all county councils in England and Wales to press for new legislation.[110]

In January 1907 circulars were sent out requesting information on the extent of the problem elsewhere and whether support would be given for general legislation. The council received thirty-five replies, and of these only five confirmed that the problem caused by the nomadic population was a serious one.[111] The majority of counties said that there was no problem in their districts and that regulation was either not necessary or was already covered by existing legislation, whether local or national. The small glimmer of hope for Surrey Council to be obtained from the replies was that more counties demanded legislation than those who stated it was a problem, and the feeling was that it should be general and not confined to a particular county or counties. On the strength of this the matter was taken to the County Council Association so that a Bill might be prepared.

In many respects the resulting Moveable Dwellings Bill was very like its predecessors. Clauses in the Bill provided for registration, the separation of the sexes, 'convenience of accommodation', cleanliness, the prevention of the spread of infectious disease and the education of the children. But there was one very significant departure from the earlier Bills of George Smith. Clause 5 stated:

Where it appears to the registration authority that the encampment of occupiers of moveable dwellings on any specified place or places within their area would be dangerous to the public health, or constitute a nuisance to the neighbourhood, the registration authority may by bye-law prohibit such encampment on such specified place or places; and any person acting in contravention of any bye-law made under this section shall be guilty of an offence under this Act.[112]

This therefore covered all moveable dwellings on private land or on land leased or hired, and not just vans and tents situated on common land. The initiative to move on the Gypsies, and to prosecute them, could thus now come from the local authority, and not only from the lord of the manor or the owner of the land. Mr John Pedder, chief clerk in the Home Office, expressed his belief, in his evidence to the 1909 Select Committee, that this clause was unnecessarily harsh and worked against the remainder of the Bill, which could be seen to act in the interests of the van-dwellers:

It does not help the gipsies or van-dwellers; it practically makes outlaws of them if the local authority decides that such and such a place is not to be entered by a van-dweller . . . The effect of the clause . . . seems to be that if a County Council thinks a van-dweller would be a nuisance (it is only 'would be', which is very vague), then and there a van-dweller is prohibited from 'being'; and although the van-dweller might be able to show that he was quite willing to conform to all the regulations and laws, and to prevent himself from being a nuisance, still, if the edict had once gone forth that that was a place where there would be a nuisance, he could not go there.[113]

The logical extension of the application of this clause would be to exclude

Gypsies and van-dwellers from the whole of the county council area, effectively leading to the total suppression of the Gypsies and their way of life.[114]

The Bill was presented by Lord Clifford of Chudleigh to the House of Lords for the first time on 18 February 1908 and it passed a second reading but was eventually withdrawn because a major part of it was being dealt with more thoroughly in a Children's Bill then being debated. It was reintroduced the following year, less the education clauses. Lord Clifford defended the proposals contained in the Bill by arguing that sentimental feelings about a nomadic way of life should not cloud the real issues of sanitary and hygienic rules, and he stressed the need to control the Gypsies by one set of uniform regulations. Clause 5 proved to be the most debated aspect of the Bill and Lord Allendale, speaking in support of the principle behind the proposals but against certain clauses he considered unworkable, expressed his fear that some of the provisions would effectively lead to the extermination of the Gypsies.[115] He concluded that the Bill went further than was reasonable or practicable. Nevertheless, it continued its passage through Parliament, receiving a second reading before being referred to a Select Committee, which eventually sat and took evidence, much of it in relation to Clause 5.

In 1910, when Lord Clifford again presented the Bill, it was moved that it be returned to the Select Committee to allow for a report. The Committee concluded that a case had been made for further legislation regarding moveable dwellings but it was not prepared to accept the Bill in its existing form. The clause demanding registration was struck out despite nearly every witness to the Committee speaking in its favour. Their argument was that this was already adequately covered by the 1835 Highway Act and that it was both unreasonable and impractical to apply such a requirement to all moveable dwellings, thus including every tarpaulin stretched over stakes and every holiday-maker who took, temporarily, to the outdoor life. But the Committee did believe there ought to be power to prohibit encampments in places where it was thought they might endanger public health or be a nuisance, and the amended Bill amounted to little more than Clause 5.[116]

This did not mean that the Committee favoured unreservedly such persecution of the Gypsies as this would possibly lead to, for they also came out strongly in support of the proposals of Sir Reginald Bray that county councils should provide camping grounds under conditions set out by the Local Government Board. In this way, the Committee could not be accused of sanctioning the persecution and harassment of the Gypsies, while at the same time they favoured provisions that would bring the Gypsies under the close supervision of the local authorities. This was incorporated into their amendments by imposing certain limits on the exercise of powers by the county councils. Any such powers had to be approved by the Local Government Board and before they could be applied the council had to have already provided suitable, alternative camping grounds. The provision of such sites would necessarily limit the places where Gypsies could legally camp, and so facilitate the process of supervision by the police, and sanitary and education officers. The argument that the amended Bill was a diluted version of the earlier proposals fails to recognise the importance of the new powers given to the local authorities and the police. The former could declare as unfit for encampments not only open spaces and common land, but private land also, and Clause 2 of the Bill involved a 'wide and rather questionable extension of the functions of the police', by allowing the latter to remove from commons and private lands any person who encamped there without authority.[117] Captain Sant's objections to acting outside the law by moving on the Gypsies on behalf of private interests would thus have been removed. The amended Bill was presented in 1911, 1912 and 1914, but failed to pass both Houses.

On the one hand the Bill can be regarded as representing little more than a call for county councils to provide camping grounds for the Gypsies but it was also an attempt to establish by law the further regulation and supervision of the Gypsy way of life by the local authorities who were called on to deal with the problem on a day-to-day basis. County council enthusiasm for the Bill waned with the realisation that the increased powers they were seeking to enable them to get rid of the Gypsy nuisance would be granted only if they also accepted the responsibility for the supervision of controlled camps. For example, the progress of the Bill had been carefully monitored by the Surrey General Purposes Committee and a steady diminution in their enthusiasm is clearly discernible. Not only was regret expressed that the provisions of the Bill had been amended in a way to remove the original intentions but it was also realised that it had little chance of being passed by both Houses. Surrey Council then resumed their campaign for local and private legislation,[118] again unsuccessfully, while other local authorities seem to have accepted the official ruling that the correct and efficient application of existing powers was sufficient. The truth behind this ruling is especially apparent from a study of specific actions of various local authorities against the Gypsies.

The owners of the land on which the Gypsies encamped were legally required to provide certain minimum sanitary arrangements, and failure to do so could result in their prosecution. The threat of this may often have been sufficient for the owner to refuse the Gypsies permission to stay or to move them on by his own methods if warned by the relevant authorities. At times this was neither practicable nor possible. By way of example, in 1888 Thomas Cuffey was summonsed for not abating a nuisance in one of his yards in Handcroft Road, Croydon, which contained seven caravans and two tents. The Sanitary Committee had instigated the proceedings in an attempt to discourage landowners from allowing Gypsies to camp in the neighbourhood. The owner's defence was that the Gypsies were away for the fruit-picking season and he had no way of contacting them to get them to remove their horses and dwellings. The case was adjourned until 19 June to allow him to take other steps. He somehow managed to comply with this deadline by clearing the yard of all the vans, and further consented to a future order of prohibition.[119]

The most common method was to proceed against the Gypsies, and this was done in many places under a variety of pretexts. In 1879 four Gypsies who camped on waste land in Walton Breck Road, Everton, were summonsed for failing to supply themselves with water, as required by the Public Health Act.[120] The Health Committee had been prompted into securing the summons by the landowners, who were attempting to avoid the trouble and cost of removing the Gypsies by passing the matter into the hands of the local authority. The magistrate decided strongly in favour of the complainant and gave the Gypsies seven days to 'clear out' of the district, and told them that if they had not gone of their own free will by the end of that time they would be removed. At Eastwood, in 1909, they were prosecuted for neglecting to dwell in a tent in a reasonably watertight condition, for not having sufficient privy accommodation or a sufficient water supply, not having a covered ash-pit and a dustbin, and for failing to have a suitable dry floor in the tent.[121] Overcrowding, sleeping out and the charge that they were likely to cause a nuisance was also used against them. Repeatedly the Gypsies were moved on by either the sanitary inspectors or the police and successful evictions were secured throughout Berkshire, at Limehurst, Reigate, Bedminster Down (Bristol), Hartlebury Common (Stourport), Neath and Nottingham.[122] Additionally, the matter was discussed in many other places, with authority being delegated to various officials who presumably took very similar steps.[123]

These various methods of treating the Gypsy problem were taken one step further, and reached their logical conclusion, when the councils, their agents, the police, landowners and local residents moved together and brought about the successful evictions of Gypsies from long-established encampments at Epping Forest, Blackpool, Birmingham and elsewhere. In these instances legality and illegality merged together and the depth of the antipathy shown to the Gypsies expressed itself in violent language and actions.

The effectiveness of such concerted actions in removing the Gypsies was seen in 1894 in Epping Forest. Although the Home Office rejected the application of local legislators for bye-laws making it illegal to camp in the Forest, the local councils were not deterred and in any case, new powers were not needed. Under existing laws the Gypsies were required to have a satisfactory water supply and proper sanitary accommodation in their camps. But the provision of such facilities would have contravened Forest laws, and so the Gypsies were caught in an impossible situation, bound to break the law whichever path they chose. Notices were served on the Gypsies stating that if the minimum sanitary requirements were not met then they would be expelled. When the first of the notices expired a body of police, forest keepers and local residents proceeded to evict the Gypsies, and eventually they were all forced to pack their caravans and were driven to the edge of the forest.[124]

A similar eviction took place at Black Patch, Handsworth, in Birmingham, in the early years of the twentieth century. The Gypsies had been camped on waste land there for more than half a century, and were such a permanent feature of the landscape that they had even come to be regarded as a recognised section of the community. Moreover,

their presence in the parish was certainly in keeping with the traditions of the locality; for till the era of Boulton and Watt had transformed the appearance of the place, old Handsworth Heath had been dotted with a number of miserable huts, the homes of an idle beggarly people who lived a precarious life by doing as little work as possible, eking out their existence by thieving and poaching all over the country side.[125]

However, between 1904 and 1905 the Gypsies were engaged in a series of tangles with the local authorities and with the owners of the land. The former wanted to transform part of the area from waste land into pleasure grounds, contemporaneously described as 'public lungs and children's playground', while the landowners thought in terms of property building.[126] The Gypsies had to be removed before either objective could be achieved.

By October 1904 there had already been five attempts at eviction, the first of which had been thwarted by the actions of the Gypsy women who threw their children in front of the horses and wagons and dared the drivers to trample on them. The fifth of this wave of attempts came at the beginning of October when fifty navvies, escorted by half a dozen policemen, attacked the camp, only again to be defeated by the ferocity of the Gypsy women's response.[127] The next assault was not until June 1905 when both the High Sheriff and Chief Constable of Staffordshire visited the camp with more than fifty sheriff's officers and policemen. Many of the Gypsies were away pea-picking and so the task of eviction was made much easier. Some of the Gypsies were secure as the land had been rented, but this applied to only a few. Of the remainder, some left peaceably, fearing violence, but others were more reluctant. One Gypsy was reported to have shouted at the would-be evictors: 'I don't want to use no violence, but I shan't allow you to do this. I've been here long enough to claim this land. Why didn't you come before? I've had no summons. If you wanted the land that bad, why didn't you behave like gentlemen and summons us? You don't frighten me, mind you.'[128] Such determination and despair was answered by the sheriff's men moving in to remove the Gypsies by force. Five Gypsies were arrested as the aggressors, and they soon realised they were heavily outnumbered and that further resistance was futile. All traces of the encampment were removed, except for a few vans remaining on the land rented by a Gypsy called Smith.[129] In February 1909 the Park Committee watched over the eviction of these

No. 2596—Vol. 82.   August 5, 1905.

THE PENNY
ILLUSTRATED PAPER
AND ILLUSTRATED TIMES

LIVERPOOL ELECTRIC RAILWAY DISASTER; TRUMBLE'S BROTHER MURDERED BY NATIVES; LIONESS ESCAPES FROM A CIRCUS IN SCOTLAND; SPECIAL PICTURES INSIDE.

GYPSIES AND POLICE AT BIRMINGHAM: AN EXCITING FIGHT.

12 The forcible eviction of the Gypsies from their site at Black Patch, in Birmingham, in 1905.

remaining Gypsies and the land was eventually opened as a recreation ground on 20 June 1911.[130]

The Gypsies who camped on the South Shore, Blackpool, suffered a similar fate. It was said that they had camped there for more than eighty years, and many of those on the sands in 1908 had been there for around half a century.[131] They followed a variety of occupations from bookmakers and waiters to labourers, scissor-grinders, hawkers and attendants at the fairground. Their camp was a local attraction to the many holiday-makers and the miniature railway operated a circular route around the camp, with a stop at Gipsyville station.[132] Regular prosecutions for fortune-telling and other offences had proved ineffective in either removing the Gypsies or preventing the offence from being repeated. Yet in April 1908 the Blackpool Corporation reversed the decision of the previous year and, by a majority of one and several abstentions, the decision was taken to remove the Gypsies.[133]

Pressure was put on the landowners to evict the Gypsies by refusing to pass plans for buildings on other parts of the owners' holdings. The owners had little choice but to agree to cooperate, and by March 1909 many of the Gypsies had already moved, while the remainder were preparing to do so. This they did with a great deal of reluctance, and were still there some six weeks later, the last not leaving until April 1910. One of their number even addressed an appeal to the King:

To his Majesty – I am very sorry to have to trouble you, but it is for a cause of necessity. It concerns all the gipsies at Blackpool. We have been resident here for the past forty years, and have always been encamped on one plot of ground. We all pay £20 to £25 for the season, and also pay rates and taxes. Our tents were the first thing on the show ground, and now they want to get rid of us by giving us only one week's notice.

It is very hard for us all. It is driving us from our homes after being here for so many years. Most of our children have been born, christened and educated here. We appeal to His Majesty for his kind help and sympathy, we are English gipsies, and we look to our King for justice.[134]

The King's Secretary passed on the appeal to the Local Government Board and no more was heard of it. As elsewhere, the Gypsies' fate was sealed. Some went to live in houses in Blackpool, others rented land on which they were entitled to encamp on the outskirts of the town, while others moved on to Preston. Although many returned to the showgrounds each summer to ply their trades, the South Shore was no longer available to them as a site for their tents and vans. A roller-coaster was later built on the site.[135]

The eviction of the Gypsies from Llanelly in 1912 provides a final instance of local authority antagonism towards the Gypsies. At the meeting of the local Health Committee, on 23 February 1912, the Gypsy camp on the Robinson Estate excited much discussion, and a resolution was passed that the council apply for an injunction to prevent the owners of the land from letting the land to the Gypsies so as to cause 'a nuisance and menace to the health of the community'.[136] By March there was still a large number of vans and tents on the property and pressure was being put on the council by local inhabitants to take more effective action. They had been annoyed by the council's apparent powerlessness, and had threatened to take proceedings against them for neglecting their duty. It was resolved that the Gypsies be given notice to quit within twenty-four hours, or suffer to be forcibly removed, 'by steam-roller, if necessary'.[137] Some Gypsies heeded the notice, but about sixty, comprising a camp of some fifteen vans and twelve 'wigwams', did not. On the expiration of the notice the Superintendent of the Police, constables and county officials arrived at the camp and threatened to turn the hose-pipe on the Gypsies if they did not remove themselves willingly. The preparation of the hose-pipe in readiness for such an occurrence left the Gypsies in no doubt that the threat would be carried out, and little opposition was shown. Within a matter of a few hours all the Gypsies had been removed from the estate.

The position of the Gypsy in society is thus perhaps nowhere made more clear than when the responses to this nomadic group are considered in the specific and local context. From the foregoing pages it is apparent that the Gypsy has always been treated as a problem and a nuisance. Although the individuals concerned with remedying the problem may have held to a belief in the 'real', Romany Gypsy, it was widely believed that this group was rapidly disappearing. The cause of the problem came from travellers who, each year, were 'less and less real gipsies',[138] and who conformed to the opposite stereotype of the Gypsy as the dirty and depraved itinerant. An editorial which appeared in the *Romanitshels', Didakais' and Folk-Lore Gazette* at the time of the Llanelly eviction parodied this latter picture:

he is regarded as a marauding robber, wholly without morals of any kind, as one who lives the life of a savage, in fine, something not far short of a cannibal. At best he is a filthy leper who never washes, and suffers from half the diseases to which flesh is heir. Therefore he is hunted from pillar to post.[139]

Such stereotypes persisted with vigour and it is little wonder that the response to Gypsy-travellers was usually one of vitriolic antipathy. Always regarded as a pest to society, and increasingly so from around the mid-century on, the laughter that greeted the suggestion put forward at a meeting of the Llanelly Rural District Council that steam-rollers and hose-pipes should be turned against the Gypsies is but a single example of the general contempt in the way they were viewed and treated.[140] There were some instances of the Gypsies being tolerated, but these were few. More commonly they met hostility and pressures to move from wherever they appeared, whether from lords of the manors, local residents, local authorities or the police. The picture is of everyone moving against the Gypsies, through a variety of means, to carry out an effective persecution. The methods varied from gentle persuasion to the threat of prosecution and forcible eviction; legal justification and backing were mixed at times with illegal methods. In practice these methods were not alternatives but complements.

The intentions of these various bodies and agencies were somewhat contradictory. Although the general feeling was that the Gypsy-travellers must be made to settle in order to curb and control the many offensive habits of which they were accused, an equally strong feeling was that their settlement should be encouraged and situated elsewhere. Their presence in large camps on the urban periphery could not be, and was not, tolerated by local authorities concerned with standards of health, sanitation, and the efficient use of valuable land resources. Their antipathetic response was further guided by age-old stereotypes which distanced the Romany (never met by officials) as a romantic if rather lawless race and relegated the non-Romany traveller (always met) to the level of a vagrant and degenerate people. Essentially, the local authority response to the problem was not to solve it but to move it on. A problem that animated all to violent language and gestures was often speedily forgotten when the Gypsies had moved out of the district.

In all this the Gypsies had no means of redress and could turn to virtually no body, agency or law for support. Laws and bye-laws were to protect sedentary society from the travellers, and not the reverse. The Gypsy Lore Society and other Gypsy lorists were the only voices, apart from the occasional statement of support in the local press, that spoke in favour of the Gypsies, and then only for the topmost part of the travellers' hierarchy. Even so, by the early twentieth century the Gypsy-travellers had been under such prolonged assault for more than twenty years, culminating in revived demands for registration and 'definite' solutions to the problem, that the reluctant and defensive lorists were provoked into a verbal attack on the Gypsy protagonists. Forceful action by the police and local authorities was merely one of the peaks of an almost continuous drive against the nomadic population. There is an impression that the grossly severe legislation of the sixteenth to eighteenth centuries had been repealed and replaced by less harsh provisions but the consistent and varied persecution of the Gypsies in the local context reveals this as an illusion. The persistence of the problem is rooted in the incompatibility between the travelling and settled ways of life. Many methods have been tried, involving great numbers of people, to understand the problem and attempt a solution, yet even today the conflict remains between sedentary society and the nomadic community. Too often the attempts to reconcile groups with contrasting habits, customs, values and attitudes have become diverted and obscured by a host of misleading stereotypes, superstitions and assumptions. The aim must be to remove the myths of race and misinterpretations of culture before any reconciliation is possible.

8

Summary and conclusion

Gypsy-travellers in the nineteenth and early twentieth centuries were a distinctive group, marked off from settled society by their types of employment and the nature of their way of life. Although, in general terms, visibly separate as an identifiable group, they were also varied according to the details of their existence and habits.

All such travellers were united by standing outside the dominant economic and social institutions of society, though also necessarily interacting with them to some extent. The three chief ways in which they remained marginal to settled society were by virtue of their migrancy, the mobility of their dwellings and by their reliance on family-based self-employment rather than on participation in the system of wage-labour. But to point to their independence from 'formal' economic structures should not be taken to mean either that their own system was chaotic and unstructured, or that changes in the wider economy did not affect them.

Far from being the spontaneous and care-free roving some commentators would have us believe, their migrancy was regulated and systematic, organised around a cycle of temporary seasonal labour, regular attendance at annual feasts and fairs and by maintaining the same circuits for their hawking ventures. The extent of migrancy varied greatly among the travellers. Some covered great distances while others restricted themselves to the immediate vicinity of their homes. The summer months witnessed the peak of the migrancy range with more travellers being on the roads than at any other time. During the period of bad weather itinerancy was curtailed and the Gypsy-travellers migrated inwards to the cities, living either in rented accommodation alongside the sedentary 'street-gutter rabble' or in the many semi-permanent van-towns, where they continued to work at various street-trades.[1] Related to the extent of itinerancy was variation in the nature of the encampment and of dwellings used, ranging from tents to disused tramcars and caravans, located either in temporary roadside halts or semi-permanent sites on urban waste land.

In different ways this heterogeneous group was able to make a significant contribution to the economic and social life of the host society. Indeed, in

181

their special relationship with the rural community can be seen reasons for the qualified tolerance accorded the Gypsy-travellers in the early decades of the nineteenth century. In order to ensure the continued existence of a market for their goods, services and, occasionally, labour they necessarily had to maintain some degree of good relations and harmony with the settled inhabitants. This was made possible when they were able to form one element in the social life of the village, perhaps as conveyors of news or as the talented musicians at village feasts and fairs. By this means the country-dwellers came to accept and expect the Gypsies, who were joined economically and socially in a reciprocal relationship with the rural community. They did not interfere with or threaten the established trades of the community, nor did they establish any rights. Moreover, their stay was temporary: here today, there tomorrow. Contact was limited and overt persecution was not necessary to remove them. The Gypsy-travellers fitted, if not entirely comfortably then at least without excessive conflict, into the rural economic and social structure.

Antipathy and fear were also features of the response, though in the early part of the century these elements did not have the forceful dominance they were to achieve when the balance in society had shifted from the rural to the urban sector. Whereas the early nineteenth-century Gypsy-travellers could have been tolerated as an integral part of the wider mechanisms operating within a developing industrial society, by the later decades their functions were thought to have been superseded. Their structural relationship with settled society had changed and the balance turned violently against what was seen as the unwanted, parasitical and anachronistic traveller. When based in urban van-towns, and so more noticeable to greater numbers, contact with city-dwellers was of a different nature to that which existed in the country, not containing the element of reciprocity achieved through irregular economic and social transactions.[2] Even so, it would be misleading to suggest that the relations with country-dwellers had been anything other than one of functional necessity and tolerance, and certainly not of positive acceptance. In the country and in the city antipathetic responses were never far from the surface of any contact or relationship with the Gypsies.

Despite being self-employed Gypsies were not self-supporting and depended for their livelihood on maintaining close contact with settled society, the market for their goods and services. Thus, any changes affecting the ability to buy, the nature of demand, and alterations in the market conditions in which the Gypsies operated, would necessarily have repercussions in the travellers' camps. For example, they came to be replaced as temporary, seasonal labourers by the tendency of farmers to employ regular, permanent workers and by technological developments which slowly transformed agriculture into a capital rather than labour intensive sector of the economy. Likewise, the growth of retail outlets which provided cheap, industrially manufactured, non-durable goods encroached on the Gypsies' traditional market. Hawking became more difficult, less remunerative and progressively anachronistic. The travellers were pushed from dependence on the rural sector by increased competition for their goods and services. Tinkers and itinerant entertainers were no longer in such demand when tin ware could be replaced cheaply from local shops and when altered leisure pursuits and social intercourse had reduced the numerical and cultural significance of fairs and feasts to the country-dwellers. From living in and around the cities in the winter months, made attractive by the large population concentrations and so mass markets, to setting up a more or less permanent urban base was a short, inevitable step.

Other general changes, not directed specifically at the travellers, also acted to circumscribe their mobility and activities. Perhaps the most notable was the enclosure movement, which had the effect of taking from the Gypsies many of their traditional camping grounds. In London the process began at Norwood at the beginning of the century and progressed steadily through to the eviction of the Gypsies from Epping Forest at the end.

Thus the position of Gypsy-travellers in settled society was conditioned by wider developments and pressures occurring within society as a whole. This, though, is just one part of the picture. Equally important in terms of their relations with settled society was how the travellers were perceived and how the different perceptions brought about a series of contradictory responses. From these emerged a complete range of other pressures aimed directly at the travellers, intended specifically to solve the problem of the existence of a travelling group in a sedentary-based society, a group whose condition of life was considered to be in 'direct contradiction to what you suppose every man's life in England must be'.[3] These pressures resulted from a response conditioned by the stereotypes which revolved around the perennial conflict between the settled and travelling ways of life, and is illustrated by antipathy to travellers coming from all classes and sections of society:

These are the people who hate them, and would control and banish them, the officials, the prose people, the mechanical minds. The law-givers hate them, the stationary powers hate them, the people who wear uniforms and take wages hate them . . . that is to say the main part of the civilised world, hate them.[4]

In the capitalist political economy of nineteenth-century England and Wales it was inevitable that arguments demanding control over this group would take on the tone and moral force of the complaint that the travellers and their itinerant life-style were incompatible with the ideology and organisation of that system. Itinerants were seen as unproductive labourers, overtly rejecting hard toil, thrift and permanency:

John Bull dislikes keeping the idle, bastard children of other nations. He readily protects all those who tread upon English soil, but in return for this kindness he expects them, like bees, to be all workers . . . If the Gipsies and others of the same class in this country will begin to 'buckle to', and set themselves out for real hard work, instead of cadging from door to door, they will find, notwithstanding they are called Gipsies, John Bull extending to them the hand of brotherhood and sympathy, and the days of persecution passed.[5]

It was the responsibility of the formal and informal agencies of that ideology to ensure conformity and bring about the effective control of the travellers.

In the early part of the century travellers were grouped together as rogues and vagabonds, living a criminal and irreligious life. The association of Gypsy-travellers with gangs of marauding robbers was commonly made. It was further suggested they were united in a closed brotherhood, a criminal Masonic-type lodge, entered into by swearing oaths of allegiance and maintained in its secrecy and exclusiveness by the use of a cant language among its members.[6] Such an impression was possible as the travellers were thought to disregard conventional notions of law and order, especially in regard to property rights. Anything that grew naturally or lived in the wild was considered by them as belonging to no man, the property of all. Raw materials for the making of craft items were taken without conscience from forests and roadsides, contents for the cookpot were poached freely from the fields. This disrespect of rights of ownership was then said to extend also to the property of individuals.

The responsibility for controlling this 'free-wheeling' and 'menacing' itinerant population fell to the many associations for the prosecution of felons, magistrates and the rural constabulary, the latter unorganised and highly parochial at least up to 1839. Their response was to come down with force on these roving vagabonds, applying without remorse such persecution as permitted by, for example, the 1824 Vagrancy Act.

Coexisting with this police surveillance and control was the work undertaken by the various missionaries and religious reformers. Not only were travellers considered to be hardened criminals but they were also completely lacking in any sense of religion or morality for to the 'common-sense' Englishman 'eccentricity and unconventionality smack . . . of moral obliquity'.[7] Various individuals and organisations, motivated by a feeling of evangelistic duty, sought to remedy the state of affairs existing in the camps of these 'savages' living on the fringes of settled society. The travellers had to be taught the word of God and settled, introducing them to the virtuous, respectable and industrious habits of the majority. Religious agencies and the representatives of law and order were working towards identical ends though by different means.

The limited achievements of the evangelists, the changing structural position of itinerancy in settled society and the growth of scientific enquiry and knowledge resulted in a shift of emphasis in the argument against the travellers. New perspectives became dominant and other agencies entered into the fray. The age of religion and superstition gave way to the age of science and new myths and stereotypes developed, allegedly based on empiricist objectivity derived from fact-finding missions to the Gypsies' camps. Travellers were now 'proved' to be dirty, illiterate, insanitary, a threat to health and generally an affront to the principles of civilised society. Indeed, living in tents was described as 'the crown of all crimes against respectable society'.[8]

The method of attack likewise changed with the emphasis moving away from a stated desire to convert and rather towards attempting to bring travellers within the accepted standards and conventions of the settled population. Although the intention in both cases had been to enforce conformity and sedentarisation, the arguments to justify this had been modified. No longer were the Gypsies a tolerated component of the rural economy. Their position had been substantially transformed by wider changes in such a way as to make their existence entirely unacceptable: 'The old order of gipsy life has, in England at any rate, become something of a nuisance. It has ceased to be even picturesque.'[9] Romantic notions about a healthy, outdoor rural way of life gave way to a realisation that urban-dwelling travellers lived mainly in appalling, insanitary conditions. The developing machinery of the state thus began to extend its influence to control the 'problems':

local government operates without any sympathy for their picturesque past, and is driving them bit by bit within the pale, insisting on certain hygienic regulations, ordering the children to school, and searching the law-books for a pretext to deprive them of their pitching-ground.[10]

A more efficient and effective police force assisted in this endeavour.

Alongside these responses to a travelling population there emerged with great force and conviction the notion of a hierarchy among travellers. This may have been expressed in terms of a distinction between *bona fide* travellers pursuing some ostensible employment and the unworthy tramp. More frequently and apparently more persuasively, differences were also established according to racial origins, contrasting the 'pure' blood Romany with others of mixed blood. Growing from the roots of romanticism and the new biological sciences, notions of racial purity became the basis for constructing a hierarchy among travellers dependent on the possession of 'true' blood. Each stage of the pyramidal construct was said to have its own distinctive characteristics, way of life and culture. The Romany Gypsies were placed securely on the top. No longer the rogues and vagabonds of former years they had now been transformed into an exclusive race. Elusive to all except the Gypsy lorists they were deemed the aristocrats of the road, yet inevitably doomed to extinction by marriage outside the tribe.

To attempt to impose rigid characterisations on a travelling population divided according to degrees of racial purity is to misconstrue and simplify. Any catch-all terms for occupational groups or social classes mislead more than they assist by the implication of the existence of easily observable and definable boundaries. No such convenient criteria were able to be applied to the nineteenth-century Gypsy except in terms of romanticised, mythically constructed, ideal images of a separate race of Romanies. The association of a Gypsy with a member of a clearly defined homogeneous race of people, identifiable by reference to notions of blood purity, rests on false assumptions, weak methodology, factual inaccuracy and general inapplicability. Nineteenth-century travellers derived from indigenous tinkers, pedlars and basketmakers as much as from an oriental race. To become obsessed with tracing pedigrees as an essential stage in identifying a separate race is to be diverted from the key issue of the relationship between the travelling and settled societies.[11]

Nevertheless, it should be noted that the methods and arguments of the gypsiologists were very much in keeping with their time, reflecting the Victorian obsession with questions of origin, race and 'alien' cultures. Too often these theories were crude and simplistic, perverted by a desire to reduce people and cultures to easily definable and controllable categories.[12]

We are left with a three-fold definition of Gypsies, identifying them as people of a nomadic disposition, or as the romantic Romany or as a degenerate race. Stereotypes from each coexisted and complemented each other, with any contradictions explained by reference to blood purity. 'True' Gypsies excited sentimental pity and sympathy, but the rest of the travellers were dismissed as the off-scourings of society, needing to be swept away. The existence of contradictory stereotypes was not only possible but likely, perpetuated by the various sources which formed impressions, from poetry and fiction to newspapers, nursery rhymes and hearsay: 'it is to be remembered that so little has been written of gipsies which did not in the main tend to fortify the popular prejudice, that it was next to impossible to form any opinion as to their character in which the evil elements did not preponderate over the good'.[13] Mixed stereotypes worked together to outrage standard and accepted moral and religious sentiments, to appeal to nationalistic and xenophobic feelings, to challenge conventional ways of life and norms, to strengthen psychological needs such as the scapegoat mechanism and to arouse hatred, jealousy and fear of an unknown and peculiar group.[14] The plethora of impressions constructed around the Gypsies, whether as mere travellers or as an alien race, gave rise to a variety of cultural and racial stereotypes that hindered the practical expression of sentiments or responses other than those of suspicion and general antipathy.

It should be apparent that although responses to Gypsies were consistent in their objectives, they were justified and explained in many different ways. The reformer could approach the 'problem' from various paths: economic,

religious, legal, racial, educational or medical. The range of pressures working on the Gypsies to conform to a sedentary way of life, general and specific,
formal and informal, was thus extensive. The effects of these on the travellers
were uneven, and were felt with various degrees of force in different areas
and according to different perceptions by the travellers of the actual threat to
their itinerant way of life. The result was a mixture of adaptation, evasion,
conformity and conflict. Some yielded to the logic of the pressures and gave
up travelling in favour of conformity with a sedentary existence. Others
continued as before, though adapting their specific life-style and employments to fit in with demand. Still others fled to America, while many
compromised by continuing to live in vans and tents, following itinerant
employments, and yet rarely moving from one, semi-permanent location.
Their survival is a tribute to their adaptability to a changed environment and
resilience to a variety of pressures.

The failure of the attempts to achieve a more effective circumscription of
the travellers and their way of life must be attributable to defects in the form
and methods of the enterprise, the handling of the pressures by the travellers
themselves and the obvious difficulties of controlling a moving population.
To begin with, persecution was qualified by the realisation that the Gypsies
performed a significant economic and social function. When the importance
of this diminished the onus for solving the 'problem' rested with a number of
agencies, between whom disputes arose over the location of ultimate
responsibility. The perceptions of the Gypsies were remarkably consistent in
their antipathy, but proposals for a solution were greatly at variance: whether
to legislate or harass, to stay within the confines of the law or to exceed it, to
remove the Gypsies forcibly or wait for them voluntarily to move on.
Inconsistency was a qualification to persistent persecution. Although considered an undesirable anachronism, a malignant plague-spot, no workable
remedy was found that satisfactorily answered the fundamental problem of
how to accommodate a travelling population within a sedentary-based
society. The nomadic way of life was thought to conflict with and challenge
essential foundations of settled society and so had to be curtailed, but beyond
this no uniform agreement could be reached.

Gypsy-travellers pursued an alternative way of life that presented them as
a readily identifiable group. They received little support or sympathy from
members of settled society and lacked political or economic muscle, permitting an antipathetic response fed and conditioned by a host of mostly adverse
stereotypes. The ferocity of the opposition was rooted in a fear of the general
threat posed by the travellers to the values of a sedentary society, reinforced
by the common belief that a Gypsy presence promised only dirt, disease,
begging and stealing. Such fears were perennial and, unlike responses to
other minority groups, appear to have been little affected by specific changes
in the economy and society such as periods of high unemployment.

The exaggerated and often contradictory claims of contemporary commentators contributed to the formation of stereotypes that mixed hearsay with fact, romanticism with condemnation. These impressions provide some indication of the nature of the travelling way of life if read critically but, perhaps more important, they tell us a great deal about the aspirations and intentions of those who voiced them. Their picture of the Gypsies distorted reality by imposing on the travellers a general character, temperament and appearance drawn from specific cases and limited experience. Only in rare instances were Gypsy-travellers able to challenge such stereotyping and antipathy to any effect.

Numerically the travellers represented only a small proportion of the total population. But while this perhaps goes some way to explain their powerlessness in relation to settled society it was not the case that hostility was conditional on absolute numbers. The question of the size of the travelling population was always raised when the issue of itinerancy was discussed, yet the problem of definition and the absence of reliable statistics meant that figures were no more than wild 'guesstimates'. The arguments against itinerancy rested not on the issue of absolute numbers but rather on the travellers' concentration in certain areas and the belief that numbers were increasing.

These questions concerning the power relationship between minority and majority groups; the source, nature and validity of stereotypes; and recourse to a 'numbers game' to highlight a threat, problem or tendency are themes that recur in all minority studies. Although the central purpose of this work has been the reconstruction of the way of life of the Gypsy-travelling community in the nineteenth century and its relationship with the host structures, it is hoped this necessary groundwork can form the basis for continued discussion of these major issues.

Appendix 1 Major legislation relating to Gypsies, 1530–1908

Statute Reference and year	Short title	Description
22 Henry VIII, c.10 1530	Egyptians Act	Imposed ban on the immigration of 'Egipcions' and notice given to all Egyptians in England to leave the country.
5 & 6 Edw. VI, c.21 1551–2	Pedlars Act	Forbade tinkers, pedlars and such like vagrant persons, 'who are more hurtful than necessary', to travel from place to place without licence from the justices, under penalty of fourteen days' imprisonment.
1 & 2 Philip and Mary,c.4 1554	Egyptians Act	Gypsies forbidden to enter the country. Made provisions for the capital punishment of Egyptians if they remained in the country for more than one month.
5 Eliz., c.20 1562	Egyptians Act	Extended the penalties of 22 Henry VIII, c.10 and 1 & 2 Philip and Mary, c.4.
39 Eliz., c.4 1596	Poor Law Act	Declared as rogues and vagabonds 'all tynkers wandering abroade . . . and all such p'sons, not being Fellons, wandering and p'tending themselves to be Egipcyans or wandering in the Habite Forme or Attyre of counterfayte Egipcians'.

Statute Reference and year	Short title	Description
17 Geo. II, c.5 1743	Justices Commitment Act	'All Persons pretending to be Gypsies, or wandering in the habit and form of Egyptians, or pretending to have skill in palmistry, or pretending to tell fortunes' were to be dealt with as rogues and vagabonds.
23 Geo. III, c.51 1783	Egyptians Act	Repealed previous laws re Gypsies.
23 Geo. III, c.83 1783	Rogues and Vagabonds Act	Extended provisions dealing with rogues and vagabonds.
50 Geo. III, c.41 1810	Hawkers and Pedlars Act	Necessitated the purchase of licence for hawkers and pedlars.
3 Geo. IV, c.40 1822	Vagrancy Act	Simplified previous laws re vagrants, rogues and vagabonds, etc., and consolidated them into one Act. Repealed former Acts but re-enacted most of their provisions.
3 Geo. IV, c.126, s.121 1822	Turnpike Roads Act	Any Gypsy encamping on side of turnpike road was liable to a fine of 40s.
5 Geo. IV, c.83 1824	Vagrancy Act	Any one pretending to tell fortunes by palmistry, or otherwise to deceive; any one wandering abroad and lodging under any tent or cart, not having any visible means of subsistence, and not giving a good account of himself, liable to penalty of three months' imprisonment. Removed by statute the reward which 3 Geo. IV, c.46 gave to a constable or other party who apprehended a vagrant.
5 & 6 Will. IV, c.50, s.72, 76 1835	Highway Act	Penalised Gypsies who camped on the highway to a fine of 40s.

Statute Reference and year	Short title	Description
34 & 35 Vict., c.96 1871	Pedlars Act	Extension of 50 Geo. III, c.41.
34 & 35 Vict., c.112, s.15 1871	Prevention of Crimes Act	Made applicable to Scotland the section re Gypsies of 5 Geo. IV, c.83.
38 & 39 Vict., c.59, s.9 1875	Public Health Act	Provisions re accommodation for hop-pickers. See 48 & 49 Vict., c.72, s.9.
39 & 40 Vict., c.56, s.29 1876	Commons Act	Empowered local authorities to make bye-laws effectively closing commons to Gypsies.
44 & 45 Vict., c.45 1881	Pedlars Act	Extension of 34 & 35 Vict., c.96
45 & 46 Vict., c.23 1883	Public Health (Fruit Pickers Lodgings) Act	Extended Public Health Act re accommodation for pickers of fruit and vegetables.
48 & 49 Vict., c.72, s.9 1885	Housing of the Working Classes Act	Applied provisions of 38 & 39 Vict., c.59 to nuisances in tents, vans, etc. District councils empowered to make bye-laws in this respect.
51 & 52 Vict., c.33 1888	Hawkers Act	Extended previous Acts re hawkers.
52 & 53 Vict., c.72, s.13 1889	Infectious Diseases (Notification) Act	Provisions of Act apply to moveable dwellings just as it applies to houses.
52 & 53 Vict., c.50, s.57 1889	Local Government Act	Allowed county councils to make bye-laws for the prevention of vagrancy.
54 & 55 Vict., c.76, s.95 1891	Public Health (London) Act	Sanitary regulations re vans, tents, etc.
56 & 57 Vict., c.73 1894	Local Government Act	Parish councils empowered to regulate village greens and open spaces.

Statute Reference and year	Short title	Description
62 & 63 Vict., c.30 1899	Commons (Inclosure) Act	District councils can apply to Board of Agriculture to make bye-laws for the regulation of commons.
8 Edw. VII, c.67, s.118 1908	Children's Act	Enforced compulsory education for children of travellers.

Sources: Sir F. M. Eden, *The State of the Poor* (1797; abridged and edited by A. G. L. Rogers, 1928), pp. 55–6; L. O. Pike, *A History of Crime in England* (1876), pp. 75–7; C. J. R. Turner, *A History of Vagrants and Vagrancy and Beggars and Begging* (1887), pp. 905–6; W. Axon, 'Laws Relating to the Gipsies', in W. Andrews (ed.), *Legal Lore: Curiosities of Laws and Lawyers* (1897), pp. 171–2; H. T. Crofton, 'Early Annals of the Gypsies in England', *J.G.L.S.*, Old Ser., Vol. 1, No. 1 (1888), pp. 5–24; 'The Law as to Gypsies', *Local Government Journal* (18 July 1896), p. 465; H.M.S.O., *Chronological Table of Statutes* (1979).

Appendix 2
'A Gipsy Diary of Five Weeks and a Day – 1911'

Saturday, November 25
This morning a number of gipsies arrived at Newlands Corner. I counted at least four children of school age among them and some younger children. They had with them three large vans, two tilt-carts, seven horses and a number of dogs, these latter of a sporting breed, rather like a rough-haired greyhound.

Sunday, November 26
The gipsies have not gone from the main encampment, and today we noticed two independent camps east and west of them. None of these people are real gipsies; they are at best what Borrow would have called 'half-breds', and some of them are, I am sure, trampers pure and simple.

Monday, November 27
This morning the main camp had not moved. The gipsies had lighted large fires and strewn the ground with their refuse. The ground will, I am afraid, be very foul for some long time to come, or at least until we get heavy rain.

My father and I riding to the east along the ridge of the Downs, saw a large encampment near Sir H.R.'s house (about two and a half miles from Newlands Corner). It consisted of three vans and three or four tilt-carts. Judging from the number of blanket tents we saw (at least half a dozen) there must have been a great many gipsies belonging to it. We only saw the 'camp guards', however, for no doubt the 'main body' of gipsies were out begging, hawking clothes-pegs, telling fortunes, or otherwise furthering the 'affairs of Egypt'. We did see five children of school age, however, and some toddling babies who looked extremely dirty and unhealthy. This afternoon the main camp moved from Newlands Corner.

A propos of the health of gipsy children, I was told at a hospital that gipsy children suffering from diseases resulting from dirt, exposure and underfeeding, have of late been fairly frequently admitted. On one occasion, I was told, some gipsies brought in an unfortunate child suffering from severe bronchial-pneumonia and in a high fever, but the gipsies could not be induced to leave the child in hospital for so much as one night but insisted on taking it to almost certain death in the caravans or tents.

Tuesday, November 28
Today I went out walking and tried in vain to prevent my two dogs from sniffing round some old gipsy camping-ground where there were a number of dirty rags, bits of mouldy food, burnt-out fires, &c. I am afraid that they may pick up some infection, as the gipsies' dogs, and apparently the gipsies themselves, may have had almost anything the matter with them, and any disease, from mange to plague, might be spread in this way.

Wednesday, November 29
Out riding this morning I saw a new encampment near Newlands Corner, consisting of three large blanket tents and one small cart. Two dogs guarded the camp and there were two horses grazing near by. I saw two children of school age returning to the camp with water.

Thursday, November 30
Today the camp, which was pitched near Newlands Corner on Wednesday, trekked on to the east and I saw the whole *ménage*. There were two particularly dirty and forbidding-looking men, three lads of about fifteen years of age, a young girl of perhaps seventeen or eighteen, a boy of ten and two other children. They cannot possibly all belong to the same family and I cannot help feeling sorry for the young girl, who is rather pretty and not as brutalised looking as these women often are. She will not have much chance, poor thing.

Friday, December 1
I was in London all day and therefore saw nothing of these poor travesties of Borrow's Egyptians. One cannot help wondering what Mr. Petulengro or Tawno Chickno, 'The World's Beauty', would have thought of calling these tramps gipsies simply because they had tents and vans.

Saturday, December 2
Today out riding we saw a family encamped in a thick 'bosky' or clump of trees and undergrowth near Newlands Corner. They had got a rather large blanket tent with them and had lighted a particularly big fire. Fortunately the undergrowth is very wet and there is therefore not much danger of its catching alight. Had the weather been frosty and dry it might easily have set that part of the Downs on fire. There were three children among the party, two of them of school age.

Sunday, December 3
A new encampment has been made further along the Downs to the east than Newlands Corner. It consists of two tents and a small cart, the bushes near-by are absolutely covered with clothes, or rather pieces of stuff apparently hung there to dry, and the gipsies have lighted a large fire.

Monday, December 4
The gipsies of the 'washing' moved on today, but we saw another small camp in a little hollow about a mile and a half from Newlands Corner (more exactly about half-way between Newlands Corner and One Tree Hill). We noticed no less than four children

of school age among the party* and we also observed that they had chosen, apparently because they preferred it, a particularly foul site for their camp. Whole generations of gipsies have camped in this hollow, the floor of which is by now covered with horribly evil-smelling rags, hay which has been originally used for bedding, and is now sodden with the rain, old worn-out boots, their leather cracking and mouldy, brims of straw hats, hunks of gnawed bread, old bones, horribly greasy tins blackened by the fire and smelling of rancid fat, cinders of burnt-out fires, and mouldering horse-dung. These are the kind of surroundings which the gipsies and trampers seem to like best as they almost always camp on an old site. We also saw a man and woman today with a perambulator (a favourite substitute for a cart), the woman with a very young baby in her arms. I saw another of the children from the bosky a long way away with a woman. They have all therefore probably moved on.

Tuesday, December 5

I did not see any gipsies today, having been for a walk in the morning in a district which is always fairly free from them. Last year, at about this time or a little later, gipsies were encamped in quite extraordinary numbers at Newlands Corner. I remember counting no less than thirteen separate encampments (not single vans but groups of two or three) at one time. It was one of the most remarkable sights that I have ever come across to see all the children playing together. They must have numbered from fifteen to twenty of all ages, all extremely ragged and dirty and apparently in a large proportion suffering from diseases of the eyes and skin.

Wednesday, December 6

I was in London all day and so saw no gipsies.

Thursday, December 7

A remarkably wet day today. Walking down the road to the Silent Pool we met a tramping man and woman who had a very young baby in a perambulator with them. We also met another tramp, a man, who did not like the look of our bull-terrier at all.

Friday, December 8

This afternoon the turf was too hard and slippery after the frost for riding and I did not go near the gipsies' haunts. In the morning, however, we had a great deal of trouble with the bull-terrier, who, puppy-like, will go and smell out all the decaying food which the gipsies leave about, and lick the horrible rags and filth. One thing is particularly disgusting about their old camps, that is that after they have struck their tents, they leave their beds of dried grass or hay scattered about on the ground, and these must literally swarm with vermin.

Saturday, December 9

Today my father and I rode along the top of the hill to Netley Heath where we saw two gipsy camps. The first consisted of two large blanket tents and a four-wheeled cart; and the second appeared to consist of tents also. We did not happen to pass very close to

* Two of these children are those who have moved on from the bosky, I think.

the latter and so did not see it very clearly, but it was probably larger than the first as we saw two horses belonging to it.

Sunday, December 10
It has been extraordinarily wet all day and although we went for a walk, we saw no gipsies. The hill seems too exposed for them in this bad weather.

Monday, December 11
A number of gipsies arrived this afternoon. This morning my father and I rode out and not a gipsy was to be seen at Newlands Corner, only the usual dirty rags, &c. By the afternoon, when my mother and I went out for a stroll, a large camp was established at Newlands Corner, consisting of three big vans with probably three but certainly two horses. We also saw another smaller camp a little further along to the west, consisting of two blanket tents. There are belonging to this encampment one woman, two men, a baby and two large dogs.

Tuesday, December 12
This morning I started for Yorkshire and I shall be away for nearly a week.

Last year the gipsies did an extraordinarily annoying thing. Whilst we were away they turned a number of horses into the garden (I am told about six). All the gates were, I believe, shut as usual, so that it would have been impossible for the horses to have strayed in. The gipsies must have intentionally opened one of the gates and driven them through. Fortunately the horses did not get into the main part of the flower garden, which is mostly up one or two steps, but they did considerable damage to grass paths, &c., before the gardener discovered their presence and drove them out.

Wednesday, December 13
I have not heard if any gipsies were seen today. Where I am staying in Yorkshire they seem to be quite free from them.

Thursday, December 14
I hear that there were a party of gipsies at Newlands Corner today consisting of two women, three men, and three small children, who all appeared to be exceedingly ragged and dirty.

Friday, December 15
I do not know of any gipsies being seen today. Probably my informant did not go farther than Newlands Corner. I wish that I could hear when the encampment of Monday was moved but I cannot find out.

Saturday, December 16
Today my father tells me he saw a small party of gipsies about a quarter of a mile west from Newlands Corner. They had pitched a blanket tent and had a horse with them.

Sunday, December 17
I came home late yesterday evening. Today it was extremely wet and we happened to

take our one walk on the Merrow Downs, which are 'regulated' and have a 'common' keeper, who sees to it that the gipsies are prevented from contaminating these Downs with their squalid leavings. The contrast between the two stretches of land is most remarkable.

Monday, December 18
Today was exceedingly wet and the Downs soaking. My father and I, therefore, kept to the roads during our ride and we saw no gipsies.

Tuesday, December 19
My mother and brother saw a large encampment about a hundred yards east of Newlands Corner. It consisted of one horse, one small van, and one large blanket tent. They strangely enough saw no people belonging to it.

Wednesday, December 20
This afternoon we saw a large encampment at Newlands Corner. There were no less than four vans, a cart, a blanket tent, and four horses, and we saw three children of school age and several men and women. Tuesday's small camp was still there and apparently the whole of the washing of the two communities was spread to dry upon the adjacent bushes. I suppose that it was washing, for although not immaculately clean, the garments, or portions of garments, of which it consisted were not really dirty.

Thursday, December 21
Some of the gipsies have moved from Newlands Corner, but although two of the four vans have gone, curiously enough there seem to be the same number of horses as before. The place where the van stood is now extraordinarily filthy considering for how short a time it remained. Two of the children begged from us and so did some of the women.

Friday, December 22
One van still remains at Newlands Corner though the others have apparently gone away. I hope that they really have gone and have not just moved on further.

Saturday, December 23
Today the one van was moved on about fifty yards, I suppose in order to be out of sight of the road that the gipsies might be disturbed by no passing policemen. Every time they move they leave the ground in a most horrible condition, and I expect that if those that are left go on thus, moving a very little at a time, they will make an almost continuous track of dirty rags and sordid refuse along the Downs, for their dirty patches will soon be linked up with other rubbish-strewn areas.

Sunday, December 24
The gipsies have not moved on again but I find that there are many more people belonging to the van than I had supposed; especially I noticed about six very villainous looking men collected near the camp east of Newlands Corner. The gipsies of

Thursday the 21st had not moved far. I find they had only gone a little way along the Downs to the west. We saw three horses grazing about but could not at first see their owners. Then we turned a corner and came upon them – a van with a patched and dirty canvas cover drawn up by the side of the green track under an old yew tree, with a fire burning in the door of the van; a dirty smoke-stained sacking tent also with a fire inside it, numberless rags, tin cans, and old boots strewn about, and amongst it all the half-clothed, unhealthy, grimy, uncared-for children running and tumbling. Half concealed in a thick clump of trees was another tent, the bright fire within it lighting up the interior. I hear that there are yet more gipsies in the little hollow between One Tree and Newlands Corner.

Monday, December 25
All the gipsies remained on today. There is now a line of them at regular intervals of about 200 yards for a mile or so along the hill top.

Tuesday, December 26
Today as we rode to the meet eastwards towards Dorking, we saw a number of gipsies besides those encamped near Newlands Corner. There were two tents and one van at 'The Ladies' Mile', which is about three miles from Newlands Corner, and four large vans and a very large number of gipsies on Ranmore Common about five miles away.

I was told the other day by a neighbour why it is that gipsies are specially fond of mutilating and spoiling holly trees. It is because they provide the best kind of wood for making skewers, which commodity the gipsies sell to butchers in the neighbourhood. Not that gipsies by any means confine their depredations to hollies. They also tear branches from small oaks, beeches, ash trees, &c., but they seem to be always hacking at the unfortunate hollies. The same neighbour, an authority, also told me that the gipsies do a great deal of ferreting on dark nights, much to the annoyance of the local farmers. He says that the gipsies threatened to kill one farmer because he had caught them poaching. According to local report, they are very fond of threatening people and using bad language.

Wednesday, December 27
Today my brother and I rode along the ridge of the Downs to the west. We counted no less than four separate encampments within one mile from Newlands Corner. The first consisted of one van, a cart, and a tent; the second consisted of three vans and one tent; the third of one tent, and the fourth of one tent and one cart. We noticed in all five children of school age. Two of these encampments have been there since yesterday and the third and fourth have been in their places certainly since Saturday, and possibly since Friday. The filth has become dreadful, and lately the caravans have moved on a little every day or two and have thus covered an enormous amount of ground with their leavings. We saw two carts with ponies and a large number of gipsies coming up the hill in the evening. They were obviously going to camp.

Thursday, December 28
A policeman and a keeper by their united efforts succeeded in 'moving on' most of the gipsies today. We saw them 'like the sands of the sea for multitude' pouring down off

the hill top. Two vans passed our gate on their way towards Clandon (north). Three or four caravans went down towards Merrow (west) and two (south) to Albury. The gipsies who went to Albury were sitting by the side of the village street when we went down, and had their van drawn up on the road and were apparently begging of each person who passed them. We went on to Albury Heath where a tramping gipsy woman with a baby in her arms begged of us in a most piteous way. It is very difficult to resist a woman with a baby, but I believe if one once begins to give these people either food or money, one tramper tells another that you are 'good for a copper', or its equivalent, and your house is besieged by a set of thieving and bullying vagrants. We have been specially warned by the police that, living far away from any village in a very lonely situation, we must not give anything to tramps. If we do, the word will be passed down and we shall be worried out of our lives by vagrants of all sorts.

Friday, December 29
There are still some gipsies walking about at Newlands Corner today, though I saw none who had camped. I hear that a week or two ago there were some gipsies encamped just outside the coachman's house. His wife tells me that their language was extraordinarily lurid. I wonder if they were really talking Romany or Jargon?

Saturday, December 30
I did not see any gipsies today, but I hear that some came to Newlands Corner in the afternoon.

Sunday, December 31
This morning we saw the gipsies who came here yesterday. They have camped just by the side of the road. The encampment consists of four large vans and four horses. There are a number of children, three or perhaps four of an age to go to school; a younger child and a baby. There are a good many people belonging to it; three or four women and apparently about six or more men and a girl of about fourteen. Further along the Downs to the west we saw another camp, this time a small one, consisting of one tent and a little cart. Later on in the morning we saw a van and a cart being driven over the Downs by some gipsies, the cart hung with rabbit skins and with a furtive and predatory dog running near it.

Source: reproduced from J. Strachey, 'The Gipsy Scandal and the Danger to the Commons', *National Review*, Vol. 59 (1912), pp. 469–71.

Appendix 3
The Gypsy 'nuisance' in Surrey, 1898

(A) STATEMENT OF M. W. POOLE, HUNTSMAN TO THE WEST SURREY
STAGHOUNDS, 2 JUNE 1898

. . . owing to my present house being isolated and abutting on Epsom Common we have a lot of trouble with the gipsies who have often mustered in considerable numbers with as many as eight or nine vans and tents pitched at our very gates for three weeks at a time, and when I am absent from home they are very bold and cause my wife a great deal of trouble and annoyance by begging for water hot and cold (and we have to fetch our drinking water from a distance), food, money, and even milk for their babies, which if she refuses she only meets with abuse.

My children attend school at Epsom and their journeys to and fro are a source of anxiety to my wife and myself because of the gipsies. They have often begged the children's pocket pence and the gipsies' children do the same; they even try to obtain from my children the dinner they take to school. When the gipsies are about my little ones are really afraid to go to school.

My wife is afraid of the gipsies when I am away.

This road to Epsom and Chessington is a favourite walk especially on Sundays but I have often seen pedestrians obliged to turn back on coming to the gipsy encampments.

My wife and daughter are accosted and begged from when returning from Church by gipsy women with babies and on a refusal their begging is quickly followed by curses and bad language.

The vans and tents of these people (being pitched as they are in our parish, close to the roadside) and the smoke from their fires are dangerous to drivers of young or restive horses. I have experienced much difficulty in this respect myself – many horses shy whenever they pass them.

We have often been kept awake all night when the gipsies have pitched near our house owing to the quarrelling, and their language is too abominable to hear; their general behaviour is disgusting; their women have changed their clothes in sight of my house, and neither sex trouble to go to cover to relieve themselves.

When the gipsies have made a move the place where they have been is generally strewn with rubbish, rags, filthy old garments, broken tins, utensils as well as vegetable refuse, whilst the turf has been destroyed by their fires.

I have to get up at night when the gipsies are about, being warned by my dog that they have been prowling round the premises.

I have suffered damage by broken hedges and fences which damage is without a doubt caused by the gipsies but one can never catch them at it.

I have had fruit and vegetables stolen by them. On one occasion I missed some choice apples that I intended for show, and – strange to say – we never got any windfalls when the gipsies are near us.

(B) STATEMENT OF MR E. F. LANGDALE, 2 JANUARY 1898

As I live quite close to the high road and at one corner of crossroads, I unfortunately have great opportunities both of hearing and seeing gipsies when they are encamped and 'at home'. Such opportunities as cannot possibly be obtained by many of the neighbouring gentry whose premises are extensive and so well closed in that the inmates of their houses cannot be subjected to the same annoyance than their less well to do neighbours are.

I have found that gipsies, although in many instances, appearing to wish to keep within bounds of the law, are often really very lawless. They will graze their cattle in your fields at night, pull stakes out of your hedges, cut your trees down for green wood to make clothes pegs of and ride when it suits them on the pathway and not get off it to let pedestrians pass. I have however never missed anything but wood, though I keep fowls. At certain seasons of the year gipsies become very numerous in the neighbourhood of Kingswood and they are accustomed to encamp on a delta of grass right opposite and within twenty yards of my house. The windows of which even in the height of summer, have often to be closed to prevent my family hearing the foulest language that could be uttered. As regards this part of my evidence I feel I should certainly not generalise; I therefore affirm that the staple words used, are f———, s—d, b————, b————, not any of them at all desirable to be heard, specially by womenfolk and children.

Gipsies make frequent requests, not to say demands, for water, boiling water for preference, and if refused, as they sometimes must be at homes whose supply of water is entirely dependent upon the rainfall, they become insolent and abusive. But of course not all are alike; many appear to be grateful and are civil and I wish to avoid confounding with the ordinary gipsy horse coper, the vendor of 'fairings' (gifts bought from fairs) and sweets who also travels about in a caravan. The former class are a great source of annoyance and very often unintentionally or not frighten women, by importuning them for assistance and children by their rough manner toward them.

Gipsies seem to be less audacious in stealing than they were some few years ago, and I do not think they would come into anyone's garden now and not mind the owner seeing them dig up her potatoes and cut her cabbages as they once did do at my servant's mother's house near Banstead.

I have usually found the police most prompt, when informed of the annoyance, in moving on gipsies who encamp opposite my house but as the local constable lives two miles off and has a good long beat I cannot always obtain his assistance quickly.

Surrey has long been the favourite ground of gipsies, but I am informed on good authority that in Reigate, particular encouragement is given them by the servants at large houses, for they purchase so many little things of gipsy women who come round to hawk their wares. Is a hawker's licence necessary, and if so is it strictly enforced?

Whilst fully recognising the fact that the gipsy class must rest somewhere by the side of the road, if, as I believe to be the case, they are not permitted by County Councils to encamp on common lands, I would with all deference suggest that they should not be permitted to go within three or four hundred yards or earshot of houses.

I think too that all gipsies' caravans, carts and tents should be conspicuously numbered so that in the event of any cause for complaint arising the public can assist the police in identifying the offenders, who under the present system get clear off very often; being here today and gone tomorrow miles away.

Further, I might suggest that as gipsies, no doubt, map out their itinerary they should be compelled or required to report to the nearest police station where they encamped the previous 24 hours and where they intend to do so during the next 24 hours.

Source: from a file containing circular letters, statements and other items re tent-dwellers, Gypsies, etc., 1897–8 (Surrey Record Office, CC28/101).

Notes

1 Introduction

1 See *Notes and Queries*, 7th Ser., Vol. 4 (12 November 1887), p. 397, and Vol. 5 (16 June 1888), p. 480. It was claimed that MacRitchie first showed that 'Gypsy' was derived from 'Egyptian' and so should be spelt with a 'y' and not an 'i' (C. G. Leland, 'What We Have Done', *Journal of the Gypsy Lore Society* (hereafter *J.G.L.S.*), Old Ser., Vol. 3, No. 4 (1892), p. 193).

2 Printed circular, undated, in a box of miscellaneous items, Gypsy Lore Society Archive. See also E. R. Pennell, *Charles Godfrey Leland, A Biography*, 2 vols. (1906).

3 H. E. J. G[ibbins], *Gipsies of the New Forest, and Other Tales* (Bournemouth, [1909]), pp. 41–2.

4 *The Tribune*, 3 January 1908, p. 6. I have been unable to discover any information confirming that this meeting took place.

5 'They Steal Children, Don't They?' was the title of a *Man Alive* programme shown on B.B.C.2 on 28 October 1980. The petrol bomb solution was proposed by an Anti-Gypsy Group at North Swansea, who were allowed to present their views on a *Brass Tacks* programme transmitted on B.B.C.2 on 12 July 1978.

6 J. James, 'The Future for the Gypsies: "They Want What Many Will See as the Best of Both Worlds"', *The Listener* (6 November 1980), p. 607.

7 G. Carley, *The Memoirs of Gaius Carley, a Sussex Blacksmith, Written by Himself* (Chichester, 1963), p. 11.

8 See J. Burnett, D. Vincent and D. Mayall (eds.), *The Autobiography of the Working Class: An Annotated Critical Bibliography, Vol. 1: 1790–1900* (Brighton, 1984).

9 *Smoke in the Lanes* (1958); *No Place Like Home* (1960); *Whichever Way We Turn* (1964).

10 C. Smith, *The Life-Story of Gipsy Cornelius Smith* (1890); R. Smith, *Gipsy Smith. His Life and Work. By Himself* (1902), and *From Gipsy Tent to Pulpit: The Story of My Life* [1901]. See also Petulengro, *Gypsy Fiddler* (1936); Lovell, 'My Life: By a Gipsy', *Home Chat* (18 April 1908); G. 'Lazzy' Smith, *Incidents in a Gipsy's Life . . . The Royal Epping Forest Gipsies* (Liverpool, 1886; Leicester, [1892]).

11 D. Binns, *A Gypsy Bibliography* (Chorltonville, 1982); *A Catalogue of the Gypsy Books Collected by the Late Robert Andrew Scott Macfie* (University of Liverpool, 1936); 'Additions to Black's Gypsy Bibliography and the Catalogue of the Scott Macfie Gypsy Collection in the University of Liverpool, Compiled chiefly from the collection of Davidson Cook', *J.G.L.S.*, 3rd Ser., Vol. 19, Nos. 1–2 (1940), pp. 20–33; addenda to the Scott Macfie catalogue, unpublished list, Sydney Jones Library,

University of Liverpool; *A Catalogue of Books, Pamphlets, Prints, Old Broadsides, &c., Comprised in the Gypsy-Lore Section of the Library of the Gypsy and Folk-Lore Club* (privately printed, near Bristol, 1917?); *A Catalogue of the Romany Collection, Brotherton Library, University of Leeds* (Edinburgh, 1962).

12 E. B. Trigg, 'Magic and Religion amongst the Gypsies of Britain', D.Phil., University of Oxford (1967) and his *Gypsy Demons and Divinities: The Magical and Supernatural Practices of the Gypsies* (New Jersey, 1973).

13 J. Crabb, *The Gipsies' Advocate* (1831; 3rd edn with additions, 1832); J. Hoyland, *A Historical Survey of the Customs, Habits and Present State of the Gypsies, Designed . . . to Promote the Amelioration of their Condition* (York, 1816).

14 See *I've been a Gipsying: Or, Rambles among our Gipsies and their Children* (1883; 1885) and *Gypsy Children: Or, a Stroll in Gypsydom. With Songs and Stories* [1889].

15 See, for example, T. Acton, *Gypsy Politics and Social Change* (1974); B. Adams, *et al.*, *Gypsies and Government Policy in England* (1975); C. Holmes, 'The German Gypsy Question in Britain, 1904–6', in K. Lunn (ed.), *Hosts, Immigrants and Minorities: Historical Responses to Newcomers in British Society 1870–1914* (1980); D. Sibley, *Outsiders in Urban Societies* (Oxford, 1981); J. Okely, *The Traveller-Gypsies* (Cambridge, 1983).

2 Itinerancy as a way of life

1 J. H. Swinstead, *A Parish on Wheels* (1897), pp. 4–6.

2 J. Sampson, 'The Gypsies', paper read to the Warrington Literary and Philosophical Society, 15 March 1897 (Warrington, 1897), pp. 3–4. A swaddler was a pedlar, especially those given to robbery with violence. A driz fencer was a lace-seller and/ or receiver of stolen lace. An umbrella-mender was also commonly known as a mush faker or mush fakir, and crocus pitcher was slang for an itinerant 'quack' doctor. Mumper became corrupted from meaning a beggar (1670–1720) to a sponger (1720–1830) to a half-bred Gypsy (1870–1900). These definitions were taken from E. Partridge, *The Routledge Dictionary of Historical Slang*, abridged by J. Simpson (1973).

3 H. Mayhew, *London Labour and the London Poor*, Vol. 1 (1861; New York, 1968), p.2.

4 See R. Samuel, 'Comers and Goers', in H. J. Dyos and M. Wolff (eds.), *The Victorian City, Images and Realities*, Vol. 1 (1973; 1976), pp. 152–3. This article provides an excellent introduction to nineteenth-century wayfaring life.

5 Canal-dwellers can also be placed in this group. From around the middle of the nineteenth century they followed an itinerant life-style and travelled as families on the canals, with each member contributing to the family income by sharing the work burden. However they constitute a distinct research topic in their own right and for this reason will be excluded from this study. By way of an introduction to the topic see C. Hadfield, *British Canals* (1950); H. Hanson, *The Canal Boatmen, 1760–1914* (Manchester, 1979); L. T. C. Rolt, *Narrow Boat* (1944), *Navigable Waterways* (1969).

6 On occasions the lines of demarcation between the groups could be crossed. When no opportunities for work existed in his own trade, a 'distressed hand-loom weaver' from Dundee temporarily took to an itinerant way of life. He secured a living by selling miscellaneous items, second-hand books and poems written by

himself. There is no reason to suspect that this temporary and partial solution to impoverishment was unique (Anon., *A Chapter in the Life of a Poor Man. Written by a Distressed Hand-Loom Weaver* (1845?). A copy of this rare item is held at the University College Library, London). A valuable insight into the lonely life of the tramping artisan is provided by William Edwin Adams in his *Memoirs of a Social Atom* (1903; New York, 1968).

7 J. Hoyland, *A Historical Survey of the Customs, Habits and Present State of the Gypsies, Designed . . . to Promote the Amelioration of their Condition* (York, 1816), p. 187. See also 'Gipsies', *The Literary and Scientific Repository*, Vol. 3 (1821), p. 404.

8 Judith Okely identified each of these factors as relating to present-day travellers (see 'Gypsies Travelling in Southern England', in F. Rehfisch (ed.), *Gypsies, Tinkers and Other Travellers* (1975), p. 70).

9 *Royal Commission on the Housing of the Working Classes, First Report* (1884–5), p. 56; *Select Committee on the Temporary Dwellings Bill, Minutes of Evidence*, of Sir H. Owen (1887), p. 1, paras. 6–10; J. Crabb, *The Gipsies' Advocate* (1831; 3rd edn with additions, 1832), p. 137; G. Smith, *I've Been a Gipsying: Or, Rambles among our Gipsies and their Children* (1885), pp. 281–2; A. Melton, 'The True-Born Gypsy Folk: Will the Ancient Romany People Disappear?', *Sunday Chronicle*, 11 August 1907, p. 2.

10 K. Bercovici, *The Story of the Gypsies* (1930), p. 243; E. O. Winstedt, 'Gypsy Civilisation', *J.G.L.S.*, New Ser., Vol. 1, No. 4 (1908), p. 331; H. T. Crofton, 'Affairs of Egypt, 1908', *J.G.L.S.*, New Ser., Vol. 3, No. 4 (1910), p. 278; 'Anglo-Romani Gleanings', *J.G.L.S.*, 3rd Ser., Vol. 8, No. 3 (1929), pp. 105–20; H. Malleson, 'A Sweet Street Sanctuary', *J.G.L.S..*, New Ser., Vol. 4, No. 1 (1910); F. S. Atkinson, 'Gypsies in East Anglia', *The Kendalian*, Vol. 11 (1911), p. 13; R. Samuel, 'Quarry Roughs', in R. Samuel (ed.), *Village Life and Labour* (1975); G. Smith, *I've Been a Gipsying*, p. 95.

11 *R.C. on Housing, First Report*, p. 56.

12 J. H. Swinstead, *op. cit.*, p. 194.

13 V. S. Morwood, *Our Gipsies in City, Tent and Van* (1885), p. 89.

14 See especially the works by James Crabb, Samuel Roberts and brief references in articles published in the *J.G.L.S..*

15 J. Crabb, *op. cit.*, p. 183; J. Hoyland, *op. cit.*, pp. 168, 187. Hoyland even produced a list, compiled by James Corder, of some of the Gypsy lodgers in Westminster and Borough (pp. 84–5).

16 Annual report of a London city missionary, 1859, in *London City Mission Magazine*, Vol. 25 (2 January 1860), p. 30.

17 J. Flanagan, *Scenes from my Life* (1907), p. 105; F. H. Groome, *In Gipsy Tents* (Edinburgh, 1880; Wakefield, 1973), p. 13; Rev. G. Hall, *The Gypsy's Parson, his Experiences and Adventures* (1915), pp. 2–3, 157, 173; R. Jefferies, *Field and Hedgerow, being the Last Essays of R.J. Collected by his Widow* (1889), p. 163; C. G. Leland, *The Gypsies* [1882], p. 141; T. W. Thompson, 'Affairs of Egypt, 1909', *J.G.L.S.*, New Ser., Vol. 5, No. 2 (1911), pp. 121, 128; T. W. Thompson, 'The Uncleanness of Women among English Gypsies', *J.G.L.S.*, 3rd Ser., Vol. 1, No. 1 (1922), p. 17; 'Notes and Queries', *J.G.L.S.*, 3rd Ser., Vol. 1, No. 3 (1922), p. 144; 'Anglo-Romani Gleanings', *J.G.L.S.*, 3rd Ser., Vol. 3, No. 3 (1924), p. 118; T. W. Thompson, 'Samuel Fox and the Derbyshire Boswells', *J.G.L.S.*, 3rd Ser., Vol. 4, No. 1 (1925),

p. 25; Rev. G. Hall, 'Notes on the Boss Pedigree', *Romanitshels', Didakais' and Folk-Lore Gazette*, Vol. 1, No. 4 (October 1912), p. 120; Rev. G. Hall, 'The Gipsies of England', *Sunday at Home* (April 1912), p. 415.

18 W. H. Hudson, *A Shepherd's Life: Impressions of the South Wiltshire Downs* (1910), pp. 265–6. When the inhabitants of these and other non-moveable dwellings adopted full-time sedentary employments, and so became completely 'gaujified' in the eyes of the lorists, is the time they fall from the scope of this study.

19 I am grateful to David Smith, Honorary Editor of the *J.G.L.S.* for this reference, which he discovered during his researches, still in progress, into the question of settled travellers. I am similarly informed by Mr V. Tyrell, Principal Area Librarian, Stoke, that Tinkersclough was a place name for a part of Hanley, near Stoke, at least by the 1660s.

20 A. Esquiros, *The English at Home*, translated and edited by L. Wraxall (1861), pp. 205–6; J. Hoyland, *op. cit.*, p. 244; *Christian Guardian*, Vol. 4 (1812), pp. 98–101; Vol. 5 (1813), pp. 412–14; T. W. Thompson, 'Samuel Fox', *loc. cit.*, p. 21; W. A. Dutt, 'In Lavengro's Country', *Macmillan's Magazine*, Vol. 84 (1901), p. 145. One traditional camp lost to the Gypsies was at Oulton, near Lowestoft, close to where the novelist George Borrow once lived.

21 Lord Eversley (G. J. S. Lefevre), *Commons, Forests and Footpaths, the Story of the Battle during the Last Forty-Five Years for Public Rights over the Commons, Forests and Footpaths of England and Wales* (rev. edn, 1910), p. 4.

22 A. Beale, 'Gipsying', *Argosy*, Vol. 16 (1873), p. 271. For similar laments see A. Esquiros, *op. cit.*, p. 177; C. G. Leland, *The English Gipsies and their Language* (1873; 1874), p. 2; W. R. S. Ralston, 'A Gipsies' Christmas Gathering', *Good Words*, Vol. 9 (1 February 1868), p. 100.

23 Lovell, 'My Life: By a Gipsy', *Home Chat* (18 April 1908), p. 267. The role of the rural police and of local authority officials in enforcing a range of laws against the travellers will be discussed in chapter 7.

24 W.B., 'Gipsies and their Friends', *Temple Bar Magazine*, Vol. 47 (May 1876), pp. 70–1. Likewise, railway extensions and building operations had obliterated effectively the encampment which used to be sited on the rushy wastes on the northern verge of Croydon Common, and a patch of ground near Addison Road Station was covered with tents and wagons in 1875 and by houses and other buildings by 1880 (see T. Frost, *Reminiscences of a Country Journalist* (1886), p. 8; F. H. Groome, *op. cit.*, p. 102).

25 H. Woodcock, *The Gipsies* (1865), pp. 162–3. See also A. Esquiros, *op. cit.*, p. 191; *Select Committee of the House of Lords on the Moveable Dwellings Bill, Minutes of Evidence*, of Mr E. Farr, Medical Officer of Health of the Andover Rural District Council (1909), p. 74, paras. 1468–9.

26 C. G. Leland, *The English Gipsies*, p. 2. See also Rev. G. Hall, *op. cit.*, pp. 157ff; T. W. Thompson, 'Samuel Fox,' *loc. cit.*, p. 23, for an account of the emigration of from sixty to seventy Bosses, Boswells, Herons, Grays, Smiths and Williams, between 1855 and 1870. By the late nineteenth century Henry Crofton thought that emigration had led to a massive drop in the numbers of Gypsies travelling through Lancashire and Cheshire, and estimated that only around 300 remained. Although his estimate is not supported by the census figures, the trend is nevertheless clear (H. T. Crofton, 'Gypsy Life in Lancashire and Cheshire',

Manchester Literary Club, Papers, Vol. 3 (Manchester, 1877), p. 33; T. W. Thompson, 'The Social Polity of the English Gypsies', *J.G.L.S.*, 3rd Ser., Vol. 2, No. 3 (1923), p. 134).

27 J. Simson, Preface, in W. Simson, *A History of the Gipsies: With Specimens of the Gipsy Language* (London [printed], Edinburgh, 1865).

28 G. Smith, *Gipsy Life: Being an Account of our Gipsies and their Children, with Suggestions for their Improvement* (1880), pp. 45–7.

29 See J. Crabb, *op. cit.*, p. 144; A. Esquiros, *op. cit.*, p. 219; E. Hodder, *George Smith of Coalville: The Story of an Enthusiast* (1896), pp. 143–4; J. Hoyland, *op. cit.*, pp. 169, 254; V. S. Morwood, *op. cit.*, p. 6; J. Simson, 'Disquisition on the Past, Present and Future of Gipsydom', in W. Simson, *op. cit.*, p. 449; B. Skot (pseud. of R. A. S. Macfie), *A Brief Account of Gypsy History* (Liverpool, 1909), p. 36; Rev. J. West, *To the Nobility, Clergy and Magistrates of the County of Dorset: A Plea for the Education of the Children of the Gypsies* (Farnham and London, 1844), p. 29.

30 *Census of England and Wales, General Report, 1861* (1863), p. 7.

31 *Census of England and Wales, General Report, 1891*, Vol. 4 (1893), pp. 24–5; *Area, Houses and Population, 1891*, Vol. 2, Table 8 (1893), p. xxxv; *General Report, 1901* (1904), pp. 164–5; *Summary Tables and Index, 1901*, Table 23 (1903), p. 137.

32 F. H. Groome, *op. cit.*, p. 58; J. Hoyland, *op. cit.*, pp. 155–6; E. O. Winstedt, 'The Norwood Gypsies and their Vocabulary', *J.G.L.S.*, New Ser., Vol. 9, Nos. 3–4 (1916), pp. 148–9.

33 Guildford Muniment Room and Surrey Record Office have copies of the county council census returns taken on the nights of 22 June and 31 August 1913. The census was part of the Surrey County Council's campaign against the Gypsies, and is discussed in chapter 7.

34 *Sel. Cttee on Temp. Dw., Minutes of Evidence*, of George Smith of Coalville, p. 21, para. 364.

35 *Illustrated Times*, 13 April 1861, p. 241. See also *Illustrated London News*, 29 November 1879, p. 503.

36 *Census of England and Wales, General Report, 1881*, Vol. 4 (1883), p. 14; *General Report, 1891*, Vol. 4 (1893), pp. 24–5.

37 R. C. De Crespigny and H. G. Hutchinson, *The New Forest: Its Traditions, Inhabitants and Customs* (1895; Wakefield, 1975), p. 85.

38 R. W. S. Griffith, 'The Gipsies of the New Forest', *Hampshire Field Club: Proceedings*, Vol. 2, paper read at field meeting on 22 July 1893 (Southampton, 1894), p. 277.

39 *Ibid.*, pp. 277–8.

40 'Account of the Gypsies of the New Forest by Miss Bowles', in W. Howitt, *The Rural Life of England* (1840), p. 186.

41 R. W. S. Griffith, 'The Gipsies', *loc. cit.*, p. 278.

42 'Account of Miss Bowles', in W. Howitt, *op. cit.*, p. 186.

43 H. E. J. G[ibbins], *Gipsies of the New Forest, and Other Tales* (Bournemouth, [1909]), p. 19. See also F. Cuttriss (pseud.), *Romany Life, Experienced and Observed during Many Years of Friendly Intercourse with the Gypsies* (1915), and review of same in *J.G.L.S.*, 3rd Ser., Vol. 1, No. 1 (1922), pp. 43–6.

44 The attempt to draw a direct correlation between purity of language and purity of blood is examined in chapter 4.

45 See R. C. De Crespigny and H. G. Hutchinson, *op. cit.*, p. 82; A. Esquiros, *op. cit.*,

p. 182; R. W. S. Griffith, 'The Gipsies', *loc. cit.*, pp. 277–82; J. R. Wise, *The New Forest: Its History and Scenery* (1880), p. 160.

46 *J.G.L.S.*, 3rd Ser., Vol. 4, No. 2 (1925), p. 95.

47 R. W. S. Griffith, 'The Gipsies', *loc. cit.*, p. 281.

48 *Ibid.*, p. 278.

49 H. E. J. G[ibbins], *op. cit.*, pp. 11–13.

50 Note from A. E. Gillington, in *J.G.L.S.*, 3rd Ser., Vol. 4, No. 2 (1925), p. 95.

51 H. E. J. G[ibbins], *op. cit.*, p. 54.

52 R. W. S. Griffith, 'The Gipsies', *loc. cit.*, p. 281.

53 *The Times*, 12 October 1842, p. 3. See also 'Account of Miss Bowles', in W. Howitt, *op. cit.*, pp. 184–6; J. Myers, 'Drab', *J.G.L.S.*, New Ser., Vol. 2, No. 3 (1909), pp. 199–207.

54 H. E. J. G[ibbins], *op. cit.*, p. 5.

55 See chapter 5 for an assessment of the New Forest Good Samaritan Charity.

56 J. De Bairacli Levy, *Wanderers in the New Forest* (1958), p. 53.

57 E. O. Winstedt, 'Gypsy Civilisation', *loc. cit.*, p. 331; *Christchurch Times*, 15 June 1907, p. 5; *Morning Leader*, 3 June 1907, p. 7.

58 *Morning Leader*, 12 June 1907, p. 7.

59 Annual report of a London city missionary, 1858, in *London City Mission Magazine*, Vol. 25 (2 January 1860), pp. 17–18.

60 A. M. Galer, *Norwood and Dulwich: Past and Present, with Historical and Descriptive Notes* (1890), p. 11; J. Hoyland, *op. cit.*, p. 180.

61 N. N. Solly, *Memoir of the Life of David Cox, with Selections from his Correspondence and some Account of his Works* (1873), p. 21.

62 'A Gipsy Colony at Dulwich', *The Builder*, 11 November 1876, p. 1094.

63 'Metropolitan Gipsyries', *All the Year Round*, New Ser., Vol. 21 (1878), p. 393; *Weekly Times*, 26 October 1876, p. 5.

64 J. J. Sexby, *The Municipal Parks, Gardens and Open Spaces of London* (1898), pp. 237–8.

65 Charles Booth, MSS, B.366, pp. 185, 190; E. Brewer, 'Gipsy Encampments in the Heart of London', *Sunday at Home* (1896), p. 113; *Building Trade News* (December 1894), p. 11.

66 T. W. Wilkinson, 'Van-Dwelling London', in G. R. Sims (ed.), *Living London*, Vol. 3 (1903), p. 322.

67 *Weekly Times*, 8 February 1880, p. 2.

68 'Anglo-Romani Gleanings', *J.G.L.S.*, 3rd Ser., Vol. 3, No. 3 (1924), p. 116.

69 C. Booth, *Life and Labour of the People in London*, 3rd Ser., Vol. 3 (1902), pp. 151–2.

70 F. H. W. Sheppard, *Survey of London: Northern Kensington*, Vol. 37 (1973), p. 342.

71 *Ibid.*

72 *Ibid.*, p. 340.

73 F. M. Gladstone, *Notting Hill in Bygone Days* (1924), p. 143.

74 *Suburban Press*, 28 February 1880, p. 2.

75 'Anglo-Romani Gleanings', *J.G.L.S.*, 3rd Ser., Vol. 3, No. 3 (1924), p. 116.

76 Rev. G. Hall, *op. cit.*, p. 198. See also G. Smith, *Gipsy Life*, pp. 122ff; *Illustrated London News*, 13 December 1879, p. 545.

77 See 'Reminiscences of J. Munday', in R. Blunt, *Red Anchor Pieces* (1928), p. 110; E. Hodder, *op. cit.*, pp. 196–7; C. Smith, *The Life-Story of Gipsy Cornelius Smith* (1890), p. 52; G. Smith, *Gipsy Life*, pp. 267–77; G. Smith, *I've Been a Gipsying*, pp. 26, 35–6,

280; 'Anglo-Romani Gleanings', *J.G.L.S.*, 3rd Ser., Vol. 3, No. 3 (1924), p. 117; 'The Present State of the Gipsies', *Sunday at Home* (1884), p. 119; *R.C. on Housing, First Report*, p. 56; *Minutes of Evidence*, of George Smith, p. 526, para. 14031; C. Booth, MSS, B.346, pp. 165, 233; B.348, p. 97; B.371, pp. 55–7, 241.

78 *Notes and Queries*, 6th Ser., Vol. 2 (4 December 1880), p. 444.

79 George Smith of Coalville also contrasted the Christian Gypsy with the majority in order to show what could be achieved.

80 C. Booth, *op. cit.*, 3rd Ser., Vol. 5 (1902), pp. 197, 206; V. S. Morwood, *op. cit.*, pp. 339–40; H. Woodcock, *op. cit.*, pp. 144–7; *Building Trade News* (December 1894), p. 11; C. Booth, MSS., B.298, pp. 91–7; B.366, pp.183–5, 190.

81 J. Greenwood, *Low-Life Deeps* (1881), p. 213.

82 J. Crabb, *op. cit.*, p. 137; F. H. W. Sheppard, *op. cit.*, p. 333.

83 J. Crabb, *op. cit.*, p. 137; J. Hoyland, *op. cit.*, p. 186; W. Howitt, *op. cit.*, pp. 175–6.

84 E. Chase, *Tenant Friends in Deptford* (1929), p. 96.

85 Quoted in G. Smith, *Gipsy Life*, pp. 117–19.

86 'Metropolitan Gipsyries', *loc. cit.*, p. 391. See also *Christian World*, 19 December 1879, p. 809.

87 E. O. Winstedt, 'The Norwood Gypsies and their Vocabulary', *J.G.L.S.*, New Ser., Vol. 9, Nos. 3–4 (1916), p. 132.

88 Rev. G. Hall, *op. cit.*, pp. 200–1; H. T. Crofton, 'Affairs . . . 1907', *loc. cit.*, p. 129. Under the arches of London Bridge D. Kirwan came across what he described as the 'perfect gypsy encampment', though it is unclear from the text whether the shelterers were vagrants or Gypsy-travellers (D. Kirwan, *Palace and Hovel* (1870; 1963), pp. 64–5, 199).

89 J. Hollingshead, *Ragged London in 1861* (1861), pp. 29–30, 73–4; C. Booth, MSS, B.298, pp. 93–7.

90 J. Crabb, *op. cit.*, pp. 136–7; R. Samuel, 'Comers and Goers', pp. 132–3; H. T. Crofton, 'Affairs . . . 1892–1906', *loc. cit.*, pp. 367–8. Woolwich can be compared with the Notting Hill district in its function as a resting-place for Gypsy-travellers on their journeys to and from London in the south-east (see C. Booth, *op. cit.*, 3rd Ser., Vol. 5, 1902, pp. 90–1).

91 J. Thompson and A. Smith, *Street Life in London* (1877–8; Wakefield, 1973), pp. 1–2.

92 A. R. Bennett, *London and Londoners in the Eighteen–Fifties and Sixties* (1924), pp. 49–50.

93 T. Frost, *op. cit.*, pp. 4, 8.

94 *Ibid.*, p. 8.

95 H. Woodcock, *op. cit.*, p. 144.

96 *Notes and Queries*, 6th Ser., Vol. 2 (4 December 1880), p. 444.

97 A. R. Bennett, *op. cit.*, p. 52.

98 J. Thompson and A. Smith, *op. cit.*, pp. 28–9. The authors also give a valuable insight into the reasons for the growth of this trade: 'At High Wickam [*sic*, i.e. Wycombe], the centre of cheap chair manufacture, common beech chairs are made which are actually retailed in the East of London at less than £1 per dozen . . . [But] the wood of these cheap chairs has not been properly dried; they crack, and shrink, part at the joints, and fall to pieces . . . Having thus introduced into London a constant supply of cane-bottomed chairs, another industry, namely that

of mending the chairs when the cane had worn out, sprung up simultaneously. This was probably first originated by the gipsies.'

99 J. Thompson and A. Smith, *op. cit.*, pp. 75–6.

100 H. Mayhew, *op. cit.*, Vol. 1, pp. 87–9. It is interesting to note that some Gypsies were said to be employed in the street-selling of oranges, an occupation generally regarded as the monopoly of the Irish.

101 V. S. Morwood, *op. cit.*, pp. 190–1.

102 For a description of the traditional method of making clothes-pegs see G. Smith, *Gipsy Life*, pp. 117–19.

103 See H. T. Crofton, 'Affairs . . . 1907', *loc. cit.*, p. 129; 'Metropolitan Gipsyries', *loc. cit.*, pp. 390–3; *Weekly Times*, 8 February 1880, p. 2.

104 Quoted in J. Thompson and A. Smith, *op. cit.*, p. 3. The cash sum mentioned seems highly improbable.

105 *Weekly Times*, 8 February 1880, p. 2.

106 From a description of Wandsworth Gypsies given in 1864 by an anonymous author, quoted in C. J. R. Turner, *A History of Vagrants and Vagrancy and Beggars and Begging* (1887), pp. 503–5. See also 'Metropolitan Gipsyries', *loc. cit.*, pp. 390–3.

3 From fortune-telling to scissor-grinding

1 D. L. Woolmer, 'Gipsies in their Winter Quarters', *The Quiver* (1903), p. 530.

2 E. J. Hobsbawm has contributed to this impression by referring to the anti-work and anti-social aspects of the Gypsy way of life ('Work and Leisure in Industrial Society', *Past and Present*, No. 30 (1965), p. 100). See also J. Crabb, *The Gipsies' Advocate* (1831; 3rd edn with additions, 1832), p. 38; A. Symons, 'In Praise of Gypsies', *J.G.L.S.*, New Ser., Vol. 1, No. 4 (1908), p. 298.

3 See B. Adams, *et al.*, *Gypsies and Government Policy in England* (1975), pp. 114ff. Although Okely's concern is chiefly with the present day, the model she presents is also well suited to the nineteenth-century situation. Many of her findings have echoes in the earlier period and so provide a useful foil and balance to a historical survey.

4 Annual report of a London city missionary, 1859, in *London City Mission Magazine*, Vol. 25 (2 January 1860), p. 31.

5 F. Thompson, *Lark Rise to Candleford* (Oxford, 1968), pp. 122–3. W. H. L. Tester also noted that the 'pathetic appeals' of a woman were likely to have more effect than similar pleas from a man. For this reason it was common practice for itinerant traders to travel with a female companion, known by the slang term 'doxy' (*Holiday Reading. Sketches of La Teste's Life on the Road* (Elgin, 1882), p. 37).

6 M. K. Ashby, *Joseph Ashby of Tysoe, 1859–1919* (1974), pp. 201–2; W. H. Davies, *The Autobiography of a Super-Tramp* (1908; 1955), p. 154; G. Smith, *Gipsy Life: Being an Account of our Gipsies and their Children, with Suggestions for their Improvement* (1880), p. 249.

7 R. E. Chatfield, 'The English Gipsies', *Theosophical Review* (April 1899), p. 108.

8 G. Smith, *I've Been a Gipsying: Or, Rambles among our Gipsies and their Children* (1883; 1885), p. 108.

9 V. S. Morwood, *Our Gipsies in City, Tent and Van* (1885), pp. 131–2.

10 W. G. Willis Watson, 'Pestiferous Carbuncles in Somerset', *J.G.L.S.*, 3rd Ser., Vol. 12, No. 2 (1933).

11 Account of visit given to W. Brockie in his *The Gypsies of Yetholm* (Kelso, 1884), pp. 92–3.

12 T. Taylor, 'Gypsey Experiences', *Illustrated London News*, 29 November 1851, p. 655. See also H. T. Crofton, 'Gypsy Life in Lancashire and Cheshire', *Manchester Literary Club, Papers*, Vol. 3 (Manchester, 1877); Note from F. H. Groome, *Notes and Queries*, 6th Ser., Vol. 1 (17 January 1880), p. 49.

13 A. Somerville, *The Autobiography of a Working Man, by 'One who has Whistled at the Plough'* (1848), p. 55. In the Border regions the terms 'tinker', 'tinkler', 'tinkler-gypsy' and 'gipsy' were synonymous.

14 *Parliamentary Debates, House of Commons*, Vol. 338 (31 July 1889), col. 1840.

15 H. Mayhew, *London Labour and the London Poor*, Vol. 1 (1861; New York, 1968), p. 9.

16 'Account of the Gipsies', *Chambers's Miscellany of Useful and Entertaining Tracts*, Vol. 16, No. 139 (1847), p. 11.

17 *Ibid*.

18 'The Autobiography, 1793–1824', in J. W. and A. Tibble (eds.), *The Prose of John Clare* (1951), p. 38.

19 E. J. Brabazon, *A Month at Gravesend* (1863), p. 90; H. Woodcock, *The Gipsies* (1865), p. 53.

20 J. Sandford, *Gypsies* (1975), p. 44.

21 Quoted in F. H. Groome, *In Gypsy Tents* (Edinburgh, 1880; Wakefield, 1973), p. 380.

22 H. T. Crofton, 'Affairs of Egypt, 1907', *J.G.L.S.*, Vol. 2, No. 2 (1908), p. 125.

23 C. G. Leland, *The Gypsies* [1882], pp. 136–7. Leland associated this practice less with the 'true' Gypsies and more with the *didakais* and half-bloods. See also A. Esquiros, *The English at Home*, translated and edited by L. Wraxall (1861), p. 192.

24 G. Smith, *I've Been a Gipsying*, pp. 117–18.

25 'Notes and Queries', *J.G.L.S.*, Old Ser., Vol. 3, No. 4 (1892), p. 245.

26 A. Melton, 'The True-Born Gipsy Folk: Will the Ancient Romany People Disappear?', *Sunday Chronicle*, 11 August 1907, p. 2; Rev. G. Hall, *The Gypsy's Parson, his Experiences and Adventures* (1915), pp. 152–3; T. W. Thompson, 'The Social Polity of the English Gypsies', *J.G.L.S.*, 3rd Ser., Vol. 2, No. 3 (1923), p. 123.

27 G. Smith, *Gipsy Life*, p. 215; T. W. Thompson, 'Borrow's Gypsies', *J.G.L.S.*, New Ser., Vol. 3, No. 3 (1910), p. 166; T. W. Thompson, 'Samuel Fox and the Derbyshire Boswells', *J.G.L.S.*, 3rd Ser., Vol. 3, No. 4 (1924), p. 178. For an etymological discussion of the words 'tinker' and 'tinkler' and their relationship with certain stereotypes see T. Acton, 'The Development of Ethnic Ideology and Pressure Politics in Gypsy-Gaujo Relations in England and Wales from Victorian Reformism to Romani Nationalism', D.Phil., University of Oxford (1973). Note also that North Country tinkers, ballad-singers and itinerant beggars were called 'randies' or 'randy-beggars' (F. W. Hackwood, *The Good Old Times* (1910), p. 228; D. MacRitchie, *Scottish Gypsies under the Stewarts* (Edinburgh, 1894), p. 12).

28 From an interview with Mrs Cooper in the Rev. T. W. Norwood's notebook, 1860, quoted in Lady A. Grosvenor, 'A Pilgrim's Progress', *J.G.L.S.*, New Ser., Vol. 3, No. 3 (1910), p. 214.

29 G. Smith, *Gipsy Life*, p. 248, *I've Been a Gipsying*, p. 209.

30 D. Townsend, *The Gipsies of Northamptonshire: Their Manner of Life* . . . *Fifty Years Ago* (Kettering, 1877), p. 11. This is an interesting account of Gypsy life in verse. See also R. A. S. Macfie, 'Gypsy Lore', *University Review*, Vol. 7 (1908), p. 105.

31 B. Skot (pseud. of R. A. S. Macfie), *A Brief Account of Gypsy History* (Liverpool, 1909), p. 55; *Bedfordshire Times and Independent*, 30 August 1907, p. 9.

32 D. Townsend, *op. cit.*, p. iv.

33 R. Samuel, 'Quarry Roughs', in R. Samuel (ed.), *Village Life and Labour* (1975), p. 147.

34 J. Crabb, *op. cit.*, p. 37. This contradicts an earlier claim (pp. 33–4) that Gypsy parents were anxious to preserve the purity of morals of their children and so, presumably, would not be keen to introduce them to these alleged houses of vice and immorality. See also the annual report of a London city missionary, 1859, in *London City Mission Magazine*, Vol. 25 (2 January 1860), p. 31.

35 V. S. Morwood, *op. cit.*, p. 119.

36 E. O. Winstedt and T. W. Thompson, 'Gypsy Dances', *J.G.L.S.*, New Ser., Vol. 6, No. 1 (1912), p. 20.

37 E. R. Pennell, 'A Gypsy Piper', *J.G.L.S.*, Old Ser., Vol. 2, No. 5 (1891), pp. 266–77.

38 E. Grey, *Cottage Life in a Hertfordshire Village* (St Albans, 1935), pp. 207–9.

39 *Ibid.*; T. W. Thompson, 'Borrow's Gypsies', *J.G.L.S.*, New Ser., Vol. 3, No. 3 (1910), p. 167; *Notes and Queries*, 4th Ser., Vol. 3 (15 May 1869), p. 461. Another Draper (Frederick) was well known for his fiddling at inns, wedding feasts and harvest suppers about Hitchin. However, the local Quakers considered his music 'almost as dangerous as gun-powder', which threatened to disrupt the quiet disposition of the town. Pressure was brought to bear on farmers and landowners to prevent Draper from encamping on their land and he was continually moved on. His response to this persecution was to fiddle 'diabolically and excruciatingly' in front of his persecutors' houses. He then disappeared from the region and later died at the age of 104 after a period in Reading Workhouse (R. L. Hine, 'Gypsy Draper, 1797–1902', *J.G.L.S.*, 3rd Ser., Vol. 11, Nos. 3–4 (1932), pp. 120–4).

40 G. 'Lazzy' Smith, *Incidents in a Gipsy's Life* . . . *the Royal Epping Forest Gipsies* (Liverpool, 1886; Leicester, [1892]), pp. 6–7.

41 W.C., 'Transformation of the Gipsies', *Once a Week*, Vol. 11 (22 October 1864), p. 498.

42 *Ibid.*, p. 501.

43 K. Bercovici, *The Story of the Gypsies* (1930), pp. 247–8.

44 *Jackson's Oxford Journal*, 25 March 1871, p. 5.

45 See, for example, E. O. Windstedt and T. W. Thompson, 'Gypsy Dances', *loc. cit.*, pp. 27ff; 'A Gipsy Ball', *Every Saturday*, New Ser., Vol. 2 (1872), pp. 691–3; *Daily News*, 19 October 1872, p. 5.

46 F. Cuttriss (pseud.), *Romany Life, Experienced and Observed during Many Years of Friendly Intercourse with the Gypsies* (1915), pp. 262–3.

47 R. Jefferies, *Field and Hedgerow, being the Last Essays of R.J. Collected by his Widow* (1889), pp. 10–11; *Daily Chronicle*, 18 January 1908, p. 6; F. Cuttriss, *op. cit.*, p. 104.

48 C. G. Leland, *op. cit.*, p. 117.

49 H. Wolff, *Sussex Industries* (Lewes, 1883), pp. 151–3.

50 *Ibid.*; see also S. J. Marsh, *Ashdown Forest* (privately printed, 1935), pp. 12–23.

51 See C. G. Leland, *The English Gipsies and their Language* (1873; 1874), p. 210; G. Smith, 'Our Gipsies and their Children', *London Society*, Vol. 47 (1885), p. 38.

52 W. Raymond, *English Country Life* (1910), p. 319.

53 G. Smith, *I've Been a Gipsying*, pp. 281–2; I. Montagu, 'Rambles with the Romany', *Good Words*, Vol. 23 (1882), p. 818; H. T. Crofton, 'Affairs of Egypt, 1908', *J.G.L.S.*, New Ser., Vol. 3, No. 4 (1910), p. 284; G. Smith, 'Our Gipsies', *loc. cit.*, p. 38.

54 A. Beale, 'Among the Gypsies', *Sunday Magazine* (1875), p. 49.

55 V. S. Morwood, *op. cit.*, pp. 266–7; G. Smith, *I've Been a Gipsying*, pp. 26, 71; F. H. Groome, *op. cit.*, pp. 265–6.

56 H. H. Malleson, *Napoleon Boswell, Tales of the Tents* (1913), p. 113.

57 *First Report of the Commissioners Appointed to Inquire as to the Best Means of Establishing an Efficient Constabulary Force in England and Wales* (1839), p. 18.

58 Letter from R. Hargreaves to Dorothy McGrigor Phillips, 29 January 1940, but dated 1939 (Romany Collection); D. Harvey, *The Gypsies: Wagon Time and After* (1979), p. 116; Rev. G. Hall, 'To Brough Hill Fair and Back', *Romanitshels', Didakais' and Folk-Lore Gazette*, Vol. 1, No. 4 (1912), pp. 134–7; *Daily Mail*, 30 September 1908, p. 3; V. S. Morwood, *op. cit.*, p. 263; G. Smith, *I've Been a Gipsying*, pp. 39–59; *Manchester City News*, 13 June 1908, p. 6.

59 G. Smith, *Incidents*, p. 5; see also J. Hoyland, *op. cit.*, pp. 175–8.

60 *Rpt of Comm. on Constab. Force*, p. 105, para. 127.

61 F. Anstey, 'A Gypsy Fair in Surrey', *Harper's New Monthly Magazine* (1888), pp. 625–33.

62 R. W. Muncey, *Our Old English Fairs* (1939), pp. 100–2.

63 Quoted in G. V. Cox, *Recollections of Oxford* (1868), pp. 287–8. See also G. Smith, *Gypsy Children: Or, a Stroll in Gypsydom. With Songs and Stories* [1889], pp. 27–8.

64 B. Skot, *op. cit.*, p. 53; E. O. Winstedt, 'Gypsy Civilisation', *J.G.L.S.*, New Ser., Vol. 1, No. 4 (1908), p. 322; *Notes and Queries*, 6th Ser., Vol. 2 (18 December 1880), p. 494.

65 J. Crabb, *op. cit.*, p. 60; H. Woodcock, *op. cit.*, pp. 161–2.

66 W. H. Hudson, *A Shepherd's Life: Impressions of the South Wiltshire Downs* (1910), p. 265.

67 *Ibid.*, pp. 263–4.

68 Extract from J. Crabb's speech at the laying of the foundation stone of the Farnham Gipsy Asylum, 1845, quoted in J. Rudall, *A Memoir of the Rev. James Crabb, Late of Southampton* (1854), p. 154; T. W. Thompson, 'Affairs of Egypt, 1909', *J.G.L.S.*, New Ser., Vol. 5, No. 2 (1911), p. 123; 'Notes and Queries', *J.G.L.S.*, New Ser., Vol. 1, No. 2 (1907), p. 187.

69 F. Cuttriss quotes a Hampshire Gypsy who described the summer 'run', beginning with potato-planting and cleaning and ending with pea-picking (*op. cit.*, p. 68).

70 J. Crabb, *op. cit.*, pp. 136–7; J. Hoyland, *A Historical Survey of the Customs, Habits and Present State of the Gypsies, Designed . . . to Promote the Amelioration of their Condition* (York, 1816), p. 187; W. M. Adams, 'The Wandering Tribes of Great Britain', *Cassell's Family Magazine* (1883), p. 730; 'The Present State of the Gypsies', *Sunday at Home* (1884), p. 119; V. S. Morwood, 'Plans Suggested for the Reclamation of Gipsies', *Victoria Magazine*, Vol. 14 (1870), p. 76; *Select Committee of the House*

of Lords on the Moveable Dwellings Bill, Minutes of Evidence, of Dr R. Farrar, Medical Officer of the Local Government Board (1909), p. 20, paras. 341–5. Note that hop farming was practically restricted to the six counties mentioned in the text. The official returns for 1907 gave the following acreages for these counties: Kent, 28,169; Hereford, 6,143; Sussex, 4,243; Worcester, 3,622; Hampshire, 1,842; Surrey, 744. This left less than 200 acres under hop not in these counties (*Select Committee on the Hop Industry, Report* (1908), p. xxx, para. 29).

71 *Reports of Medical Inspectors to the Local Government Board, No. 252: Dr Reginald Farrar's Report to the Local Government Board on the Lodging and Accommodation of Hop-Pickers and Pickers of Fruit and Vegetables* (1907), pp. 28–30.

72 *Ibid.; Sel. Cttee on Mov. Dw., Minutes of Evidence*, of Dr R. Farrar (1909), p. 20, para. 346.

73 R. Samuel, 'Comers and Goers', in H. J. Dyos and M. Wolff (eds.), *The Victorian City, Images and Realities*, Vol. 1 (1973; 1976), p. 135.

74 *Dr Farrar's Rpt to the L.G.B.*, p. 28; *Sel. Cttee on Mov. Dw., Minutes of Evidence*, of Mr J. Beck (1909), p. 37, para. 787.

75 An interesting description of the Sussex hoppers appears in H. Wolff, *op. cit.*, pp. 97–8.

76 *Ibid.*, p. 100.

77 Rev. J. Y. Stratton, *Hops and Hop-Pickers* [1883], p. 133; M. J. Winstanley, *Memories of Life in Kent at the Turn of the Century* (Folkestone, 1978), pp. 81ff.; *Labour News and Employment Advertiser*, 28 February 1874, pp. 2–3. The claim that nearly all the English Gypsies migrated to the hop fields in September is clearly an exaggeration, though it does indicate the high number of nomadic families among the hoppers.

78 Rev. J. Y. Stratton, *op. cit.*, p. 89; *Sel. Cttee on Mov. Dw., Minutes of Evidence*, of Dr Farrar (1909), p. 20, paras. 341–6. See also Mrs Reynold's account in M. Lewis (ed.), *Old Days in the Kent Hop Gardens* (Tonbridge, 1962).

79 Even this account has not given a complete picture of the range of occupations pursued by the Gypsy-travellers. They can also be found to have worked as shrimpers, coalminers, bell-hangers, domestic servants, models, slipper-makers, menders of glass and china, rifle-range attendants, bathing-machine attendants, cab proprietors, prize-fighters and inn-keepers. See F. H. Groome, *op. cit.*, p. 48; S. Roberts, *The Gypsies* (1836), pp. 211–14; G. Smith, *Gipsy Life*, pp. 237, 291; 'Notes and Queries', *J.G.L.S.*, Old Ser., Vol. 3, No. 3 (1892), pp. 191–2; E. O. Winstedt, 'Gypsy Civilisation', *loc. cit.*, p. 340; 'Anglo-Romani Gleanings', *J.G.L.S.*, 3rd Ser., Vol. 3, No. 3 (1924), p. 115; T. W. Thompson, 'Borrow's Gypsies', *loc. cit.*, p. 165; T. W. Thompson, 'Gypsies who Hunted with the Badsworth Hounds', *J.G.L.S.*, 3rd Ser., Vol. 7, Nos. 3–4 (1928), p. 152; T. W. Thompson, 'English Gypsies as Bell-Hangers', *J.G.L.S.*, 3rd Ser., Vol. 10, No. 4 (1931), pp. 187–94; 'Notes and Queries', *J.G.L.S.*, 3rd Ser., Vol. 14, No. 3 (1935), p. 165; F. S. Atkinson, 'Gypsies in East Anglia', *The Kendalian*, Vol. 11 (1911), p. 14; *Notes and Queries*, 4th Ser., Vol. 3 (12 June 1869), p. 558; *Notes and Queries*, 6th Ser., Vol. 1 (17 January 1880), p. 49; T.A.T., 'The Gipsy of To-Day', *The Sketch*, Vol. 1 (4 September 1895), p. 329.

80 Gas-stoking, itself a job subject to seasonal change, was taken up primarily by the Battersea Gypsies. See D. L. Woolmer, 'Gipsies in their Winter Quarters', *loc. cit.*, pp. 534–5.

81 V. S. Morwood, *op. cit.*, p. 167. See also B. Adams, *et al.*, *op. cit.*, pp. 129–53; J. Okely, 'Trading Stereotypes: The Case of English Gypsies', in S. Wallman (ed.), *Ethnicity at Work* (1979), pp. 17ff.

82 Letter from C. G. Leland to the *Standard*, 19 August 1879, p. 6.

83 R. A. S. Macfie, 'The Gypsies: An Outline Sketch', *Romanitshels', Didakais' and Folk-Lore Gazette*, Vol. 1, No. 3 (1912), pp. 81–2.

84 Lovell, 'My Life: By a Gipsy', *Home Chat* (18 April 1908), p. 267.

85 See especially P. Bailey, *Leisure and Class in Victorian England: Rational Recreation and the Contest for Control, 1830–1885* (1978).

86 'The Norwood Gypsies', *The Literary Lounger* (1826), p. 88.

87 See R. Samuel, 'Village Labour', in R. Samuel (ed.), *Village Life and Labour* (1975), and also his article 'Comers and Goers', in Dyos and Wolff (eds.), *The Victorian City*.

88 C. Whitehead, *Retrospections* (Maidstone, 1913), p. 7.

89 See for example D. Farmer, *Under a Spreading Chestnut Tree: The Reminiscences of a Village Blacksmith* (Hull, 1981).

4 Romany or traveller – definitions and stereotypes

1 See, for example, W. H. Ainsworth, *Rookwood: A Romance* (1850); G. Borrow, *Lavengro; the Scholar, the Gypsy, the Priest*, 3 vols. (1851), *The Romany Rye; a Sequel to 'Lavengro'*, 2 vols. (1857); C. Dickens, *The Mystery of Edwin Drood* (1870); Sir Walter Scott, *Guy Mannering* (1817); 'The Gipsy Queen's Revenge', *The Aldine Half Holiday Library*, No. 419 (n.d.); 'The Gipsy Queen's Legacy', *The Aldine Cheerful Library*, No. 139 (n.d.); 'A Gipsy Bride', *Aunt Kate's Penny Stories*, No. 5 (Dundee, 1901); 'Gipsy Jack', *The Boys' First-Rate Pocket Library*, No. 55 (c. 1891).

2 See G. Borrow, *Romano Lavo-Lil* (1888), together with the works cited above; A. Compton-Rickett, *The Vagabond in Literature* (1906), p. 6; J. Simson, 'Disquisition on the Past, Present and Future of Gipsydom', in W. Simson, *A History of the Gipsies: With Specimens of the Gipsy Language* (London [printed], Edinburgh, 1865), pp. 523–4; Rev. S. B. James, 'English Gipsies', *Church of England and Lambeth Magazine* (6 October 1875), p. 226; T. Taylor, 'Gypsey Experiences', *Illustrated London News*, 29 November 1851, p. 665; C. M. Bowen, 'George Borrow', *Westminster Review*, Vol. 173 (1910), pp. 286–304.

3 'The Roumany-Chai or Gipsies', *Illustrated London News*, Vol. 29 (1856), p. 304.

4 See W. Howitt, *The Rural Life of England* (1840), pp. 165–72; C. G. Leland, *The Gypsies* [1882], pp. 9–17; G. White, *The Natural History of Selborne* (1788), p. 201; A. Bates, 'Gipsy George', *Atlantic Monthly*, Vol. 100 (1907), p. 479; 'Who Are the Gipsies?' *Church of England Magazine* (1842), p. 293; 'The Yetholm Gipsies', *Hogg's Instructor*, New Ser., Vol. 10 (1853), p. 75; *Clarion*, 19 August 1910, p. 1; *First Report of the Committee for the Reformation of the Gipsies in Scotland* (Edinburgh, 1839), p. 6.

5 See B. C. Smart and H. T. Crofton, *The Dialect of the English Gypsies* (2nd edn enlarged, 1875), p. xvi. One of the first writers to set up the comparison between the Gypsies and those who lived in the expanding cities was Samuel Roberts. He was undoubtedly a fervent Gypsy romanticist who admired the simplicity of their pastoral way of life, seeing them as one of the few groups standing opposed to industrial progress. He asked his readers to compare their natural way of life with

the bitterness and degradation that characterised the lower classes in the manufacturing districts (see his 'A Word for the Gipsies', in *The Blind Man and his Son: A Tale for Young People* (1816), p. 116). By 1836 he even claimed 'the Gypsies are by far more intelligent and civilised than the depraved part of the lower ranks in large towns' (*The Gypsies* (1836), p. 57). See also C. Holmes, 'Samuel Roberts and the Gypsies', in S. Pollard and C. Holmes (eds.), *Essays on the Economic and Social History of South Yorkshire* (Barnsley, 1976), pp. 233–46; S. Roberts, 'Samuel Roberts of Park Grange, Sheffield, 1763–1848', *J.G.L.S.*, New Ser., Vol. 5, No. 3 (1912), pp. 161–6.

6 See A. Symons, 'In Praise of Gypsies', *J.G.L.S.*, New Ser., Vol. 1, No. 4 (1908), pp. 296–7.

7 G. Smith, *I've Been a Gipsying: Or, Rambles among our Gipsies and their Children* (1883; 1885), Prefatory note, p. 34.

8 See, for example, A. Esquiros, *The English at Home*, translated and edited by L. Wraxall (1861), pp. 145–6; A. H. Japp, 'The Gypsies as Seen by Friendly Eyes', *Gentlemen's Magazine*, Vol. 255 (1883, Vol. 2), p. 584; S. B. James, 'Gipsies', *The Graphic*, Vol. 10 (19 September 1874), p. 289; *Hampshire Advertiser*, 1 January 1842, p. 2.

9 'In Gipsy Tents', *Chambers's Journal*, No. 882 (20 November 1880), p. 738.

10 An old Gypsy quoted in F. H. Groome, *In Gipsy Tents* (Edinburgh, 1880; Wakefield, 1973), pp. 101–2.

11 While the works of the Gypsy lorists were intended in some measure to counter Smith's uncompromising attacks, their views were in reality not so far distant. Smith also held a vision of the 'true' Romany. He talked of one settled Gypsy as being 'as pure a gypsy as it is possible to find at this late day' (*I've Been a Gipsying*, p. 236). Another encounter took place in the vans of the Gypsy owner of a coconut establishment. The vans were so clean that Smith concluded the owner must have had at least three parts Romany blood in his veins (*ibid.*, p. 272). However Smith was not consistent and at times diverged radically from the lorists by denying racial variation and simply equating Gypsyism with travelling, hence the title of his book. In *I've Been a Gipsying* he added an appendix in which he stated that two-thirds of the children then travelling the country were of parents who once followed town and settled employments. His interpretation was thus confused and contradictory, at one moment upholding the idea of the Romany and the next stating that an acquaintance had been a Gypsy 'nearly all his life' (letter from George Smith to the *Standard*, 14 August 1879, p. 6).

12 See W. A. Dutt, 'English Gypsies', *Cassell's Magazine*, Vol. 53 (1911), p. 60; J. Sampson, 'English Gypsy Songs and Rhymes', *J.G.L.S.*, Old Ser., Vol. 2, No. 2 (1890), p. 80; A. Beale, 'Among the Gypsies', *Sunday Magazine* (1875), p. 49.

13 Letter from J. R. T. Mayer, quoting from a manuscript in his possession by V. S. Morwood, to *Notes and Queries*, 3rd Ser., Vol. 9 (13 January 1866), p. 49. See also E. Deutsch, 'Gypsies', *Chambers's Encyclopaedia*, Vol. 5 (1863), p. 172.

14 See J. Crabb, *The Gipsies' Advocate* (1831; 3rd edn with additions, 1832), p. 24; E. Deutsch, 'Gypsies', *loc. cit.*, p. 172.

15 C. G. Leland, 'Visiting the Gypsies', *Century Magazine*, Vol. 25 (April 1883), p. 908.

16 R. Numelin, *The Wandering Spirit: A Study of Human Migration* (1937), p. 279.

17 Rev. G. Hall, *The Gypsy's Parson, his Experiences and Adventures* (1915), pp. 3–4. See also H. Woodcock, *The Gipsies* (1865), p. 40.

18 J. Simson used this idea to argue for a secret society of Gypsies, united in a world-wide brotherhood by the Romany language. See his preface to W. Simson, *op. cit.*, p. 12.

19 'Account of the Gipsies', *Chambers's Miscellany of Useful and Entertaining Tracts*, Vol. 16, No. 139 (1847), pp. 22–3.

20 V. S. Morwood, *Our Gipsies in City, Tent and Van* (1885), pp. 137–43; T. W. Thompson, 'Gypsy Marriage in England', *J.G.L.S.*, 3rd Ser., Vol. 5, No. 1 (1926).

21 W. Simson, *op. cit.*, pp. 260–3. See also E. B. Trigg, 'Magic and Religion amongst the Gypsies of Great Britain', D.Phil., University of Oxford (1967), and his book *Gypsy Demons and Divinities: The Magical and Supernatural Practices of the Gypsies* (New Jersey, 1973).

22 W.B., 'The Gipsies of the Border', *Monthly Chronicle of North Country Lore and Legend* (1891), pp. 205–8.

23 See, for example, W. Crooke, 'The Burning of the Property of the Gypsy at Death', *Folk-Lore*, Vol. 20 (1909), p. 353; H. T. Crofton, 'Affairs of Egypt, 1892–1906', *J.G.L.S.*, New Ser., Vol. 1, No. 4 (1908), pp. 366–7; H. T. Crofton, 'Affairs of Egypt, 1908', *J.G.L.S.*, New Ser., Vol. 3, No. 4 (1910), p. 283; *Notes and Queries*, 2nd Ser., Vol. 3 (6 June 1857), pp. 442–3; *Notes and Queries*, 9th Ser., Vol. 12 (19 December 1903), p. 496.

24 C. G. Leland, *The English Gipsies and their Language* (1873; 1874), p. 58; note from C. H. J. Anderson in *Notes and Queries*, 4th Ser., Vol. 3 (29 May 1869), p. 518.

25 B. Skot (pseud. of R. A. S. Macfie), *A Brief Account of Gypsy History* (Liverpool, 1909), p. 52.

26 J. Crabb, *The Gipsies' Advocate*, pp. 28–9; V. S. Morwood, *op. cit.*, p. 174; H. T. Crofton, 'Affairs . . . 1892–1906', *loc. cit.*, p. 358; *Notes and Queries*, 8th Ser., Vol. 6 (13 October 1894), p. 286; *Notes and Queries*, 9th Ser., Vol. 12 (28 November 1903), p. 428.

27 W. Crooke, 'The Burning', *loc. cit.*, p. 353.

28 See T. W. Thompson, 'The Uncleanness of Women among English Gypsies', *J.G.L.S.*, 3rd Ser., Vol. 1, No. 1 (1922).

29 For an excellent and thorough survey of present-day Gypsy life see J. Okely, *The Traveller-Gypsies* (Cambridge, 1983).

30 There is an interesting parallel here with the Jews. Both were seen as a displaced people, united by common origin, living in an alien and hostile environment. There are also echoes of the theory of the world-wide Jewish conspiracy in the various claims made concerning the purpose of the Gypsies' secretive language, internal cohesion and strict polity.

31 C. G. Leland, *The English Gipsies*, p. 173.

32 'Who Are the Gypsies?', *County Gentleman and Land and Water Illustrated* (1906), p. 1076.

33 The word didakai, ditakei, or diddecoy, was said to have derived from the mispronunciation of the common Gypsy word 'Dik akei', meaning 'look here!'. The earliest record of the use of the word, spelt 'didykois', is thought to be found in Rev. J. Clay, *Chaplain's Twenty-Eighth Report on the Preston House of Correction*,

Presented to the Magistrates of Lancashire, 1851 (Preston, 1852), p. 53. See also Rev. G. Hall, *op. cit.*, p. 77; H. T. Crofton, 'Gipsy Life in Lancashire and Cheshire', *Manchester Literary Club, Papers*, Vol. 3 (Manchester, 1877), p. 32. For a full and interesting discussion of these terms see T. Acton, 'The Development of Ethnic Ideology and Pressure Politics in Gypsy-Gaujo Relations in England and Wales from Victorian Reformism to Romani Nationalism', D.Phil., University of Oxford (1973), pp. 131–59.

34 See A. Melton, 'The True-Born Gypsy Folk: Will the Ancient Romany People Disappear?', *Sunday Chronicle*, 11 August 1907, p. 2.

35 M. Howitt (ed.), *Mary Howitt, an Autobiography* (1891), p. 50; Rev. G. Hall, 'The Gipsies of England', *Sunday at Home* (April 1912), pp. 414–16; T. Taylor, 'Gypsey Experiences', *loc. cit.*, 29 November 1891, pp. 655–6; 13 December 1891, pp. 715–16; 27 December 1891, pp. 777–9.

36 Rev. S. B. James, 'English Gipsies', *loc. cit.*, (18 September 1875), p. 161. See also W. H. Hudson, *A Shepherd's Life: Impressions of the South Wiltshire Downs* (1910), p. 266.

37 C. Stein, 'Our Gypsy Visitors', *Baily's Magazine of Sports and Pastimes*, Vol. 70 (1898), pp. 21–3.

38 J. Sampson, 'The Gypsies', *Warrington Literary and Philosophical Society: Papers*, No. 6 (Warrington, 1896–7), pp. 16–17. See also Rev. G. Hall, *op. cit.*, p. 181; F. H. Groome, *op. cit.*, p. 30; B. S. Fitzgerald, *Gypsies of Britain. An Introduction to their History* (1944; 1951), p. 42.

39 Lovell, 'My Life: By a Gipsy', *Home Chat* (18 April 1908), p. 267.

40 G. Smith, *I've Been a Gipsying*, p. 163. See also *Select Committee on the Temporary Dwellings Bill, Minutes of Evidence*, of George Smith (1887), p. 24, paras. 404–7.

41 W.B., 'Gipsies and their Friends', *Temple Bar Magazine*, Vol. 47 (1876), p. 71. See also S. L. Bensusan, 'How the Other Half Lives', *English Illustrated Magazine*, Vol. 17 (1897), p. 646.

42 A. Symons, 'In Praise', *loc. cit.*, p. 295.

43 See 'The Gipsy's Grave', *Church of England Magazine* (1843), p. 75.

44 As a race they were reported to prefer to eat animals that had died by the hand of God rather than by the hand of man. This conflicts with the frequent assertions that they poisoned and killed animals for their own consumption, termed 'drabbing'. It was also claimed they ate their own parents! See F. Grose, *A Classical Dictionary of the Vulgar Tongue* (1785; 1796; edited by E. Partridge, 1931), pp. 175–8; E. Deutsch, 'Gypsies', *loc. cit.*, p. 172; 'Gipsies', *The Literary and Scientific Repository*, Vol. 3 (1821), p. 405.

45 See A. Esquiros, *op. cit.*, p. 143; F. Grose, *op. cit.*, pp. 175–8; J. G. Kohl, *England and Wales* (1844; 1968), p. 190; 'Account of the Gipsies', *Chambers's Miscellany of Useful and Entertaining Tracts*, Vol. 16, No. 139 (1847), pp. 8–9; 'Gypsies', *Edinburgh Encyclopaedia*, Vol. 10 (1830), p. 597; G. C. Renouard, 'Gypsy', *Encyclopaedia Metropolitana*, Vol. 20 (1845), pp. 54–9; Annual report of a London city missionary, 1858, in *London City Mission Magazine*, Vol. 25 (2 January 1860), pp. 16–22; 'Gipsies', *New Monthly Magazine*, Vol. 35 (1832), pp. 375–7; 'The Passing of the Gipsy', *Outlook* (1 June 1907), pp. 721–2; A Wanderer, 'The Gipsies', *The Quiver*, Vol. 6 (1871), pp. 668–70; 'Gipsies', *Penny Cyclopaedia*, Vol. 11 (1836), pp. 255–6; *Whitby Gazette*, 22 March 1912, p. 4. The references could be multiplied many

times. Those included have been selected to show the appearance of racial stereotypes in a broad cross-section of works.

46 *First Report of the Commission Appointed to Inquire as to the Best Means of Establishing an Efficient Constabulary Force in England and Wales* (1839), p. 56, para. 30, also p. 21.

47 Rev. J. Clay, *op. cit.*, Appendix 12, p. 59. See also D. J. V. Jones, 'A Dead Loss to the Community: The Criminal Vagrant in Mid-Nineteenth Century Wales', *Welsh History Review*, Vol. 8, No. 3 (1977), pp. 312–44.

48 'The Norwood Gypsies', *The Literary Lounger* (1826), p. 91.

49 See W. Simson, *op. cit.*, p. 72; letter from 'Scoto-Montanus', in *Wesleyan Methodist Magazine*, 3rd Ser., Vol. 7 (1828), pp. 242–4.

50 *Philip Hine's Journal*, 9 November 1825, p. 63. See also Mr Ellis, 'The Nuisance and Prejudice of the Gypsy Vagrant to the Farmer', in V. Bell, *To Meet Mr Ellis: Little Gaddesden in the Eighteenth Century* (1956), pp. 74–8; H. M. G. Grellmann, *Dissertation on the Gipsies*, translated by M. Raper (1787), p. 92; F. Thompson, *Lark Rise to Candleford* (Oxford, 1968), pp. 472–3; A. Symons, 'In Praise', *loc. cit.*, p. 294; *Birmingham Daily Mail*, 8 October 1879, p. 2. Note also that contemporary slang placed the Gypsies alongside thieves and beggars. Consider, for example, the folowing: 'Arch Rogue' or 'Dimber Damber Upright Man': chief of a gang of thieves or Gypsies; 'King of the Gypsies': chief of a gang of misrule; in cant language called also the upright man; 'Stop Hole Abbey': rendezvous of the canting crew of beggars, Gypsies, cheats, thieves, etc. All definitions taken from F. Grose, *op. cit.*

51 This took place at the Winchester Lent Assizes in 1827. Such blatant discrimination was witnessed by James Crabb and it proved to be a major stimulus to his setting up a Committee to 'improve and assist these people'. This is dealt with in the following chapter. See J. Crabb, *The Gipsies' Advocate*, pp. 64–9; *Rpt of Comm. on Constab. Force*, p. 214, para. 146; H. Woodcock, *op. cit.*, pp. 44–5; 'Notes and Queries', *J.G.L.S.*, New Ser., Vol. 6, No. 2 (1912), pp. 158–60; W.B., 'Gipsies of the Border', *loc. cit.*, p. 163.

52 See F. W. Carew (ed.), *No. 747. Being the Autobiography of a Gipsy* (Bristol, [1891]), pp. 20, 35; 'Account of the Gipsies', *Chambers's Miscellany of Useful and Entertaining Tracts*, Vol. 16, No. 139 (1847), p. 22; H. T. Crofton, 'Gipsy Life', *loc. cit.*, p. 40; R. D. Paine, 'The Gypsy of England', *Outing*, Vol. 45 (New York, 1904), p. 334.

53 Quote from Hillyer, a member of the itinerant Frimley gang, in Rev. J. Clay, *op. cit.*, Appendix 12, p. 50.

54 *Ibid.*, pp. 45, 49.

55 *Ibid.*, p. 50.

56 'Ringing the changes' involved the switching of a valuable parcel by a worthless one, the unsuspecting victim believing that Gypsy magic would bring untold riches. The volumes of press-cuttings in the Romany Collection, Brotherton Library (University of Leeds), contain numerous instances of this alleged fraud. See also H. T. Crofton, 'Affairs of Egypt, 1892–1906', *J.G.L.S.*, New Ser., Vol. 1, No. 4 (1908), p. 369; *Police Gazette*, No. 37 (24 June 1839), p. 146. I am grateful to Dr Tony Mason for this latter reference.

57 For a sample of references to this alleged practice see A. Esquiros, *op. cit.*, pp. 158–9; J. Myers, 'Drab', *J.G.L.S.*, New Ser., Vol. 2, No. 3 (1909), pp. 199–207; *The Times*, 14 November 1842, p. 5.

58　F. Thompson, *op. cit.*, p. 36.
59　*Report of the Departmental Committee on Tinkers in Scotland* (Edinburgh, 1918), p. 5.
60　Mr Ellis, 'The Nuisance', in V. Bell, *op. cit.*, p. 76.
61　'Gipsydom', *Bow Bells*, Vol. 5 (1867), p. 275. This view contradicts the lorists' claims of tribal exclusivity in marriage.
62　As with all such claims, examples were provided. Adam Smith, the economist, was allegedly carried off by the Gypsies when only three years of age, to be rescued from obscurity by an uncle ('Account of the Gipsies', *Chambers's Miscellany of Useful and Entertaining Tracts*, Vol. 16, No. 139 (1847), p. 11; W.B., 'Gipsies of the Border', *loc. cit.*, p. 163). Again, this charge has interesting parallels in the ritual murder accusations levelled at Jews, with children from the host society being abducted for the ritual practices of an alien race. See 'The Tent Folk', *The Nation*, Vol. 2 (12 October 1907), p. 44.
63　T. Acton, 'Academic Success and Political Failure: A Review of Modern Social Science Writing in English on Gypsies', *Ethnic and Racial Studies*, Vol. 2, No. 2 (April 1979), p. 231.
64　Francis Groome attempted to extract something favourable from this by illustrating they mixed only with 'worthy' partners: '[they] wedded with the sons and daughters of the land – with peasants, miners, shopkeepers, farmers often, with native tramps and jail-birds hardly ever' (*In Gipsy Tents*, p. 250).
65　It would be too lengthy to provide references to every source where intermarriage is mentioned. The following is just a small sample. R. C. De Crespigny and H. G. Hutchinson, *The New Forest: Its Traditions, Inhabitants and Customs* (1895; Wakefield, 1975), p. 83; Lady A. Grosvenor, 'Preface', to H. H. Malleson, *Napoleon Boswell, Tales of the Tents* (1913), p. viii; 'Edinburghshire', in the *New Statistical Account of Scotland*, Vol. 1 (Edinburgh, 1845), pp. 184–5; W. A. Dutt, 'With the East Anglian Gypsies', *Good Words*, Vol. 37 (1896), pp. 120–6; E. O. Winstedt, 'Gypsy Civilisation', *J.G.L.S.*, New Ser., Vol. 1, No. 4 (1908), pp. 331–2; H. T. Crofton, 'Affairs of Egypt, 1907', *J.G.L.S.*, New Ser., Vol. 2, No. 2 (1908), p. 127.
66　F. H. Groome, *op. cit.*, pp. 250–3.
67　See, for example, J. Sampson, 'Introduction', to M. E. Lyster, *The Gypsy Life of Betsy Wood* (1926), pp. xi–xii, and pp. 2, 7; 'Pedigree of Matthew Wood', *J.G.L.S.*, New Ser., Vol. 2, No. 3 (1909), pp. 370–1; Rev. G. Hall, 'The Heron Pedigree', *J.G.L.S.*, New Ser., Vol. 7, No. 2 (1913), pp. 81–7; W. H. Rivers, 'Notes on the Heron Pedigree Collected by the Rev. G. Hall', *J.G.L.S.*, New Ser., Vol. 7, No. 2 (1913), pp. 88–104; 'Anglo-Romani Gleanings', *J.G.L.S.*, 3rd Ser., Vol. 3, No. 3 (1924), p. 113; T. W. Thompson, 'Samuel Fox and the Derbyshire Boswells', *J.G.L.S.*, 3rd Ser., Vol. 3, No. 4 (1924), pp. 158ff; Rev. G. Hall, 'Notes on the Boss Pedigree', *Romanitshels', 'Didakais' and Folk-Lore Gazette*, Vol. 1, No. 4 (1912), pp. 120ff.
68　T. W. Thompson, 'The Uncleanness', *loc. cit.*, p. 42.
69　W. H. Rivers, 'Notes on the Heron Pedigree', *loc. cit.*, p. 91.
70　The issue of self-ascription is of central importance in defining the features of this group. Judith Okely has indicated how self-definition forms a key element in locating the boundaries of the travelling community (see *The Traveller-Gypsies*).
71　C. G. Leland, *The Gypsies*, pp. 304–9.
72　See, for example, F. Cuttriss (pseud.), *Romany Life, Experienced and Observed during Many Years of Friendly Intercourse with the Gypsies* (1915), pp. 76–7; A. E. Gillington,

Gypsies of the Heath (1916), p. 17; Rev. G. Hall, *op. cit.*, p. 55; B. S. Fitzgerald, *op. cit.*, p. 77; C. Stein, 'Our Gypsy Visitors', *loc. cit.*, pp. 17–23; T.A.T., 'The Gypsy of Today', *The Sketch*, Vol. II (4 September 1895), p. 329.

73 See L. T. C. Rolt, *Narrow Boat* (1944), and the critique in H. Hanson, *The Canal Boatmen, 1760–1914* (Manchester, 1979).

74 Lady A. Grosvenor, 'A Pilgrim's Progress', *J.G.L.S.*, New Ser., Vol. 3, No. 3 (1910), p. 204.

75 H. Woodcock, *op. cit.*, pp. 148–51.

76 G. Smith, *I've Been a Gipsying*, pp. 86–7.

77 Gypsy Lore Society, printed report, undated (Gypsy Lore Society Archive). Any reliance on parish registers to establish racial identity must be treated with caution. Whether to enter a traveller under the heading 'traveller', 'Egyptian', etc., would have varied from vicar to vicar, parish to parish and also over time. Furthermore, the different spellings would have added to the confusion with Boswell becoming anything from Boss to Bosel and Bosvile, and Heron from Earne to Hurn to Horam (see Rev. S. B. James, 'English Gipsies', *loc. cit.*, 18 September 1875, p. 161).

78 The Kemp gang was said to travel the Midland Counties, along with the Lovells and Boswells (W. Howitt, *op. cit.*, p. 182).

79 'Notes and Queries', *J.G.L.S.*, New Ser., Vol. 4, No. 1 (1910), p. 80.

80 Lady A. Grosvenor, 'A Pilgrim's', *loc. cit.*, p. 216, fn. 1.

81 Broken Romany was said to be spoken by a variety of people in villages in Kent, Surrey and Sussex, including shopkeepers, publicans and stable-boys (Rev. G. Hall, *op. cit.*, p. 153).

82 C. G. Leland, 'The Tinkers' Talk', *J.G.L.S.*, New Ser., Vol. 1, No. 2 (1907), p. 169.

83 B. Skot (pseud. of R. A. S. Macfie), *op. cit.*, p. 45.

84 B. C. Smart and H. T. Crofton, *op. cit.*, p. xi; Rev. S. B. James, 'English Gipsies', *loc. cit.*, p. 225.

85 Peter Keating has expertly shown how this expeditionary enthusiasm also reached to the 'unknown' culture and way of life of the working classes. See his *Into Unknown England, 1866–1913: Selections from the Social Explorers* (1976) and *The Working Classes in Victorian Fiction* (1971).

86 Again, references to this are many. See, for example, A. H. Japp, 'The Gypsies', *loc. cit.*, p. 579; M. R. Mitford, *Our Village: Sketches of Rural Character and Scenery*, Vol. 2 (1827), p. 267; E. Brewer, 'Gipsy Encampments in the Heart of London', *Sunday at Home* (1896), p. 113; J. G. Kohl, *op. cit.*, p. 190; *First Report of the Committee for the Reformation of the Gipsies in Scotland* (Edinburgh, 1840), Appendix IV, p. 30.

87 R. C. De Crespigny and H. G. Hutchinson, *op. cit.*, p. 82. See also A. Esquiros, *op. cit.*, p. 175.

88 T. Taylor, 'Gypsey Experiences', *Illustrated London News*, 29 November 1851, pp. 655–6. Taylor stated further that painters, dramatists and novelists frequently misrepresented the Gypsies and refused to paint them as they really were: 'In the pictures and drawings of them there is an entire lack of truth, which can be detected at a glance by the "aficionado", the true lover and student of Roumany life. I cannot remember a single genuine Gypsy in a novel.'

89 The following references represent only a small sample of contemporary sources which point to this conclusion. See J. Crabb, *A Condensed History of the Gypsies*

(Southampton, 1843); M. R. Mitford, *op. cit.*, p. 300; S. Roberts, *The Gypsies*, pp. 17–18; 'Gipsies and Fortune-Telling', *Bow Bells*, Vol. 16 (1873), p. 502; 'My Friend's Gipsy Journal', *Good Words*, Vol. 9 (1 November 1868), p. 704; E. Brewer, 'Gipsy Encampments', *loc. cit.*, p. 113; A. Beale, 'Among the Gypsies', *loc. cit.*, p. 50.

90 R. D. Samuel, *The Art of Jugling or Legerdemaine* (1612), pp. 6–8. See also H. Woodcock, *op. cit.*, p. 10.

91 'Account of the Gipsies', *loc. cit.*, p. 1; 'Notes and Queries', *J.G.L.S.*, Old Ser., Vol. 3, No. 2 (1891), p. 123; J. Hoyland, *A Historical Survey of the Customs, Habits and Present State of the Gypsies, Designed . . . to Promote the Amelioration of their Condition* (York, 1816), pp. 92–3; 2nd Report of Sub-Committee, November 1828, in *Southampton Committee: A Summary Account of the Proceedings of a Provisional Committee Associated at Southampton with a View to the Consideration and Improvement of the Condition of the Gipseys* (Southampton, c. 1830), p. 9; G. Smith, *I've Been a Gipsying*, p. 264; W. Simpson, *op. cit.*, pp. 534–40.

92 C. G. Leland, 'Shelta', *J.G.L.S.*, Old Ser., Vol. 2, No. 6 (1891), p. 349, fn. 3. See also Rev. G. Hall, *op. cit.*, p. 181; J. Timbs, *Popular Errors Explained and Illustrated* (1869), p. 232; 'The Children of Mystery', *All the Year Round*, New Ser., Vol. 39 (1886), p. 88.

93 H. Mayhew, *London Labour and the London Poor*, Vol. 1 (1861; New York, 1968), p. 2.

94 L. O. Pike, *A History of Crime in England, Illustrating the Changes of the Laws in the Progress of Civilisation*, Vol. 1 (1876), pp. 75–6.

95 Although the trade unionists were primarily concerned with the system of 'tramping' undertaken by their members as a response to regional trade depressions, their comments generally made broader reference to the evils of itinerancy. A considerable amount of useful material relating to this subject can be found among the extensive trade union archives held at the Modern Records Centre, University of Warwick.

96 L. O. Pike, *op. cit.*, pp. 75–6.

97 Egyptians Act, 22 Henry VIII, c. 10, 1530. See also Appendix 1 for a summary list of the main legislation applying to itinerants.

98 Egyptians Act, 23 Geo. III, c. 51, 1783; Vagrancy Act, 3 Geo. IV, c. 40, 1822; Vagrancy Act, 5 Geo. IV, c. 83, 1824. See also A Barrister, *The Vagrant Act, in Relation to the Liberty of the Subject* (2nd edn, 1824).

99 It should be remembered that, at least for the early part of the century, villages were an introspective community and hostility could exist between up-towners and down-towners, neighbouring villages and counties. In a context where myths developed about people dwelling a few miles across a county border, any stranger would have been treated with some suspicion. See J. Lawson, *Progress in Pudsey* (1887; Firle, 1978).

100 G. Smith, *I've Been a Gipsying*, p. 263.

101 A. Somerville, *The Autobiography of a Working Man, by 'One who has Whistled at the Plough'* (1848), p. 54.

102 For an account of the Greek Gypsies see D. MacRitchie, 'The Greek Gypsies at Liverpool', *Chambers's Journal*, 5th Ser., Vol. 3 (September 1886), pp. 577–80; F. H. Groome, *Gypsy Folk Tales* (1899), pp. xlii–xliii; A. M'Cormick, *The Tinkler-Gypsies of Galloway* (Dumfries, 1906; Dumfries, 1907), p. x. For the German Gypsies see C. Holmes, 'The German Gypsy Question in Britain, 1904–6', in K. Lunn (ed.), *Hosts,*

Immigrants and Minorities: Historical Responses to Newcomers in British Society 1870–1914 (1980), pp. 134–59; R. Hargreaves, 'A Brief History of the German Gypsies, Brough Hill, 1908', in his letters to Mrs McGrigor Phillips, 13 November 1939–29 January 1940 (Romany Collection, Brotherton Library); J. Simpson, 'The German Gypsies at Blackpool', *J.G.L.S.*, New Ser., Vol. 1, No. 2 (1907), pp. 111–21. For the Calderari coppersmiths see Andreas (Mui Shuko), pseudonym of R. A. S. Macfie, *Gypsy Coppersmiths in Liverpool and Birkenhead* (Liverpool, 1913); E. O. Winstedt, 'The Gypsy Coppersmiths Invasion of 1911–13', *J.G.L.S.*, New Ser., Vol. 6, No. 4 (1913), pp. 244–303; E. O. Winstedt, 'Coppersmith Gypsy Notes', *J.G.L.S.*, New Ser., Vol. 8, No. 4 (1915), pp. 246–66; W. T. Searle, 'The Calderari Gypsy Coppersmiths', *Romanitshels', Didakais' and Folk-Lore Gazette*, Vol. 3, No. 1 (1914), pp. 6–32.

103 C. J. R. Turner, *A History of Vagrants and Vagrancy and Beggars and Begging* (1887), pp. 216, 259–60.

104 See HO45/9340.

105 Current work into the question of definition is assisted by the ability of the researchers to undertake a detailed enquiry into the issue of self-ascription. As previously mentioned, Judith Okely provides a most useful analysis of this. Historical studies are subject to serious limitations in this area because of the insufficiency of remaining records by Gypsies which could reliably inform this topic. For this reason my survey has necessarily concentrated on a critical treatment of how others defined the Gypsy rather than on how the Gypsies defined themselves. The Gypsy-travellers identified in this work exist as a group broader in scope than the racial definition of the pure Romany would allow and narrower than the categories of itinerants and travellers referred to by Swinstead and others, discussed in chapter 2.

5 Evangelism and the reforming mission

1 *Sheffield and Rotherham Independent*, 23 August 1869, p. 3. The incident took place at York. I am grateful to Dr John Field for this reference.

2 G. Smith, *Gipsy Life: Being an Account of our Gipsies and their Children, with Suggestions for their Improvement* (1880), pp. 153–5. The offence was not recorded.

3 *Ibid.*, p. 153.

4 Quoted in 'Notes and Queries', *J.G.L.S.*, New Ser., Vol. 2, No. 1 (1908), p. 92.

5 Even by the opening decade of the twentieth century this reasoning could still be heard. The real Romany of Eastern origins could not be reformed, it was claimed, for it would require a change in their nature, whereas the vagrant had merely to alter his habits (see *Departmental Committee on Vagrancy, Minutes of Evidence*, of Mr J. G. Legge, 1906, p. 155, para. 4495).

6 See G. Smith, *Gipsy Life*, pp. 154–5.

7 'Gypsies in England', *Christian Observer*, Vol. 7 (February 1808), pp. 91–2; Vol. 8 (August 1809), pp. 286–7; Vol. 9 (May 1810), pp. 278–80; Vol. 9 (September 1810), pp. 554–5; see also Vol. 14 (January 1815), pp. 23–5, 141; Vol. 14 (September 1815), pp. 590–1; Vol. 20 (March 1821), p. 159. An abridged copy of the correspondence contained in Volumes 7, 8 and 9 also appears in J. Hoyland, *A Historical Survey of*

the Customs, Habits and Present State of the Gypsies, Designed . . . to Promote the Amelioration of their Condition (York, 1816), pp. 199–219.

8 *Christian Observer*, Vol. 9 (May 1810), pp. 278–80.

9 It would seem that sometime in the late eighteenth century there was an early example of parish responsibility for settling and accommodating the Gypsies. The overseers of the parish were required by magisterial order to find a house for Aaron Smith, owing to the fact that his father had settled there some seventy or eighty years previously. Since that time the descendants of this man appeared periodically in the parish and demanded relief payments which, if refused, were followed by a threat to force the overseers to find them houses also. Sometimes they were threatened with the workhouse and so withdrew their demands, but at other times they were given money in return for their hasty removal from the parish. (See *Report from His Majesty's Commissioners for inquiring into the Administration and Practical Operation of the Poor Laws*, Appendix A, Report of J. J. Richardson, Assistant Commissioner (1834), p. 402).

10 *Northampton Mercury*, 29 June 1814, p. 4; 9 July 1814, p. 1; 23 July 1814, p. 2.

11 J. Hoyland, *op. cit.*

12 *Northampton Mercury*, 25 June 1814, p. 4.

13 *Ibid.*, 9 July 1814, p. 2.

14 See J. Hoyland, *op. cit.*, pp. 158–68, for a reproduction of the questionnaire and replies.

15 *Ibid.*, p. 251.

16 S. Roberts, 'A Word for the Gipsies', in his *The Blind Man and his Son: A Tale for Young People* (1816). See also, by the same author, *Parallel Miracles; or, the Jews and the Gypsies* (1830), later re-published as *The Gypsies; their Origin, Continuance, and Destination, as Clearly Foretold in the Prophecies of Isaiah, Jeremiah, and Ezekiel* (1836), *The Jews, the English Poor, and the Gypsies; with a Proposal for an Important Improvement in the British Constitution* (1848). See also S. Roberts, 'Samuel Roberts of Park Grange, Sheffield, 1763–1848', *J.G.L.S.*, New Ser., Vol. 5, No. 3 (1912), pp. 161–6; C. Holmes, 'Samuel Roberts and the Gypsies', in S. Pollard and C. Holmes (eds.), *Essays on the Economic and Social History of South Yorkshire* (Barnsley, 1976), pp. 233–46. Although Roberts believed the Gypsies were a separate and distinctive race of people, though originating from Egypt and not from the Suder caste of Hindu from North India as claimed by Hoyland, he conceded that they had no superstitious observances, forms or ceremonies (see his *The Gypsies*, p. 182).

17 Such a response was largely a product of Roberts' belief that the Gypsies had a Divine mission, and were symbols of a Divine power, and so caution and consideration were essential. (See C. Holmes, in S. Pollard and C. Holmes (eds.), *op. cit.*, pp. 240–1; E. B. Trigg, 'Magic and Religion amongst the Gypsies of Great Britain', D.Phil., University of Oxford (1967), pp. 255–7).

18 A Clergyman of the Church of England, *The Gipsies: Or a Narrative, in Three Parts, of Several Communications with that Wandering and Scattered People: With Some Thoughts on the Duty of Christians to attempt their Insruction and conversion* (York, 1822).

19 Letter from 'Scoto-Montanus', in the *Wesleyan Methodist Magazine*, 3rd Ser., Vol. 7 (1828), p. 244.

20 A Clergyman of the Church of England, *op. cit.*, p. 44. This device of publishing

works which illustrated that reform was indeed possible even with the most outcast elements of society was common practice by reformers of every description. See, for example, the anonymously-written novel, *The Gipsies* (1842).

21 Letter from 'Scoto-Montanus', *loc. cit.*, p. 244. The author believed, wrongly, that this had already taken place in Scotland, and that the Gypsies had been absorbed.

22 Letter from 'J.P.' of Cambridge, in the *Christian Observer*, Vol. 9 (May 1810), pp. 278–80.

23 Quoted in J. Hoyland, *op. cit.*, p. 173.

24 *Ibid.*, p. 174.

25 *Ibid.*, pp. 174–5.

26 'Gipsies', *The Literary and Scientific Repository*, Vol. 3 (1821), p. 404. G. Smith wrote that this took place in the 1820s, and when a question of religion arose the children were sent back to their Gypsy parents (*Gipsy Life*, pp. 274–5). Trigg apparently confuses this even further by claiming the Gypsies were sent to St Patrick's charity school in London in 1809, but when some difficulty arose over the question of religion they were sent to a school for the Irish ('Magic and Religion', p. 237). Trigg does not provide a source for this.

27 See J. Crabb, *The Gipsies' Advocate* (1831; 3rd edn with additions, 1832), p. 134.

28 Letter from Rev. C. Hyatt to Rev. J. Crabb, quoted in J. Rudall, *A Memoir of the Rev. James Crabb, Late of Southampton* (1854), pp. 135–8.

29 Letter from Rev. C. Hyatt, in *ibid.*, p. 136.

30 I have references to articles in the *Home Missionary Society Magazine* for 1820, 1821, February 1829 and December 1837, but have been unable to confirm these as the volumes were either missing from the collections or from the shelves at the British Library and at the University Libraries of Oxford and Cambridge. I have been unable to locate them elsewhere. Those I have seen are for September 1836, pp. 44–5; July 1838, pp. 118–19; December 1838, pp. 200–1; December 1841, p. 303; March 1845, p. 60. See also *Home Missionary Quarterly Chronicle* (Midsummer 1827), pp. 71–2.

31 *Home Missionary Society Magazine* (February 1829), quoted in E. B. Trigg, 'Magic and Religion', p. 265.

32 For an account of Crabb's early life, see J. Rudall, *op. cit.*; also I. H. S. Stratton, 'The Work and Ideas of John West, 1778–1845', M.A., University of Durham (1977), pp. 64–5.

33 Quoted in J. Rudall, *op. cit.*, p. 132.

34 J. Crabb, *op. cit.*, p. 65.

35 *Southampton Committee: A Summary Account of the Proceedings of a Provisional Committee Associated at Southampton with a View to the Consideration and Improvement of the Condition of the Gipseys* (Southampton, c. 1830), p. 2.

36 *A Summary Account of the Southampton Provis. Cttee*, p. 2. It was called 'The Southampton Committee instituted for the amelioration of the state of the Gipsies; and for their religious instruction and conversion.'

37 The similarity with Hoyland's method was no coincidence, for Crabb acknowledged his debt to this author. Moreover, the similarity did not end there, as Crabb also published the information collected in a book. *The Gipsies' Advocate* was an unqualified success, and ran to three editions.

38 Second Report of the Sub-Committee, 12 November 1828, in *A Summary Account of the Southampton Provis. Cttee*, p. 8 (both the First and Second Reports of the Sub-Committee are to be found in this publication).

39 Letter from Rev. Cobbin, quoted in J. Crabb, *op. cit.*, pp. 187–8.

40 Quoted in J. Rudall, *op. cit.*, pp. 188–9.

41 J. Crabb, *op. cit.*, p. 95.

42 *Ibid.*, pp. 130–3.

43 First Report of the Sub-Committee, 3 May 1828, *loc. cit.*, pp. 2–5.

44 J. Crabb, *op. cit.*, pp. 135–6.

45 First Report of the Sub-Committee, 3 May 1828, *loc. cit.*, p. 4.

46 V. S. Morwood, *Our Gipsies in City, Tent and Van* (1885), pp. 336–7.

47 Second Report of the Sub-Committee, 12 November 1828, *loc. cit.*, p. 8.

48 *A Summary Account of the Southampton Provis. Cttee*, p. 11.

49 J. Rudall, *op. cit.*, pp. 141–2. Any Gypsy new to the Southampton area would not have escaped their attentions either, as money was given to children who reported the presence of any new Gypsy camp to a member of the Committee (J. Crabb, *op. cit.*, p. 128).

50 *Hampshire Advertiser*, 1 January 1842, p. 2.

51 J. Rudall, *op. cit.*, p. 145.

52 *Derby Mercury*, 4 January 1843, p. 4. See also J. Crabb, *op. cit.*, p. 149; W. Simson, *A History of the Gipsies: With Specimens of the Gipsy Language* (London [printed], Edinburgh, 1865), p. 369.

53 J. Rudall, *op. cit.*, p. 140.

54 *Ibid.*, p. 224.

55 *Home Missionary Society Magazine* (July 1838), pp. 118–19.

56 See *A Summary Account of the Southampton Provis. Cttee; Report from the Southampton Committee for the Amelioration of the State of the Gipsies; and for their Religious Instruction and Conversion, Aug. 1827–May 1832* (Southampton, 1832).

57 Second Report of the Sub-Committee, 12 November 1828, *op. cit.*, p. 6.

58 J. Rudall, *op. cit.*, p. 140.

59 *Rpt of the Southampton Cttee*, p. 9.

60 E. O. Winstedt, 'Gypsy Civilisation', *J.G.L.S.*, New Ser., Vol. 1, No. 4 (1908), p. 335.

61 J. G. Kohl, *England and Wales* (1844; 1968), p. 191.

62 See 'Gipsy Reformation', *Scottish Christian Herald*, 2nd Ser., Vol. 1 (6 April 1839), pp. 216–17.

63 *Home Missionary Society Magazine* (July 1838), pp. 118–19.

64 Quoted in J. Rudall, *op. cit.*, p. 157.

65 W. Howitt, *The Rural Life of England* (1840), p. 186.

66 Similarly, the Gypsy hoppers at Farnham told Stanley they thought the children at school were all confined and waiting to be transported (J. Crabb, *op. cit.*, pp. 139, 155).

67 'Gossip about the Gipsies', *Leisure Hour*, Vol. 10 (1861), p. 447.

68 J. A. Fairley, *Bailie Smith of Kelso's Account of the Gypsies of Kirk Yetholm in 1815* (Hawick, 1907), p. 3. Only thirty copies of this pamphlet were privately printed. This pamphlet provides a fuller version of the replies of William Smith, Bailie of

Kelso, to Hoyland's circular, which the latter reproduced in his book (*op. cit.*, pp. 98–103).

69 W. Baird, *Memoir of the Late Rev. John Baird, Minister of Yetholm, Roxburghshire: With an Account of his Labours in Reforming the Gipsy Population of that Parish* (1862), p. 17.

70 See W. Brockie, *The Gypsies of Yetholm* (Kelso, 1884), pp. 39–40; W. A. Chatto (S. Oliver), *Rambles in Northumberland and on the Scottish Border* (1835), pp. 270–1; letters from a clergyman in Scotland (Rev. J. Baird), in J. Crabb, *op. cit.*, pp. 113–17; J. A. Fairley, *op. cit.*, p. 3; J. M. M'Whir, 'The Muggers of the Border', *Glasgow Herald*, 5 May 1906, p. 9; *Notes and Queries*, 2nd Ser., Vol. 11 (9 March 1861), pp. 196–7; letter from R. Harrison, in the *Standard*, 20 August 1879, p. 2.

71 J. Baird, *The Scottish Gipsy's Advocate: Being a Short Account of the Gipsies of Kirk Yetholm* (Edinburgh, 1839), p. 12; W. Brockie, *op. cit.*, p. 41; Sir G. Douglas, 'Essays on Kirk Yetholm Gypsies', in his *Diversions of a Country Gentleman* (1902), p. 283; W.B., 'The Gipsies of the Border', *Monthly Chronicle of North Country Lore and Legend* (1891), p. 55; *First Report of the Committee for the Reformation of the Gipsies in Scotland* (Edinburgh, 1840), p. 18.

72 J. Baird, *op. cit.*, pp. 14–15; W. Howitt, *op. cit.*, pp. 179–80; W.B., 'The Gipsies of the Border', *loc. cit.*, p. 54.

73 Letter from a clergyman from Scotland, quoted in J. Crabb, *op. cit.*, pp. 113ff; see also Rev. J. Baird, *op. cit.*, pp. 11–12; *Notes and Queries*, 3rd Ser., Vol. 8 (30 December 1865), p. 537; *Globe*, 17 June 1898, pp. 1–2; C. G. Leland Manuscript Collection: letter from D. MacRitchie, 15 January 1890 (37174).

74 J. Baird, *op. cit.*, pp. 12–13.

75 The game was played from 2 p.m. till dark between married and single men, and was started traditionally by a local landowner dropping the ball. After the end of the game the combatants retired to the inns to eat and drink in excess (W. Brockie, *op. cit.*, p. 23; J. A. Fairlie, *op. cit.*, p. 4).

76 W. Brockie, *op. cit.*, pp. 134–5.

77 W. Baird, *op. cit.*, p. 11; J. A. Fairlie, *op. cit.*, p. 4.

78 A 'well-informed gentleman', quoted in W. Brockie, *op. cit.*, p. 40.

79 From a letter quoted in J. Crabb, *op. cit.*, pp. 115–16.

80 W. Baird, *op. cit.*, p. 13.

81 J. Baird, quoted in W. Baird, *op. cit.*, pp. 19–20.

82 *First Rpt of the Scottish Cttee*, p. 21.

83 J. Baird, *op. cit.*, pp. 15–16.

84 *Ibid.*, p. 16.

85 Quoted in W. Baird, *op. cit.*, pp. 24–5.

86 *Ibid.*, pp. 27–8.

87 *First Rpt of the Scottish Cttee*, p. 3.

88 It was hoped that the cost per child could be reduced to no more than 1s. 6d. a week. Any extra expense was to be borne by the parents. (Report by J. Baird to the Cttee, 1841, quoted in W. Baird, *op. cit.*, p. 33.)

89 *First Rpt of the Scottish Cttee*, p. 10.

90 Quoted in W. Baird, *op. cit.*, p. 41.

91 J. Baird, *op. cit.*, pp. 42–3.

92 W. Baird, *op. cit.*, p. 55.

93 Letter from Rev. A. Davidson, quoted in W. Brockie, *op. cit.*, pp. 109–10.

94 Even in 1840 the Committee noted that there were too many travelling families seeking out a living by the same means to sustain them all: 'A few families may be said to be useful in supplying remote country districts with besoms, baskets, pottery ware, and such other things in which they deal. But there are, at least, more than four times the number who follow this occupation, than is at all consistent with any purposes of utility' (*First Rpt of the Scottish Cttee*, p. 17).

95 For a full account of the life of John West, see I. H. S. Stratton, 'The Work and Ideas'. Stratton presents West as a man wholly committed to his faith, with a strong belief in the close relationship between the Christian gospel and the spread of civilisation, and who also held the view that subordination acted as a social cement. He would have experienced contact with the Gypsies who were employed by his father as seasonal hoppers on his farm in Surrey, but the stimulus to attempting their reform was undoubtedly provided much later by Crabb.

96 J. Rudall, *op. cit.*, pp. 147–58; I. H. S. Stratton, 'The Work and Ideas', pp. 65–6; *Dorset County Chronicle*, 31 July 1845, p. 3.

97 From the speech given by Rev. J. Crabb at the laying of the foundation stone of the Farnham Gipsy Asylum and Industrial School, quoted in J. Rudall, *op. cit.*, p. 154.

98 Reproduced in the *Dorset County Chronicle*, 31 July 1845, p. 3.

99 At the time this donation was heralded as an important step towards receiving royal and Parliamentary recognition that the Gypsy children were entitled to state protection and care. Indeed, this does appear to have been the first grant to come from any monarch or government intended to do good for the Gypsies, thus perhaps reflecting some change in attitude and approach to the problem (see *ibid.*).

100 Letter from Rev. J. West to Rev. R. Smith, of W. Stafford, near Dorchester, 13 December 1844 (Romany Collection); *Dorset County Chronicle*, 18 December 1845, p. 1.

101 For an account of the Farnham Committee's earlier sponsorship of missionary activities with the Gypsies see J. Rudall, *op. cit.*, p. 158.

102 J. M. Weylland, *Round the Tower; or, the Story of the London City Mission* [1875], pp. 224–5; 'The Missionary to the Gypsies', *London City Mission Magazine*, Vol. 25 (2 January 1860), p. 1; *Notes and Queries*, 2nd Ser., Vol. 12 (7 September 1861), pp. 197–8.

103 V. S. Morwood, *op. cit.*, pp. 339–40.

104 'The Gypsy Tea-Party', *Missing Link Magazine* (1 May 1865), pp. 122–5; A. Beale, 'Among the Gypsies', *Sunday Magazine* (1875), p. 49. For details of similar tea parties and missionary activity see 'Meeting of the Gipsies: Another of Mrs. Bayly's Thoughtful Plans', *Weekly Record of the National Temperance League*, No. 253 (2 February 1861), p. 40; C. Booth, *Life and Labour of the People in London*, 3rd Ser., Vol. 5 (1902), pp. 157–8, 205–6; C. Smith, *The Life Story of Gipsy Cornelius Smith* (1890), p. 45; H. Woodcock, *The Gipsies* (1865), p. 144.

105 D. L. Woolmer, 'Gipsies in their Winter Quarters', *The Quiver* (1903), p. 530; E. Brewer, 'Gipsy Encampments in the Heart of London', *Sunday at Home* (1896), p. 113.

106 D. L. Woolmer, 'Gipsies', *loc. cit.*, p. 532.

107 R. W. Vanderkiste, *Notes and Narratives of a Six Years Mission* (1851), p. 307.

108 D. L. Woolmer, 'Gipsies', *loc. cit.*, p. 532.

109 *Notes and Queries*, 6th Ser., Vol. 11 (4 December 1880), p. 444.

110 See H. Murray, *Sixty Years an Evangelist: An Intimate Study of Gipsy Smith* [1937]; and, by the same author, *Gipsy Smith: An Intimate Memoir* (Exeter, [1947]); R. Smith, *From Gipsy Tent to Pulpit: The Story of my Life* [1901]; and also his *Gipsy Smith. His Life and Work. By Himself* (1902). It is probable that the evangelists on Wanstead Flats were Smith's father and two brothers.

111 See V. S. Morwood, *op. cit.*, p. 340; A. Beale, 'Among the Gypsies', *loc. cit.*, p. 311; 'Meeting of the Gipsies', *loc. cit.*, p. 40.

112 E. O. Winstedt, 'Gypsy Civilisation', *loc. cit.*, p. 336.

113 C. G. Leland Manuscript Collection: letter from F. H. Groome, undated, 1873? (37173).

114 R. C. De Crespigny and H. Hutchinson, *The New Forest: Its Traditions, Inhabitants and Customs* (1899; Wakefield, 1975), p. 96.

115 R. W. S. Griffith, 'The Gipsies of the New Forest', *Hampshire Field Club: Proceedings*, Vol. 2, paper read at field meeting on 22 July 1893 (Southampton, 1894), p. 282.

116 H. E. J. G[ibbins], *Gypsies of the New Forest, and Other Tales* (Bournemouth, [1909]), p. 33.

117 The *J.G.L.S.* quotes from the 19th Annual Report, 1907–8, of the New Forest Gipsy Mission, which is presumably the same as the New Forest Good Samaritan Charity ('Notes and Queries', *J.G.L.S.*, New Ser., Vol. 2, No. 3, 1909, pp. 278–9). Extracts from the 10th Annual Report of the Charity, undated, are to be found in A. Symons, 'In Praise of Gypsies', *J.G.L.S.*, New Ser., Vol. 1, No. 4 (1908), p. 294, and in H. T. Crofton, 'Affairs of Egypt, 1908', *J.G.L.S.*, New Ser., Vol. 3, No. 4 (1910), p. 277. If I am wrong in linking the missions then, clearly, the New Forest Good Samaritan Charity did not commence until 1898. Unfortunately, I have been unable to locate any of these reports, other than these brief references, or any other archival material relating to the Mission.

118 T. W. Thompson, 'Affairs of Egypt, 1909', *J.G.L.S.*, Vol. 5, No. 2 (1911), p. 122.

119 H. T. Crofton, 'Affairs, 1908', *loc. cit.*, p. 277; H. E. J. G[ibbins], *op. cit.*, pp. 27–9.

120 Quoted in H. E. J. G[ibbins], *op. cit.*, pp. 48–9.

121 Quoted in A. Symons, 'In Praise of Gypsies', *loc. cit.*, p. 294.

122 See chapter 2.

123 See S. Alder, *Work among the Gipsies; being an Account of Twelve Years Mission Work amongst the Gipsies* (Chobham, 1893); *West Surrey Times*, 30 December 1882, p. 5; Letter from S. Alder, in *Surrey Advertiser and County Times*, 9 January 1886, p. 6. Alder also published, in 1890, a penny tract entitled *From a Turf Hut to a Mansion*, and although it sold 400 copies at the time none appear to have survived (*West Surrey Times*, 27 December 1890, p. 7).

124 See 1st to 11th Reports, 1881–92, which comprise the volume by S. Alder.

125 See, for example, *West Surrey Times*, 30 December 1882, p. 5; 27 December 1890, p. 7.

126 See, for example, correspondence in the *Surrey Advertiser*, 20 January 1883, p. 5; 10 February 1883, p. 3.

127 7th Report, 1887–8, in S. Alder, *op. cit.*, p. 28.

128 9th Report, 1889–90, in *ibid.*, pp. 37–8.

129 8th Report, 1888–9, in *ibid.*, pp. 32–3.

130 See E. W. L. Davies, *Memoir of the Rev. J. Russell, and his Out-of-Door Life* (1878), pp. 203–8; Rev. J. H. Swinstead, *A Parish on Wheels* (1897), pp. xiv, 165; 'The Gipsy's Grave', *Church of England Magazine*, Vol. 14 (1843), p. 91; *Hampshire Advertiser*, 1 January 1842, p. 2.

131 E. Grey, *Cottage Life in a Hertfordshire Village* (St Albans, undated, 1935?), p. 201; H. Woodcock, *op. cit.*, pp. 120–1.

132 See F. Cuttriss (pseud.), *Romany Life, Experienced and Observed during Many Years of Friendly Intercourse with the Gypsies* (1915), p. 217; J. Denvir, *The Irish in Britain* (1892), p. 154; F. Vidgen, 'Hop Pickers' Memories', in M. Lewis (ed.), *Old Days in the Kent Hop Gardens* (Tonbridge, 1962); J. E. Revington-Jones, *Among Kentish Hoppers* (1901); *Reports of Medical Inspectors to the Local Government Board, No. 252: Dr Reginald Farrar's Report to the Local Government Board on the Lodging and Accommodation of Hop-Pickers and Pickers of Fruit and Vegetables* (1907), p. 27; Annual report of a London city missionary, 1859, in *London City Mission Magazine*, Vol. 25 (2 January 1860), p. 36.

133 Quoted in *London City Mission Magazine* (2 January 1860), p. 36.

134 See S. Chinn, *Among the Hop-Pickers* [1887].

135 Lord Wolmer, quoted in *ibid.*, p. 204.

136 Chairman of the Alton bench of magistrates, quoted in *ibid.*, p. 205.

137 Quoted in *ibid.*, pp. 207–8.

138 J. Baird, *op. cit.*, p. 7.

139 A. Esquiros, *The English at Home*, translated and edited by L. Wraxall (1861), p. 203.

140 *Ibid.*, p. 220.

141 See B. Street, *The Savage in Literature: Representations of Primitive Society in English Fiction, 1858–1920* (1975).

142 See 'Magic and Religion'. Note that Trigg's thesis was supervised from within the Department of Theology, University of Oxford.

143 See *ibid.*, pp. 413–15. His uncritical acceptance of the writers involved in the missionary attempts is further evidence of Trigg's methodological descent.

144 This offshoot of the racist myth has been discussed fully in the previous chapter.

145 See E. B. Trigg, 'Magic and Religion', pp. 425–6; E. O. Winstedt, 'Gypsy Civilisation', *loc. cit.*, p. 334; *Yorkshire Post*, 24 August 1907, p. 11. Note that the attempts to convert the Jews met with a similar superficial acceptance, but inward rejection, by the receiving group (see C. Holmes, *Anti-Semitism in British Society, 1876–1939* (1970), pp. 251–2, fn. 90 to chapter 4, and the references contained therein).

6 George Smith of Coalville and the legislative attack

1 A scheme was proposed by Rev. W. C. Fenton, of Mattersey, near Bawtry, to set up a school for Gypsy children in central England, but nothing came of it (*Scottish Christian Herald*, 2nd Ser., Vol. 1, Supplement (1839), p. 48; 'Notes and Queries', *J.G.L.S.*, New Ser., Vol. 2, No. 1, 1908, pp. 92–3). Similarly, in 1894, the journal *Caravan* raised subscriptions for a travelling van school, but this also appears to have come to nothing (E. O. Winstedt, 'Gypsy Civilisation', *J.G.L.S.*, New Ser., Vol. 1, No. 4 (1908), p. 342). Concern was also expressed by the Salisbury Diocese, eventually resulting in travelling mission work, and by the Presbyterians of

Breadalbane, Scotland, who petitioned Parliament on the matter in 1884 (J. H. Swinstead, *A Parish on Wheels* (1897), pp. xiv, 165; G. Smith, *I've Been a Gipsying: Or, Rambles among our Gipsies and their Children* (1883; 1885), p. 289).

2 *Parliamentary Debates, House of Commons*, Vol. 300 (11 August 1885), cols. 1705–6.

3 *Weekly Times*, 8 February 1880, p. 2.

4 E. Hodder, *George Smith of Coalville: The Story of an Enthusiast* (1896), pp. 18–22.

5 *Ibid.*, p. 26; *Dictionary of National Biography*, Vol. 53 (1898), p. 41.

6 E. Hodder, *op. cit.*, p. 28. It is an irony that in later life, as an employer of child labour, he refused on humanitarian grounds to allow his own workers to labour at nights or on Sundays, preventing them from taking the same escape route from manual labour.

7 *Ibid.*, p. 36. Smith also refused to employ any girls or women, or boys aged under thirteen years (or twelve years, as stated on p. 40).

8 *Ibid.*, p. 63. Elsewhere, it was stated that he was dismissed from his job having aroused considerable ill-will from within the trade. It would seem that his essential humanitarianism in attacking the use of child labour was believed to amount to an assault on the vested interests not only of his own employers but also of the manufacturing class. Although it would be entirely wrong to label Smith as an opponent of the methods and structure of industrial capitalism, it is possible to see how his criticism of one of its exploitative ingredients could be construed and exaggerated in this way (see *D.N.B.*, Vol. 53 (1898), p. 41).

9 E. Hodder, *op. cit.*, pp. 68–9.

10 *Ibid.*, p. 5.

11 *Derby Daily Telegraph and Reporter*, 16 August 1879, p. 2.

12 E. Hodder, *op. cit.*, p. 93.

13 For example, whenever Smith began a sentence, 'Some time ago . . .', meaning anything from eighty years to a few months, it is more than probable that what followed was taken directly from another author. Smith employed this device frequently, without acknowledgement or conscience.

14 E. O. Winstedt, 'Gypsy Civilisation', *loc. cit.*, p. 343.

15 As observed by one of his contemporaries: 'Mr. Smith never takes up more than one thing at a time, and upon the accomplishment of it he concentrates all his energies . . . he becomes thoroughly possessed by his subject, and the most important event that may happen for the country, or for the world loses all value in his eyes unless it bears directly upon the accomplishment of the object in hand . . . from the time we sallied out together in search of a gipsy camp, until the moment we parted at night, Mr. Smith thought of nothing, spoke of nothing, remembered nothing, saw nothing but what had some relation to the gipsies and their mode of life' ('Gipsies near London', *Weekly Times*, 26 October 1879, p. 5).

16 Webster Lee, quoted in 'Anglo-Romani Gleanings', *J.G.L.S.*, 3rd Ser., Vol. 3, No. 3 (1924), pp. 112–13. Lee has here accused Smith of the same complaints levelled by the latter against the Gypsies. Webster Lee was a founder and leader of the United Kingdom Van Dwellers' Protection Association, which was at the forefront of the opposition to Smith's Moveable Dwellings Bill.

17 E. Hodder, *op. cit.*, p. 136.

18 Quoted in *ibid.*, pp. 136–8. See also, Rev. E. N. Hoare, *Notable Workers in Humble Life* (1887), p. 217; *Pall Mall Gazette*, 21 November 1884, pp. 4–5.

19 *D.N.B.*, Vol. 53 (1898), p. 41; E. Hodder, *op. cit.*, pp. 161–2.

20 *D.N.B.*, Vol. 53 (1898), pp. 41–2.

21 E. Hodder, *op. cit.*, pp. 29, 94.

22 *Ibid.*, pp. 29–30.

23 G. Smith, *Gipsy Life: Being an Account of our Gipsies and their Children, with Suggestions for their Improvement* (1880), p. 167.

24 G. Smith, *I've Been a Gipsying*, p. 34.

25 Letter from G. Smith in the *Daily Chronicle*, 20 November 1879, p. 5. Yet despite the unquestionable venom of his remarks T. Acton has argued that Smith thought of the Gypsies as his equals, and spoke to them and treated them as human beings and not as inferiors. Insofar as Smith was clearly opposed to the travelling way of life and the vices it encouraged rather than to the people themselves, then Acton is correct. However, the nature of his propaganda hardly permits us to believe that Smith saw and treated them as equals (see T. Acton, 'The Development of Ethnic Ideology and Pressure Politics in Gypsy-Gaujo Relations in England and Wales from Victorian Reformism to Romani Nationalism', D.Phil., University of Oxford (1973), pp. 220–1).

26 See G. Smith, 'The Conditions of our Gipsies and their Children, with Remedies', paper read at the Social Science Congress, Nottingham, 26 September 1882, quoted in his *I've Been a Gipsying*, p. 239; letters from G. Smith in the *Daily Chronicle*, 20 November 1879, p. 2; the *Standard*, 14 August 1879, p. 6.

27 G. Smith, 'The Conditions of our Gipsies', in *I've Been a Gipsying*, p. 239; *Royal Commission on the Housing of the Working Classes, Minutes of Evidence*, of George Smith (1884–5), p. 526, paras. 14038–41.

28 Letter to the *Standard*, 14 August 1879, p. 6.

29 *Ibid.*; G. Smith, 'The Conditions of our Gipsies', in *I've Been a Gipsying*, p. 239; *R.C. on Housing, Minutes of Evidence*, of George Smith (1884–5), p. 526, para. 14040.

30 Letter to the *Standard*, 14 August 1879, p. 6; G. Smith, 'Our Gipsies and their Children', *London Society*, Vol. 47 (1885), p. 40.

31 G. Smith, 'The Conditions of our Gipsies', in *I've Been a Gipsying*, p. 239.

32 G. Smith, quoted from a paper presented to the Social Science Congress at Manchester, October 1879, in F. H. Groome, *In Gipsy Tents* (Edinburgh, 1880; Wakefield, 1973), pp. 240–2.

33 Letter from 'J.W.B.' to *May's Aldershot Advertiser*, 13 September 1879, quoted in G. Smith, *Gipsy Life*, pp. 87–90. See also the letter from G. Smith to the *Standard*, 21 August 1879, p. 6; E. Hodder, *op. cit.*, p. 150–6.

34 *Derby Daily Telegraph and Reporter*, 16 August 1879, p. 2.

35 Letter from G. Smith in the *Daily News*, 5 September 1882, p. 2. Consider also the following comment fom G. Smith: 'It is not creditable to us as a Christian nation to have had for centuries these heathenish tribes in our midst. It does not speak very much for the power of the Gospel, the zeal of the ministers of Christ's Church, and the activity of the schoolmaster, to have had these plague spots continually flitting before our eyes, without anything being done to effect a cure' (quoted in E. Hodder, *op. cit.*, p. 142).

36 G. Smith, *Gipsy Life*, p. 193.

37 Letter to *May's Aldershot Advertiser*, 13 September 1879.

38 E. Hodder, *op. cit.*, p. 258.

39 See, for example, *Birmingham Daily Mail*, 8 October 1879, p. 2; *Daily News*, 6 September 1879, p. 7; 13 September 1879, p. 3; 6 October 1879, p. 4; 5 September 1882, p. 2; *Derby Daily Telegraph and Reporter*, 16 August 1879, p. 2; *Daily Chronicle*, 14 August 1879, p. 5; 20 November 1879, p. 5; *Graphic*, 13 March 1880, p. 275; *Morning Post*, 11 October 1882, p. 2; *Standard*, 14 August 1879, p. 6; 15 August 1879, p. 5; 16 August 1879, p. 3; 19 August 1879, p. 6; 20 August 1879, p. 2; 21 August 1879, p. 6; 30 August 1879, p. 3; 10 September 1879, p. 5; 12 September 1879, p. 2; *Sunday School Chronicle*, Vol. 8, No. 270, 19 December 1879, p. 640; *Suburban Press*, 28 February 1880, p. 2; *Weekly Dispatch*, 12 October 1879, p. 1; *Weekly Times*, 26 October 1879, p. 5; 11 January 1880, p. 2; 8 February 1880, p. 2.

40 Smith was already experienced in the art of public speaking, having lectured many times on behalf of the brickyard children and canal-dwellers (see E. Hodder, *op. cit.*, pp. 48–9, 157, 179; F. H. Groome, *op. cit.*, pp. 240–2; G. Smith, *I've Been a Gipsying*, pp. 238–40).

41 Cf. his *Gipsy Life*, also *Gypsy Children: Or, a Stroll in Gypsydom. With Songs and Stories* [1889].

42 E. Hodder, *op. cit.*, pp. 54–7.

43 Dated 4 July 1884, quoted in *ibid.*, pp. 130–1.

44 G. Smith, *Gypsy Children*, Part 1, p. 1.

45 E. Hodder, *op. cit.*, pp. 115–16.

46 *Christian Herald*, 31 March 1880, quoted in F. H. Groome, *op. cit.*, pp. 259–60.

47 Quoting a Gypsy named Winter, who lived in Bulwell Forest. Note how Smith has transcribed the (imaginary?) conversation in order to convey the ignorance and illiteracy of the Gypsy, who was speaking, as Smith noted, not in Romany but in a Staffordshire dialect (G. Smith, *I've Been a Gipsying*, pp. 234–5).

48 G. Smith, *Gypsy Children*, Part 2, pp. 11–12.

49 E. Hodder, *op. cit.*, pp. 183–5; 'Notes and Queries', *J.G.L.S.*, Old Ser., Vol. 1, No. 3 (1889), p. 176; *Graphic*, 4 May 1889, p. 476; *Manchester Examiner*, 26 November 1888, p. 2; *Newcastle Daily Chronicle*, 16 May 1889, p. 6.

50 Letter to the *Standard*, 16 August 1879, p. 3.

51 See *Weekly Dispatch*, 12 October 1879, p. 1.

52 1884–5 (239) iii, 479; 1887 (256) vi, 303; 1887 (370) vi, 315, amended by Select Committee; 1888 (200) v, 251; 1889 (316) v, 403; 1889 (206) viii, 231; 1890 (170) vi, 795; 1890–1 (222) vii, 137; 1892 (212) iv, 597; 1894 (298) vii, 39.

53 F. H. Groome, *op. cit.*, pp. 261ff. Quite how this would operate, and why registration was necessary for this purpose, was not made clear by Groome.

54 G. Smith, *Gypsy Children*, Part 2, p. 17.

55 *Ibid.*, and also his *I've Been a Gipsying*, pp. 288–9, 292.

56 *Parliamentary Debates, House of Commons*, Vol. 339 (2 August 1889), col. 264. The Liberty and Property Defence League was formed in 1882 by Lord Elchs (later Lord Wemyss), Herbert Spencer and others. It aimed to uphold the principle of liberty, to guard the rights of threatened and weak bodies against undue state intervention, and 'for resisting overlegislation, for maintaining Freedom of Contract, and for advocating Individualism as opposed to Socialism irrespective of Party Politics' (see volume of *Annual Reports, 1888–94*, p. 57). Its motto was 'self-help versus state-help'. During its life it gave rise to other laissez-faire and vehemently anti-socialist associations, notably the Employers' Parliamentary Council, the Free

Labour Protection Association (1898) and the Middle Class Defence League (see the journals of the League, *Jus* (1887–8), and the *Liberty Review* (1893–1909); also N. Soldon, 'Laissez faire as Dogma: The Liberty and Property Defence League, 1882–1914', in K. D. Brown, ed., *Essays in Anti-Labour History* (1974), pp. 208–33).

57 *Parliamentary Debates, House of Commons*, Vol. 338 (31 July 1889), cols. 1839–40.

58 *Ibid.*

59 G. Smith, *Gypsy Children*, Part 2, p. 17.

60 Letter from the County Magistrate of Danbury, Essex, to G. Smith, 1881, quoted in the latter's *I've Been a Gipsying*, pp. 288–9.

61 Quoted in *ibid.*, pp. 291–2.

62 Quoted in E. Hodder, *op. cit.*, p. 206.

63 See Canal Boats Act, 40 & 40 Vict., c. 6, clause 5, 1877; Canal Boats Act, 47 & 48 Vict., c. 75, s.4, 1884; Housing of the Working Classes Act, 48 & 49 Vict., c. 72, 5, 9, 1875; Public Health Act, 38 & 39 Vict., c. 55, clauses 72–89, 1875.

64 G. Smith, *Gypsy Children*, Part 2, pp. 9, 16.

65 Quoted in G. Smith, *I've Been a Gipsying*, p. 296.

66 *Ibid.*, pp. 297, 336–8.

67 G. Smith, *Gypsy Children*, Part 2, p. 10.

68 G. Smith, quoted in F. H. Groome, *op. cit.*, p. 262.

69 *Caravan* (October 1890), p. 4.

70 Quoted in G. Smith, *Gypsy Children*, Part 2, p. 13.

71 E. Hodder, *op. cit.*, p. 174.

72 Extract from G. Smith's diary, quoted in E. Hodder, *op. cit.*, p. 222.

73 G. Smith, *Gypsy Children*, Part 2, p. 2.

74 *Ibid.*, Part 2, p. 4.

75 *Ibid.*; Extract from G. Smith's diary, May 1886, quoted in E. Hodder, *op. cit.*, pp. 178–9; E. O. Winstedt, 'Gypsy Civilisation', *loc. cit.*, pp. 343–4. Groome related the story of a Gypsy who, on hearing Smith's description of Gypsies and his proposals to reform them, hurled a teapot against a wall and exclaimed, 'I wish to *mi-Duvel* George Smith's head were in it' (F. H. Groome, *op. cit.*, p. 224).

76 Extract from G. Smith's diary, 15 June 1983, quoted in E. Hodder, *op. cit.*, pp. 222–3.

77 Quoted in J. Myers, 'Lazzy Smith in Egglestone's Notebook', *J.G.L.S.*, 3rd Ser., Vol. 16, Nos. 1–2 (1937), p. 4.

78 *Liberty Review* (2 December 1893), pp. 1–2; (20 January 1894), p. 114.

79 *Annual Reports of the L.P.D.L.*, 1892–3, p. 51.

80 E. Hodder, *op. cit.*, p. 177.

81 Quoted in T. Murphy, *A History of the Showmen's Guild, 1889–1948* (privately printed, Oldham, 1949), p. 32.

82 Quoted in *ibid.*, pp. 23–4.

83 G. Smith, *Gypsy Children*, Part 2, pp. 2–3.

84 Murphy stated that Smith attended the 1890 meeting, but does not mention his presence at that of 1891 (T. Murphy, *op. cit.*, pp. 28–9). Smith gave the date of the meeting as February 1891 (*Gypsy Children*, Part 2, pp. 2–3), while Hodder dated it at 28 January 1891 (*op. cit.*, p. 207). Elsewhere it was reported that the attacks on Smith were more verbal than physical, and it was probable that Smith's picture of drunken men and women clambering over seats and each other in order to inflict

violence on his person was again an image coloured by imaginative exaggeration (E. O. Winstedt, 'Gypsy Civilisation', *loc. cit.*, pp. 342–3).

85 T. Murphy, *op. cit.*, pp. 29, 45–9.
86 Mr Healy, quoted in *Parliamentary Debates, House of Commons*, Vol. 299 (22 July 1889), cols. 1512–13; Vol. 300 (11 August 1885), cols. 1705–6.
87 E. Hodder, *op. cit.*, pp. 174–81.
88 *Ibid.*
89 G. Smith, *Gypsy Children*, Part 1, p. 46.
90 G. Smith, *Gypsy Children*, Part 2, p. 10; E. Hodder, *op. cit.*, p. 177.
91 E. Hodder, *op. cit.*, p. 200.
92 G. Smith, *Gypsy Children*, Part 1, pp. 13–14.
93 See D. Dallas, *The Travelling People* (1971), p. 26.
94 Although the list covers mainly the nineteenth century, some earlier and later enactments have also been included. This list is necessarily abbreviated, for it would be an impossible task to list every Act relating to, for example, commons regulation or vagrancy which would have a direct or indirect effect on the travellers.
95 *Departmental Committee on Vagrancy, Minutes of Evidence*, of Capt. H. McHard, Chief Constable of Ayrshire (1906), p. 258, para. 7706; *Report of the Commission Appointed to Inquire as to the Best Means of Establishing an Efficient Constabulary Force in England and Wales* (1839), p. 36.
96 R. D. Paine, 'The Gypsy of England', *Outing*, Vol. 45 (New York, 1904), p. 330.
97 A Barrister, *The Vagrant Act, in Relation to the Liberty of the Subject* (1824), pp. 3–4.
98 Quoted in *ibid.*, p. 4.
99 *Ibid.*, p. 45.
100 See V. S. Morwood, *Our Gipsies in City, Tent and Van* (1885), p. 45.
101 See W. Simson, *A History of the Gipsies: With Specimens of the Gipsy Language* (London [printed], Edinburgh, 1865), p. 352.
102 *Departmental Committee on Vagrancy, Minutes of Evidence* (1906), p. 262, para. 7727.
103 Quoted in Rev. E. N. Hoare, *op. cit.*, p. 214.
104 A. Thesleff, 'Report on the Gypsy Problem', *J.G.L.S.*, New Ser., Vol. 5, No. 2 (1911), p. 94. See also J. W. Adamson, *English Education, 1789–1902* (Cambridge, 1930).

7 The Gypsy versus magistrates, police and local authorities

1 Letter to the *Northampton Mercury*, quoted in J. Hoyland, *A Historical Survey of the Customs, Habits and Present State of the Gypsies, Designed . . . to Promote the Amelioration of their Condition* (York, 1816), pp. 244–5.
2 Printed notice, held at the East Sussex Record Office.
3 *Sheffield Mercury*, 9 September 1815, p. 4.
4 *Ibid.*
5 Quoted in *New Monthly Magazine*, Vol. 8 (1817), p. 462; see also *Bedfordshire Times and Independent*, 30 August 1907, p. 9.
6 See Reports of Chief Constables (Public Record Office, HO45/9340/22208); also, C. J. R. Turner, *A History of Vagrants and Vagrancy and Beggars and Begging* (1887), pp. 308–9.

7 See *Chelmsford Chronicle*, 20 October 1882, p. 7; Letter from the Clerk of the Peace for Norfolk to the Under Secretary of State, 14 July 1911 (P.R.O., HO45/10995/158231/17).

8 J. Hoyland, *op. cit.*, p. 230.

9 See J. Crabb, *The Gipsies' Advocate* (1831; 3rd edn with additions, 1832), pp. 58–62. It will be remembered that the discriminatory treatment meted out to Gypsy horse-stealers by the Winchester Justices of Peace caused Crabb to become involved with this group.

10 *Cornish Telegraph*, 18 May 1864, p. 2.

11 *Ibid.*

12 *Parliamentary Debates, House of Commons*, Vol. 175 (May 1864), cols. 193, 461–2; *The Times*, 14 May 1864, p. 8.

13 Elsewhere it was reported that the party consisted only of the mother and her six children. See G. L. Boase and W. P. Courtney (eds.), *Bibliotheca Cornubiensis*, Vol. 2 (1878), p. 729; H. Woodcock, *The Gipsies* (1865), p. 14; 'Notes and Queries', *J.G.L.S.*, New Ser., Vol. 4, No. 4 (1911), pp. 318–19; *Cornish Telegraph*, 4 May 1864, p. 3; 11 May 1864, p. 2; 18 May 1864, p. 2; *The Times*, 10 May 1864, p. 8; 14 May 1864, p. 8.

14 *Cornish Telegraph*, 18 May 1864, p. 2.

15 *Parliamentary Debates, House of Commons*, Vol. 175 (9 May 1864), col. 193.

16 *First Report of the Commission Appointed to Inquire as to the Best Means of Establishing an Efficient Constabulary Force in England and Wales* (1839), p. 198.

17 See *First Report of the Society for the Suppression of Mendicity* (1819).

18 J. Hoyland, *op. cit.*, p. 230.

19 J. Crabb, *op. cit.*, pp. 58–62. However, Crabb also provided a few instances, drawn from his experience of policing in the locality, of the police acting humanely. On one occasion a group of constables, having first driven off the Gypsies' horses and donkeys and then fined their owners, felt remorse for their victims and returned the fines levied. One of the constables, a carpenter by trade, even offered a coffin for an unburied child among the party if the parish refused to bury it (*ibid.*, pp. 61–2).

20 J. Hoyland, *op. cit.*, p. 100; 'Gipsies', *The Literary and Scientific Repository*, Vol. 3 (1821), pp. 401–11.

21 F. H. Groome, *In Gipsy Tents* (Edinburgh, 1880; Wakefield, 1973), p. 116; J. Lucas, *The Yetholm History of the Gypsies* (Kelso, 1882), p. 135; E. O. Winstedt, 'The Norwood Gypsies and their Vocabulary', *J.G.L.S.*, New Ser., Vol. 9, Nos. 3–4 (1916), p. 139.

22 The three Gypsies arrested on suspicion of murder were later acquitted. The murder was later confessed to by Isaac Evans, on his deathbed at Lewisham Workhouse, February 1809. See R. S. Kirkby, *The Wonderful and Scientific Museum*, Vol. 1 (1803), pp. 53–67; *Gentleman's Magazine*, Vol. 73, Part 1 (1803), pp. 84, 280; E. O. Winstedt, 'The Norwood Gypsies', *loc. cit.*; *Leicester Journal*, 1 April 1803, p. 2; *London Chronicle*, 28–30 December 1802, p. 629; 4–6 January 1803, p. 18; 13–15 October 1803, p. 367; *The Times*, 6 January 1803, p. 3; 20 January 1803, p. 3; 25 January 1803, p. 3.

23 M. Howitt (ed.), *Mary Howitt, an Autobiography* (1891), p. 50; N. N. Solly, *Memoirs*

of the Life of David Cox, with Selections from his Correspondence and some Account of his Works (1873), p. 21.

24 *Niles' Weekly Register*, Vol. 9 (16 September 1815), p. 41; see also J. Hoyland, *op. cit.*, p. 180; H. T. Crofton, 'Gypsy Life in Lancashire and Cheshire', *Manchester Literary Club, Papers*, Vol. 3 (Manchester, 1877), pp. 36–7.

25 See A. M. Galer, *Norwood and Dulwich: Past and Present, with Historical and Descriptive Notes* (1890), pp. 9–12, 38, 61, 117; E. O. Winstedt, 'The Norwood Gypsies', *loc. cit.*, p. 152; *The Builder*, 11 November 1876, p. 1094; *Guardian*, 15 November 1876, p. 1490; *The Times*, 30 December 1878, p. 4; 'Gossip about the Gipsies', *Leisure Hour*, Vol. 10 (1861), p. 464.

26 See R. Smith, *Gipsy Smith. His Life and Work. By Himself* (1902), pp. 61–2; D. Townsend, *The Gipsies of Northamptonshire: Their Manner of Life . . . Fifty Years Ago* (Kettering, 1877), p. 30; H. Woodcock, *op. cit.*, p. 39; W.B., 'Gipsies and their Friends', *Temple Bar Magazine*, Vol. 47 (May 1876), pp. 70–1; R. E. Chatfield, 'The English Gipsies', *Theosophical Review* (April 1899), p. 106.

27 F. S. Atkinson, 'Gypsies in East Anglia', *The Kendalian*, Vol. 11 (1911), p. 10; *The Times*, 30 November 1841, p. 3; signed manuscript by H. T. Crofton, 1873, verso engraving of a Gypsy encampment (Scott Macfie Collection).

28 R. A. S. Macfie, 'The Gypsies: An Outline Sketch', *Romanitshels', Didakais' and Folk-Lore Gazette*, Vol. 1, No. 2 (1912), p. 45.

29 Correspondence between E. Henry, Commissioner of Police of the Metropolis, and the Under Secretary of State, 1909 (P.R.O., HO45/10995/158231/5).

30 *Select Committee of the House of Lords on the Moveable Dwellings Bill, Minutes of Evidence*, of Dr A. Haynes (1909), pp. 29–30, para. 581; of Mr Pedder (1909), p. 53, para. 1078.

31 Diaries were kept by the following police stations: Fernhurst (1898–1903); Burgess Hill (1912–13); Glynde (1989–1913); Upper Beeding (1898–1914); Burwash Common/Weald (1898–1925); Burwash (1898–1926). I am grateful to the Archives and Public Relations Department, East Sussex Constabulary, for this information.

32 See 'Gipsies and Dwellers in Tents, Vans, &c.': synopsis of replies received from district councils and Superintendents of Police in East Suffolk, February 1899 (Surrey Record Office, hereafter Su. R.O., CC28/158).

33 See A. Shubert, 'Lest the Law Slumber in Action: Associations for the Prosecution of Felons in England, 1744–1978', M.A., University of Warwick (1978). It is interesting to note here that in the late sixteenth century in Scotland, under various statutes passed in the reign of James VI, coal and salt masters were empowered to apprehend all vagrants and put them to labour in the mines, with the result that Simson was able to claim that some of the colliers of the Lothians were of Gypsy extraction (W. Simson, *A History of the Gipsies: With Specimens of the Gipsy Language* (London [printed], Edinburgh, 1865), p. 111).

34 Quoted in J. Hoyland, *op. cit.*, p. iv.

35 *Hampshire Telegraph and Sussex Chronicle*, 26 January 1818, p. 3.

36 *Surrey Times*, 1 June 1907, p. 3.

37 W. G. W. Watson, 'Pestiferous Carbuncles in Somerset', *J.G.L.S.*, 3rd Ser., Vol. 12, No. 2 (1933), pp. 82–3.

38 *Preston Herald*, 31 October 1874, p. 6.

39 Rev. J. H. Barker, 'The Gipsy-Life of Northumberland', in W. Andrews (ed.), *Bygone Northumberland* (1899), p. 239.

40 *Sel. Cttee on Mov. Dw., Minutes of Evidence*, of Mr R. Bray (1909), p. 63, para. 1299.

41 *Ibid.*, of Lord Clifford of Chudleigh (1909), pp. 76–7, paras. 1553–5.

42 T. W. Thompson, 'Affairs of Egypt, 1909', *J.G.L.S.*, New Ser., Vol. 5, No. 2 (1911), p. 125.

43 *Select Committee Appointed to Inquire into the Best Means of Preserving for the Public Use the Forests, Commons, and Open Spaces in and around the Metropolis, Minutes of Evidence*, of Earl Spencer (1865), pp. 18–19, paras. 397–407.

44 *Sel. Cttee on Open Spaces, Minutes of Evidence*, of Earl Spencer (1865), pp. 18–19, paras. 397–407; see also *ibid.*, Appendix 3, p. 82.

45 Letter from 5th Earl Spencer to Mr C. Hutton, 30 December 1861 (Romany Collection).

46 *Sel. Cttee on Open Spaces, Minutes of Evidence*, of Mr W. S. Forster (1865), p. 37, para. 910.

47 Under the Statute of Merton the lord of the manor could enclose common land without either the assent of the commoners or the sanction of Parliament. This statute remained in force until 1893, despite the recommendations of the Select Committee on Open Spaces, urging that it be repealed in 1865.

48 Lord Eversley, (G. J. S. Lefevre), *Commons, Forests and Footpaths, the Story of the Battle during the Last Forty-Five Years for Public Rights over the Commons, Forests and Footpaths of England and Wales* (rev. edn, 1910), pp. 20–1.

49 *Sel. Cttee on Open Spaces, Minutes of Evidence*, of Mr W. S. Forster (1865), p. 37, para. 509; of Rear Admiral B. J. Sulivan (1865), p. 51, para. 1228.

50 See S. J. Marsh, *Ashdown Forest* (privately printed, 1935); R. Samuel, 'Village Labour', in R. Samuel (ed.), *Village Life and Labour* (1975), p. 8; H. Wolff, *Sussex Industries* (Lewes, 1883), pp. 151–3; letter from A. Lee to the *South Bucks Standard*, 29 May 1908, p. 8.

51 Letter from the Commissioner of the Metropolitan Police to the Clerk of the Surrey County Council, 6 September 1913 (Su.R.O., CC28/249A). Many of the Gypsies found in Surrey were said to have come from Battersea and were 'mostly Londoners, bred and born' (Rev. G. Hall, *The Gypsy's Parson, his Experiences and Adventures* (1915), pp. 200–1). Others were said to have travelled from Sussex, where the authorities had been successful in driving them out (typescript copy of R. Bray's evidence to the Sel. Cttee on Mov. Dw. (1909) – P.R.O., HO45/10999/158231/9).

52 Letter from the Commissioner of the Metropolitan Police to the Clerk of the Surrey County Council, 6 September 1913 (Su. R.O., CC 28/249A); letter from Captain Sant, Chief Constable of Surrey, to the Under Secretary of State, 1 July 1910 (P.R.O., HO 45/10995/158231/25).

53 'The Surrey Gipsies', *The Spectator*, Vol. 79 (18 December 1897), pp. 894–5.

54 See *Sel. Cttee on Mov. Dw., Minutes of Evidence*, of Capt. M. Sant (1909), p. 71, paras. 1406–8; *Surrey Times*, 8 June 1907, p. 4; County Council Census of the Nomad Population, 1911 and 1913 (held at the Guildford Muniment room; hereafter G.M.R.).

55 *Sel. Cttee on Mov. Dw., Minutes of Evidence*, of Colonel the Hon. Charles Hay Drummond (1909), p. 65, paras., 1258–62; Lord Farrer speaking in support of the Moveable Dwellings Bill, quoted in *Parliamentary Debates, House of Lords*, Vol. 187

(1908), cols. 492–3; typescript copy of R. Bray's evidence to the Sel. Cttee on Mov. Dw. (1909) (P.R.O., HO45/10995/158231/9); *Census of England and Wales, Administrative Areas, 1911*, Vol. 1 (1912), table 22, p. 636; H. T. Crofton, 'Affairs of Egypt, 1908', *J.G.L.S.*, New Ser., Vol. 3, No. 4 (1910), p. 284.

56 J. Strachey, 'The Gipsy Scandal and the Danger to the Commons', *National Review*, Vol. 59 (1912), p. 461. See also B. Marsh, 'The Tent-Dwellers', *Argosy*, Vol. 63 (1897), pp. 679–82. In the winter of 1911 a diary was kept of the Gypsies' presence at Newlands Corner, North Downs, and this interesting account is reproduced in Appendix 2.

57 G.M.R., 85/29/8.

58 Such correspondence is to be found in the archive documents 85/29/8 and 173/18/16 at the G.M.R.

59 P.R.O., HO45/10995/158231/9.

60 Letter from Bray to the Secretary of State, 30 March 1910 (P.R.O., HO45/10995/158231/9); letter from Bray to the Clerk of the Peace, County of Surrey, 27 September 1911 (G.M.R., 85/29/8).

61 This correspondence is also collated in the archive collection at the G.M.R.

62 T. W. Thompson, 'Affairs of Egypt, 1909', *J.G.L.S.*, New Ser., Vol. 5, No. 2 (1911), pp. 117–18.

63 G.M.R., 85/29/8; *Graphic*, Vol. 79 (1909), p. 529; *Surrey Times*, 20 February 1909, p. 4.

64 Editorial, *Liverpool Courier*, 5 February 1909, p. 6.

65 Letter from Bray, undated; printed notice re the Surrey Anti-Vagrants and Prevention of Heath Fires Association. (Both items to be found at the G.M.R., 85/29/8.)

66 *Sel. Cttee on Mov. Dw., Minutes of Evidence*, of Sir R. Bray (1909), p. 64, paras. 1248–51.

67 Draft question by Earl Onslow to the Home Secretary, undated (G.M.R., 173/19/91); see also letter from Bray to the Secretary of State, 30 March 1910 (P.R.O., HO45/10995/158231/9).

68 See, for example, letter from J. H. S. Walker, of the Worcester County Constabulary, 27 June 1910 (G.M.R., 173/19/92).

69 Letter from Bray to the Clerk of the Peace, County of Surrey, 27 September 1911 (G.M.R., 85/29/8); letter from Captain Sant to Earl Onslow, 9 June 1910 (G.M.R., 173/19/82).

70 Letter from Sant to Bray, 23 March 1910 (P.R.O., HO45/10995/158231/9); letter from the Under Secretary of State to Bray, 10 May 1910 (G.M.R., 85/29/8). The correspondence between Bray, Sant and the Home Office extended to many lengthy and bitter exchanges, to be found at the locations mentioned in this note.

71 Letter from Sant to the Home Office, 5 July 1910 (P.R.O., HO49/10995/158231/15).

72 Report of F. Smallpiece, Steward of Manor, to Lord Onslow, 21 June 1910 (P.R.O., HO45/10995/158231/15). For Sant's account of this episode, see letter from Sant to the Under Secretary of State, 1 July 1910 (P.R.O., HO45/10995/158231/15).

73 Letter from Sant to the Home Secretary, 19 April 1910 (P.R.O., HO45/10995/158231/25).

74 Draft letter from the Secretary of State to Lord Onslow, 27 August 1910 (P.R.O., H045/10995/158231/15).

75 Letter from Sant to Bray, 9 April 1913 (G.M.R., 85/29/21).

76 Instructions for the Special Constable, 1913 (G.M.R., 85/29/21).

77 Letter from W. Joynson-Hicks to Bray, 15 May 1913 (G.M.R., 85/29/21); see also letter from Mr Lovelace to Bray, 21 March 1913 (G.M.R., 85/29/21).

78 County Council Census of the Nomad Population, 31 August 1913 (G.M.R., 85/29/21).

79 F. H. Groome, *op.cit.*, p. 265; 'Affairs of Egypt', *Romanitshels', Didakais' and Folk-Lore Gazette*, Vol. 1, No. 3 (1912), p. 87.

80 See W. H. Hudson, *A Shepherd's Life: Impressions of the South Wiltshire Downs* (1910), p. 266; R. Smith, *Gipsy Smith*, p. 16; *Surrey Mirror*, 15 May 1908, p. 2.

81 'Affairs of Egypt', *Romanitshels', Didakais' and Folk-Lore Gazette*, Vol. 1, No. 3 (1912), p. 87.

82 *Romanitshels', Didakais' and Folk-Lore Gazette*, Vol. 2, No. 2 (1913), p. 44.

83 *Ibid.*

84 See 'Attorney-General v. Stone', 1895, *Justice of the Peace*, Vol. 60 (1896), pp. 168–9; also *Oldham Chronicle*, 30 November 1907, p. 8; 11 January 1908, p. 9; *Departmental Committee on Vagrancy* (1906), Appendix 34.

85 Quoted in 'Attorney-General v. Stone', *loc. cit.*, pp. 168–9.

86 Quoted in *ibid*.

87 *Select Committee on the Temporary Dwellings Bill, Minutes of Evidence*, of Sir H. Owen, Secretary to the Local Government Board (1887), p. 2, para. 26.

88 *Local Government Journal* (2 January 1897), p. 6.

89 Quoted in *Parliamentary Debates, House of Lords*, Vol. 187 (1908), col. 449.

90 *Dptal Cttee on Vag., Report*, p. 109.

91 See *Sel. Cttee on Mov. Dw., Minutes of Evidence*, of Mr H. Monro, on behalf of the Local Government Board (1909), p. 1, para. 9.

92 *Reports of Medical Inspectors to the Local Government Board, No. 252; Dr. Reginald Farrar's Report to the Local Government Board on the Lodging and Accommodation of Hop-Pickers and Pickers of Fruit and Vegetables* (1907), p. 25.

93 West Parley Parish Council, *Minutes of Meeting*, 7 December 1896, 18 April 1904, 13 June 1904, 17 April 1905, 11 June 1906, 12 November 1906.

94 *Ibid.*, 12 February 1912.

95 *Ibid.*, 27 March 1912.

96 *Ibid.*, 13 May 1912, 9 September 1912, 13 October 1912.

97 *Dptal Cttee on Vag.*, Appendix 34, p. 167.

98 *Sel. Cttee on Mov. Dw., Minutes of Evidence*, of Mr Pedder (1909), p. 51, para. 1056.

99 P.R.O., HO45/10995/158231/36.

100 Middlesex County Council Act, 6 Edw. VII, c.174, 1906. See also *Sel. Cttee on Mov. Dw., Report*, Appendix 3 (1909), p. 88; *Parliamentary Debates, House of Lords*, Vol. 187 (1908), p. 88; *Parliamentary Debates, House of Lords*, Vol. 187 (1908), cols. 447–66. Note that this Act incorporates the finding of the High Court mentioned earlier.

101 Quoted in T. Murphy, *A History of the Showmen's Guild, 1889–1948* (privately printed, Oldham, 1949), p. 64.

102 Reply from the Home Office, April 1904, quoted in 'Nuisance by Gipsies', a memorandum prepared by the Deputy Clerk of Essex County Council, 1904 (Su. R.O., CC28/158).

103 Reply from the Secretary of State, July 1893 and March 1902, quoted in *ibid*.

104 Reply from the Home Office, 16 December 1902, quoted in *ibid*. See also *Local Government Journal* (2 January 1897), p. 2; (9 January 1897), p. 22.

105 'The Surrey Gipsies', *loc. cit.*, pp. 894–5.

106 Letter from the Deputy Chief Constable of Surrey to the Clerk of the Surrey Council, 4 September 1913 (G.M.R., 85/29/21).

107 Surrey County Council: printed notices re conference called to discuss regulation of 'Gipsies, Tent and Van Dwellers, &c.', 14 December 1897 (Su. R.O., CC28/154A).

108 Su. R.O., CC 28/101. Two such statements are reproduced in Appendix 3.

109 Typescript extracts from the Reports and Minutes of the County Council in reference to Moveable Dwellings, 1893–1911 (Su. R.O., CC 28/249A).

110 Report of Sub-Committee to the General Purposes Committee of Surrey County Council, 20 December 1906 (Su. R.O., CC28/154A).

111 Hampshire, East Suffolk, West Suffolk, Essex, Worcester (Su. R.O., CC 28–158). The *Surrey Times* reported that thirty-seven replies were received (1 June 1907, p. 4).

112 Reprinted in *Parliamentary Debates, House of Lords*, Vol. 187 (1908), cols. 449–52. See also W. M. Gallichan, 'The State versus the Gypsy', *J.G.L.S.*,. New Ser., Vol. 1, No. 4 (1908), pp. 356–8.

113 *Sel. Cttee on Mov. Dw., Minutes of Evidence*, of Mr J. Pedder (1909), pp. 48–9, para. 1021.

114 *Ibid.*, p. 53, para. 1074.

115 *Parliamentary Debates, House of Lords*, Vol. 1 (1909), para. 118.

116 See *Select Committee of the House of Lords on the Moveable Dwellings Bill, Report*(1910), pp. v, vi; *Parliamentary Debates, House of Lords*, Vol. 7 (1911), cols. 97–110.

117 *Sel. Cttee on Mov. Dw., Minutes of Evidence*, of Mr J. Pedder (1909), p. 49, para. 1029.

118 Draft circular letter from Surrey County Council, undated, 1911? (Su. R.O., CC28/249A).

119 *Croydon Chronicle*, 2 June 1888, p. 2; 23 June 1888, p. 2.

120 'Mr. Raffles and the Gipsies', *Porcupine*, Vol. 21 (1879), p. 409.

121 T. W. Thompson, 'Affairs . . . 1909', *loc. cit.*, p. 114–15.

122 *Dptal Cttee on Vag., Minutes of Evidence*, of Major A. F. Poulton, Chief Constable of Berkshire, p. 166, paras. 4181–22; H. T. Crofton, 'Affairs of Egypt, 1907', *J.G.L.S.*, New Ser., Vol. 2, No. 2 (1908), pp. 122, 129; *Manchester Courier*, 17 May 1907; p. 8; *Parliamentary Debates, House of Lords*, Vol. 7 (1911), col. 108; *Surrey Mirror and County Post*, 15 May 1908, p. 2; Bristol Health Committee, *Minutes of Meetings*, 3 November 1908; 4 January 1910; 1 February 1910; 1 March 1910; *Bristol Echo*, 3 November 1908, p. 3; H. T. Crofton, 'Affairs of Egypt, 1908', *J.G.L.S.*, New Ser., Vol. 3, No. 4 (1910), p. 282; T. W. Thompson, 'Affairs . . . 1909', *loc. cit.*, p. 122.

123 For example, in Worcestershire (*Sel. Cttee on Mov. Dw., Minutes of Evidence*, of Dr G. Haynes Fosbroke, County Medical Officer for Worcestershire (1909), pp. 25–6, paras. 481–84); at Oldham (*Oldham Chronicle*, 30 November 1907, p. 8; 7 December 1907, p. 9; 11 January 1908, p. 9); in Cardiff (Cardiff Watch Committee, *Minutes of Meeting*, 11 December 1889; Cardiff Property, Markets etc. Committee, *Minutes of Meetings*, 1 March 1893, 1 May 1906); in Depwade, Norfolk (Depwade Rural District Council, *Minutes of Meeting*, 15 March 1909); and at Cheddar (Cheddar Parish Council, *Minutes of Meetings*, 17 November 1911; 1 December 1911).

124 *Clarion*, 20 August 1897, p. 279.

125 F. W. Hackwod, *Handsworth Old and New* (Birmingham, 1908), p. 64.

126 *Ibid.*

127 *Daily Graphic*, 13 October 1904, p. 4.

128 Quoted in the *Birmingham Daily Post*, 27 July 1905, p. 11.

129 *Ibid.*; *Penny Illustrated Paper*, 5 August 1905, p. 1.

130 T. W. Thompson, 'Affairs . . . 1909', *loc. cit.*, p. 118.

131 *Blackpool Gazette and News*, 25 December 1908, p. 3; *Lancashire Post*, 23 April 1908, p. 4.

132 B. Turner and S. Palmer, *The Blackpool Story* (Blackpool, 1976), p. 98.

133 *The Standard*, 17 April 1908, p. 7.

134 Quoted in T. W. Thompson, 'Affairs . . . 1909', *loc. cit.*, pp. 115–16.

135 B. Turner and S. Palmer, *op. cit.*, p. 100.

136 Llanelly Health Committee, *Minutes of Meeting*, 23 February 1912.

137 *Llanelly Mercury*, 7 March 1912, p. 3. See also *Llanelly and County Guardian*, 7 March 1912, p. 4; *Llanelly Mercury*, 14 March 1912, p. 3; *South Wales Echo*, 8 March 1912, p. 4; 9 March 1912, p. 2.

138 Letter from Bray to the Secretary of State, 30 March 1910 (P.R.O., HO45/10995/158231/9).

139 Vol. 1, No. 2 (1912), pp. 35–6.

140 See *Llanelly and County Guardian*, 7 March 1912, p. 4; 'Affairs of Egypt', *Folk-Lore Gazette*, Vol. 1, No. 3 (1912), p. 95.

8 Summary and conclusion

1 G. Smith, *Gipsy Life: Being an Account of our Gipsies and their Children, with Suggestions for their Improvement* (1880), p. 21.

2 *Select Committee of the House of Lords on the Moveable Dwellings Bill, Minutes of Evidence*, of Dr H. M. Chester (1909), p. 40, para. 840.

3 C. G. Leland, *The English Gipsies and their Language* (1873; 1874), p. 8.

4 A. Symons, 'In Praise of the Gypsies', *J.G.L.S.*, New Ser., Vol. 1, No. 4 (1908), p. 294.

5 G. Smith, *Gipsy Life*, pp. 11–12.

6 See D. V. Jones, 'A Dead Loss to the Community: The Criminal Vagrant in Mid Nineteenth Century Wales', *Welsh History Review*, Vol. 8, No. 3 (1977), pp. 312–44.

7 A. Compton-Rickett, *The Vagabond in Literature* (1906), p. 3.

8 A. H. Japp, 'The Gypsies as Seen by Friendly Eyes', *Gentleman's Magazine*, Vol. 255 (1883, Vol. 2), p. 576.

9 Editorial, *Daily News*, 6 October 1879, p. 4.

10 'Gipsies in Hainault Forest', *Outlook* (20 August 1898), p. 76.

11 See 'Gypsies', *New Edinburgh Review*, Vol. 1 (1844), pp. 11–12.

12 See C. Bolt, *Victorian Attitudes to Race* (1971); B. Street, *The Savage in Literature: Representations of Primitive Society in English Fiction, 1858–1920* (1975); G. Watson, *The English Ideology: Studies in the Language of Victorian Politics* (1973), chapter 11; M. D. Biddiss, 'Myths of Blood: European Racist Ideology, 1850–1945', *Patterns of Prejudice*, Vol. 9, No. 5 (September/October 1975), pp. 11–18; B. Zawadzki,

'Limitations of the Scapegoat Theory of Prejudice', *Journal of Abnormal and Social Psychology*, Vol. 43 (1948), pp. 127–41.

13 'In Gipsy Tents', *Chambers's Journal*, No. 882 (20 November 1880), p. 737. See also J. O. Halliwell-Phillips, *Popular Rhymes and Nursery Tales* (1849; Michigan, 1968), p. 131; W. C., 'Transformation of the Gipsies', *Once a Week*, Vol. 11 (22 October 1864), p. 498.

14 See W. M. Gallichan, 'The State versus the Gypsy', *J.G.L.S.*, New Ser., Vol. 1, No. 4 (1908), pp. 350–2.

Bibliography

BIBLIOGRAPHICAL NOTES

A number of *guides* have been published which are invaluable in identifying the many printed works containing some reference to Gypsies and travellers. The most important of these is that compiled by G. F. Black, provisionally issued in Liverpool in 1909 before being published in Edinburgh in 1914 under the title *A Gypsy Bibliography*. A short supplement appeared in the *Journal of the Gypsy Lore Society* in 1940 (3rd Ser., Vol. 19, Nos. 1–2, pp. 20–3) and has been recently updated by Dennis Binns, who published his *A Gypsy Bibliography* from Manchester in 1982. Other guides have catalogued the important Gypsy Lore Society archive and Scott Macfie Collection at the Sydney Jones Library, University of Liverpool (*A Catalogue of the Gypsy Books Collected by the Late Robert Andrew Scott Macfie, Sometime Editor and Secretary of the Gypsy Lore Society*, Liverpool, 1936; an unpublished addenda is also held at the library), and the Romany Collection at the Brotherton Library, University of Leeds (*A Catalogue of the Romany Collection, Brotherton Library, University of Leeds*, Edinburgh, 1962). These undoubtedly form the most substantial collections relating to Gypsy material, containing an excellent selection of printed works, extensive correspondence relating to the Gypsy Lore Society and assorted photographs and ephemera.

Other useful *archival* material can be found in the Department of Manuscripts, British Library (C. G. Leland Collection), the British Library of Political and Economic Science (Charles Booth MSS), the Guildford Muniment Room and the Surrey Record Office (an extensive selection of material relating to the Surrey Gypsy problem of 1894–1914), and the Public Record Office (Home Office correspondence, HO45). Elsewhere the sources are more sparse though some references can be found in minutes of parish meetings, bye-laws, parish registers and items relating to vagrancy.

Parliamentary Papers: despite the problems with census reports discussed in the second chapter these nevertheless offer the most useful and substantial indication of the numbers and distribution of the travelling population. Of major importance are reports of various Committees of Enquiry, notably *The Report of the Select Committee on the Temporary Dwellings Bill*, 1887 (279), the *Report from the Select Committee of the House of Lords on the Moveable Dwellings Bill*, 1909 (H.L. 199), and the *Report from the Select Committee of the House of Lords on the Moveable Dwellings Bill*, 1910 (H.L.146). Also of value are the reports concerning the administration of the Poor Laws (1834), the Constabulary Force (1839), the Housing of the Working Classes (1884–5) and Vagrancy (especially 1906).

The *Journal of the Gypsy Lore Society* stands out as the single most important of all the printed sources. The advantages and disadvantages of this periodical have been discussed previously. Individual authors and articles have been referenced in the notes. Of great assistance in identifying particular articles of interest is the *Index of the Old Series of the Journal of the Gypsy Lore Society, 1888–92* (1914) by A. Russell, and the index for the issues of 1907–33 in E. L. Mullins (ed.), *A Guide to the Historical and Archaeological Publications of Societies in England and Wales* (1968).

Newspapers also contain many short references of value. My own study drew on a large number over an extensive geographical area for the whole of the period under review. It is probable that a more systematic survey of a particular area or for a limited period would reveal much additional information.

Theses: for a fuller bibliography see my own 'Itinerant Minorities in England and Wales in the 19th and Early 20th Centuries: A Study of Gypsies, Tinkers, Hawkers and Other Travellers', Ph.D. thesis, University of Sheffield (1981). Other theses of relevance, some of which have been published in revised forms, include T. Acton, 'The Development of Ethnic Ideology and Pressure Politics in Gypsy-Gaujo Relations in England and Wales from Victorian Reformism to Romani Nationalism', D.Phil. thesis, University of Oxford (1973); D. Guy, 'The Attempt of Socialist Czechoslovakia to Assimilate its Gypsy Population', Ph.D. thesis, University of Bristol (1957); I. H. S. Stratton, 'The Work and Ideas of John West, 1778–1845', M.A. thesis, University of Durham (1977); E. B. Trigg, 'Magic and Religion amongst the Gypsies of Great Britain', D.Phil. thesis, University of Oxford (1967); R. Worrall, 'Gypsies, Education and Society: Case Studies in Conflict', M.Ed. thesis, University of Birmingham (1977).

The following select bibliography of *printed works* lists only the most important and substantial of the works available. Many further references can be extracted from the *guides* mentioned earlier. The selection of articles published in periodicals has been arranged alphabetically by journal because of the large number of anonymous items.

SELECT BIBLIOGRAPHY OF PRINTED WORKS

BOOKS (PUBLISHED IN LONDON UNLESS OTHERWISE STATED)

Acton, T., *Gypsy Politics and Social Change. The Development of Ethnic Ideology and Pressure Politics among British Gypsies from Victorian Reformism to Romany Nationalism* (1974).

Adams, B., et al., *Gypsies and Government Policy in England: A Study of the Travellers' Way of Life in Relation to the Policies and Practices of Central and Local Government* (1975).

Alder, S., *Work among the Gipsies; being an Account of Twelve Years Mission Work amongst the Gipsies* (Chobham, 1893).

Alexander, W., *Notes and Sketches Illustrative of Northern Rural Life in the Eighteenth Century* (Edinburgh, 1877).

Andreas (Mui Shuko), pseud. of R. A. S. Macfie, *Gypsy Coppersmiths in Liverpool and Birkenhead* (Liverpool, 1913).

Anon., *The Gipsies* (1842).

Gypsies: On the Origin of the Gypsies (1863).

George Smith of Coalville: A Chapter in Philanthropy [1881].

Axon, W. E. A., 'Laws Relating to the Gipsies', in W. Andrews (ed.), *Legal Lore: Curiosities of Law and Lawyers* (1897).

Baird, J., *The Scottish Gipsy's Advocate: Being a Short Account of the Gipsies of Kirk Yetholm* (Edinburgh, 1839).

Baird, W., *Memoir of the Late Rev. John Baird, Minister of Yetholm, Roxburghshire: With an Account of his Labours in Reforming the Gipsy Population of that Parish* (1862).

Barker, J. H., 'The Gipsy-Life of Northumberland', in W. Andrews (ed.), *Bygone Northumberland* (1899).

A Barrister, *The Vagrant Act, in Relation to the Liberty of the Subject* (2nd edn, 1824).

Bell, V., *To Meet Mr. Ellis: Little Gaddesden in the Eighteenth Century* (1956).

Bennett, A. R., *London and Londoners in the Eighteen-Fifties and Sixties* (1924).

Bercovici, K., *The Story of the Gypsies* (1930).

Booth, C., *Life and Labour of the People in London* (1902–4).

Borrow, G., *Lavengro; the Scholar, the Gypsy, the Priest*, 3 vols. (1851).

  The Romany Rye; a Sequel to 'Lavengro', 2 vols. (1857).

Boswell, S. G., *The Book of Boswell: Autobiography of a Gypsy*, edited by J. Seymour (1970).

Bradburn, E., *Dr. Dora Esther Yates: An Appreciation* [Liverpool, 1975].

Brockie, W., *The Gypsies of Yetholm* (Kelso, 1884).

Burton, Sir R., *The Jew, The Gypsy and El Islam*, edited with a preface and brief notes by W. H. Wilkins (1898).

Carew, F. W. (ed.), *No. 747. Being the Autobiography of a Gipsy* (Bristol, [1891]).

Chambers, R., *Exploits and Anecdotes of the Scottish Gypsies, with Traits of their Origin, Character and Manners* (Edinburgh, 1821).

Chance, Sir W., *Vagrancy: Being a Review of the Report of the Departmental Committee on Vagrancy, 1906, with Answers to Certain Criticisms* (1906).

Chinn, S., *Among the Hop-Pickers* [1887].

Clay, Rev. J., *Chaplain's Twenty-Eighth Report on the Preston House of Correction, Presented to the Magistrates of Lancashire, 1851* (Preston, 1852).

Clebert, J.-P., *The Gypsies*, translated by C. Duff (1963).

A Clergyman of the Church of England, *The Gipsies: Or a Narrative, in Three Parts of Several Communications with that Wandering and Scattered People: With Some Thoughts on the Duty of Christians to Attempt their Instruction and Conversion* (York, 1822).

Crabb, J., *The Gipsies' Advocate; or, Observations on the Origin, Character, Manners and Habits of the English Gipsies: To which are Added, many Interesting Anecdotes, on the Success that has Attended the Plans of Several Benevolent Individuals who Anxiously Desire their Conversion to God* (1831; 3rd edn with additions, 1832).

  A Condensed History of the Gypsies (Southampton, 1843).

Cuttriss, F. (pseud.) [i.e. Frank R. Hinkins and R. Cuttriss Hinkins], *Romany Life, Experienced and Observed during Many Years of Friendly Intercourse with the Gypsies* (1915).

Davidson, A., *Present State of the Gipsies in Yetholm* (Yetholm?, [1862]).

Davies, W. H., *The Autobiography of a Super-Tramp* (1908).

De Crespigny, R. C. and Hutchinson, H. G., *The New Forest; its Traditions, Inhabitants and Customs* (1895; Wakefield, 1975).

De Peyster, J. W., *Gypsies, some Curious Investigations* (Edinburgh, 1887).

Dodds, N., *Gypsies, Didikois and Other Travellers* (1966).

Douglas, Sir G., 'Essays on Kirk Yetholm Gypsies', in his *Diversions of a Country Gentleman* (1902).

Esquiros, A., *The English at Home*, translated and edited by L. Wraxall (1861).

Evens, E., *Through the Years with Romany* (1946).

Eversley, Lord (G.J.S. Lefevre), *Commons, Forests and Footpaths, the Story of the Battle during the Last Forty-Five Years for Public Rights over the Commons, Forests and Footpaths of England and Wales* (rev. edn, 1910).

Fairley, J. A., *Bailie Smith of Kelso's Account of the Gypsies of Kirk Yetholm in 1815* (Hawick, 1907).

Fitzgerald, B. S., *Gypsies of Britain. An Introduction to their History* (1944).

Frost, T., *Reminiscences of a Country Journalist* (1886).

Fuller, R., *The Beggar's Brotherhood* (1936).

Galer, A. M., *Norwood and Dulwich: Past and Present, with Historical and Descriptive Notes* (1890).

G[ibbins], H. E. J., *Gipsies of the New Forest, and Other Tales* (Bournemouth, [1909]).

Grellmann, H. M. G., *Dissertation on the Gipsies, being an Historical Enquiry Concerning the Manner of Life, Economy, Customs and Conditions of this People in Europe, and their Origin*, translated by M. Raper (1787).

Grey, A. M., *The Gipsy's Daughter, a Novel* (1852).

Grey, E., *Cottage Life in a Hertfordshire Village* (St Albans, 1935).

Groome, F. H., *In Gipsy Tents* (Edinburgh, 1880; Wakefield, 1973).

The Gypsies (Edinburgh, 1881).

Two Suffolk Friends (Edinburgh, 1895).

Gypsy Folk-Tales (1899).

Grose, F., *A Classical Dictionary of the Vulgar Tongue* (1785; 1796; edited by E. Partridge, 1931).

Hall, Rev. G., *The Gypsy's Parson, his Experiences and Adventures* (1915).

Hanson, H., *The Canal Boatmen, 1760–1914* (Manchester, 1979).

Harvey, D., *The Gypsies: Waggon-Time and After* (1979).

Hoare, Rev. E. N., *Notable Workers in Humble Life* (1887).

Hodder, E., *George Smith of Coalville: The Story of an Enthusiast* (1896).

Holmes, C., 'Samuel Roberts and the Gypsies', in S. Pollard and C. Holmes (eds.), *Essays on the Economic and Social History of South Yorkshire* (Barnsley, 1976).

'The German Gypsy Question in Britain, 1904–5', in K. Lunn (ed.), *Hosts, Immigrants and Minorities: Historical Responses to Newcomers in British Society, 1870–1914* (1980).

(ed.), *Immigrants and Minorities in British Society* (1978).

Howitt, M. (ed.), *Mary Howitt, an Autobiography* (1891).

Howitt, W., *The Rural Life of England* (1840).

Hoyland, J., *A Historical Survey of the Customs, Habits and Present State of the Gypsies, Designed . . . to Promote the Amelioration of their Condition* (York, 1816).

Hudson, W. H., *A Shepherd's Life: Impressions of the South Wiltshire Downs* (1910).

Jefferies, R., *Field and Hedgerow, being the Last Essays of R.J. Collected by his Widow* (1889).

Kenrick, D. and Puxon, G., *The Destiny of Europe's Gypsies* (1972).

Kohl, J. G., *England and Wales* (1844; 1968).

Lane, E. W., *An Account of the Manners and Customs of the Modern Egyptians*, 2 vols. (1836).

Leland, C. G., *The English Gipsies and their Language* (1873; 1874).
  The Gypsies [1882].
Leland, C. G., Palmer, E. H. and Tuckey, J., *English-Gipsy Songs, in Romany with Metrical English Translations* (1875).
Levy, J. de Bairacli, *Wanderers in the New Forest* (1958).
Lewis, M., ed., *Old Days in the Kent Hop Gardens* (Tonbridge, 1962).
Loftie, W. J., *In and Out of London; or, the Half-Holidays of a Town Clerk* [1875].
Lucas, J., *The Yetholm History of the Gypsies* (Kelso, 1882).
Lyster, M. E., *The Gipsy Life of Betsy Wood* (1926).
M'Cormick, A., *The Tinkler-Gypsies of Galloway* (Dumfries, 1906).
McMillan, A., *Gipsy Hawkins. Shoeblack, Cobbler, 'Boy Preacher', Evangelist and Soulwinner* [1939].
MacRitchie, D., *Scottish Gypsies under the Stewarts* (Edinburgh, 1894).
Malleson, H. H., *Napoleon Boswell, Tales of the Tents* (1913).
Marsh, S. J., *Ashdown Forest* (privately printed, 1935).
Mayhew, H., *London Labour and the London Poor*, 4 vols. (1861; New York, 1968).
Mitchell, T., *History of Thomas Mitchell, Born and Educated among the Gipsies, Afterwards a Soldier in the 21st Regiment of Foot, or Royal North British Fusiliers* (Edinburgh, 1816).
Mitford, M. R., *Our Village: Sketches of Rural Character and Scenery* (1827).
Morwood, V. S., *Our Gipsies in City, Tent and Van* (1885).
Murphy, T., *A History of the Showmen's Guild, 1889–1948* (privately printed, Oldham, 1949).
Murray, H., *Sixty Years an Evangelist: An Intimate Study of Gipsy Smith* [1937].
  Gipsy Smith: An Intimate Memoir (Exeter, [1947]).
Murray, R., *The Gypsies of the Border* (Galashiels, 1875).
Okely, J., 'Gypsy women: Models in Conflict', in S. Ardener (ed.), *Perceiving Women* (1975).
  'Trading Stereotypes: The Case of English Gypsies', in S. Wallman (ed.), *Ethnicity at Work* (1979).
  The Traveller-Gypsies (Cambridge, 1983).
Pennell, E. R., *Charles Godfrey Leland, a Biography*, 2 vols. (1906).
Pike, L. O., *A History of Crime in England, Illustrating the Changes of the Laws in the Progress of Civilisation*, 2 vols. (1873–6).
Potter, H. T., *A New Dictionary of all the Cant and Flash Languages, both Ancient and Modern, Used by Gipsies, Beggars, Swindlers . . . and Every Class of Offenders, from a Lully Prigger to a High Tober Glosh* (1797).
Reeve, D., *Smoke in the Lanes* (1958).
  No Place Like Home (1960).
  Whichever Way We Turn (1964).
Rehfisch, F. (ed.), *Gypsies, Tinkers and Other Travellers* (1975).
Roberts, S., 'A Word for the Gipsies', in his *The Blind Man and his Son: A Tale for Young People* (1816).
  Parallel Miracles; or the Jews and the Gypsies (1830).
  The Gypsies; their Origin, Continuance and Destination, as Clearly Foretold in the Prophecies of Isaiah, Jeremiah and Ezekiel (1836; 5th edn enlarged, 1842).
Rolt, L. T. C., *Narrow Boat* (1944).
  Navigable Waterways (1969).

Rudall, J., *A Memoir of the Rev. James Crabb, Late of Southampton* (1854).

Samuel, R., 'Comers and Goers', in H. J. Dyos and M. Wolff (eds.), *The Victorian City, Images and Realities*, Vol. 1 (1973; 1976).

'Quarry Roughs', in R. Samuel (ed.), *Village Life and Labour* (1975).

Sandford, J., *Gypsies* (1975).

Sanger, 'Lord', G., *Seventy Years a Showman: My Life and Adventures in Camp and Caravan the World Over* [1908].

Sheppard, F. H. W., *Survey of London: Northern Kensington* (1973).

Simson, W., *A History of the Gipsies: With Specimens of the Gipsy Language*, edited, with a preface, introduction, notes and a disquisition on the past, present and future of Gypsydom, by J. Simson (London [printed], Edinburgh, 1865).

Skot, B. (pseud. of R. A. S. Macfie), *A Brief Account of Gypsy History; otherwise titled The Romanichels: A lucubration*, by Tringurushi Juvalomursh (Liverpool, 1909).

Smart, B. C. and Crofton, H. T., *The Dialect of the English Gypsies* (2nd edn, enlarged, 1875).

Smith, C., *The Life-Story of Gipsy Cornelius Smith* (1890).

Smith, G., *Gipsy Life: Being an Account of our Gipsies and their Children, with Suggestions for their Improvement* (1880).

I've Been a Gipsying: Or, Rambles among our Gipsies and their Children (1883, 1885).

A Lecture ([on] the Brickyard, Canal, Gipsy, Van and Other Travelling Children) Delivered before the Association of Public Sanitary Inspectors [1888].

Gypsy Children: Or, a Stroll in Gypsydom. With Songs and Stories [1889], pp. 27–8.

Smith, G. 'Lazzy' (alias Lazzy Buckley, alias Ambrose Smith), *Incidents in a Gipsy's Life . . . the Royal Epping Forest Gipsies* (Liverpool, 1886; Leicester, [1892]).

Smith, R., *From Gipsy Tent to Pulpit: The Story of My Life* [1901].

Smith, R., *Gipsy Smith. His Life and Work. By Himself* (1902).

Solly, N. N., *Memoir of the Life of David Cox, with Selections from his Correspondence and some Account of his Works* (1873).

Somerville, A., *The Autobiography of a Working Man, by 'One who has Whistled at the Plough'* (1848).

Steggall, J. H., *John H. Steggall: A Real History of a Suffolk Man, who has Been a Gypsy &c., Narrated by Himself*, edited by R. Cobbold (1857).

Stratton, Rev. J. Y., *Hops and Hop-Pickers* [1883].

Street, B., *The Savage in Literature: Representations of Primitive Society in English Fiction, 1858–1920* (1975).

Swinstead, J. H., *A Parish on Wheels* (1897).

Thompson, F., *Lark Rise to Candleford* (Oxford, 1968).

Thompson, J. and Smith, A., *Street Life in London* (1877–8; Wakefield, 1973).

Townsend, D., *The Gipsies of Northamptonshire: Their Manner of Life . . . Fifty Years Ago* (Kettering, 1877).

Trigg, E. B., *Gypsy Demons and Divinities: The Magical and Supernatural Practices of the Gypsies* (New Jersey, 1973).

Turner, C. J. R., *A History of Vagrants and Vagrancy and Beggars and Begging* (1887).

Vanderkiste, R. W., *Notes and Narratives of a Six Years' Mission, Principally Among the Dens of London* (1852).

Van Hare, G., *Fifty Years of a Showman's Life, or the Life and Travels of Van Hare by Himself* (1888).

Wedeck, H. E. and Baskin, W., *Dictionary of Gipsy Life and Lore* (1973).

West, Rev. J., *To the Nobility, Clergy and Magistrates of the County of Dorset: A Plea for the Education of the Children of the Gypsies* (Farnham and London, 1844).

Weylland, J. M., *Round the Tower; or, the Story of the London City Mission* [1875].

Wilkinson, T. W., 'Van-Dwelling London', in G. R. Sims (ed.), *Living London*, Vol. 3 (1903).

Wise, J. R., *The New Forest; its History and Scenery* (1880).

Wolff, H., *Sussex Industries* (Lewes, 1883).

Wood, M. F., *In the Life of a Romany Gypsy*, edited by J. A. Brune (1973).

Woodcock, H., *The Gipsies: being a Brief Account of their History, Origin, Capabilities, Manners and Customs; with Suggestions for the Reformation and Conversion of the English Gipsies* (1865).

ARTICLES AND PERIODICAL PUBLICATIONS (ARRANGED ALPHABETICALLY BY TITLE OF JOURNAL)

Groome, F. H., 'Review of G. Smith's Gipsy Life', *Academy*, Vol. 18 (1880), pp. 20–1.

Norwood, T. W., 'Tramps' Language', *Academy*, Vol. 31 (1887), pp. 11–12.

'At the court of the King of the Gipsies', *All the Year Round*, Vol. 6 (1862), pp. 69–72.

'An Immense Gipsy Party', *All the Year Round*, Vol. 15 (1866), pp. 224–9.

'Gipsy Glimpses', *All the Year Round*, New Ser., Vol. 1 (1869), pp. 536–40.

'Metropolitan Gipsyries', *All the Year Round*, New Ser., Vol. 21 (1878), pp. 390–3.

'The Children of Mystery', *All the Year Round*, New Ser., Vol. 39 (1886), pp. 86–91.

Axon, W. E. A., 'The English Gypsies in 1818', *Antiquary*, New Ser., Vol. 3, No. 5 (1907), pp. 181–4.

Beale, A., 'Gipsying', *Argosy*, Vol. 16 (1873), pp. 270–4.

Marsh, B., 'The Tent-Dwellers', *Argosy*, Vol. 63 (1897), pp. 679–82.

Hake, A. E., 'Recollections of George Borrow', *Athenaeum*, No. 2807 (1881), pp. 209–10.

Watts-Dunton, T., 'Reminiscences of George Borrow', *Athenaeum*, Nos. 2810–11 (1881), pp. 307–8, 336–8.

Watts-Dunton, T., 'The Tarno Rye', *Athenaeum*, No. 3878 (1902), pp. 243–6.

Bates, A., 'Gipsy George', *Atlantic Monthly*, Vol. 100 (1907), pp. 473–9.

'Gipsy Bride', *Aunt Kate's Penny Stories*, No. 5 (1901).

Stein, C., 'Our Gypsy Visitors', *Baily's Magazine of Sports and Pastimes*, Vol. 70 (1898), pp. 17–23.

Myers, J., 'Gypsies', *The Barrovian: The Magazine of the Secondary School for Boys*, Vol. 2 (1909), pp. 15–16.

Myers, J., 'The Other Half', *The Barrovian: The Magazine of the Secondary School for Boys*, Vol. 3 (1909), pp. 15–17.

Biograph (May 1879), pp. 316–38.

'Notices Concerning the Scottish Gypsies', *Blackwood's Edinburgh Magazine*, Vol. 7 (1817), pp. 43–58, 154–61, 615–20.

Cunningham, A., 'Adventures with the Gypsies', *Blackwood's Edinburgh Magazine*, Vol. 7 (1820), pp. 48–57, 157–68.

'Gipsies', *Blackwood's Edinburgh Magazine*, Vol. 99 (1866), pp. 565–80.

M., 'The Wandering Population of the West Highlands', *Blackwood's Edinburgh Magazine*, Vol. 175 (1904), pp. 537–45.

'Gipsydom', *Bow Bells*, Vol. 5 (1867), p. 275.

'Gipsies and Fortune-Telling', *Bow Bells*, Vol. 16 (1873), p. 502.

'Gipsy Jack', *Boys' First Rate Pocket Library*, No. 55 (c.1891).

Norwood, T. W., 'On the Race and Language of the Gipsies', *British Association for the Advancement of Science: Notes and Abstracts* (1859), p. 195.

Gilliat-Smith, B. J., 'Gypsies', *Caian: The Magazine of Gonville and Caius College*, Vol. 16, No. 3 (Easter 1907), pp. 192–201.

Adams, W. M., 'The Wandering Tribes of Great Britain', *Cassell's Family Magazine* (1883), pp. 728–31.

'An Adventure with Gipsies', *Cassell's Illustrated Family Paper*, Vol. 4 (1857), p. 22.

Dutt, W. A., 'English Gypsies', *Cassell's Magazine*, Vol. 53 (1911), pp. 53–60.

Leland, C. G., 'Visiting the Gypsies', *Century Magazine*, Vol. 25 (1883), pp. 905–12.

Leland, C. G., 'A Gypsy Beauty', *Century Magazine*, Vol. 32 (1886), pp. 539–42.

Deutsch, E., 'Gypsies', *Chambers's Encyclopaedia*, Vol. 5 (1863), pp. 170–3.

Groome, F. H., 'Gypsies', *Chambers's Encyclopaedia*, New Ser., Vol. 5 (1893), pp. 485–90.

'In Gypsy Tents', *Chambers's Journal* (November 1880), pp. 737–40.

'Queen Esther Faa Blyth and the Yetholm Gypsies', *Chambers's Journal* (August 1883), pp. 518–20.

MacRitchie, D., 'The Greek Gypsies at Liverpool', *Chambers's Journal* (September 1886), pp. 577–80.

'Account of the Gipsies', *Chambers's Miscellany of Useful and Entertaining Tracts*, Vol. 16, No. 139 (1847), pp. 1–32.

Wotherspoon, G., 'A Word for the Romany Chals', *Cheltenham College Magazine* (April 1874), pp. 109–11.

'Gypsies in England', *Christian Observer*, Vol. 7 (1808), pp. 91–2, 496–7, 712; Vol. 8 (1809), pp. 286–7; Vol. 9 (1810), pp. 82–3; 278–80, 554–5; Vol. 14 (1815), pp. 23–5, 141, 590–1; Vol. 20 (1821), p. 159.

Andrews, W., 'Some Curious Gleanings', *Christian World Magazine* (December 1887), pp. 476–9.

'Who Are the Gipsies?', *Church of England Magazine* (1842), pp. 163–4, 292–4.

'The Gipsy's Grave', *Church of England Magazine* (1843), pp. 75–7, 90–3.

James, S. B., 'English Gipsies', *Church of England and Lambeth Magazine*, Vol. 79 (1875), pp. 97–100, 161–4, 225–30, 289–94, 353–7.

Drake, O., 'A Strange People and a Strange Language', *Churchman's Shilling Magazine* (1876), pp. 31–8.

'Gypsies', *The Cottage Magazine, or Plain Christian's Library*, Vol. 15 (1826), pp. 325–32, 397–404; Vol. 16 (1827), pp. 1–7, 37–45.

Gillington, A. E., 'The Gypsies Pass', *Country Life*, Vol. 28 (1910), p. 740.

'Who Are the Gipsies?', *County Gentleman and Land and Water Illustrated* (1906), p. 1076.

MacAlister, Sir D., 'Romany', *The Eagle: A Magazine Supported by members of St. John's College*, Vol. 16 (1889), pp. 23–7.

'Gypsies', *Edinburgh Encyclopaedia*, Vol. 10 (1830), pp. 597–600.

'Johnnie Faa, The Gypsey Chief, and the Countess of Cassillis', *Edinburgh Magazine* (November 1817), pp. 302–10.

Jorgenson, J., 'Travels through France and Germany, in the Years 1815, 1816 and 1817', *Edinburgh Review*, Vol. 28 (1817), pp. 371–90.

Clarke, A., 'Origin and Wanderings of the Gypsies', *Edinburgh Review*, Vol. 148 (1878), pp. 117–46.

'Gipsies', *Eliza Cook's Journal*, Vol. 10 (1854), pp. 30–2.

Watson, G., 'Race and the Socialists: The Progressive Principle of Revolutionary Extermination', *Encounter*, Vol. 47 (1976), pp. 15–23.

Groome, F. H., 'Gypsies', *Encyclopaedia Britannica*, Vol. 10 (1879), pp. 611–18.

Renouard, G., 'Gypsy', *Encyclopaedia Metropolitana*, Vol. 20 (1845), pp. 54–9.

'Gypsies', *English Cyclopaedia of Arts and Sciences*, Vol. 4 (1860), pp. 590–1.

Bensusan, S. L., 'How the Other Half Lives', *English Illustrated Magazine*, Vol. 17 (1897), pp. 643–8.

Acton, T., 'Academic Success and Political Failure: A Review of Modern Social Science Writing in English on Gypsies', *Ethnic and Racial Studies*, Vol. 2, No. 2 (April 1979), pp. 231–41.

'Gypsies', *European Magazine*, Vol. 70 (1861), pp. 240–1.

'A Gypsy Ball', *Every Saturday*, New Ser., Vol. 2 (1872), pp. 691–3.

'The Gipsey's Prophecy', *Family Herald*, Vol. 1 (1843), p. 230.

'Gipsies', *Family Herald*, Vol. 59 (1887), pp. 173–4.

Hildburgh, W. L., 'Gipsy Amulets', *Folk-Lore*, Vol. 17 (1906), pp. 470–1.

Crooke, W., 'The Burning of the Property of a Gypsy at Death', *Folk-Lore*, Vol. 20 (1909), p. 353.

Myers, J., 'Gypsy Fare', *Food and Cookery and the Catering World*, Vol. 14 (1910), p. 238.

'The Gipsy and the Dupe', *Fraser's Magazine* (1840), pp. 577–91.

Hamilton, A. H. A., 'Quarter Sessions under Charles I', *Fraser's Magazine* (1877), pp. 56–67.

M'Evoy, C., 'The Gypsy Holiday', *Fry's Magazine* (1909), pp. 381–4.

M'Cormick, A., 'George Borrow, and the Memo of his Tour thru' Galloway', *The Gallovidian*, Vol. 7 (1905), pp. 116–26.

Gentleman's Magazine, Vol. 73 (1803), pp. 84, 280.

Japp, A. H., 'The Gypsies as Seen by Friendly Eyes', *Gentleman's Magazine*, Vol. 255 (1883, Vol. 2), pp. 575–87.

Gordon, A. J., 'About Gypsies', *Gentleman's Magazine*, Vol. 287 (1899), pp. 409–12.

Stevenson, W. F., 'On Vagabonds', *Good Words*, Vol. 3 (1862), pp. 705–11.

Ralston, W. R. S., 'A Gipsies' Christmas Gathering', *Good Words*, Vol. 9 (1868), pp. 96–101.

'My Friend's Gipsy Journal', *Good Words*, Vol. 9 (1868), pp. 701–5, 745–52.

Montagu, I., 'Rambles with the Romany', *Good Words*, Vol. 23 (1882), pp. 720–3, 816–19.

Dutt, W. A., 'With the East Anglian Gypsies', *Good Words*, Vol. 37 (1896), pp. 120–6.

Holbeach, H., 'My Little Gipsy Cousin', *Good Words for the Young*, Vol. 3 (1871), pp. 294–6.

James, S. B., 'Gipsies', *The Graphic*, Vol. 10 (1874), p. 289.

G., 'Hunting for Gypsies', *The Graphic*, Vol. 40 (1889), p. 48.

'The Campaign against the Gypsies', *The Graphic*, Vol. 79 (1905), p. 529.

The Gypsy, Vol. 1, Nos. 1–2 (May 1915–May 1916).

Gypsy and Folk-Lore Gazette: see under *Romanitshels', Didakais'* and *Folk-Lore Gazette*.

Griffith, R. W. S., 'The Gipsies of the New Forest', *Hampshire Field Club: Proceedings*, Vol. 2 (Southampton, 1894), pp. 277–82.

Smith, G., 'Gipsy Children's Homes', *Hand and Heart*, Vol. 5 (December 1879), p. 170.

Smith, G., 'Gipsy and Other Travelling Children', *Hand and Heart*, Vol. 5 (June 1880), p. 584.

'Gypsies of Surrey', *Harper's Magazine*, Vol. 65 (1882), p. 654.

Anstey, F., 'A Gypsy Fair in Surrey', *Harper's New Monthly Magazine* (1888), pp. 625–33.

'The Yetholm Gipsies', *Hogg's Instructor*, New Ser., Vol. 10 (1853), pp. 57–60, 75–7.

Lovell, 'My Life: By a Gipsy', *Home Chat* (18 April 1908), pp. 267–8.

Home Missionary Quarterly Chronicle (Midsummer 1827), pp. 71–2.

Home Missionary Society Magazine (September 1836), pp. 44–5; (July 1838), pp. 118–19; (December 1838), pp. 200–1; (December 1841), p. 303; (March 1845), p. 60.

P., 'A Gipsy's Funeral, Epping Forest', in *W. Hone's Everyday Book and Table Book*, Vol. 3, Part 2 (1841), cols. 27–8.

Dyke, E. T., 'Gipsey Funeral', in *W. Hone's Year Book of Daily Recreation and Information* (1841), cols. 915–16.

'The Gipsey Mother', *Howitt's Journal*, Vol. 1 (1847), p. 296.

Jarvis, A. W. and Turtle, R., 'Gipsy Life, Illustrated from Old Prints in the British Museum', *The Idler* (October 1907), pp. 14–23.

'Gypsies', *Johnstone's Edinburgh Magazine*, Vol. 1 (1834), pp. 100–6.

Zawadzki, B., 'Limitations of the Scapegoat Theory of Prejudice', *Journal of Abnormal and Social Psychology*, Vol. 43 (1948), pp. 127–41.

Journal of the Gypsy Lore Society, Old Ser. (1888–92); New Ser. (1907–17); 3rd Ser. (1922–   ).

Jus (1887–8).

'Attorney-General v. Stone', *Justice of the Peace*, Vol. 60 (1896), pp. 168–9.

Atkinson, F. S., 'Gypsies in Westmorland', *The Kendalian*, Vol. 9 (1909), pp. 12–17.

Atkinson, F. S., 'Gypsies in East Anglia', *The Kendalian*, Vol. 11 (1911), pp. 9–14.

'Gossip about the Gipsies', *Leisure Hour*, Vol. 10 (1861), pp. 430–2, 446–8, 462–4.

'Gipsies', *Lend a Hand*, Vol. 1 (1886), pp. 581–4.

Liberty Review (December 1893), pp. 1–2; (January 1894), p. 114.

James, J., 'The Future for the Gipsies: "They Want What Many Will See as the Best of Both Worlds",' *The Listener* (6 November 1980), pp. 607–8.

'The Norwood Gypsies', *The Literary Lounger* (1826), pp. 88–96.

'Gipsies', *The Literary and Scientific Repository*, Vol. 3 (1821), pp. 401–11.

'The Law as to Gipsies', *Local Government Journal* (18 July 1896), p. 465.

Local Government Journal (2 January 1897), p. 6; (9 January 1897), p. 22.

'The Missionary to the Gypsies', *London City Mission Magazine*, Vol. 25 (1860), pp. 1–36.

'Glad Tidings from Gypsydom', *London City Mission Magazine*, Vol. 76 (1911), pp. 173–82.

'Our Gipsies and their Children', *London Society*, Vol. 47 (1885), pp. 33–42.

'Natland Potters', *Lonsdale Magazine*, Vol. 2 (1821), pp. 343–7.

'Gipsy Fortune-Telling', *Lonsdale Magazine*, Vol. 3 (1822), pp. 64–6.

Saintsbury, G., 'George Borrow', *Macmillan's Magazine*, Vol. 53 (1886), pp. 170–83.

Dutt, W. A., 'In Lavengro's Country', *Macmillan's Magazine*, Vol. 84 (1901), pp. 145–50.

Madame (16 October 1897), p. 184.

Crofton, H. T., 'Gypsy Life in Lancashire and Cheshire', *Manchester Literary Club, Papers*, Vol. 3 (Manchester, 1877), pp. 32–41.

Crofton, H. T., 'The English Gipsies under the Tudors', *Manchester Literary Club, Papers*, Vol. 6 (Manchester, 1880), pp. 93–116.

'Beggars and Gypsies', *The Miniature* (1805), pp. 294–304.

'Gipsy Anecdotes', *The Mirror*, Vol. 5 (1829), pp. 412–14.

The Mirror, Vol. 7 (March 1826), p. 152; Vol. 8 (October 1826), pp. 243–6.

'The Aged Gipsy of Agar Town', *Missing Link Magazine*, Vol. 1 (1865), pp. 100, 261–2, 336.

'The Gipsy Tea-Party', *Missing Link Magazine*, Vol. 1 (1869), pp. 122–5.

W.B., 'The Gipsies of the Border', *Monthly Chronicle of North Country Lore and Legend* (1891), pp. 54–7, 100–2, 163–5, 205–8.

Copsey, D., 'Dialect and Manners of the Gypsies', *Monthly Magazine*, Vol. 46 (1818), pp. 393–4.

'A Lily among Thorns', *Monthly Visitor*, No. 284 (1856).

'A Gipsey's Warning', *My Queen Novels*, No. 723 (1909).

'The Tent Folk', *The Nation*, Vol. 2 (12 October 1907), pp. 44–5.

Noyes, J. O., 'The Gipsies of England and Scotland', *National Magazine*, Vol. 13 (1858), pp. 104–8.

Groome, F. H., 'Gipsy Folk-Tales: A Missing Link', *National Review*, Vol. 11 (1888), pp. 659–73.

Strachey, J., 'The Gipsy Scandal and the Danger to the Commons', *National Review*, Vol. 59 (1912), pp. 459–72.

'Origin and Rites of the Gypsies', *Nature*, Vol. 81 (1909), pp. 142–3.

'Gypsies', *Nelson's Encyclopaedia*, Vol. 5 (1906), pp. 550–8.

'Gypsies', *New Edinburgh Review*, Vol. 1 (1844), pp. 11–17.

New Monthly Magazine, Vol. 8 (1817), p. 462.

H., 'Fortune-Telling', *New Monthly Magazine*, Vol. 8 (1823), pp. 336–40.

'Gipsies', *New Monthly Magazine*, Vol. 35 (1832), pp. 375–7.

Acton, T., 'True Gypsies: Myth and Reality', *New Society* (6 June 1974), pp. 563–5.

'The Gipsies', *New Statesman* (5 June 1920), pp. 245–6.

Niles' Weekly Register, Vol. 9 (16 September 1815), p. 41.

Lucas, J., 'Petty Romany', *Nineteenth Century* (October 1880), pp. 578–92.

Review of Hoyland's *A Historical Survey . . .*, *Northern Star, or Yorkshire Magazine*, Vol. 1, No. 2 (1917), pp. 132–5.

Notes and Queries (1849–).

W.C., 'Transformation of the Gipsies', *Once a Week*, Vol. 11 (22 October 1864), pp. 498–501.

Beamish, F., 'Gilderoy: Or Scenes from Gipsy Life', *Our Own Gazette*, Vol. 4 (1887), pp. 109–11, 121–3, 133–6.

Paine, R. D., 'The Gypsy of England', *Outing*, Vol. 45 (New York, 1904), pp. 329–34.

'Gipsies in Hainault Forest', *Outlook* (20 August 1898), p. 76.

'The Passing of the Gipsy', *Outlook* (1 June 1907), pp. 721–2.

Biddiss, M. D., 'Myths of Blood: European Racist Ideology, 1850–1945', *Patterns of Prejudice*, Vol. 9, No. 5 (September–October 1975), pp. 11–18.

Puxon, G., 'Forgotten Victims: Plight of the Gypsies', *Patterns of Prejudice*, Vol. 11, No. 2 (March–April 1977), pp. 23–8.

'Gipsies', *Penny Cyclopaedia*, Vol. 11 (1836), pp. 225–6.

'Gipsies', *Penny Magazine of the Society for the Diffusion of Useful Knowledge*, No. 142 (21 June 1834), p. 235.

'The Tinkers of Scotland', *Penny Magazine of the Society for the Diffusion of Useful Knowledge*, No. 303 (23 December 1836), p. 502.

'The English Gipsies', *Penny Magazine of the Society for the Diffusion of Useful Knowledge*, No. 372 (20 January 1838), pp. 17–19.

'Mr. Raffles and the Gipsies', *Porcupine*, Vol. 21 (1879), p. 409.

'Roving Life in England', *Quarterly Review*, Vol. 101 (1857), pp. 468–501.

'The Gipsies', *The Quiver*, Vol. 6 (1871), pp. 668–70.

Woolmer, D. L., 'Gipsies in their Winter Quarters', *The Quiver* (1903), pp. 530–5.

W., 'The Gipsies', *The Revivalist* (1837), pp. 294–5.

Romanitshels', Didakais' and Folk-Lore Gazette (from 1913, *Gypsy and Folk-Lore Gazette*), Vols. 1–3 (1912–14).

Munro, A., 'The Coronation of a Gipsy King', *Royal Magazine*, Vol. 2 (1899), pp. 360–4.

'Resemblance of Gypsies to Jews', *Saturday Magazine*, Vol. 12 (1838), pp. 46–7.

Watts-Dunton, T., 'Gypsies and Gypsying', *Saturday Review*, Vol. 104 (1907), pp. 695–6, 724–6.

School Guardian, Vol. 4, No. 191 (1879), p. 508.

'Gipsy Reformation', *Scottish Christian Herald*, Vol. 1 (6 April 1839), pp. 216–17.

Baird, Rev. J., 'Proposed Plan for the Reformation of the Gipsies in Scotland', *Scottish Christian Herald*, Vol. 1 (13 April 1839), pp. 231–3.

'Proposed School for Gipsies in England', *Scottish Christian Herald*, Vol. 1, Supplement (1839), p. 48.

'Gipsies', *Sharpe's London Magazine*, Vol. 7 (1848), pp. 169–72.

Joven, pseud., 'Gipsyism', *Sharpe's London Magazine*, Vol. 12 (c.1849–50), pp. 311–14.

'Yetholm and the Scottish Gipsies', *Sharpe's London Magazine/Journal*, Vol. 13 (c.1850–1), pp. 321–5.

T., 'The Gipsy of To-Day', *The Sketch*, Vol. 11 (4 September 1895), pp. 329–30.

'The Surrey Gipsies', *The Spectator*, Vol. 79 (18 December 1897), pp. 894–5.

'Origins of Gypsies', *Spirit of the Public Journals, for the Year 1824* (1825), pp. 82–4.

'The Gipsy Wife', *Sunday at Home* (1874), pp. 172–5.

'With the Gipsies', *Sunday at Home* (1874), pp. 566–8.

'The Present State of the Gipsies', *Sunday at Home* (1884), pp. 118–20.

Brewer, E., 'Gipsy Encampments in the Heart of London', *Sunday at Home* (1896), pp. 113–14.

Hall, Rev. G., 'The Gipsies of England', *Sunday at Home* (1912), pp. 413–19.

Beale, A., 'Among the Gypsies', *Sunday Magazine* (1875), pp. 49–53; 237–42; 309–12.

Harrison, M., 'Gypsies', *Sunday Magazine* (1885), p. 494.

W. B., 'Gipsies and their Friends', *Temple Bar Magazine*, Vol. 47 (May 1876), pp. 65–76.

MacManus, S., 'When the Tinkers Come', *Temple Bar*, New Ser., Vol. 1 (1906), pp. 216–23.

Chatfield, R. E., 'The English Gipsies', *Theosophical Review* (April 1899), pp. 105–16.

Thompson, T. W., 'Gipsies', *Tramp Magazine*, Vol. 2 (1910), pp. 46–53.

Bartlett, Rev. D. M. M., 'Studying Gypsies', *The Treasury* (August 1909), pp. 426–30.

Macfie, R. A. S., 'Gypsy Lore', *University Review*, Vol. 7 (1908), pp. 93–107.

Morwood, V. S., 'English Gipsies', *Victoria Magazine*, Vol. 9 (1867), pp. 291–4, 499–504; Vol. 10 (1868), pp. 140–6.

Morwood, V. S., 'Plans Suggested for the Reclamation of Gipsies', *Victoria Magazine*, Vol. 14 (1870), pp. 71–7.

Behlmer, G. K., 'The Gypsy Problem in Victorian England', *Victorian Studies*, Vol. 28, No. 2 (Winter 1985), pp. 231–53.

Sampson, J., 'The Gypsies', *Warrington Literary and Philosophical Society: Papers*, No. 6 (1896–7).

'Meeting of the Gipsies: Another of Mrs. Bayly's Thoughtful Plans', *Weekly Record of the National Temperance League*, No. 352 (2 February 1861), p. 40.

D. J. V. Jones, 'A Dead Loss to the Community: The Criminal Vagrant in Mid-Nineteenth Century Wales', *Welsh History Review*, Vol. 8, No. 3 (1977), pp. 312–44.

Scoto-Montanus, pseud., 'Gypsies in England', *Wesleyan Methodist Magazine*, 3rd Ser., Vol. 7 (1828), pp. 242–4.

'Society for the Benefit of the Gipsies at Southampton', *Wesleyan Methodist Magazine*, 3rd Ser., Vol. 7 (1828), pp. 251–2.

'The Gipsy Race – Labours for Improvement', *Wesleyan Methodist Magazine*, Vol. 10, Part 1 (June 1854), pp. 510–15; Vol. 10, Part 2 (August 1854), pp. 697–702.

Bowen, C. M., 'George Borrow', *Westminster Review*, Vol. 173 (1910), pp. 286–304.

Crichton, T., 'Tinkers and Tramps at Gauldry, Fife', *Young Scotland*, Vol. 3 (1907), pp. 86–9.

Index